ANNUAL REPORTS

$ 25.00

Text by Richard A. Lewis
Edited by Walter Herdeg

This is the first book ever written on the subject of annual reports and expressly conceived for the corporate executive who is charged with this responsibility.

Annual Reports is a gold mine of practical information. It functions as a planning manual. Each step in producing a *quality* annual report is explicitly described: writing, financial figures, charts and graphs, artwork, photography, typography, paper, printing and binding. It is filled with answers to such questions as: 'How much should an annual report cost?' 'What kind of deal should I make with photographers?' 'How can I negotiate a realistic contract with a printer?' It includes a specially designed *flow chart* giving step-by-step instructions and guidance on how to get an effective annual report—*on time!*

There are 204 pages, containing five text chapters and 405 illustrations (75 of them in full color) of outstanding annual report design.

All texts are in English, French, and German. This volume belongs on the shelf of every executive in charge of producing the report. It will be useful to public relations firms, designers, printers, photographers and paper companies.

Three great companion volumes…

GRAPHIS ANNUAL

International Annual of Advertising Graphics
Edited by Walter Herdeg

Since 1952 this leading annual in its field has recorded the best and most significant advertising from all media and from over 500 artists / graphic designers / art directors. 'This international annual of advertising graphics has been a valuable guide in the field of advertising design for more than a decade and a half—not only for its authoritative selection but also for its excellent presentation and flawless production.'—Printing Magazine/National Lithographer. Graphis Annual is published each September/October. 244 pages, about 1000 illustrations with more than 100 in color.

PHOTOGRAPHIS

International Annual of Advertising Photography
Edited by Walter Herdeg

The photographic companion to Graphis Annual continues to reflect the finest in graphic design. It concentrates on the use of photography, specifically its use in advertising, with examples from all parts of the world. Always lavishly printed, it shows the best examples of photographic work in advertising, calendars, booklets, magazines, posters and record covers. Published each year in April/May. 260 pages, over 900 photographs.

GRAPHIS PACKAGING 2

Edited by Walter Herdeg

This volume shows the massive changes in packaging over the past decade—changes brought about by a bewildering variety of new materials and the increasing complexity of a consumer age. A cross-section of the best work being done today, with illustrations grouped under eleven categories, ranging from food products to industrial containers, from pharmaceuticals to cosmetics. Introductory texts written by such experts as Carl Fink, president of the Package Designers Council, Walter Stern, technical director of Raymond Loewy/William Snaith, Inc., and industrial designer George Nelson. 9½"×12", 1085 illustrations, 260 black-and-white and 72 color pages, fully indexed.

VISUAL COMMUNICATION BOOKS

Hastings House, Publishers, Inc.
10 East 40th Street, New York, N.Y. 10016
Printed in Switzerland

ANNUAL REPORTS

CONCEPTION AND DESIGN
OF ANNUAL REPORTS

KONZEPTION UND
GESTALTUNG
VON JAHRESBERICHTEN

CONCEPTION ET DESIGN DE
RAPPORTS ANNUELS

TEXTS BY/TEXTE VON/TEXTES DE
RICHARD A.LEWIS

EDITED BY/HERAUSGEGEBEN VON/REALISE PAR
WALTER HERDEG

GRAPHIS

62697

Contents

Abbreviations

AUL	Australia
CAN	Canada
FRA	France
GER	Germany
GB	Great Britain
HKG	Hong Kong
NOR	Norway
SWE	Sweden
SWI	Switzerland
USA	United States of America

Inhalt

Sommaire

Abkürzungen

Abréviations

AUL	Australien
GER	Deutschland
FRA	Frankreich
GB	Grossbritannien
HKG	Hong Kong
CAN	Kanada
NOR	Norwegen
SWE	Schweden
SWI	Schweiz
USA	Vereinigte Staaten von Amerika

GER	Allemagne
AUL	Australie
CAN	Canada
USA	Etats-Unis
FRA	France
GB	Grande-Bretagne
HKG	Hong Kong
NOR	Norvège
SWE	Suède
SWI	Suisse

Distributed in the United States by

Hastings House

Publishers
10 East 40th Street, New York, N. Y. 10016

PUBLICATION No. 124 (ISBN 8038-2650-8)

© Copyright under Universal Copyright Convention
Copyright 1971 by Walter Herdeg, The Graphis Press,
45 Nüschelerstrasse, 8001 Zurich, Switzerland
Paper/Papier: Biber Kunstdruck SK3 Admiro hochweiss, 120 gm²
und Werkdruckpapier SK3 Biber Offset, hochweiss maschinen-
glatt, 120 gm²
Printed in Switzerland

■ The editor and the author wish to express their sincere thanks to all who have in any way contributed to this book, above all to the designers, studios and corporations who answered our call to submit their best annual reports. We also would like to express our gratitude to those individuals who have given assistance and advice of one kind or another, especially to Jack J. Kunz for his important part in the preparation of this book; to J. A. Messina, Director of the Mead Library of Ideas in New York, for giving us access to the wealth of material from the Library's Annual Report Exhibits; to Leslie A. Segal, creative director of Corporate Annual Reports, Inc., for his advice and perspective, derived from nine years of annual report design experience, and to Ann Dunham for her writing and editing assistance to Richard A. Lewis, and to Roger J. Gaulon, Director of S. D. E.-Conseils en Information in Paris, for reviewing the French translation of the text.

■ Herausgeber und Autor möchten all jenen herzlich danken, die auf irgendeine Weise zum Gelingen dieses Buches beigetragen haben, speziell allen Designern, Agenturen und Unternehmen, die uns auf unsere Einladung hin ihre besten Jahresberichte sandten. Bei dieser Gelegenheit möchten wir auch denjenigen Mitarbeitern unseren besten Dank aussprechen, die uns mit Rat und Tat zur Seite standen, vor allem Jack J. Kunz für seine Vorarbeiten zu diesem Buch; J. A. Messina, Direktor der Mead Library of Ideas, der uns Einsicht gewährte in die reiche Materialsammlung der Jahresberichts-Ausstellungen der Mead Library; Leslie A. Segal, Creative Director der Corporate Annual Reports, Inc., für seine wertvollen Anregungen, die er uns dank seiner langjährigen Erfahrung als Jahresberichtgestalter geben konnte, und Ann Dunham für ihre Mitarbeit am Text und Roger J. Gaulon, Direktor der S. E. D.-Conseils en Information in Paris, für die Durchsicht der französischen Übersetzungen.

■ L'éditeur et l'auteur adressent leurs remerciements à tous ceux qui d'une manière quelconque ont contribué à la réalisation de cet ouvrage; tout particulièrement les designers, studios et entreprises qui, en réponse à notre invitation, nous ont envoyé leurs meilleurs rapports annuels. Nous tenons d'autre part à remercier très sincèrement toutes les personnes qui nous ont prêté leur assistance et leurs conseils, en particulier Jack J. Kunz qui assuma une part d'une certaine importance dans l'élaboration de ce livre; J. A. Messina, Directeur de la Mead Library of Ideas, New York, qui a bien voulu nous donner accès à l'immense collection de rapports annuels des expositions de la Mead Library; Leslie A. Segal, Directeur Créatif de Corporate Annual Reports, Inc., qui grâce à neuf ans d'expérience en tant que designer de rapports, nous a donné de précieux conseils, ainsi que Roger J. Gaulon, Directeur de S. D. E.-Conseil en Information de Paris, qui a bien voulu revoir toutes les traductions françaises des textes.

GRAPHIS / ANNUAL REPORTS

Editor and Art Director: Walter Herdeg
Text by Richard A. Lewis
Assistant Editor: Stanley Mason
Project Manager: Jack J. Kunz

Editor's Foreword

In the days when private enterprise really was private the annual report was no more than a financial summary of operations, often meant for the eyes of a select few. In the present century companies have grown in size and influence till they are now major forces in economic and social life. As such they need contacts with society, they need an image by which they can be recognized, and the annual report has offered itself as a tool by which image and contacts can be created. As a result the annual report has far outgrown its mere financial function, becoming a corporate communication of the first magnitude. It has also become big business: some companies spend up to half a million dollars on a single issue. Since it aims at the widest possible appeal and wants to be read not only by company shareholders but by almost everybody, from government leaders to prospective employees, it has opened up a vast new field to the skills of the designer, writer, photographer, illustrator, layout man and printer.

This book on the conception and design of annual reports is the first comprehensive work on the subject so far published. It sets out to describe the genesis of the medium, to review its headlong development in the last few decades and to give all those involved in its presentation hints and advice on how to go about the job. In the pictorial section, our illustrations are less documentation of the text than examples of outstanding annual report design.

Since the annual report was, up to a few years ago, chiefly an American phenomenon, much of what is said relates specifically to the United States. The author of the text, Richard A. Lewis, ranks among the very foremost authorities in the field and is President of *Corporate Annual Reports, Inc.*, a creative team that has planned, written, designed and produced over 250 reports in the past nine years.

While emphasis on America reflects the status quo, it does not make this book any the less international. This point is underlined by the reproduction of numbers of good examples of report design from other countries. For the fact is that the rise of the annual report to prominence in America is now rapidly being followed by a parallel development in Europe and elsewhere. The annual report thus presents a growing challenge to corporations, designers and communicators all over the world. This book is meant as a stimulant and a standby to them in their endeavors.

Vorwort des Herausgebers

Avant-propos de l'éditeur

Als man die freie Wirtschaft wirklich noch frei nennen konnte, war der Jahresbericht nichts anderes als eine finanzielle Zusammenfassung von Geschäftsvorgängen, oft nur für die Augen einer auserwählten Minderheit bestimmt. Im gegenwärtigen Jahrhundert haben die Unternehmen an Grösse und Einfluss zugenommen, bis sie zu einem heute sehr bedeutenden Faktor im wirtschaftlichen und sozialen Leben geworden sind. In dieser Eigenschaft aber brauchen sie den Kontakt mit der Gesellschaft, brauchen sie ein Image, das sie unverwechselbar kennzeichnet. Der Jahresbericht hat sich hier als das geeignete Mittel angeboten, mit dessen Hilfe sich Image und Kontakte schaffen lassen. Als Folge davon ist er seiner rein finanziellen Funktion längst entwachsen und zu einem umfassenden Informationsmittel ersten Ranges geworden. Er hat sich ausserdem zu einem sehr wichtigen Geschäft entwikkelt: Manche Unternehmen stecken bis zu einer halben Million Dollar in einen einzigen Jahresbericht. Da er nicht nur von den eigenen Aktionären, sondern von so gut wie jedermann gelesen werden will, vom leitenden Regierungsbeamten bis zum zukünftigen Angestellten des Unternehmens, hat sich hier ein weites Feld für die gestalterischen Fähigkeiten von Designern, Fachschriftstellern, Photographen, Illustratoren und Druckern aufgetan.

Dieses Buch über Konzeption und Gestaltung von Jahresberichten hat sich zum Ziel gesetzt, den Werdegang dieses Mediums zu beschreiben, seine stürmische Entwicklung in den letzten Jahrzehnten einer kritischen Betrachtung zu unterziehen und all denen, die sich mit seiner Herstellung befassen, Hinweise und Ratschläge für ihre Arbeit zu geben.

Der Verfasser des Textes, Richard A. Lewis, gehört zu den bedeutendsten Autoritäten auf diesem Gebiet. Als Präsident der *Corporate Annual Reports, Inc.* hat er mit seinem Team über 250 Jahresberichte konzipiert, geschrieben und produziert. Die Darstellungen im Bildteil sind weniger Illustrationen des Textes als vielmehr Beispiele hervorragender Jahresberichtsgestaltung.

Da der Jahresbericht bis vor ein paar Jahren hauptsächlich ein amerikanisches Phänomen war, bezieht sich vieles des hier Gesagten ganz speziell auf die Vereinigten Staaten. Es ist aber nicht mehr zu übersehen, dass dem grossen Bedeutungszuwachs des Jahresberichtes in Amerika eine parallele Entwicklung in Europa und anderswo auf dem Fusse folgt. Der Jahresbericht stellt deshalb eine wachsende Herausforderung für Unternehmer, textliche und künstlerische Gestalter in aller Welt dar. Dieses Buch ist als Inspiration und Hilfsmittel in ihren Bemühungen gedacht.

Aux beaux jours de l'entreprise privée au sens complet du terme, un rapport annuel se présentait comme un simple résumé financier des opérations à l'intention de quelques rares privilégiés. Notre siècle a vu les grandes sociétés acquérir une dimension et une influence qui en font des facteurs essentiels de la vie économique et sociale. Il s'avère donc nécessaire qu'elles soignent leurs contacts avec le public ainsi que leur image globale. Or, le rapport annuel est un excellent outil de contact et de création d'image. Devenu moyen important de communication, il ne s'en tient plus à un simple état des faits financiers. Certains groupes y consacrent près d'un demi-million de dollars par an, et pour cause. Il s'agit de s'adresser non seulement aux actionnaires, mais en somme au public tout entier, des représentants du gouvernement aux employés prospectifs. C'est ainsi que le rapport annuel est devenu un champ de manœuvre intéressant pour les graphistes, rédacteurs, photographes, illustrateurs, maquettistes et imprimeurs de talent.

Le présent ouvrage sur la conception et le design de rapports annuels est le premier du genre à traiter ce sujet de manière exhaustive. On y examine les origines du médium, puis retrace son foudroyant essor au cours des dernières décennies pour finalement offrir à tous ceux qui participent à la création de tels rapports des indications et conseils des plus utiles pour leur réalisation. La partie illustrative présente une documentation qui, en fait, est une sélection de brillants exemples du design de rapports annuels.

Jusqu'à une date récente, le rapport annuel était l'apanage des grandes sociétés américaines, d'où la forte proportion d'exemples américains. La rédaction du texte a été confiée à l'un des grands spécialistes en la matière, Richard A. Lewis, le président de *Corporate Annual Reports, Inc.*, dont l'équipe créatrice et dynamique a conçu, rédigé et illustré ces neuf dernières années plus de 250 rapports pour les entreprises les plus diverses.

Malgré l'importance de la production américaine dans ce domaine, nous nous sommes attachés à inclure dans ce volume le meilleur de la production du reste du monde, de nombreuses sociétés en Europe et ailleurs emboîtant le pas aux précurseurs américains. Le rapport annuel représente un champ d'activité d'importance croissante pour les entrepreneurs, les designers et spécialistes des communications du monde entier. Puisse ce volume les encourager et les aider dans leur tâche stimulante!

Chapter 1

The Phenomenon of Change

Modern technology has created an age of incredible change and fantastic pace. Some 90 per cent of all the scientists who ever lived are now alive. Half of all the energy consumed by man in the past 2000 years has been consumed in the past 100. And in technologically advanced societies, the total output of goods and services doubles every 15 years.

In the United States the industrial super-boom really began in the mid-1950's, a time when computers started to spawn new technology, stock prices began to rise sharply, and the economy generally was picking up speed. The Gross National Product, which stood at $ 364 billion[1] in 1954, accelerated at a dizzying pace to the $ 1 trillion[1] level in 1971, as American corporations moved through ever-quickening phases of growth and change. Consider examples of what has happened to three companies since 1954:

W. R. Grace & Co., with 1954 sales of $ 413 million, was primarily a shipping and Latin America trading company. By 1970, sales had soared to $ 1.9 billion and the company was almost totally transformed – the shipping line had been sold, Latin American activities were greatly reduced, and Grace had become the nation's fifth largest chemical company.

Litton Industries, one of the great growth companies of American industry, was founded in 1954. It took only until 1967 for the company to reach $ 1 billion in sales, reflecting its successful entry into such diverse areas as office machines, shipbuilding, paper manufacture, publishing, electronics, and X-ray equipment. By 1970, Litton sales had swollen to $ 2.4 billion.

In 1954 *International Business Machines (IBM)*, standing on the verge of the computer age, earned impressive profits of $ 46.5 million from its office machines business; by 1970 the company was the world's foremost producer of computers and profits were a fantastic $ 1 billion.

Not by accident, the middle 1950's were also a point of departure for a completely new type of annual report.

The IBM annual report most dramatically illustrates the new genre. In 1954 the IBM report was essentially unchanged from those issued since the company's founding 42 years earlier. It had a stiff brown paper cover, 20 plain inside pages with only bare financial information – and no photographs or attempts at design.

The following year, IBM modernized its annual report, and has led the field in design and corporate communications ever since. Through the mid and late 1950's, innovation continued with a few corporate leaders, and by the 1960's most major American corporations had joined the vast switch-over to the modern annual report.

The annual report, the key corporate document

What happened in essence was that the annual report – by default – became the prime and often the only tool to help corporate managements define and report on the change and growth that was in effect creating a new company each year. Corporations were experiencing the transience – temporariness, compression – that Alvin Toffler spotlights in his book *Future Shock*. With identity booklets and company films outdated by the time they are produced, the legal deadline of the annual report provides the impetus for top corporate executives to sit down for the only time each year and define their company for the public.

One result of this top management involvement is a willingness to spend large sums to produce the best possible annual report. Companies hire the finest graphic designers and photographers to create the look of their annual report, and they use the best quality paper and printing.

Together, these corporations form a multi-million-dollar annual report market: More than 50000 American companies have shares that are traded publicly. *American Telephone & Telegraph* has the most shareholders – some 3.1 million – and runs off about four million copies, spending about $ 575000 on printing and design.

The GRAPHIS Annual Report Survey[2] of America's 1000 largest corporations shows that most companies – except those with very large print runs – spend $1 a copy or more for the design and printing of their annual reports. Large companies (300000 to four million copies) reported spending 33 cents a copy; middle-sized companies (55000 to 63000 copies) spend 96 cents per copy; and small companies (4500 to 12000 copies) spend an average of $ 1.19 a copy.

Even a unit cost of $ 2 apiece for some 5000 reports is usually a good investment for new, small companies, because for them the annual report is especially important. Large firms have long-established relationships with investors, suppliers, and customers – and, usually, active public relations and advertising programs as well. Many small companies, on the other hand, have no effective way to communicate except through the annual report.

If annual reports have a favorable influence on investment decisions, they have an even more specific value to all kinds of companies. If an annual report can help raise the price/earnings ratio (see Chapter 2) of a medium-sized company like *Joy Manufacturing* (1970 sales of $ 273 million) by even one point this translates into a $ 10-million increase in total stock value. For *AT & T*, the increase would be about $ 2 billion.

To strengthen the communications effectiveness of their annual reports an increasing number of companies are including a corporate identity paragraph, usually placed on the opening spread. This written definition of the company – updated as it is each year – can

---

[1] The terms "billion" and "trillion", are used in this book in their American sense, i.e. one billion = 1000000000, one trillion = 1000000000000.

[2] To gather original data for this book The Corporate Communications Report, in behalf of Graphis Press, surveyed the 1000 largest corporations in the United States. Results of this Graphis Annual Report Survey, believed to be the most comprehensive of its type ever done, are incorporated into the text that follows.

replace hours of verbal communication by top management throughout the year.

The annual report enjoys this primacy for several reasons. Its honesty is assumed: The chief executive officer signs his name to the document, the accountants audit its financial information, and the regulatory agencies in the securities industry review it.

The annual report is the preferred communications document of the men in top management because they have primary control over it (unlike prospectuses, often written by lawyers). An indication of management's own feeling about the annual report is the fact that companies usually print two to three times as many reports as they have shareholders. In addition to its primary function of meeting legal requirements and informing shareholders, the annual report is used regularly for such purposes as recruiting employees, selling products and services, attracting acquisitions, and, increasingly, as a "corporate calling card" when dealing with foreign businessmen.

Westinghouse Electric Corporation, for example, printed 400 000 copies of its 1969 annual report, distributing 166 000 to listed stockholders and another 33 000 to unlisted shareholders whose stock is held by brokers or nominees. In addition the company mailed reports to all employees for the first time, using 142 000 reports. It reserved 12 000 reports for training and recruiting work, 3500 for mailing to analysts, banks, universities and libraries, and 3700 for public and community relations. The company held the remaining 40 000 reports for general corporate purposes.

The annual report's regular issuance and systematic distribution – as it is incorporated into official files throughout the investment community – give it the substance of a fixture or institution. The annual report is history, it is record, it is the all-encompassing source document of the corporation.

The leading edge of corporate thinking is often first disclosed in the annual report, either through a direct policy statement or indirectly, depending on what is emphasized in its pages. *American Can Company's* 1969 report, featuring on page one a large photo of an attractive young woman consumer, underscored and signaled the company's increasing emphasis on the consumer market. One of the most important audiences for this kind of communication is the company's own executives, who otherwise get lost in the headlong rush into the future.

The annual report also serves as a catalyst for formalizing various situations in a rapidly changing company – many a major management decision is made in order to expedite production of the annual report. An organization chart may lack a name to head a particular group; the executive will often be appointed as the deadline approaches. Vague and confusing titles for people, and functions for operating units, frequently get straightened out in time for the annual report.

Because the annual report always involves top corporate management in the activity of communication, executives often use it to make special points or meet special communication needs as they come up. Some examples:
• *Ethyl Corporation*, faced with increasing demands to eliminate lead additives in gasoline as a means of reducing air pollution, in its 1969 annual report included a special booklet advocating Ethyl's alternative solution to the problem.

• The *Fidelity Corporation* 1968 report was specifically designed to attract acquisitions. The presentation was in two main parts – a dialogue on the company's acquisitions policy between the two top officers, and a series of testimonials by heads of acquired companies discussing their relationship with Fidelity Corporation.
• The 1967 *J.C. Penney Co.* annual report was designed to recruit young executives by correcting a prevalent impression that there was no chance for ambitious young people to advance in the company. This report pictured and named young executives and described their jobs, making the point that Penney's offers a wide variety of interesting and challenging job opportunities to college graduates.
• *Litton Industries* translated 3000 copies of its 1963 annual report into Russian and sent them to Russian and American ambassadors around the world as well as key readers in the Soviet Union. The move was a calculatedly indirect bid for favorable attention from a certain handful of American ambassadors and from the British banking community, a preliminary step to an overseas expansion program that Litton launched the next year.
• The *US Industries* 1969 annual report was designed to give recognition and prestige to chief executive officers of 130 acquired companies who serve, in USI, as independent entrepreneurial managers. The report featured several pages of group photos of these managers.

American business today is faced with an unprecedented challenge: a growing body of people who question its very right to exist. These people – youth, clergymen, stockholders – are concerned with race problems and poverty, worried about pollution and suspicious of the military-industrial complex. Businessmen today must both defend what is right about American capitalism and assure the public that they are working to correct what is wrong. In part, this message is being communicated in annual reports. *Crown Zellerbach* included a 12-page portfolio on corporate social responsibility in its 1968 annual report. *Southern California Edison* enclosed with its 1969 annual report a special 16-page booklet: "Edison and the Environmental Crisis". *Bank of America*, the country's largest bank, printed its 1970 annual report on recycled paper, sparing 600 to 1000 trees, while *Outboard Marine* printed an essay entitled "The Quality of Life... and what we are doing about it".

The annual report must communicate basic strengths

Although the annual report is an effective tool for serving specialized communication needs, it should be primarily concerned with presenting a company's basic strengths, those assets that will help bring future growth. This message is, of course, directed most importantly to potential buyers of the company's common stock; but it is also aimed at employees, bankers, suppliers, customers, and at businessmen and government officials in other countries. Among the basic strengths companies try to communicate are:

Technology In a world of rapid change, it is essential that companies have the competence to keep up. *Weyerhaeuser* imparted an impression of high technology in its 1968 annual report, illustrated with dramatic double-page microphotographs. The text welcomed change: "A laboratory idea conceived today can create a new industry tomorrow. And, in the process, render old ways obsolete. At Weyerhaeuser, we like it that way. Half of our sales this year were of products we didn't make 15 years ago."

Financial strength   Disclosure by such major corporations as the *Penn Central Railroad*, *Lockheed Aircraft* and *Ling-Temco-Vought* of massive financial difficulties has shattered the automatic assumption that big companies are rich companies. Companies that possess financial strength have turned to the annual report as the logical document in which to underscore this strength. While this has generally been accomplished in the text, the 1970 annual report of *Tishman Realty & Construction Co.* devoted a two-page spread to a dramatic chart presentation of the assets underlying the company's cash flow.

Productivity   Much of the growth of the 1960's was fueled by the increasing productivity that corporations were able to achieve through automated equipment and other capital investments. In the 1970's, productivity increases will be harder to come by, but they will remain a fundamental influence on profit potential. Where they can, companies are using annual reports to demonstrate their ability to increase productivity.

Research   The *Squibb Beech-Nut* 1969 annual report, by focusing on research, assured readers that the company has the technological basis for developing new proprietary and ethical products, and also indirectly reminded the public and the Government that the high cost of developing new drugs justifies the high retail price of such drugs.

Overseas markets   Since many overseas markets are growing faster than domestic markets, an increasing number of corporations are emphasizing their strong position abroad. *First National City Bank*, for one, underscored the importance of its foreign operations by printing its 1970 annual report in French, Spanish, and English.

Acquisitions   In 1967, *SCM Corporation's* annual report dealt with the problem of explaining to shareholders the sudden acquisition of *The Glidden Company*, a major producer of paints and chemicals — which doubled the company's size but diluted its image in the glamorous field of copying machines. By devoting four pages to a dialogue entitled "The Meaning of Glidden: An SCM Forum", the company was able to have nine executives of the two companies explain in their own words why they believed the merger would strengthen SCM. The explanation was picked up by the financial press and widely circulated.

Markets   In order to win proper recognition from security analysts and other professional investors, it is important for a company to clearly describe the markets it serves, particularly if they offer above-average growth. *Berkey Photo* devoted a special feature in its 1967 annual report to describing the video and motion picture market, then identifying Berkey's position within the market. Taking a particularly imaginative approach, the 1965 *Motorola* report devoted nine pages to showing how Motorola serves the city of San José, California — making the impressive point that "Motorola can touch the lives of everyone, one way or another".

Management   Most professional investors consider good management the number one criterion for corporate success. It is no surprise, then, that annual reports consistently work at presenting management in the best possible light. The annual report itself is, in fact, an important measure of management's taste, sophistication, and credibility. Modern annual reports tend to use casual, unposed-looking photographs of their executives in place of formal portraits.

But even the 12-month span between annual reports is sometimes too long in this age of transience, and corporations are increasingly using new forms of communication in an effort to keep their identity as up-to-date as possible. *General Electric*, an innovator and leader in the modern annual report field, has divided its annual report into what are in effect four quarterly magazines, so that it can report to stockholders in a meaningful way on a more current basis. *Pan American World Airways*, concerned with employee morale in the midst of financial problems for the airlines, installed a recorded telephone message from the President, available to all employees and changed periodically. At least one corporation is planning a similar telephone approach for shareholder communications.

And new media will bring new types of messages — the video cassette, for example, will undoubtedly open new opportunities for timely corporate reporting in the near future.

But as corporations continue trying more effective and timely ways to communicate, the annual report will almost certainly remain the chief source document of the corporation each year. As such, it will continue to be used for a multitude of purposes by corporate executives who have an almost desperate need in this era of rapid change to accurately identify their company.

But even today many company presidents are not fully aware of how much they rely on the annual report for general identification and communication. Ask a chief executive officer — in the privacy of his own office — what he wants the annual report to accomplish, and he will candidly respond that he wants it to influence people to invest in his company. The magic created by investor favor is discussed in the next chapter.

Chapter 2

The Phenomenon of Growth

If the most basic function of the annual report is to communicate with investors, the most important message to them is to "buy stock". Since the mid-50's, encouraged by the modern annual report, a new breed of American stockholder has indeed been buying stock and creating the phenomenon of the growth company.

Capital growth – the prime objective

In 1954, there were six or seven million stockholders in the U. S. – largely sophisticated businessmen, people with access to good investment counseling advice. Today, some 30 million shareholders hold stock directly, and perhaps 100 million own shares through mutual funds or pension funds. Today's shareholders tend to be younger, less well established, more emotional, and more impatient with their investments. Until the 1950's shareholders were primarily interested in dividend income – capital appreciation was not their main goal. But after the mid-50's, and increasingly through most of the 1960's, capital growth had become the primary objective for most investors, and the old reliable stocks with their steady dividends had lost favor.

And no wonder. In 1961, an investor could have purchased *IBM* stock at $ 100 a share and sold it at $ 158 later in the same year, or bought shares of *Litton Industries* at $ 17 and sold them for $ 33. With a chance to double their money, shareholders cared little about dividends.

So investors began searching eagerly for growth companies. And the companies, just as eagerly, sought to be identified as growth companies. The GRAPHIS survey asked the chief executives of 146 of America's 1000 largest companies what adjective described the impression they wanted the annual report reader to form about their company. The most popular answer, given by 57 company presidents, was, "growth-oriented". Only 20 executives listed "honest", and a single respondent listed "blue chip". This overwhelming preference for a growth company image explains why corporations lavish so much time and money on the annual report.

The importance of the growth image

It is necessary to understand the price-earnings multiple, commonly called the P/E, to comprehend the fervor with which corporations pursue the image of a growth company.

The price-earnings multiple is the number that when multiplied by a company's earnings establishes a theoretical price that the stock should properly sell for. While closing prices of a stock vary daily, the P/E over the long run tends to establish the selling price range. Multiples are rather mysteriously assigned by a consensus of security analysts and other members of the financial community, but they are almost always based on the projected growth rate of future earnings.

Thus a company producing pulp and paper might be assumed to have only an average growth potential and would be assigned a P/E of 10. But an electronics company, with special knowledge in an exciting new technology, might be assumed to have extraordinary growth potential and would be assigned a P/E of 50. If the paper company and the electronics company each earned $ 1 a share, the multiples would cause the paper company stock to sell for $ 10 and the electronics company stock to sell for $ 50. Should both companies increase earnings to $ 2 a share, the paper company's multiple would move its stock price up to $ 20, whereas the electronics company's multiple would push its price to $ 100.

The magic of conglomerate growth

It was in the early 60's that certain companies learnt the magic of how to parlay high multiples into conglomerate growth. It works like this: Electronics Company A, with two million shares outstanding, has earnings of $ 4 million, or $ 2 a share. Because of its 50-times multiple, investors are paying $ 100 a share. Electronics Company A then approaches Paper Company B and proposes a merger. Company B has the same earnings and the same shares outstanding, but has a multiple of only 10, so that its shares are selling for $ 20. Company A buys Company B for a dollar value of 10 times the earnings of Company B, or $ 40 million. But Company A doesn't pay in cash, it pays with its own $ 100-a-share stock, which requires issuing 400 000 shares to the owners of Company B. The result is that Company A now has 2 400 000 shares outstanding and earnings of $ 8 million, or $ 3.33 a share. Applying the 50-times multiple to these new earnings pushes Company A's stock from $ 100 to $ 166.50.

The growth company look

Not all companies, of course, needed mergers to achieve growth or to command high P/Es. Three of the greatest growth companies of the 60's – *IBM, Xerox* and *Polaroid*, each dominating a field of high-growth technology – generated rapid internal growth. In fact it is these companies, particularly IBM, that established the "growth company look" so much in evidence in today's annual reports.

Thomas Watson, Jr., who became President of IBM in 1951, brought Paul Rand into the company to head a new graphics program. Rand, one of the world's leading graphic designers, has produced the IBM annual reports since 1957. His innovations have included paper (discarding the old shiny blue-white sheets used in letterpress printing in favor of a rich dull-coated stock); a beautiful and refined type face; different format sizes from the standard 8½ by 11 inch report, and many other subtle design factors. But Paul Rand's greatest contribution to annual reports has been in his use of photography. Working with some of the world's greatest photojournalists, men like Erich Hartmann and Ernst Haas of *Magnum*, Rand pioneered a new, slightly mysterious and impressionistic industrial photography that seems to express the spirit of *IBM*'s kind of technology. Along with the dramatic color photography went a generous use of white space and other visual elements that added up to the new growth look.

Another innovative company in this respect was *General Dynamics*, whose 1958 annual report was the most advanced graphically at that time. Designed by designer Erik Nitsche, the report interleaved rich black-and-white photos of airplanes, rockets and submarines with half-pages containing full-color photographs, many of them abstract industrial designs. Three printing processes were used: gravure for the black-and-white photos, letterpress for the color, and lithography for the cover and text. (See figs. 394, 401–403.)

Unfortunately, three years after its lavish 1958 annual report, General Dynamics managed to lose more money than any American industrial corporation had ever lost – $143 million – reflecting an unsuccessful entry into the commercial jet aircraft market. That year's annual report was understandably Spartan, and for a few years the company ceased to be a pace-setter in annual reports.

Meanwhile, annual reports were drawing increasing attention in the graphic arts field. Prominent commercial art shows began including categories for annual reports. An important influence was the *Mead Library of Ideas* International Annual Report Exhibit.[3] Started in 1956 by the *Mead Paper Company*, the exhibit today consists of five traveling shows that visit more than 100 cities in the U. S. and Canada. Entries for possible inclusion in the show are judged by leading graphic designers and others involved in corporate graphics.

General Electric Company's procedure for building a growth company image was not based primarily on graphics. GE took a very methodical, logical approach to the annual report, shaping it to meet corporate objectives. By the mid-50's, GE had recognized the importance of growth and made it a major theme of company communications – so successfully that, despite a lackluster growth record of around four per cent a year during the 60's, the company's healthy P/E ratio continued and GE is still popularly considered a major growth company.

GE's annual reports have been scientifically produced, incorporating numerous innovations suggested by the readership surveys conducted nearly every year since 1953. The surveys showed, for example, that readership of the Chairman's Letter could be increased many times by reducing the text to a single page, and by including the Chairman's picture. They also showed that readership could be sustained by running color photos throughout the report.

But General Electric's chief contribution was its emphasis on achieving specific communications objectives by integrating photos, captions, headlines and text to support specific annual report themes. One year's theme in the early 60's, for example, was aimed at establishing GE as a company with superior "systems capability", a phrase that at the time was closely identified with growth companies. Since companies are increasingly trying to achieve specific communications objectives with their annual reports, GE's approach may turn out to have the most lasting influence on the modern annual report.

The glamorous annual report

If *IBM* led the way with good design and *General Electric* introduced scientific research, then *Litton In-* dustries must earn its place in history for the glamorous annual report. As a new company and a conglomerate, Litton possessed neither General Electric's long-established reputation as a producer of consumer products nor the clear-cut technological image provided by IBM's computers, *Xerox's* copying machines, or *Polaroid's* self-developing cameras. Litton directly faced the problem of building a corporate image to go along with its intended growth. Almost from the beginning of its corporate existence in 1954, Litton was striving to look like the billion-dollar company that founder Tex Thornton was planning to build.

For its annual reports, Litton's strategy was elaborate editorial themes combined with spectacular graphic design. Crosby Kelly, until 1965 Litton's Manager of Investor Relations and the spearhead behind the reports, describes Litton's communications problem this way: "In effect, we had to tell people 'We're coming, we'll be there.' Building faith and confidence in the company was the biggest single mission of the annual report," he says, and he aimed to achieve it with all audiences – employees as well as stockholders. "I feel you have to have something that symbolizes the corporation – something like a flag," says Kelly. "One of the problems in industry relates to failure to have a symbol to rally behind. If I want you to take me on faith, how do I do it? Fly a flag. And that flag was the annual report."

Litton was in effect highlighting the future before it had gotten there – a technique that was to have many imitators. Teaming with Kelly to produce the early Litton reports was Robert Miles Runyan, whose brilliant and flamboyant approach to graphic design resulted in the most dramatic and imaginative series of annual reports ever produced.

The 1959 Litton report, the first to contain distinctive graphics and an elaborate theme, featured three two-page spreads combining still-life photos with theme-setting statements. One spread, illustrated with antique scientific instruments, implied Litton's technological leadership and asserted that American industry must meet the challenge of foreign competition "with higher productivity, superior quality, and with ingenuity and resourcefulness in product design". A second spread, illustrated with a toy cannon, ancient weapons and a copy of the Declaration of Independence, declared, "Our country must continue to maintain its defenses strong," and went on to describe Litton as "a major industrial citizen serving well the defense needs of our country". The third spread, illustrated with an antique treasure chest and some Litton stock certificates, assured investors of Litton's concern with financial management that, among other things, ensures "that there is an adequate profit on sales to provide a sound return on investment for the stockholder".

This report was among the first to present the "big picture" – the major social and economic trends of the times – and then to show how the individual company fits within this framework. "Just giving the facts is not enough," says Kelly, "because if the readers come to the wrong conclusion, you've failed in your responsibility." Kelly admits to having had little interest in clearly explaining the company. He preferred to have the an-

---

[3] The Mead Library of Ideas International Annual Report Exhibit is the major showcase for outstanding graphic design. A call for entries is sent out in April; the deadline is July 31. Normally the five judges – all experts in graphic design – screen the entries in August. The exhibit takes place in September or October in New York. Then traveling exhibits are sent around the country. Send entries to Mead Library of Ideas, 200 Park Avenue, New York, N. Y. 10017.

nual report arouse the interest of security analysts enough for them to visit Litton's Los Angeles headquarters for the full story. Kelly says he was complimented when one analyst told him, "Crosby, I read the whole annual report before I realized you hadn't told me a damn thing".

The Litton reports became increasingly grand in scope. The 1962 report, for example, contained on the cover a stunning photo of the Acropolis in Athens and was dedicated to freedom — "to the day when all mankind will have leaped over The Wall". Photos throughout the report illustrated historic scenes relating to man's quest for freedom. The mystique of the annual report, however, was nothing compared to the mysterious force that was pushing Litton's stock price higher and higher, and was attracting the interest and envy of other enterprising businessmen.

Soon the tactics pioneered by Litton Industries spawned new corporate conglomerates. Litton's own executives were among the first who began to understand the technique. If you acquired a lot of small companies and were able to maintain your own high P/E ratio and apply it to the acquisitions, you could have a fantastic new "growth company". And many of these executives left to start their own firms, among them *City Investing*, *Walter Kidde*, *Teledyne* and *KDI Corporation*.

Robert Miles Runyan aggressively sought out these new companies as clients. He called them LIDO'S (Litton Industries Drop-Outs). Because of the Runyan touch, a great number of mystique-oriented annual reports appeared in the mid-1960's.

Such reports often subordinated and even sacrificed content to design. One beautiful Teledyne report featured full-color abstract technology photos dropped out of a dark gray page — with the text printed in black ink against the same dark gray background. The City Investing annual report for 1968 was a whole book full of pictures — without a single caption. The pictures, and a calendar of world events that ran across the tops of the pages, provided drama but not much information.

Other non-LIDO conglomerates that tended toward mystique-building graphics were *Gulf and Western Industries*, *A-T-O*, and *Ling-Temco-Vought (LTV)*. The 1965 LTV annual report is a classic, and not in the way it was intended. The cover has embossed white Grecian columns against a dark background, followed inside by many pictures from ancient Greece and a statement that concluded: "Thus, we have drawn from the Hellenic Golden Age to illustrate 'Building Lasting Values' — our corporate goal and the theme of this report." The LTV people had tried to copy the style of the Litton report, but they lacked the flair, and the result was decidedly *nouveau riche*.

Conglomerates lose their magic

Then came 1968 and the beginning of a sharp downtrend in the stock market. Conglomerates could no longer work magic and their stocks led the rest of the market into a precipitous decline, shattering the dreams of thousands of investors. Conglomerate stocks were hurt worst of all and at least one, *KDI Corporation*, filed for bankruptcy.

The stock market hit bottom in mid-1970 and then rebounded sharply within months. Real growth companies, like IBM, and companies with valuable resources, like the oil producers, were in the forefront of the upswing. The conglomerates dragged, and many were busy selling off money-losing companies.

The investing public in general was left in a sober mood. People talked about "getting back to basics". Companies highlighted in their annual reports such virtues as liquidity and productivity and unique competitive advantages. But while the language had changed, surprisingly few companies actually cut back on the quality appearance of their annual reports. The majority of the companies surveyed in 1970 planned to spend as much, if not more, for their annual reports as they had for their 1969 reports. Companies continued to want to look like growth companies. And investors were still looking for growth companies, though demanding more evidence.

The trend is toward fuller disclosure

Fortunately for investors, the trends within the financial industry are toward greater readability, clarity, and disclosure of facts. In front-of-the-book text sections, companies are shortening the copy: the 1969 *Westinghouse* annual report has only 3500 words — 50 per cent of the text length of the previous year.

There is increasing pressure by the Securities and Exchange Commission and others to require corporations to disclose more interpretative financial information on an equal basis to everyone. For example, the SEC wants more accurate disclosure of sales and earnings from a company's various operations, or product groups. This will prevent a company that derives most of its profit from rubber, for example, from implying that it is really an aerospace company.

More subtle pressure for better shareholder information has come from another quarter: the weekly FINANCIAL WORLD magazine, which since 1941 has issued awards each year for annual reports[4], and has for the past several years favored companies giving such product group breakdowns.

FINANCIAL WORLD'S influence is considerable, since each year it judges some 5000 annual reports, awarding Bronze trophies (the award is a single bookend) in more than 90 industries, a dozen Silver awards in broader industry categories and one Gold award for the year's most outstanding annual report. The 1970 Gold Oscar-of-Industry award went to Westinghouse Electric, whose 1969 report for the first time broke out sales and earnings for its five major operating units; in previous years the company had merely provided percentages of total sales by broad product category.

The Accounting Principles Board, also, has recommended many changes aimed at providing investors with more reliable data. Companies are responding to this form of pressure and providing more and better information in annual reports.

And the financial statements are yielding in other ways to the trend toward greater clarity and disclosure. Historically, companies have been required to submit a "legal" annual report to the Government in the form of a 10K annual reporting form. Recently the Government has begun demanding considerably more

---

4 Financial World Magazine each year evaluates over 5000 annual reports. In late June, Merit Award certificates are sent to about 2000 companies that have met minimum standards. Reports are judged 50% — information for the stockholder, 25% — content for the security analyst and professional investor, and 25% — general appearance. The security analysts who serve as judges, however, tend to have conservative tastes in graphic design. In late October, results of the final judging are announced at an awards banquet attended by as many as 1500 corporate executives. Nearly 300 companies, representing 90 industry categories, receive awards. To enter, mail two copies of your annual report by May 31st to: Annual Report Survey, Financial World, 17 Battery Pl., New York, 10004.

information than must be included in the annual report to shareholders. To eliminate this inequity, a growing number of companies have started to include in their annual report to shareholders the same information that is required in the 10K report.

Even the footnotes, traditionally printed in tiny type and obscure to almost everyone except accountants, are becoming more readable. A proposed rule will require them to be printed in the same size type as the rest of the report.

Another trend is toward eliminating footnotes, as such, by incorporating them into the body of the annual report text. General Electric, which has followed this practice for a number of years, includes the footnotes in a Financial Review section that runs alongside the financial tables. This tends to make for dull reading, but it is a worthwhile step in that all financial text material would be certified by the accountants. *J. C. Penney*, following GE's lead with its 1969 report, not only incorporated footnotes into a Financial Review but went a step further by eliminating some of the dull prose. Instead of relating all the details on leased properties, something of interest only to a professional analyst, Penney's merely noted in the Financial Review that a memo on the subject was available on request. All these efforts are commendable trends toward making the entire annual report an even more reliable and accurate source document.

Chapter 3:   **Creating a Quality Annual Report**

The growth company look was an exciting new graphic approach to annual reports, and a new approach to the written word arose with it. Together they formed the new corporate journalism, one that heavily borrowed techniques from the newspapers, magazines, and television programs that were clamoring around it for readers' attention. It was high time that annual reports discovered the need for excitement: the average person is bombarded with several times the 10 000 to 20 000 edited words he actually "ingests" each day, Alvin Toffler reports in *Future Shock*.

And annual reports compete directly with each other: One *General Electric* survey showed that the average GE stockholder owns shares in 16 different companies. As a result, he spends less than 10 minutes on each annual report. Competition is even keener within an industry group, where the favorable reaction of the security analysts, as they compare annual reports with each other, is all-important.

The writing   With competition this stiff, top professional talent is required to create a successful annual report. For one thing, it is essential to have a trained professional writer and/or editor, whether an outside specialist or a member of the corporation.

The writer's first and most obvious value to the company is in researching, interviewing, and organizing the vast and often rambling topics to be covered, then forming them into a first and second draft. The still widely held idea that no outside person can learn enough about a company to write about it is erroneous. Most insiders suffer from knowing so much about their company that they are unable to isolate the pertinent facts. Once the basic text is written, the other executives can then edit and rewrite as they see fit. The writer's skill and experience at the preliminary stage save many executive hours, and result in a much more readable and focused manuscript, one that covers the essentials and eliminates trivia.

The writer makes his contribution in several ways.

"The greatest harm a company can do to itself with its annual report is to gild the lily," declares Dan Lufkin, former security analyst and co-founder of *Donaldson, Lufkin & Jenrette, Inc.*, one of Wall Street's most successful young firms. The company that misleads financial analysts into making overly bullish projections will win long-lasting enmity from the professionals it has fooled. So the job of presenting the company is extremely delicate. On the one hand the writer should present the company in the best possible light; on the other hand, he risks doing great harm if he overstates the case.

A subtle but important contribution of the experienced writer is writing that has the desired "right-sounding" effect. In the case of annual reports, the copy often should probably sound a little like the straightforward prose found in THE WALL STREET JOURNAL or BUSINESS WEEK, two publications that have become the standard reading material of the American business public. Writers with advertising backgrounds often fail with annual reports, because they lack the touch of understatement that is necessary for credibility. And lawyers and businessmen often have trouble producing a short, direct sentence.

Photography   If straight text sections in an annual report must avoid an unrealistically rosy impression, the graphic elements can dramatize whatever inherent excitement the company may possess. High-quality photography has been one of the most important ingredients in the successful or growth company look, and one of the reasons for the high cost of producing the modern annual report. Most established annual report photographers working in the major metropolitan areas charge from $ 300 to $ 700 for each day of actual location shooting. Studio photographers may charge $ 1000 a day or more. Such expenses as transportation, lodging, and film and processing costs are billed in addition to the day rate.

Corporate executives often consider these fees excessive, yet "obtaining good photography on time" was listed by those in the GRAPHIS survey as the second greatest source of frustration in producing the annual report (the first: reconciling viewpoints of senior management). Therein lies the answer: the top photographers deliver dependability, creativity, and overall professionalism. In addition to their shooting days, they confer with the designer and learn the basic objectives of the annual report (time that is not billed), another reason why their photos almost always give the desired result. It is also important to hire a photographer accustomed to dealing with highly placed executives; such businessmen are rightfully impatient with reshooting or any suggestion of amateurishness. Companies that hire the first available photographers are taking a chance on the entire visual look of the product as well as the reputation of the team producing the annual report.

It must be made clear at the outset what specific rights the company has to the photographer's coverage. Professional photographers' associations have established a code that makes photographs available only for the purpose for which they were taken. In practice, the company generally receives the right to use the photos for all kinds of collateral purposes—in the company magazine, in press releases and other promotion. Advertising usage requires a separate transaction; the agency negotiates with the photographer and pays him an additional fee, representing the money saved by not having to shoot the picture from scratch.

Design An even more important factor in a quality annual report is the designer, who must understand the company's communications goal, pick the right shots from the vast selection, then crop and otherwise utilize them most effectively. Sometimes he elects to forgo photography and use high-quality illustrations, especially if the corporation is a financial institution or other kind of company lacking photographic subjects. If properly conceived, illustrations can often convey intangibles better than photographs. In its 1968 report, *St. Joe Minerals Corporation* wanted to show the company's substantial capital investment in new mines and smelting facilities. A photographer would have faced the nearly impossible task of showing the cluttered and unimpressive interiors of mines and huge but not visually dramatic smelting facilities. The illustrator was able to convey the magnitude of these projects and communicate their importance for St. Joe.

As companies look for increasingly novel ways to present their corporate images, they go beyond traditional illustrative approaches. The 1969 *Scovill* annual report featured assemblages made of wood, glass, and other materials that dramatically pictured the markets Scovill was in. Companies can use such works afterwards to brighten up corporate headquarters, but again must clearly establish the ultimate ownership of the original art. Another approach was the inclusion in the *Ansul Company's* 1968 annual report of three fold-out posters, designed by leading poster artists. The posters served as an integral part of the annual report, and Ansul offered a limited number to shareholders upon request.

Typography An element rarely understood or fully appreciated by corporate executives is typography. It frequently makes the difference between a raw, ama-teurish effect and a distinguished "quality" look. The selection of a type face for a specific report should be left to the designer, who understands the subtle, sophisticated differences between type faces.

There are fashions in type faces just as in other elements of annual reports. Modern Gothic type faces are currently very much in vogue. The use of a Gothic face by *General Electric*, whose reports won the FINANCIAL WORLD gold medals in 1961 and 1962, proved the readability of these faces and became a major factor in the growth of their use.

Headlines and other display type are also important graphic elements, and can help convey a conservative impression, a modern look, or a technological tone.

The effective application of white space is often hard to explain to corporate executives. Businessmen, accustomed to memos and other non-designed communications, often think all available space should be filled with words or pictures, and fail to realize that the use or misuse of space importantly determines the impact of the printed material itself. Generous use of white space in the *IBM* annual reports has made this part of the "look" of modern annual reports.

Charts and graphs provide another fine opportunity for graphic pacing as well as a means for amplifying key parts of the corporate message. The most valuable goal here is simplicity, and some companies have gotten quite expert at simple bar charts and alpine charts. And pie charts are becoming a common element as more and more companies disclose sales and earnings by product groups. Some companies use charts to dramatize a good year, and eliminate them when business has been bad. This transparent device could be interpreted by analysts as an indication that the company doesn't expect the charts to go upward again.

The printing paper Another subtle ingredient is the paper on which the book is printed. Weight, coating, and coloring are the characteristics of printing stock that make the difference in look and feel of the paper. *IBM* pioneered the use of dull-coated stock, and this kind of paper practically became a standard during the 1960's. Technological advances give today's designer a plethora of surfaces on which to present his message. They range from glossy coated papers, which offer brilliant photographic reproduction, to the conservative, subtle looks that can often be obtained with soft-textured colored papers. The choice of weight for the paper makes the kind of difference one immediately notices between a firm and a weak hand-shake. A flimsy annual report may negate the feeling of substance that the words are trying to convey.

Information in layers But all these graphic elements add up to very little if they are not planned to work with the written content of the annual report. The biggest challenge the editors and designers have in working together is that ubiquitous business reader, the skimmer. In the length of time spent by the average shareholder, it is impossible to convey any great detail about the company's performance. The annual report must therefore impart the most important *impression* of the company's strength, solidity, future growth, technological innovation, product expansion—whatever the company's main message is.

One answer is to present important information in

layers. This technique is designed for skimmers, and is not unlike the newspaper practice of presenting the most important information in the headline, the next in the first paragraph, and so on. In an annual report, the first layer of information is really the cover—it provides the most general impression. The second layer is the President's Letter, which *GE*'s surveys reveal is usually the best-read part of the report. The third layer—for readers who have found the first two interesting enough to go on—is the pictures and accompanying captions. Many people will read a caption only if the picture is sufficiently interesting. Probably the next step, or layer, is the subheads scattered through the text of the Review of Operations. This is particularly true if the subheads convey actual information—for example, "Sales Up 17 Per Cent" instead of merely "Sales". And opening paragraphs of sections that summarize the material to follow are a useful journalistic touch.

The final layers are the details of the Review of Operations, the Financial Review, and other sections, which are there for the more serious and informed investor. The integrated annual report presents the financial data, operating data, pictures, and other graphic elements in one appealing package.

Two-part annual reports Some companies take the opposite tack, separating the types of information completely, and come up with the phenomenon of the two-part annual report. *U. S. Plywood-Champion Paper* and *Ralston Purina Co.* have used two-part reports, with a separate two-color booklet stapled on the inside front cover, containing a message to shareholders and the financial statement; the picture section then reads out to the right.

Each year a few companies send out two completely separate books, a very self-defeating practice. It is too easy for the key audience, the security analysts, to file the financial book and discard the picture book. Since the objective is to interest the analyst in the growth potential of a company, and the theme, text, and photos are all directed toward conveying such a positive message about the company, the security analyst should get the whole package. The integrated annual report, certainly the most successful type of presentation, will have the information in layers—the most visible elements for the not-too-concerned stockholder, and underneath them the sophisticated and detailed information for the analyst.

The financial language Investor surveys sometimes report with alarm that most shareholders don't understand the financial language used in annual reports—terms like "convertible debenture". This is not the problem it is claimed to be. Even the shareholder who understands the terminology can't intelligently read a financial statement picked up at random, because there are too many optional ways of presenting the information. An analysis of the financial statement is best left to the professional analyst, who can interview company officials for exact meanings.

In this same vein, there is an on-going discussion on whether the annual report should be written primarily to interest "Aunt Jane", the symbolic small stockholder, or to convey financial information to the investment decision-maker, who, while usually a professional, may also be a small businessman or finan-

cially sophisticated head of household. In terms of volume of shares, all but a tiny percentage of stock-buying decisions are either made or influenced by a professional. As an audience, professional investors are easily 100 times more important than small, individual shareholders. An effective, integrated report, in any event, will be meaningful both to Aunt Jane and to the professionals.

The innovative approach The well-organized, integrated annual report has virtually become the standard that a company must meet if it is to be competitive in the financial marketplace. But once in a while, a company comes up with an approach that is so creative and innovative that it generates widespread recognition and publicity. In a field where there is tremendous paucity of truly original thinking, the business media are eager to write about something really unusual.

Unfortunately, many companies confuse true creativity with elaborate graphics or gimmicks that put off the audience instead of attracting them. Methods like printing with perfumed ink or putting the message on a phonograph record that the analyst can't file or even play are highly inappropriate in the corporate communications field.

Several companies, however, have come up with some truly original approaches to their annual reports.
• An early classic was *Charles Pfizer'*s printing its 1956 annual report as a Sunday newspaper supplement to be distributed to the 3.5 million readers of the NEW YORK TIMES, CHICAGO TRIBUNE, and LOS ANGELES TIMES. To make sure of reaching key audiences, Pfizer distributed 200,000 additional copies to members of Congress, state governors, civic and industrial leaders in Pfizer plant communities, educators, pharmacists, physicians, public libraries, non-stockholding employees, customers and suppliers, members of the financial community, plant visitors, and national opinion leaders. An Associated Press story on the event was carried in more than 100 newspapers and THE NEW YORKER magazine called Pfizer a "trailblazer". The newspaper supplement program, which was repeated the next two years, was a key part of Pfizer's investor relations program, which started in 1954 when the company had 13 000 stockholders. By the mid-1960's, the company had more than 80 000 stockholders.
• To emphasize that it was more than a tin can maker, *American Can Company* in the early 1960's sent out its annual report in a cardboard tube. The tube was one of a new diversified line of food packaging materials for the company. The company learned that well over 90 per cent of recipients opened the annual report that year, compared to a normal figure of around 60 per cent. Unfortunately, the report remained curled and was almost impossible to file, drawing some protests from security analysts. But the favorable publicity was worth it.
• "Dear Sir: I am 15 years old and I have a little money saved up that I want to invest in some company's stock ... Can you please explain ... what you are doing and why ... Sincerely, Chris Nelson." These words, from a letter reprinted on the cover of the 1963 *Bell & Howell Company* annual report, provided a perfect opening for the company to dedicate its 1963 annual report to Chris and "the many young people like you, who have such a genuine interest in the businesses of America". The company then proceeded to explain its

high-technology business in very simple terms—much to the appreciation of many adult shareholders who didn't understand the company either.

• In 1969, Philadelphia's *Girard Bank* commissioned author James Michener and artist Andrew Wyeth to create a small book called "Quality of Living". The annual report accompanying the book was rather simple and inexpensive. But the relevant and striking message contained in the handsomely packaged book by the two Pennsylvania residents drew a large amount of favorable publicity, including 5000 laudatory letters. In 1970, the bank followed its earlier success with a 64-page book called "An Urban Planet?", written by Barbara Ward, the noted international economist, and illustrated by a Philadelphia watercolorist.

• *Cybermatics, Inc.*, a small New Jersey company with some $ 6 million in annual sales, applied creativity at the opposite end of the literary spectrum. Their 1969 annual report simply did what is almost never done—it took a humorous approach to the company. The cover: "Eight impartial observers tell you how Cybermatics, Inc., *really* did in 1969." The testimonials inside are from the cleaning lady—"Trash at Cybermatics is up 630%", the lunch delivery boy—"They order seven times more cheeseburgers than the year before", and the window washer—"They look busier than last year".

• In 1970, *Combustion Engineering* "wanted to see how the company looked to someone with a fresh viewpoint", according to Robert Amen, vice president of corporate communications. Accordingly, Amen hired a 17-year-old black youth, whose winning work he had spotted in a photo contest, to take pictures of the company for 20 days. The young man, Stewart Jackson, shot pictures all over the U. S., including shots by helicopter of oil rigs in the Gulf of Mexico, and in addition each night he tape-recorded his impressions of what he had seen and done. The boy's photos were used in the annual reports, and his comments formed a major part of the text. What C-E accomplished in this simple way was an active and tangible bridge between the generations, and between business and youth.

One of the greatest contributions a company can make to the annual report field is a tasteful and original report that will create a positive impact.

Chapter 4:   Elements of the Annual Report

The bare outline of an annual report includes a Letter to Shareholders, a Review of Operations, the financial statements, footnotes, a listing of officers and directors, and the legally required auditors' certification. These elements are usually in the same order from front to back, making the annual report a challenge to design. But as a competitive tool in the marketplace, the annual report of today's sophisticated corporation usually goes beyond these essential elements to portray and dramatize the unique characteristics of the company. This chapter describes such an expanded list.

The cover

The cover, the most important graphic element in an annual report, should intrigue the reader into opening the report, and establish or reinforce the corporate image. Of the many possible approaches, the most effective covers usually employ the kind of graphic interest contained in an exciting photo. Whether on an annual report or LIFE magazine, a stimulating photo excites curiosity and draws the reader into the book.

When it is desirable to establish a conservative tone for the company, other elements may be more important—such as rich colored paper, embossing, or gold stamping. In recent years, some of the most free-wheeling conglomerates have used highly conservative covers, presumably in an effort to create a more stable image.

If an annual report has a strong specific theme, the cover can effectively highlight and introduce it. The 1967 *Chase Manhattan Bank* annual report cover featured a somewhat abstract photo of Manhattan's tra-

ditional skyscraper skyline, with the skyline of Harlem superimposed in the foreground. The President's message began: "We believe it is fitting that the cover for 1967 should merge New York's 'other' skyline with the traditional one ... Together, the two skylines illustrate New York's majesty as well as the menace of her slum. Throughout 1967, your bank labored to narrow the distance—in a figurative sense—between these two disparate ways of life ..."

The many types of modern corporations call for a wide range of cover treatments. Paul Rand of *IBM*, for example, believes the cover should not be too literal: "If we merely put a piece of equipment on the cover, we do not accurately convey the image of the company. By using a photo that is non-representational, non-recognizable, and abstruse—a bit mysterious—I am able to convey what IBM really is," he explains. Abstract photographic covers have been used quite consistently by IBM and *Xerox*.

If the cover must draw the reader into the book, the opening spread—inside front cover and page one taken together—should have some material, probably written, that solidly engages his interest in the company. A plain table of contents and title page often throw away the excellent opportunity inherent in this space to provide real impact.

The corporate identity section

Some kind of text paragraph that identifies the company in significant terms is the most effective use of the opening spread, and its use is growing. The terms may be products and markets, or perhaps the size of the company, or other strengths that provide a base for growth. In a succinct way, it tells the reader what the company is and why it is important.

The identification paragraph, for example, of the 1969 United Merchants annual report reads as follows:

"United Merchants and Manufacturers, Inc., is one of America's largest suppliers of styled fabrics for men's, women's and children's apparel and for home furnishings. United Merchants also manufactures and distributes glass fabrics and products using plastic film—including the well known Con-tact® and Kwick-Kover® lines of self-adhering materials.

"Important diversified related activities are commercial factoring and finance operations and *Robert Hall Clothes*, nationwide retail clothing chain consisting of 418 stores. Significant foreign manufacturing and related operations are located in Argentina, Brazil, Colombia, Uruguay, Venezuela, Canada, France and Great Britain.

"United Merchants operates 49 manufacturing plants in the United States and abroad, maintains sales and distribution offices in principal cities, and employs more than 36,000 people."

The table of contents

Contrary to the opinion of some annual report critics, the Table of Contents is an optional element and is in fact often superfluous. Since few annual reports run more than 36 pages, the reader can flip easily through the entire report—which is to the company's advantage, since more of the total message will be absorbed. A Table of Contents often clutters the opening spread, distracting from the impact of important identity elements, without adding anything except a list of the contents.

Some companies do use a creative contents table that adds both information and interest. The 1969 annual report of *First National City Bank* divided its contents section into eight topics, each highlighted by some six lines of descriptive copy and a thumbnail-sized illustration taken from inside the book.

The financial highlights

This is a very brief listing of the key financial figures of the past year—the briefer, the better. The 1968 *Aiken Industries* annual report featured only three items—Net Sales, Net Income, and Net Income Per Share. Some companies waste space and readers' attention by having a long, detailed Highlights section in front, then repeat most of the information in the five- or ten-year statistical summary in the back of the book. The best approach is to have a limited Highlights section and a detailed ten-year Review section.

The Highlights section can be located on the inside front cover, or on page 1, or adjacent to the President's Letter. Placed opposite the Letter, it enables the President to concentrate on interpretative and descriptive material, and merely refer to the Highlights for figures. The trend of the past ten years is toward this kind of presentation.

The letter to the stockholders

This letter, signed by the President and Chief Executive Officer, and sometimes by the Chairman of the Board as well, is the best-read section in an annual report. The Letter should be brief and interpretative, allowing the President to communicate directly to the reader the most important events of the year—inclusion of a topic in the Letter confirms its importance. Although the Letter should be short, it should cover key product, market, and financial developments, as well as any acquisitions. It should also give an indication of where the company is going in the coming year—but, except for unusual cases, should never give actual financial projections.

The Letter is the appropriate place to handle political matters and delicate questions of policy. One company that had received a good many pollution citations during 1970 had worked hard to correct the problems. After considering a special section on the firm's positive contributions to pollution control, company officials finally decided to include one paragraph on the subject in the Letter. This gave the matter the prestige position it deserved but didn't overdo an unpleasant and unfavorable subject.

In political matters, the Letter can serve as a statement of position. The 1969 *Philip Morris* annual report, for example, devoted eight paragraphs in the President's Letter to setting forth the cigarette industry's position on the tobacco and health issue.

It is wise to eliminate from the Letter the stodgy, old-fashioned practice of tacking on a final paragraph that thanks employees and managers, shareholders and customers, and even suppliers, for the company's success. Such a statement sounds quite insincere when repeated year after year.

Something else to be resisted is inclusion of a list of new officers named during the year. From the reader's viewpoint, this is one of the least interesting items in an annual report. The information should properly be included in the annual report, but it should be placed at the end of the Review of Operations. The naming of new Directors, on the other hand, should get brief mention in the Letter.

The date accompanying the Letter, often a point of confusion, should be the date the manuscript is sent to the printer—the final date after which no more changes can be made throughout the annual report. The Letter can and should report on all corporate events up to that date, and not confine itself to the calendar year that may have closed several weeks or months earlier.

The title of the person signing the Letter is always printed in type under the signature—and his name should also be included. Modern executives' signatures are so often illegible that this line is necessary for identification.

Brevity is the key to maximum readership of the Letter. Surveys indicate that readership drops sharply if the Letter exceeds two pages in length. Another way to enhance readership is to include a photograph of the official signing the Letter.

Special features

These are the elements added to the annual report beyond the minimum sections dictated by law and custom. As explained in Chapter I, special features can cover acquisitions, research, special market reports, people, or any other area of concern to the company. The 1968 *Time Inc.* annual report devoted 28 pages to a feature titled "Advertising: The Selling Process". It featured dramatic black-and-white photographs and tape-recorded comments from representative members of the company's 350-person advertising sales staff.

Undoubtedly the report served as an excellent calling card for these sales people the following year, since it presented them as articulate, attractive human beings.

Question-and-answer

An increasing number of annual reports include some form of Question-and-Answer section. *The Gillette Company* has included a Q&A in its annual reports for more than a decade. In 1969 *General Electric* in its new annual report of quarterly magazine format inaugurated an "Investors Are Asking" section that passes on to all shareholders answers to questions being asked in share-owner correspondence and at stockholder meetings and inquiries from professional analysts. The Q&A has several important advantages. For one, it gets directly to the heart of the matter. The 1968 *Olin* annual report provides a clear and reasonable answer after posing the sharp question: "Will earnings nosedive when the shooting stops in Vietnam?" Q&A is easy to skim: The questions work like subheads, enabling the reader to skip along until he finds a question that interests him. And Q&A is a means of imparting some of the human character and personality of the key executives. In the 1965 *Scovill* annual report, the company's colorful President Malcolm Baldrige said, "In looking over our choices there are so many ways to go that sometimes I feel like a blind dog in a butcher shop," in response to a question about future market opportunities.

Review of operations

This section varies from the depth coverage possible with a small and simply organized company to the mere hitting of highlights with a large, complex organization. In general, the Review should try to cover in some detail what the company did in the preceding year in terms of new products, new markets, sales and earnings—and discuss why the company performed as it did. The Review should also discuss capital investments, and give some clue to what the company is expected to accomplish in the year ahead.

This section is often crammed with operating detail and technical jargon, lacking the perspective to give the shareholder what he needs: facts and trends that will influence per-share earnings in the years ahead.

The financial review

An increasing number of companies are including this important section in their annual reports. It helps satisfy growing pressures for more disclosure and provides a much better place to put detailed financial information that used to clutter the President's Letter.

The Financial Review is provided for the security analyst and other professional investors. It should make the analyst's work easier by providing ratios and other information he would otherwise have to extract from the financial statements. It should also interpret the financial information—give reasons why earnings were higher, why working capital dropped, why less than the full rate of taxes was paid.

Just what should be included in the Financial Review depends on the nature of the individual company, but here are some possibilities: sales; income; extraordinary items; cash flow; foreign exchange; acquisition terms; capital expenditures; dividends; long-term debt; working capital; stockholders' equity; return on investment; convertible securities and dilution, and employment costs.

The financial statement

There is little variation in the way these are presented. They usually include a statement of income, a statement of earned surplus (retained earnings), a balance sheet or statement of financial position, and a statement of source and application of funds.

Footnotes

As noted in Chapter Two, these essential appendages to the financial section are undergoing several changes designed to make them more complete and more readable. The Government has proposed that they be set in type no smaller than 10 point (comparable to the text type used in magazines). While such a practice could make the annual report unduly long, the motive behind it is commendable. Another fruitful contemporary trend is toward the incorporation of footnotes in the Financial Review.

Accountant's certification

This statement, required by law, certifies that an independent public accountant has reviewed the financial statements and finds the presentation correct and in accordance with generally accepted accounting practices. Occasionally it will include an exception which may be a tip-off that something is seriously wrong with the company's financial presentation. This certification usually comes right after the footnotes. The accounting firm's name should be set in type rather than printed in handwriting, an old-fashioned custom that can cause last-minute delays and other problems.

The long-term financial summary

This optional section is included in most annual reports. The most common form is a ten-year summary, but a company that has changed drastically in a short time usually prefers a five-year summary. Few companies extend the summary 15 years or longer—ancient history in this era of rapid change.

There are many ways to present the summary information: one well-organized approach is to begin with Earnings Statistics (essentially, information from the income statement), followed by Balance Sheet Statistics, then Per Common Share figures (including such items as net income, cash dividends, and book value). These would be followed by a section called Other Statistics, which would include such items as cash flow, number of common stockholders, and number of employees. It is also extremely useful to the security analyst to include the price range of the common stock for the past ten years, and such ratios as capitalization as a per cent of long-term debt; capitalization as a per cent of stockholders' equity; net earnings as a per cent of sales; and net earnings as a per cent of stockholders' equity.

The listing of officers and directors

This listing is included in all annual reports, usually on the last page or the inside back cover. It is important to give the directors' other affiliations and titles; absence of such information indicates either an almost total in-house Board or one composed largely of retired people.

Corporate data section

This section should include all the information that will be helpful to the annual report's many audiences. The address of corporate headquarters is basic; and many companies include the phone number as well; a statement telling whom to write to for more information is also helpful. The date, time, and place of the annual meeting should be included, and the corporate data usually also includes the names of the transfer agents and registrars, and perhaps the general counsel or auditors. The names of exchanges where the stock is listed—including foreign and regional stock exchanges—should be indicated. *Indian Head* even includes in this section the number of people holding each kind of security the company has (common stocks, two series of preferred stocks, convertible debentures, subordinated debentures, and warrants).

A statement of company trademarks is a useful addition, and more efficient than using the registered trademark symbol beside each appearance of a trade name. The 1970 Olin annual report handles it this way: "Product names italicized in this report are trademarks of *Olin Corporation.*"

An increasing number of annual reports give a credit line for the designer and photographer in or near the corporate data section. It is especially used when "name" talents have been used, helps provide a thank-you and an incentive, and incidentally enhances the company's prestige.

The corporate directory

A directory that sorts out the company by operating units is useful when the company is small or simple enough to present all the pertinent information within two pages or so. The directory will usually contain the name of the operating division and the key products it makes, and should if possible include the address and phone number of each operating unit, as well as perhaps the name of that unit's manager. Such information can be very useful within the company, especially if no corporate phone directory is handy.

The outside back cover

Some companies like a decorative back cover with a photo, but this cover is usually—and best—left for the company name and corporate address. With all the handling annual reports get, it is desirable that the back cover provide quick identity.

Chapter 5:

Producing the Annual Report

"From a publishing standpoint, the annual report is the most amateurish job undertaken by corporate management," says the public relations director of a large, diversified company. Many executive traits tend to make it so: "Management wants stilted language—the annual report is a monument to corporate gobbledygook," says another executive. "Management gets literary and self-conscious," says another, "but they avoid detail and don't say anything." Clearance is another major stumbling-block—"Fighting an annual report through an Executive Committee of a major corporation is a bloody battle," says a veteran of the experience. Worst of all, top management is often unhappy at the result.

Why does the annual report, which costs so much money and takes so much time and effort, end up being such a disappointing document so often? Here are the most common reasons:

1. The chief executive officer does not assign the project to a man in whom he has confidence. As a result, this man is the victim of all the conflicting opinions of people who outrank him.

2. The chief executive officer doesn't get involved early in the planning stages, when his opinions could have a major effect. Instead, he often makes hasty and ill-conceived changes at the last minute.

3. The writer of the annual report text doesn't complete the first draft in time for careful consideration by top management.

4. The text is written on time, but the chief executive officer and other key executives put off reading it until there is a crisis.

5. The accountants don't deliver the financial statements on time, with the result that there is an impossible squeeze between the time the figures are finally delivered and the time the book must be off the press and mailed.

6. After the design is set and the type is in galley form, a new group of people—such as lawyers, directors, assorted vice presidents and possibly even the President's wife—start making a whole series of new comments, with no understanding of the basic concept on which the annual report was initially developed.

7. The chief executive officer panics at the last minute. This is particularly true if Number 6 takes place, when a lot of new opinions have suddenly been thrown in. This usually destroys the theme—the copy is hastily rewritten and only released because the final deadline has arrived. The resulting compromise almost guarantees that something very mediocre will go to press.

Most of these problems could be prevented at the outset if it is admitted that an annual report can only really speak for one man—and he must be the man who runs the company—the President, or chief executive officer. He must be close to the project from the outset, and must delegate its execution to someone who has his complete confidence and backing. Increasingly, the annual report project is going to the new, stronger communications chiefs being designated at corporations. These people often have the title of Vice President of Corporate Communications. The GRAPHIS survey found the annual report to be the responsibility of the Communications or Public Relations Director in 75 per cent of the companies responding; other titles mentioned were Financial Vice President, 17 per cent, and Secretary, eight per cent.

Sometimes it is efficient to bring in an outside consultant, the weight of whose experience can be added to that of the company man in charge. Advertising agencies often refuse this job: it is too detailed and arduous for the fee they can charge, and they'd rather avoid the possibility of antagonizing a valuable advertising client.

With an experienced man in charge and enjoying the confidence of the chief executive officer, the following concrete steps are necessary to get out the annual report:

Developing the schedule and the plan

For a large company, it will take some six or seven months from first planning until the annual reports are in the mail. For a company whose fiscal year ends December 31, with mailing scheduled for March, preparation should begin in September. If possible, some work—especially photography—should begin earlier. Often only summer photos, especially of outdoor scenes, convey the look a company wants.

The schedule should be complete and realistic. The flow chart accompanying this chapter (page 27/28) contains the basic items to include; the best system would incorporate both a flow chart and a simpler schedule. An annual report can and should be produced much like a newspaper or magazine, with an early and a late closing section.

The pivotal date that determines when the reports are actually printed is the date when the accountants deliver the financial statements. Before that date, most of the creative work of text, photographs and graphic design can be done. After that date, the process speeds up to complete the late-closing sections: the Financial Review, the President's Letter, and the financial statements themselves. At this point, the schedule is extremely tight; every half-day is figured to complete an important step forward. Executives who put out annual reports rank "obtaining audited figures on time" as their third greatest problem. It is obvious that preliminary work must be completed before the financials are received, and that the accountants must meet their vital deadline. Any changes made in these final stages are sure to throw the report into costly overtime studio production work and overtime printing.

The final deadline for issuing the annual report is fixed by the stock exchanges—90 days after the close of the fiscal year for companies listed on the New York Stock Exchange, 120 days for companies listed on the American Stock Exchange. Companies whose shares trade over-the-counter, while under no specific deadline, should also get their report out in 120 days. If a listed company is faced with missing its deadline, it must apply to the stock exchange for an extension, an indication of bad management and a step most companies are loath to take. Therefore, the scheduled deadline should be considered inviolable, and if a delay takes place the schedule must be realistically revised—but never abandoned.

At the time the original schedule is concei[...] executives' winter vacations should be checked, the schedule or the vacation adjusted according[ly], since many a company has deeply regretted trying to fly the final draft of annual report copy to the Bahamas under deadline pressure.

The plan for the annual report is different from the *schedule.* The plan should incorporate a series of objectives that have been determined after interviews both inside and outside the company. The inside thinking should come from key executives who share the overall view of the chief executive officer. The outside point of view comes from financial analysts who are familiar with the company and its industry.

The objectives should be aimed at three basic communications goals: to emphasize the company's strengths; to clear up misconceptions; and to introduce new information. Of course, the report will cover the past year's results.

The objectives will often suggest a theme, a highly desirable goal in itself. A theme unifies the message and increases its impact on the reader. It also provides a framework around which to select photographs and written material, and provides a handy defense against people who would change the text.

After the plan and its objectives have been formulated, the project should be thought out to an actual page-by-page breakdown showing how the report is going to be prepared. This information should be submitted to the President in memo form sometime in September, and many an annual report executive will find the preparation of the plan the most intellectually demanding step in the whole project. This early planning pays off, though, because in a well-organized company the preliminary meeting with the President results in a plan of action that will remain essentially unchanged. Whether the chief executive approves the initial plan as presented, makes major changes, or calls for a completely different approach, the important thing is that early in the project the President will be committed to a firm plan that he will back against any last-minute second-guessing by executives beneath him.

Gathering the creative ingredients – photography, design and writing

These steps, which go on concurrently, will reasonably take three months. For the visual elements, companies are increasingly hiring a professional designer, who will in turn select an appropriate photographer for the project. The growing trend to use one photographer for the entire job has distinct advantages: The photographer is familiar with the goal and theme, so the photos will have a common perspective, and sometimes certain economies can be achieved, especially if planning is done in advance.

Insufficient planning and preparation of photographs is one of the biggest wastes of money and sources of frustration in an annual report project. The photographer must have specific information on his subjects before setting out across the country or around the world, and once he's there, someone should escort him, arrange for needed equipment, and get him past any possible barriers. At the common rate of $ 500 or $ 600 a day, a company can waste a lot of money if the photographer has to wait at the location before he can start shooting.

One photography-related subject—often raised by lawyers at the last minute—is whether the company must have releases from the individuals whose photographs are appearing in the annual report. While it is prudent for the photographer to obtain photo releases, there is little danger of lawsuits. A New York law firm researched the subject extensively in 1969 and determined that no one has ever sued a company because his picture appeared in its annual report. Even if an individual did sue, the lawyers noted, he probably couldn't collect much in damages, since it would be hard to prove pain, suffering or embarrassment; also, the annual report is not used for commercial purposes but is given away.

The designer's primary work begins, of course, after the photographs are delivered, when he selects specific shots, including the cover. In our sample schedule, the photographer receives his assignment on September 25 and the photos are due on November 16, about two months later. During that time, the designer allocates the space for each section, and formulates a rough design for the book.

Meanwhile, the writer of the annual report usually talks directly with the vice presidents heading different operating units, which helps the men feel they are actively participating in the development of the annual report, and ensures accuracy. An interview should include the following:

• How did the division do during the year in sales and earnings? What were the major factors influencing this performance?
• What were this division's capital expenditures during the year? What are the capital expenditures planned for the year ahead? How will these expenditures affect the division's capacity to provide profits?
• What new products or services did the division initiate during the year? And for the year ahead?
• Are there any social or economic trends that are influencing the performance of this division, either on the plus or minus side?

Once this information is obtained, it should be written into a first draft and submitted to the vice president interviewed. Each executive should see the information covering only his own area. It is important to be very firm about getting this material returned on schedule, so that there is no delay in preparing a revised draft for the chief executive officer.

Solicit bids from printers

Even before dummy preparation begins, it is a good idea to solicit preliminary bids from printers based on the previous year's annual report. Bids can and should then be revised as soon as the President approves the dummy (see below), so a final decision may be made on printers. There are many pitfalls in selecting a printer, and the judgment of the designer—whether he is within the corporation or an outside professional—should be strongly relied upon.

In soliciting competitive bids, it is important to compare printers of similar quality and capabilities. The lowest bidder might simply be the poorest quality printer. On the other hand, a high-caliber printer might submit a higher bid than others because he habitually works hard to help the client keep overtime and other extra charges down—a type to seek as vigorously as one avoids his opposite number, the printer who makes excessive profits from clients' inefficiencies.

To ensure a more accurate bid, there should be agreement on the number of days the printer will have to print the book—usually between nine and 15 working days—and what those days will be. The importance of developing the schedule and plan initially is underscored here. An unrealistically low bid may be based on more working time than your schedule permits.

In deciding how many annual reports to print, consider such factors as: number of reports required for listed shareholders; reports to be delivered to brokerage houses for Street name share-owners; reports for shareholders of new acquisitions; and employees who will receive reports in connection with a new stock plan. Also determine whether you will make a special mailing to security analysts or run a newspaper advertisement offering annual reports upon request. Add to this total the estimated number required for general corporate purposes. Most companies print two to three times the number of reports they distribute to shareholders. It is an embarrassing and costly error to print too few annual reports: it may cost five times as much to reprint an extra few thousand reports as it does to have them run off initially. When getting printing bids always ask for the cost per additional thousand in case you want to order more reports at the last minute.

A footnote to printers' billing: It is normal, ethical practice for printers to deliver up to 10 per cent either fewer or more books than the contract called for, and to bill accordingly. In practice good printers rarely come in low and usually don't overrun more than five per cent. Nevertheless, the extra charge can be a source of misunderstanding.

Presenting the dummy and the copy

The dummy should have photos, captions, and headlines in type and in place, and the typewriter text should include all of the copy except the late-closing sections that depend on the accountants' final figures. These early-closing sections include the Review of Operations or any special feature article; the identification paragraph; the Table of Contents; and all corporate data not subject to late financial figures. It is a great advantage to show the chief executive the dummy along with the copy, so he can visualize where the information is going and how much space it will occupy, and can begin to see how the written and visual elements will combine. Our sample schedule calls for this meeting with the chief executive officer to take place December 10.

At this point, the President or chief executive officer may invite in some of his advisors—perhaps the Financial Vice President, the Executive Vice President, or the Chairman of the Board. The President's role is both crucial and delicate, since he is familiar with the original concept. He should now perform the function of defending the project to advisors who have not seen it before. If he can't or won't defend it, it is highly likely that the creative team will have to start again from the beginning.

Printer, envelopes, distribution

The confusion and frustration surrounding distribution of the annual report can be avoided with advance scheduling and planning. At the same time as the dummy book and copy are prepared, the printer should be given a written list of the distribution points for the finished annual reports, and told in what order the deliveries are to be made.

The envelopes, seemingly a simple aspect, often become a headache because they are forgotten or postponed till the last minute. The main job is to determine the type of paper, decide on a design, and select a printer. If a professional designer is handling the annual report, it makes sense for him to design a compatible attention-getting envelope as well. The envelopes should be designed and printed well in advance and delivered to the mailing house two weeks before the annual reports arrive, so the mailer can address them before the arrival of the reports.

An increasing number of companies are dispensing with the envelope and using a self-mailing annual report. One important advantage is that the shareholder is less likely to ignore the annual report, since he doesn't have to remove it from the envelope. Dispensing with envelopes can also be used as evidence of corporate frugality, often desirable if shareholders have criticized advertising or other expenses.

A factor in deciding about envelopes, and in timing the final stages of scheduling, is by what class mail the annual reports will be sent. With mailing rates high and going still higher, the difference between first and third class can easily be 20 to 40 cents per annual report, or $ 2000 to $ 4000 per 10,000 reports. The only reason for using first class is that accountants often deliver the figures too late. Using third class mail, the company should mail the annual report to shareholders six weeks (minimum, five weeks) before the annual meeting.

Color transparencies to printer

As soon as the dummy is approved by the chief executive officer, the transparencies go out to be made into color separations. Allowing enough time to make proper color separations, and then to correct and refine them, is one of the essential ingredients of true quality control in any printing project. Printers in the New York metropolitan area require at least three weeks to make color separations, and any changes take another couple of weeks, making five weeks in all.

Type and mechanicals for early-closing sections

Setting these early text sections in type and making mechanical boards (camera-ready art) of them for the printer should go smoothly, since all key people have previously passed the contents. And these sections have purposely been written to avoid dependence on the last-minute financial information.

The cover should also be released for printing at this point—a separate printing job that can be done in advance. In designing the report, avoid putting the Financial Highlights on the inside front cover, as this would require waiting for last-minute figures and would delay printing of the cover.

Prepare late-closing sections

The writing of these pieces of copy, the President's Letter, Financial Highlights, and Financial Review, can begin while the mechanicals of the earlier-closing sections are being made. The President's Letter is the most critical part of the annual report and the one he will spend the most time on. It should be written in rough form and delivered to him as soon as possible—ideally, over the Christmas holidays—allowing him

time to look at it. Naturally, the message will be refined and updated when final figures become available.

Accountants deliver figures – project goes into final stages

The financial figures should be delivered between the time the chief executive officer reviews the draft and the day the final draft goes out for type. The same timing holds good for the financial review section, perhaps with the Financial Vice President approving it instead of the President. The Financial Review and President's Letter should be final but in typewritten copy until the financial statements arrive, at which point the figures can be inserted as needed and the three elements can be sent for type together as a late editorial package.

From this point on, nothing should be allowed to delay getting the entire report to the printer except the working time required to receive and check type, order reproduction proofs ("repros"), make and check the mechanicals, and collect all the elements for the printer. Two weeks should be allowed to perform these functions, once the financial statements have been delivered by the accountants. Sometimes, however, the job is pushed through in a week.

If the accountants have delivered their figures in time, and if all company clearances have been firm and final, these steps can proceed smoothly. But if other aspects of the job have been postponed until this stage, and all the segments of the job come together at the last minute, there can be tremendously expensive last-minute crises.

Changes in the text once it has been set in type, called author's alterations, represent one of the most avoidable costs in annual report production—and one of the highest of such costs. Type costs have been soaring for the past several years, and no letup is in sight. It is not unheard of for a company to spend $ 2000 on the basic typesetting cost for an annual report, then spend another $ 10000 to $ 15000 on all kinds of last-minute changes that simply reflect lack of confidence in what's been done.

It's clear at this point how important it is to have one person responsible for the entire annual report, and that person reporting directly to the President. In very large companies, the President often delegates his own annual report function to a key management executive. The two of them should be the only ones with the right to make changes in the writing style of the book. Individual preferences in writing style account for a great number of the changes that cause such high type costs, and the text is rarely improved. It is much more likely to be harmed by the resulting jerkiness of style.

Some companies harbor frustrated editors who become obsessed with commas or other punctuation. Such an executive, in trying to make the report conform to his own idea of usage, can cause the entire report to be reset in new type—possibly without realizing it. Frequently, another comma nut in the company with an opposite point of view will redo the text back into its original form. Incorporation at the typewriter text stage of all the changes of those who should be consulted saves untold dollars later.

The distribution of galley proofs to various executives is full of pitfalls. Copy will sometimes be handed out up to a dozen times, in different versions. Sometimes a senior executive will wait until a final stage, then, after everyone else's changes have been incorporated, go over the galley in depth and make a whole series of new changes—an expensive luxury.

It is important to limit the stages of approval, and be very precise in giving everyone a "sign-off" date, after which his comments will not be incorporated. The lawyers should confine themselves to matters of law, and the accountants to financial information. The chief executive officer should be the person to be satisfied, and other executives should confine themselves to matters of fact and occasionally of interpretation.

Send mechanicals to printer

When all the boards are complete with every element in place, they go to the printer and the material comes back two or three days later in the form of a blueprint or keyline print. This copy of the report is made from film, the stage just before "burning the plates" in offset printing. It shows every element in the exact position in which it will be printed, and can and should be checked for accuracy. It is particularly important to check the blueprint for accuracy in any charts and for picture and caption placement.

Supervise printer

The book now enters the printing process—which altogether will require some nine to 15 working days. Many corporate executives don't understand why printing and binding take this long. One important reason is that during the busy annual report season of February and March at least three-quarters of all annual reports are being printed and most good printers are booked solid with them. Therefore they try to include some cushion time in their schedules, so that if problems arise they don't necessarily have to work overtime to get a specific report out.

Quality printers are just as interested in an excellent product as are their corporate clients, and know that beyond efficiency there are no shortcuts to fine printing results. The steps of platemaking, printing on each side of press sheets, binding and trimming, and preparation for shipping must be done carefully. If not, they can completely ruin the effect of six or seven months' hard work.

The financial people usually give their final approval at the blueprint stage, and don't see the annual report again until it's completely printed. The graphic designer should check the press sheets to make sure the color is coming out as anticipated. The company will usually get one or two advance, hand-stapled copies made from press sheets. They go to the executive in charge of the report, who usually shows them to the President if he's available. Then, corporate headquarters will usually get the first 100 copies that come out of the bindery. After six or seven months' work, there is a high level of tension surrounding the annual report, and all the executives want to see what it looks like. It behooves the man in charge to see that everyone who's legitimately involved gets a copy as soon as possible. If he's

prudent, he will hand-check these copies to discover any obvious printers' errors, such as binding the cover upside down.

The report is delivered and mailed

The finished books are delivered from the bindery to the mailing house, often a bank transfer agent. If arrangements have been properly scheduled, the average mailing house can get out 20000 to 25000 annual reports per day, and larger ones can handle more.

Sometimes, despite the most careful checking systems, it will be discovered that an annual report contains some kind of error. The way it is handled is determined by two factors: the significance of the error and the time, in relation to the mailing deadline, at which it is discovered. Throughout the publishing world, errors decline in importance as deadlines advance. A newspaper is never held up at press time to correct an error short of the most disastrous or perhaps libelous. However, as amateur publishers, companies are almost fanatically afraid of a mistake, to the point where management can't put into perspective the relative importance of an error in per-share earnings compared to misplaced punctuation that doesn't alter basic meaning.

Accuracy is of course an important goal in the annual report project, and it should be given top priority throughout each production step. At the very latest stages, minor errors should be ignored. One company discovered a comma in the wrong place in the address line after the covers had been printed, and decided to reprint the full-color covers—at a cost of thousands of dollars. The common and recommended solution to a factual error discovered after printing is complete but before mailing is the erratum slip. This small piece of paper can be printed and stapled to the inside cover or the specific page involved, and solves the problem inexpensively.

Even assuming the report has been perfectly produced, however, there is usually a delayed reaction on the part of top management. The President and other key executives usually want comments from friends, associates and members of the financial community before deciding just how much they like their new annual report. This reaction lag can be hard on the executive in charge of the annual report, since he has just spent six months of intensive involvement with the project.

One of the most useful activities during this waiting period, which is likely to last several weeks, is to have a meeting of the creative team—the designer, writer and any other people who were intimately involved in the annual report project. With the experience still fresh in mind, those in attendance should discuss what went wrong, what went right, and should offer preliminary suggestions for next year's report. Because of the nature of the topic, and the timing, it is recommended that this meeting be held in an excellent restaurant on a Friday when there is no imperative reason for returning to the office.

Das Phänomen des Wandels

Die moderne Technologie hat uns ein Zeitalter unfassbarer Wandlungen in immer rascherem Tempo gebracht. Annähernd 90 Prozent aller Wissenschaftler, die je auf dieser Welt gelebt haben, sind heute noch am Leben. Die Hälfte aller Energie, die die Menschheit in den vergangenen 2000 Jahren verbraucht hat, wurde in den letzten 100 Jahren aufgezehrt, und in technologisch hoch entwickelten Ländern verdoppelt sich die Produktion an Gütern und Dienstleistungen alle 15 Jahre.

In den Vereinigten Staaten hat der industrielle Super-Boom erst Mitte der fünfziger Jahre wirklich angefangen, zu einer Zeit, da Computer neue Gebiete der Technologie erschlossen, als die Aktienkurse steil anstiegen und die Wirtschaft ganz allgemein eine Beschleunigung verzeichnete. Das Bruttosozialprodukt, das 1954 noch 364 Milliarden[1] Dollar betrug, bewegte sich in rasender Geschwindigkeit auf den Stand von 1 Billion[1] Dollar im Jahre 1971 dank des immer rascheren Wachstums und Wandels der amerikanischen Unternehmen. Die Entwicklung von drei Gesellschaften seit 1954 diene als Beispiel:

W.R. Grace & Co., mit Verkäufen von insgesamt 413 Millionen Dollar im Jahre 1954, arbeitete hauptsächlich als Schiffahrtslinie und Handelsgesellschaft mit Südamerika. Bis 1970 stieg das Verkaufsvolumen auf 1,9 Milliarden Dollar, und die Firma erhielt ein fast völlig neues Gesicht – die Schiffahrtslinie war verkauft, die Geschäfte mit Lateinamerika waren stark reduziert, und Grace hatte sich in den fünftgrössten Chemiekonzern Amerikas verwandelt.

Litton Industries, eine der bedeutenden Wachstumsgesellschaften der amerikanischen Industrie, wurde erst 1954 gegründet. In der kurzen Zeit bis 1967 waren die Verkäufe der Firma bereits auf 1 Milliarde Dollar emporgeschnellt, ein Beweis dafür, dass Litton es verstanden hatte, erfolgreich in so verschiedenartigen Branchen wie Büromaschinen, Schiffsbau, Papierherstellung, Verlagswesen, Elektronik und Röntgenausrüstungen Fuss zu fassen. 1970 erreichte der Umsatz von Litton 2,4 Milliarden Dollar.

1954 standen *International Business Machines (IBM)* an der Schwelle des Computer-Zeitalters und verdienten die beträchtliche Summe von 46,5 Millionen Dollar mit ihren Büromaschinen; 1970 war die Gesellschaft der führende Hersteller von Computern in der ganzen Welt, und der Nettogewinn erreichte die fast astronomische Zahl von einer Milliarde Dollar.

Es ist kein Zufall, dass die mittleren fünfziger Jahre auch Ausgangspunkt für eine völlig neue Art von Jahresbericht wurden.

Der Jahresbericht der IBM liefert das drastischste Beispiel dieses andersartigen Stils. Der IBM Bericht von 1954 war im grossen ganzen gleich wie die früheren Berichte, die seit Gründung der Gesellschaft vor 42 Jahren herausgegeben worden waren. Er war in einen steifen, braunen Umschlag gebunden und enthielt 20 Seiten mit nacktem Zahlenmaterial und der finanziellen Berichterstattung – Abbildungen oder der Versuch einer graphischen Gestaltung fehlten völlig.

Im nächsten Jahr modernisierte die IBM ihren Jahresbericht und ist seitdem in Gestaltung und Berichterstattung führend geblieben. In der zweiten Hälfte der fünfziger Jahre haben einige wenige Gesellschaften die Neuerungen in der Struktur der Geschäftsberichte fortgesetzt, und in den sechziger Jahren hatten sich die meisten bedeutenden Aktiengesellschaften Amerikas dieser weitreichenden Umstellung auf einen zeitgemässen, modern konzipierten Geschäftsbericht angeschlossen.

Der Jahresbericht –
Schlüssel zum Wesen des Unternehmens

Was sich im Grunde genommen ereignet hatte, war einfach dies: Der Jahresbericht war, in Ermanglung anderer Möglichkeiten, das wichtigste und in vielen Fällen das einzige Mittel geworden, dessen sich die Geschäftsleitung bedienen konnte, um die Wandlungen und das Wachstum ihres Unternehmens zu umschreiben, Wandlungen, die praktisch jedes Jahr eine neue Gesellschaft entstehen liessen. Den Unternehmen kam das flüchtige, zeitlich begrenzte ihres Daseins zu Bewusstsein. Alvin Toffler hat in seinem Buch «*Der Zukunfts-Schock*» auf diese Vergänglichkeit hingewiesen. Weil Broschüren, die geschrieben, und Filme, die gedreht werden, um Charakter und Identität des eigenen Unternehmens zu umschreiben, meist bereits zum Zeitpunkt ihrer Entstehung überholt sind, bildet die gesetzlich für den Jahresbericht vorgeschriebene Frist die treibende Kraft, die die leitenden Leute veranlasst, sich einmal im Jahr zusammenzusetzen, um der Öffentlichkeit das Wesen ihrer Gesellschaft zu beschreiben und zu erläutern.

Eine der Folgen dieser direkten Beteiligung der leitenden Leute ist die Bereitschaft, bedeutende Summen für die Ausarbeitung des bestmöglichen Jahresberichtes auszugeben. Die Unternehmen engagieren die besten Graphiker und Photographen und verwenden das beste Qualitätspapier und die höchste Druckkunst, um das Gesicht ihres Jahresberichtes zu gestalten.

Insgesamt bilden diese Aktiengesellschaften einen Jahresbericht-«Markt», der viele Millionen Dollar jährlich umfasst, denn in den Vereinigten Staaten von Amerika werden die Aktien von mehr als 50000 Unternehmen öffentlich gehandelt. *American Telephone & Telegraph* besitzt die meisten Aktionäre – annähernd 3,1 Millionen. Diese Gesellschaft druckt ihren Jahresbericht in einer Auflage von etwa 4 Millionen mit einem Aufwand von 575000 Dollar jährlich für Druckkosten und graphische Gestaltung.

Eine GRAPHIS-Umfrage[2] über Jahresberichte bei

---

[1] 1 Milliarde = 1 000 000 000; 1 Billion = 1 000 000 000 000.

[2] Um die allerneuesten Angaben für dieses Buch zu erhalten, führte *The Corporate Communications Report* im Namen des Graphis Verlags bei den 1000 grössten Unternehmen in den Vereinigten Staaten eine Umfrage durch. Die Ergebnisse dieser bis heute zweifellos umfassendsten Umfrage dieser Art wurden in den nachfolgenden Text integriert.

1000 der grössten Unternehmen Amerikas hat gezeigt, dass die meisten Gesellschaften, ausgenommen die mit besonders hohen Auflagen, 1 Dollar oder mehr pro Exemplar ihres Geschäftsberichts für Gestaltung und Drucklegung ausgeben. Grosse Unternehmen (300 000 bis vier Millionen Exemplare) gaben 33 Cents als Kosten pro Exemplar an; Unternehmen mittlerer Grösse (55 000 bis 63 000 Berichte) geben 96 Cents pro Exemplar, und kleinere Gesellschaften (zwischen 4500 and 12 000 Kopien) nannten $ 1.19 als durchschnittlichen Aufwand.

Selbst eine Ausgabe von $ 2 pro Exemplar bei einer Auflage von ungefähr 5000 Geschäftsberichten bedeutet im allgemeinen eine gute Anlage für neue, kleinere Unternehmen, denn gerade für sie ist ein solcher Bericht von besonderer Bedeutung. Grössere Firmen verfügen über langjährige Beziehungen zu Anlegern, Lieferanten und Kunden; ausserdem führen sie meist aktive Werbe-, Public Relations- und Pressekampagnen durch. Demgegenüber haben viele kleine Unternehmen ausser dem Jahresbericht kein wirksames Mittel, um sich der Öffentlichkeit zu präsentieren.

Jahresberichte können nicht nur bei Anlageentscheidungen eine Rolle spielen, sondern auch für die verschiedensten Gesellschaften einen ganz speziellen Wert haben. Wenn ein Geschäftsbericht dazu beitragen kann, das Kurs-Ertrags-Verhältnis (Kapitel 2) einer mittelgrossen Firma wie *Joy Manufacturing* mit einem Verkaufsvolumen von 273 Millionen Dollar im Jahre 1970 um nur einen Punkt zu erhöhen, so bedeutet das einen 10-Millionen-Dollar-Anstieg im Kurswert aller ausstehenden Aktien der Gesellschaft. Bei der AT & T wäre die Wertsteigerung etwa 2 Milliarden Dollar.

Um die Wirkung der Aussage ihrer Jahresberichte zu verstärken, fügen eine wachsende Zahl von Gesellschaften, meistens in der Einleitung, einen Absatz bei, in dem das Bild der Firma gezeichnet wird *(Corporate Identity Paragraph)*. Diese schwarz auf weiss niedergelegte – jedes Jahr auf den neusten Stand gebrachte – Definition der Gesellschaft kann der Geschäftsleitung im Laufe des Jahres viele mündliche Mitteilungen ersparen.

Der Jahresbericht hat diese Vorrangstellung aus verschiedenen Gründen. Dass er ehrlich ist, wird vorausgesetzt: Er trägt die Unterschrift des obersten Geschäftsführers, eine Treuhandstelle prüft die finanziellen Angaben, und er wird von Überwachungsorganen des Wertschriftensektors revidiert.

Die Mitglieder der Geschäftsleitung bedienen sich mit Vorliebe des Jahresberichts als Sprachrohr, da sie eine unmittelbare Kontrolle darüber ausüben können (was bei Prospekten, die vielfach von Anwälten geschrieben werden, nicht der Fall ist). Was das Management selbst von dem Jahresbericht hält, entnimmt man der Tatsache, dass Gesellschaften im allgemeinen zwei- bis dreimal so viele Berichte drucken lassen, wie sie Aktionäre haben. Zusätzlich zu der Hauptfunktion, die darin besteht, die gesetzlichen Vorschriften zu erfüllen und die Aktionäre über den Geschäftsverlauf zu informieren, wird der Geschäftsbericht in vielen Fällen auch für so verschiedenartige Zwecke wie Personalrekrutierung, den Verkauf von Produkten und Dienstleistungen, die Anbahnung von Neuerwerbungen und immer mehr auch als «Visitenkarte» der Gesellschaft im Umgang mit ausländischen Geschäftsleuten verwendet.

Westinghouse Electric Corporation hat, um ein Beispiel zu nennen, 400 000 Exemplare ihres Jahresberichtes von 1969 drucken lassen. Davon wurden 166 000 an eingetragene Aktionäre versandt und weitere 33 000 an nicht eingetragene Aktionäre, deren Aktienbesitz von Maklern oder Treuhändern gehalten wird. Ausserdem hat die Firma zum erstenmal allen ihren Angestellten einen Jahresbericht zugestellt, womit 142 000 weitere Exemplare versandt wurden. 12 000 Berichte wurden für Ausbildungs- und Personalanwerbungszwecke bestimmt, 3500 für den Versand an Wertschriftenanalytiker, Banken, Universitäten und Bibliotheken, und 3700 Exemplare wurden für den Kontakt mit Öffentlichkeit und Gemeinden reserviert. Die restlichen 40 000 Berichte behielt die Gesellschaft für allgemein geschäftsfördernde Zwecke zurück.

Die regelmässige Veröffentlichung und systematische Verteilung des Jahresberichtes als fester Bestandteil zahlreicher offizieller Dossiers im Anlagepublikum verleiht ihm den Charakter einer ständigen Einrichtung. Er ist eine Chronik der Vergangenheit, ist Protokoll und als solches umfassendes Quellenmaterial für die Entwicklung der Gesellschaft.

Der grundlegende Gedanke der Geschäftspolitik wird im Jahresbericht vielfach erstmals dargestellt, und zwar entweder durch eine direkte Erklärung über ihre Richtung oder indirekt durch die Setzung von Akzenten im Text. Der Geschäftsbericht der *American Can Company* für 1969 mit der Aufnahme einer attraktiven jungen Kundin auf der ersten Seite illustriert die wachsende Bedeutung des Konsumentenmarktes für diese Gesellschaft. Mit zu den wichtigsten Lesern dieser Art Mitteilungen gehören die eigenen Geschäftsführer der Gesellschaft, die sonst oft im ungestümen Drang nach neuen Entwicklungen die Orientierung verlieren.

Der Jahresbericht kann jedoch auch als Katalysator für die Formulierung und Darstellung der verschiedensten Situationen und Bedingungen innerhalb eines sich rapide wandelnden Unternehmens dienen. Nicht selten werden grundlegende Führungsentscheidungen getroffen, um die Veröffentlichung des Jahresberichts voranzutreiben. So kann es vorkommen, dass einer gewissen Abteilung oder Gruppe noch ein Vorstehender fehlt; er wird oft erst dann ernannt, wenn sich der Drucktermin nähert. Es kommt auch häufig vor, dass unklare, irreführende Titel noch rechtzeitig vor der Drucklegung bereinigt werden.

Da der Jahresbericht stets eine Mitteilung der obersten Geschäftsleitung darstellt, benutzen leitende Angestellte ihn oft, um bestimmte Gedanken vorzutragen oder besondere Mitteilungen weiterzugeben. Hier einige Beispiele:

• *Ethyl Corporation*, die sich wachsenden Forderungen nach Beseitigung der Bleizusätze im Benzin im Kampf gegen die Luftverschmutzung gegenüber sah, fügte ihrem Jahresbericht für 1969 eine kleine Broschüre bei, in der Ethyls Alternativlösung für dieses Problem angepriesen wird.

• Der Geschäftsbericht der *Fidelity Corporation* für 1968 ging bewusst darauf aus, andere Gesellschaften zur Fusion mit Fidelity zu verlocken. Der Text war in zwei Hauptteile gegliedert – ein Dialog über die Aufkaufpolitik der Gesellschaft zwischen zwei Direktoren und verschiedene «Aussagen» von Leitern aufgekaufter Gesellschaften über ihre Beziehungen zur Fidelity Corporation.

• Der Geschäftsbericht für 1967 der *J.C. Penney Company* bezweckte, tüchtige junge Leute zu rekrutieren, indem er versuchte, den verbreiteten Eindruck richtigzustellen, dass für solche ehrgeizige junge Leute keine Aufstiegsmöglichkeiten bestünden. Der Bericht schilderte junge Geschäftsführer, nannte sie mit Namen, beschrieb ihre Aufgaben und betonte gleichzeitig, dass Penney über eine grosse Anzahl interessanter Beschäftigungsmöglichkeiten für Maturanden verfüge.

• *Litton Industries* liess 3000 Exemplare ihres Geschäftsberichtes für 1963 ins Russische übersetzen und schickte sie an russische und amerikanische Gesandtschaften in der ganzen Welt, wie auch an Leser in Schlüsselstellungen in der Sowjetunion. Dies war eine bewusst indirekte Werbung um die wohlwollende Aufmerksamkeit einer Anzahl amerikanischer Botschafter und der britischen Bankwelt. Sie diente als Vorbereitung für das von Litton im folgenden Jahr gestartete Übersee-Expansionsprogramm.

• Der Geschäftsbericht der *US Industries* für 1969 sollte den leitenden Angestellten von 130 neu erworbenen Gesellschaften, die im Rahmen der USI als unabhängige Unternehmer-Manager arbeiten, Anerkennung und Prestige gewähren. Der Bericht enthielt mehrere Seiten mit Gruppenaufnahmen dieser Geschäftsführer.

Amerikas Geschäftswelt steht heute einer beispiellosen Herausforderung gegenüber: ein wachsender Teil der Menschheit bezweifelt ihr Lebensrecht. Diese Leute – Jugend, Vertreter der Kirchen und Aktionäre – beschäftigen sich mit Rassenproblemen und Armut, sind besorgt über die Umweltverschmutzung und misstrauen dem militärisch-industriellen Komplex. Die Geschäftsleute müssen heute nicht nur das verteidigen, was gesund am amerikanischen Kapitalismus ist, sondern sie müssen die Öffentlichkeit auch überzeugen können, dass sie beabsichtigen, zu verbessern und abzuschaffen, was nicht in Ordnung ist. Teilweise wird diese Botschaft durch Jahresberichte vermittelt. *Crown Zellerbachs* 1968er Bericht enthielt 12 Seiten über die soziale Verantwortung der Unternehmen. *Southern California Edisons* Jahresbericht für 1969 enthielt eine 16seitige Broschüre «Edison und die Umweltkrise». Die *Bank of America*, das grösste Unternehmen dieser Art in den Vereinigten Staaten, druckte ihren Geschäftsbericht für 1970 auf aus Altpapier hergestelltem Papier, wodurch 600–1000 Bäume weniger geopfert werden mussten. Und *Outboard Marine* liess eine Abhandlung drucken mit dem Titel: «Die Schönheit des Lebens... und was wir dazu beitragen».

Der Jahresbericht muss auf die Stärke des Unternehmens hinweisen

Obwohl der Geschäftsbericht gute Dienste bei besonderen Berichterstattungsaufgaben leisten kann, besteht sein Hauptzweck darin, auf die besondere Stärke des Unternehmens hinzuweisen und die Aktiva aufzuzeigen, die künftiges Wachstum verbürgen. Solche Mitteilungen sind natürlich vor allem für potentielle Käufer von Aktien des Unternehmens bestimmt, jedoch auch für die Belegschaft, Banken, Lieferanten, Kunden und Geschäftsleute sowie Regierungsbeamte in anderen Ländern. Zu den grundlegenden Leistungen, die eine Gesellschaft der Öffentlichkeit vermitteln will, gehören:

Technologie Es ist in einer Welt der raschen Wandlungen von ausschlaggebender Bedeutung, dass Unternehmen die Fähigkeit besitzen, sich zu behaupten. *Weyerhaeuser* vermittelte den Eindruck hochentwickelter Technologie in ihrem Geschäftsbericht für 1968; ein Eindruck, der durch dramatische doppelseitige Mikro-

photographien noch verstärkt wurde. Man hiess Wandlungen willkommen: «Eine Idee, die heute im Laboratorium geboren wird, kann morgen eine neue Industrie schaffen und somit alte Methoden überholt machen. Uns bei Weyerhaeuser gefällt es so. Die Hälfte unserer Verkäufe dieses Jahres bestand aus Produkten, die wir vor 15 Jahren überhaupt noch nicht fabrizierten».

Finanzielle Stärke Die Enthüllung bedeutender finanzieller Schwierigkeiten bei so grossen Firmen wie *Penn Central Railroad*, *Lockheed Aircraft* und *Ling-Temco-Vought* haben die Annahme, dass grosse Firmen automatisch reiche Gesellschaften sind, gründlich erschüttert. Gesellschaften von finanzieller Stärke und Gesundheit bedienen sich logischerweise des Geschäftsberichtes, um diese Stärke hervorzuheben. Während dies gewöhnlich schon im Text geschieht, zeigt der Geschäftsbericht der *Tishman Realty & Construction Co.* für das Jahr 1970 zwei Seiten mit einem wirksamen Diagramm, das die dem Cash Flow der Gesellschaft zugrunde liegenden Vermögenswerte illustriert.

Produktivität Ein beträchtlicher Teil des Wachstums in den sechziger Jahren wurde durch die zunehmende Produktivität ermöglicht, die die Unternehmen dank automatischer Kontrollausrüstungen und anderen Kapitalanlagen erreichten. Produktivitätsverbesserungen werden in den siebziger Jahren schwerer erreichbar sein, sie werden jedoch weiter grundlegenden Einfluss auf das Gewinnpotential ausüben. Wo immer möglich, benützen die Gesellschaften den Geschäftsbericht, um ihre Fähigkeiten zur Produktionserhöhung unter Beweis zu stellen.

Forschungsprogramm Der *Squibb Beech-Nut* Jahresbericht 1969 hob die Forschungstätigkeit hervor und überzeugte so den Leser, dass das Unternehmen über die technischen Voraussetzungen für die Entwicklung neuer rezept- und nichtrezeptpflichtiger Arzneimittel verfügt. Gleichzeitig wurden Öffentlichkeit und Regierung darauf hingewiesen, dass die mit der Entwicklung neuer Arzneien verbundenen beträchtlichen Kosten die hohen Detailpreise dieser Produkte rechtfertigen.

Überseemärkte Da Überseemärkte oft schneller wachsen als Inlandmärkte, betonen eine immer grösser werdende Zahl von Gesellschaften ihre starke Stellung in anderen Ländern. *First National City Bank* beispielsweise unterstrich die Wichtigkeit ihrer Auslandtätigkeit dadurch, dass sie ihren Jahresbericht für 1970 auf französisch, spanisch und englisch publizierte.

Neuerwerbungen In ihrem Geschäftsbericht für 1967 erklärte die *SCM Corporation* ihren Aktionären den etwas plötzlichen Erwerb der *Glidden Company*. Glidden, ein führender Farben- und Chemikalienproduzent, verdoppelte zwar die Grösse der neuen Muttergesellschaft, schwächte jedoch ihre Stellung und ihr «Image» in der Glamour-Welt der Kopiermaschinen. Vier ganze Seiten wurden deshalb einem Dialog mit dem Titel «Die Bedeutung von Glidden: ein SCM Forum» gewidmet, welcher neun leitenden Direktoren der beiden Unternehmen die Möglichkeit gab, mit ihren eigenen Worten darzulegen, weshalb die Fusion ihrer Meinung nach zu einer Stärkung der SCM beitragen werde. Diese Erklärung wurde von der Finanzpresse weitgehend verbreitet.

Absatzmärkte Es ist wichtig für eine Gesellschaft, die Wert darauf legt, von Wertschriftenanalytikern und anderen Berufsanlegern richtig bewertet zu werden, ihre Absatzmärkte genau zu beschreiben, besonders wenn sie überdurchschnittliches Wachstum bieten. In seinem Geschäftsbericht für 1967 widmete *Berkey Photo* dem Markt für Fernsehtechnik und der Filmindustrie einen Spezialbericht, um anschliessend Berkeys Stellung und Bedeutung innerhalb dieser Sparte darzulegen. Besonders gelungen zeigt der *Motorola* Geschäftsbericht für 1965 auf ganzen neun Seiten, wie das Unternehmen die Bedürfnisse der Stadt San José in Kalifornien befriedigt. Dabei wird eindrucksvoll hervorgehoben, dass Motorola praktisch mit «jedermanns Leben in irgendeiner Weise verflochten ist».

Geschäftsleitung Die meisten professionellen Anleger betrachten eine gute Geschäftsleitung als wichtigstes Kriterium für den Geschäftserfolg. Es ist also kein Wunder, dass man sich in den Jahresberichten stets bemüht, das Management ins beste Licht zu stellen. Tatsächlich bietet der Bericht selbst einen guten Massstab für Geschmack, Intelligenz und Glaubwürdigkeit des Managements. Moderne Jahresberichte verwenden lieber ungezwungene Aufnahmen ihrer Geschäftsleiter, als sie in steifen und feierlichen Porträts zu präsentieren.

Aber sogar der Abstand von zwölf Monaten zwischen dem Erscheinen der Jahresberichte ist in unserem Zeitalter des Wandels unter Umständen zu lang, und die Unternehmen bedienen sich zunehmend neuer Formen der Berichterstattung und Kontaktaufnahme, um ihr Bild so zeitgemäss wie möglich zu halten. *General Electric*, die als führend auf dem Gebiet der Geschäftsberichterstattung gelten, haben ihren Bericht in vier Vierteljahres-Magazine eingeteilt, was ermöglicht, die Aktionäre auf wirkungsvolle Weise über laufende Geschäfte zu unterrichten.

Sinkende Arbeitsmoral, hervorgerufen durch die finanziellen Schwierigkeiten der Fluggesellschaften, hat die Leitung der *Pan American World Airways* dazu bewogen, eine aufmunternde Botschaft des Präsidenten auf Tonband aufzunehmen und sie via Telephon jedem Angestellten zugänglich zu machen. Die Botschaft wird periodisch erneuert. Mindestens eine Gesellschaft plant ähnliche telephonische Mitteilungen für Aktionäre. Ausserdem werden neue Medien auch neue Arten von Mitteilungen bringen – die Videokassette zum Beispiel wird zweifellos demnächst neue Möglichkeiten für eine aktuelle Berichterstattung der Unternehmen bieten.

Aber auch wenn die Unternehmen weiter versuchen werden, wirkungsvollere und zeitgemässe Wege der Kontaktaufnahme zu finden, wird der Jahresbericht bestimmt doch die wichtigste Dokumentation für die Tätigkeit der Gesellschaft in jedem Jahr bleiben. Und als solche wird sie auch weiterhin von den Direktoren der Gesellschaften für eine Vielzahl von Zielsetzungen benutzt werden. Denn in unserer Zeit des raschen Wandels haben sie ein geradezu dringendes Bedürfnis, der Öffentlichkeit das wahre Bild ihrer Gesellschaft zu vermitteln.

Aber selbst heute ist vielen Generaldirektoren und Präsidenten nicht ganz bewusst, wie weitgehend sie sich auf den Jahresbericht als Mittel zur Erstellung dieses Bildes und der Kommunikation verlassen. Fragt man einen Geschäftsleiter in der Stille seines Büros, was er mit dem Geschäftsbericht erreichen möchte, so wird er offen erklären, dieser sei dazu bestimmt, die Leute zu veranlassen, ihr Geld in seiner Gesellschaft anzulegen. Welche Magie die Gunst der Anleger bedeuten kann, wird im nächsten Kapitel behandelt.

Das Phänomen des Wachstums

Während der Hauptzweck des Jahresberichtes in der Orientierung des Anlegers besteht, ist sein wichtigstes Anliegen, den Kauf von Aktien anzuregen. Ermutigt durch den modernen Geschäftsbericht, hat seit den fünfziger Jahren tatsächlich eine neue Schicht amerikanischer Aktionäre Aktien erworben und damit das Phänomen der sogenannten Wachstumsgesellschaft ermöglicht.

Wertzuwachs – Hauptziel der Anleger

Im Jahre 1954 zählte man sechs bis sieben Millionen Aktionäre in den Vereinigten Staaten – grösstenteils gewiegte Geschäftsleute, denen es nicht schwerfiel, sich eine gute Anlageberatung zu verschaffen. Heute halten rund 30 Millionen Anleger Aktien direkt und etwa 100 Millionen Amerikaner sind indirekt, über Anlagefonds oder Pensionskassen, Aktienbesitzer. Der Aktionär von heute ist meist jünger, gefühlsbetonter und weniger gut gestellt, sowie ungeduldiger, was die Entwicklung seiner Anlagen betrifft. Bis in die fünfziger Jahre waren Aktionäre hauptsächlich am Einkommen aus ihren Anlagen in Form von Dividenden und anderen Ausschüttungen interessiert – der Wertzuwachs des angelegten Kapitals hielt für sie keine ausschlaggebende Bedeutung. Aber seit Mitte der fünfziger Jahre und noch stärker in den sechziger Jahren, entwickelte sich die Wertsteigerung des angelegten Kapitals zum eigentlichen Zweck für die meisten Anleger und die alten, zuverlässigen Aktien mit ihren regelmässigen Dividendenausschüttungen fanden immer weniger Gunst bei den Käufern.

Das ist kaum verwunderlich! 1961 konnte ein Anleger *IBM* Aktien zu $ 100 pro Aktie erwerben und sie im Verlauf des gleichen Jahres zu $ 158 wieder verkaufen, oder er kaufte Aktien der *Litton Industries* zu $ 17 und verkaufte sie zu $ 33. Aktionäre waren wenig an Dividenden interessiert, solange sich Gelegenheit zur Verdoppelung ihres Einsatzes bot.

Die Anleger suchten demgemäss eifrig nach Wachstumsgesellschaften. Den Unternehmen ihrerseits lag daran, als Wachstumsgesellschaft angesehen zu werden. In der GRAPHIS-Umfrage wurden die Geschäftsleiter von 146 der tausend grössten Gesellschaften Amerikas gefragt, welches Eigenschaftswort den Eindruck umschriebe, den sie dem Leser ihrer Jahresberichte vermitteln wollten. Die meistgegebene Antwort – sie wurde von 57 Gesellschaftspräsidenten erteilt – lautete: «auf Wachstum ausgerichtet». Nur 20 Geschäftsführer nannten «wahrheitsgetreu» und nur ein einziger gab «solide», oder «blue chip», wie die Amerikaner es nennen, als den gewünschten Eindruck an. Diese überwältigende Vorliebe für das Bild einer Wachstumsgesellschaft ist der Grund, warum Unternehmen dem Geschäftsbericht so viel Zeit und Geld widmen.

Wachstum als Leitbild

Um die Gründe für das leidenschaftliche Bemühen der Aktiengesellschaften um das Bild einer Wachstums-

gesellschaft zu verstehen, muss man etwas über den sogenannten Kurs-Gewinn-Multiplikator, kurz P/E genannt, wissen.

Der Preis-Gewinn-Multiplikator ist eine Zahl, die, mit dem Gewinn der Gesellschaft multipliziert, einen Betrag ergibt, der den theoretisch angemessenen Kurswert der Aktien dieser Gesellschaft darstellt. Während die Schlusskurse einer Aktie von Tag zu Tag variieren können, bestimmt über längere Zeit der P/E den Bereich dieser Schwankungen. Wertschriftenanalytiker und andere Mitglieder der Finanzwelt setzen solche Multiplikatoren in übereinstimmender Beurteilung der verschiedenen Aktien auf etwas geheimnisvolle Weise fest, stützen sich jedoch dabei fast immer auf den vermutlichen Wertzuwachs in den kommenden Jahren.

So dürften z. B. einer Papierfabrikationsgesellschaft nur durchschnittliche Wachstumschancen zugebilligt und ihr ein P/E Multiplikator von 10 zugeteilt werden. Für ein Unternehmen der Elektronikbranche, mit Spezialkenntnissen einer dynamischen neuen Technologie dagegen, könnte ein ausserordentliches Wachstumspotential angenommen und ein P/E von 50 errechnet werden. Selbst wenn die Papierfabrik und der Hersteller von elektronischen Produkten beide einen Dollar pro Aktie verdienen sollten, würden die Aktien des Papierunternehmens auf Grund des Multiplikators zu 10 Dollar und die des elektrotechnischen Unternehmens zu 50 Dollar gehandelt werden. Sollten beide Firmen ihre Gewinne auf 2 Dollar pro Aktie verbessern können, würde der Verkaufspreis einer Aktie der Papierfabrik durch den Multiplikator auf 20 Dollar und der Preis der Elektronikaktie auf die gleiche Weise auf 100 Dollar erhöht.

Das Wunder der Konglomerate

Zu Beginn der sechziger Jahre entdeckten gewisse Gesellschaften eine Zauberformel: nämlich die Umwandlung hoher Multiplikatoren in Konglomeratwachstum. Die Formel funktioniert wie folgt:

Die Elektronikgesellschaft A, mit 2 Millionen Aktien im Umlauf, verdient 4 Millionen Dollar, oder $ 2 pro Aktie. Bei einem Multiplikator von 50 müssen Käufer $ 100 pro Aktie auf den Tisch legen. Elektronikunternehmen A tritt dann an die Papiergesellschaft B heran und schlägt eine Fusion der beiden Gesellschaften vor. Gesellschaft B verdient genau so viel wie A und hat auch die gleiche Anzahl Aktien herausgegeben; auf Grund des ihr zugeschriebenen Multiplikators von nur 10 werden die Aktien der Gesellschaft B jedoch zum Preise von $ 20 gehandelt. Unternehmen A erwirbt jetzt Unternehmen B für ein Zehnfaches des Gewinnes der Gesellschaft A, d. h. für 40 Millionen Dollar. Unternehmen A, die Elektronikgesellschaft, bezahlt jedoch nicht in bar, sondern mit eigenen Aktien von $ 100 pro Stück und muss daher 400 000 Aktien an die Besitzer der Gesellschaft B übergeben. Als Ergebnis hat die Gesellschaft A nach Abschluss der Transaktion insgesamt 2 400 000 Aktien ausgegeben und kann einen Gewinn von 8 Millionen Dollar verzeichnen, also $ 3.33 pro Aktie. Nach

Anwendung des Multiplikators von 50 auf diesen neuen Ertrag wird der Preis einer Aktie der Gesellschaft A von $ 100 auf $ 166.50 erhöht.

Das Bild einer Wachstumsgesellschaft

Natürlich bedurften nicht alle Gesellschaften einer Fusion, um Wachstum zu erreichen oder ein höheres P/E Verhältnis anzugeben. Drei der bedeutendsten Wachstumsgesellschaften der sechziger Jahre – *IBM*, *Xerox* und *Polaroid*, jede führend auf einem anderen Gebiet der wachstumsintensiven Technologie – konnten rapides Wachstum durch interne Mittel erreichen. Tatsächlich sind es eben gerade diese Gesellschaften, insbesondere IBM, die das in den Geschäftsberichten von heute so offensichtliche «Bild einer Wachstumsgesellschaft» geprägt haben.

Thomas Watson Jr., der 1951 Präsident von IBM wurde, brachte Paul Rand in die Gesellschaft, um ein neues Programm für graphische Gestaltung aufzustellen und zu überwachen. Rand, einer der führenden Graphiker der Welt, gestaltet seit 1957 die IBM Jahresberichte. Von ihm durchgesetzte Neuerungen bestehen u. a. in der Verwendung von anderem Papier (er hat das im Buchdruck verwendete blau-weisse Glanzpapier durch ein elegant wirkendes, mattes Papier ersetzt); einem schönen und vornehmen Schriftbild; einem anderen Format als das für Jahresberichte übliche von 21,5×28 cm (8¹/₂×11 in.) sowie vielen anderen graphischen Einfällen. Paul Rands wichtigster Beitrag zur Geschäftsberichtgestaltung besteht jedoch aus seiner Anwendung der Photographie für diesen Bereich. Dank der Zusammenarbeit mit einigen weltberühmten Bildberichterstattern, Leuten wie Erich Hartmann und Ernst Haas von *Magnum*, hat Rand den Weg für eine neue, etwas mysteriöse und impressionistische Art der Industriephotographie gebahnt, die das Wesen der IBM Technologie besonders gut zum Ausdruck bringt. Erregende Farbphotos, grosszügige Verwendung von weissen Flächen und andere visuellen Elemente schaffen das neue Wachstums-Image.

General Dynamics, deren Jahresbericht für 1958 damals wohl als der am modernsten gestaltete gelten durfte, war eine weitere, in dieser Beziehung experimentierfreudige Gesellschaft. Vom Graphiker Erik Nitsche entworfen, wechselten sich in dem Bericht schwarzweiss Aufnahmen von Flugzeugen, Raketen und Unterseebooten mit halbseitigen, z. T. abstrakten Farbphotos ab. Dabei wurden drei verschiedene Druckverfahren verwendet: Tiefdruck für die schwarzweissen Bilder, Buchdruck für die Farbe und Lithographie für Umschlag und Text. (Siehe Abb. 394, 401–403.)

Leider brachte General Dynamics es fertig, drei Jahre nach der Publikation des verschwenderisch gestalteten Geschäftsberichtes für 1958 mehr Geld zu verlieren, als je ein anderes Industrieunternehmen, nämlich 143 Millionen Dollar als Ergebnis eines Misserfolges auf dem kommerziellen Markt für Düsenflugzeuge. Der Geschäftsbericht für dieses unglückliche Jahr war begreiflicherweise recht spartanisch und die Gesellschaft musste ihre Tätigkeit als Schrittmacher beim Gestalten von Jahresberichten für mehrere Jahre unterbrechen.

Mittlerweile wurde den Jahresberichten in der graphischen Branche grössere Beachtung geschenkt. Wichtige Ausstellungen für angewandte Kunst begannen verschiedene Kategorien von Jahresberichten aufzunehmen. Einen bedeutenden Einfluss übte in dieser Hinsicht die internationale Ausstellung für Jahresberichte aus, die von der «Mead Library of Ideas» arrangiert worden war[3]. Die von der *Mead Paper Company* zum ersten Mal im Jahre 1956 veranstaltete Schau besteht heute aus fünf Wanderausstellungen, die in mehr als 100 Städten der Vereinigten Staaten und Kanadas gezeigt werden. Die für die Einbeziehung in die Ausstellung eingereichten Berichte werden von führenden Graphikern und anderen, bei der graphischen Gestaltung von Gesellschaftspublikationen beteiligten Experten, beurteilt und zur Annahme empfohlen.

Die Bemühungen der *General Electric Company* um das Bild einer Wachstumsgesellschaft beruhten nicht in erster Linie auf graphischer Darstellung. GE bediente sich des Jahresberichtes in sehr methodischer und logischer Weise und passte seine Struktur und Gestaltung der Geschäftszielsetzung an. Die Gesellschaft hatte spätestens Mitte der fünfziger Jahre die Bedeutung des Wachstums erkannt und machte es zum Hauptgegenstand ihrer Berichterstattung. Diese Politik erwies sich als so erfolgreich, dass eine recht farblose Wachstumsquote von ungefähr 4 Prozent jährlich in den sechziger Jahren das gesunde Kurs-Gewinn-Verhältnis der Gesellschaft nicht berührte und General Electric auch heute noch allgemein als eines der bedeutenden Wachstumsunternehmen angesehen wird.

Die Jahresberichte der GE werden mit wissenschaftlicher Akribie entworfen und enthalten viele Änderungen, wie sie in den seit 1953 fast alljährlich unter den Lesern durchgeführten Umfragen vorgeschlagen werden. Diese Umfragen haben zum Beispiel ergeben, dass sich die Leserschaft des «Briefes an die Aktionäre vom Vorsitzenden des Verwaltungsrates» um ein Vielfaches erhöhen würde, wenn der Text auf eine einzige Seite gekürzt und ausserdem ein Bild des Vorsitzenden enthalten würde. Die Umfragen haben auch ergeben, dass das Interesse der Leser durch Farbphotos an vielen Stellen des Geschäftsberichtes verstärkt wird.

General Electrics hauptsächlichster Beitrag bestand jedoch aus der Bedeutung, die das Unternehmen einer bestimmten Zielsetzung in der Berichterstattung beilegte. Dies wird durch die Integration von Photos, Bildlegenden, Überschriften und Text erreicht, die die im Bericht berührten Themen wirkungsvoll unterstützen. Zu Beginn der sechziger Jahre z. B. zielte ein Thema darauf hin, GE als ein Unternehmen mit überlegener «Systems capability» – die Fähigkeit zur Ausarbeitung neuer Systeme – darzustellen. Diese «Systems capability» galt damals als charakteristisch für Wachstumsgesellschaften. Wenn man bedenkt, dass die Unternehmen sich zusehends bemühen, die Öffentlichkeit mit ihren Geschäftsberichten in einer ganz bestimmten Richtung zu beeinflussen oder ihr Informationen bestimmter Art zu vermitteln, wird die GE-Gestaltung des Jahresberichtes vermutlich den nachhaltigsten Einfluss auf die moderne Berichterstattung ausüben.

Der «blendende» Jahresbericht

Während *IBM* mit guter Gestaltung bahnbrechend war und *General Electric* das Element systematischer Forschung einführte, wird *Litton Industries* als Verfechter des blendend schönen Jahresberichtes in die Ge-

---

[3] Die von der *Mead Library of Ideas* veranstaltete internationale Ausstellung für Jahresberichte ist wohl die wichtigste Präsentation besonders wertvoller graphischer Gestaltung. Die Aufforderung, Arbeiten einzureichen, wird jeweils im April versandt; letzte Frist für die Eingabe ist der 31. Juli. Die fünf Juroren – alles erfahrene Graphiker – bewerten die Eingänge im August. Die Ausstellung selbst findet im September oder Oktober statt. Später werden Wanderausstellungen durchs Land geschickt. Die Arbeiten sollten an die «Mead Library of Ideas», 200 Park Avenue, New York, N.Y. 10017 gesandt werden.

schichte eingehen. Als neues Unternehmen und als Konglomerat, besass Litton weder General Electrics Ruf als Produzent erstklassiger Konsumgüter noch verkörperte es eindeutig den Begriff der Technologie, wie IBM das mit ihren Computern, *Xerox* mit ihren Vervielfältigungsmaschinen oder *Polaroid* mit ihren die Bilder selbstentwickelnden Kameras fertigbrachten. Litton sah sich dem Problem gegenüber, ein Bild des Unternehmens zu zeichnen, das zu dem beabsichtigten Wachstum passte. Litton hat deshalb schon fast seit der Gründung im Jahre 1954 versucht, genau wie die Milliarden-Dollar-Gesellschaft auszusehen, die ihr Gründer Rex Thornton aufbauen wollte.

Bei der Geschäftsberichterstattung bestand Littons Strategie darin, ausführliche redaktionelle Themenbehandlung mit aufsehenerregender graphischer Gestaltung zu kombinieren. Crosby Kelly, bis 1965 Leiter der Abteilung, die sich mit den Beziehungen zum Anlagepublikum befasste und massgebend beteiligt an der Gestaltung der Geschäftsberichte, beschrieb Littons Informationsproblem wie folgt: «Was wir wirklich wollten, war den Leuten zu sagen: ‹wir sind auf dem Wege, wir werden bald oben angelangt sein›; Vertrauensbildung war Hauptauftrag des Geschäftsberichtes» und er trachtete danach, allen Leserkreisen Vertrauen einzuflössen, Littons Angestellten sowohl wie den Aktionären. «Ich bin der Meinung, dass man etwas braucht, das die Gesellschaft versinnbildlicht – etwas das einer Flagge gleichkommt», sagte Kelly. «Eines der vielen Probleme in der Industrie besteht im Mangel an Symbolen, denen man Gefolgschaft leisten kann. Ich will, dass man mir vertraut, aber wie kann ich das erreichen? Indem ich eine Flagge hisse. Und diese Flagge war der Jahresbericht.»

Litton hat auf diese Weise das Bild einer Zukunft gemalt, von der die Gesellschaft noch weit entfernt war – eine Technik, die später von vielen nachgeahmt wurde. Zusammen mit Kelly arbeitete an den ersten Jahresberichten der Litton noch Robert Miles Runyan, dessen brillanter, begeisternder graphischer Stil zu der erregendsten und einfallreichsten Serie von Geschäftsberichten führte, die je geschaffen wurde.

Der Litton Bericht für 1959, der erste mit ausgeprägter Graphik und ausführlichem Thema, zeigte auf drei Doppelseiten Gegenüberstellungen von photographischen Stilleben und Ausführungen zum Thema. Einer dieser Artikel war mit Abbildungen alter wissenschaftlicher Instrumente illustriert und deutete auf Littons führende Stellung auf dem Gebiet der Technologie. Gleichzeitig wurde betont, Amerikas Industrie müsse der Herausforderung des ausländischen Wettbewerbs «durch höhere Produktivität, bessere Qualität und Erfindungsgabe, sowie Wendigkeit beim Entwurf neuer Produkte» begegnen. Eine zweite Aufschlagseite mit einer Spielzeugkanone, alten Waffen und einer Kopie der Unabhängigkeitserklärung, erklärte, dass «unser Land seine Verteidigung weiterhin stärken müsse» und beschrieb dann Litton als «einen wichtigen Industrie-Bürger, der zur Erfüllung der Verteidigungsbedürfnisse unseres Landes einen wertvollen Beitrag leistet». Die dritte Doppelseite, mit einer alten Schatztruhe und Litton Aktienzertifikaten, zeigte den Anlegern wie viel Bedeutung Litton dem finanziellen Management beimisst, einem Management, das, u. a., «einen angemessenen Gewinn aus den Verkäufen sichert, der dem Aktionär einen guten Ertrag seiner Anlagen garantiert.»

Dieser Jahresbericht zählte zu den ersten, die ein umfassendes Bild mit den wichtigsten sozialen und wirtschaftlichen Tendenzen der Zeit zeichnete und dann zeigte, wie eine bestimmte Gesellschaft in diesen Rahmen passte. «Nur die Tatsachen angeben genügt nicht», sagt Kelly, «denn wenn der Leser die falschen Schlüsse zieht, so hat man seine Aufgabe nicht erfüllt». Kelly gibt zu, dass er wenig daran interessiert war, die Gesellschaft klar zu umschreiben. Er zog es vor, mit dem Geschäftsbericht bei Wertschriftenanalytikern so viel Interesse zu erwecken, dass sie den Geschäftssitz der Litton in Los Angeles besuchten, um sich dort eine ausführliche Dokumentation zu beschaffen. Kelly empfand es als Kompliment, als ein Analytiker ihm einmal sagte: «Crosby, ich habe den ganzen Geschäftsbericht durchgelesen und erst dann ist mir klar geworden, dass Sie mir überhaupt nichts erzählt haben».

Die Litton Berichte wurden in ihrer Reichweite immer grandioser. Der Geschäftsbericht für 1962, beispielsweise, zeigte auf dem Umschlag eine atemberaubende Aufnahme der Akropolis in Athen und war der Freiheit gewidmet, «dem Tag, da die ganze Menschheit über die Mauer gesprungen sein wird». Über den ganzen Bericht verteilte Photographien bezogen sich auf historische Ereignisse, die mit der Suche der Menschen nach Freiheit in Verbindung stehen. Das Geheimnisvolle des Geschäftsberichtes war jedoch nichts im Vergleich mit der geheimnisvollen Kraft, die Littons Aktien höher und höher trieb und das Interesse und den Neid anderer unternehmungslustiger Geschäftsleute weckte.

Die von Litton auf so bahnbrechende Weise befolgte Taktik erwies sich bald als nützliche Hilfe zur Gründung neuer Konglomeratgebilde. Littons Geschäftsführer gehörten zu den ersten, die diese Technik auszuwerten verstanden. Gelang es, eine Anzahl kleiner Gesellschaften zu erwerben und gleichzeitig den eigenen hohen Kurs-Gewinn-Multiplikator beizubehalten und auf die Neuerwerbungen anzuwenden, so war es möglich eine neue «Wachstumsgesellschaft» fantastischen Ausmasses zu errichten. Viele dieser Geschäftsführer verliessen Litton, um ihre eigenen Unternehmen zu gründen. Auf diese Weise entstanden *City Investing*, *Walter Kidde*, *Teledyne*, *KDI Corporation* und andere.

Robert Miles Runyan setzte alles daran, diese neuen Gesellschaften als Klienten zu erwerben. Er nannte sie LIDO's (Litton Industries Drop-Outs). In den mittleren sechziger Jahren erschien eine grosse Anzahl dieser geheimnisvoll angehauchten Jahresberichte im Runyan Stil.

Der Inhalt solcher Berichte wurde oft der Gestaltung unterstellt oder ihr sogar geopfert. Ein besonders schöner Teledyne Bericht brachte abstrakte Farbaufnahmen aus der Welt der Technologie, vor einem dunkelgrauen Hintergrund – der Text war in schwarzer Tinte auf die gleiche schwarz-graue Seite gedruckt. Der Geschäftsbericht der City Investing für 1968 bestand aus einem ganzen Heft voller Abbildungen – ohne eine einzige Bildlegende. Die Bilder und eine Chronik der Weltereignisse quer über den oberen Teil der Seiten, lieferten Spannung, aber nicht viel Information.

Andere Konglomerate, die nicht der LIDO-Gruppe angehörten, aber ebenfalls jene mystique-bildende Gestaltung ihrer Jahresberichte anstrebten, waren *Gulf and Western Industries*, *A-T-O*, und *Ling-Temco-Vought (LTV)*. Der LTV Jahresbericht für 1965 ist klassisch aber nicht in der angestrebten Richtung. Der Umschlag zeigt weisse, erhaben geprägte griechische Säulen auf dunklem Hintergrund, im Text folgen viele Bilder aus dem Griechenland des Altertums und eine Erklärung, die mit den Worten schliesst: «Wie Sie sehen, haben wir unser Material aus dem goldenen Zeitalter der griechischen Geschichte geschöpft, um das Ziel unserer Gesellschaft und das Thema unseres Berichtes ‹Das Schaffen von beständigen Werten› zu veranschaulichen». Die Leute bei LTV hatten versucht, den Stil der Litton Berichte nachzumachen. Es fehlte ihnen aber das nötige Fingerspitzengefühl, und das Resultat kann nur als *nouveau riche* beschrieben werden.

Die Konglomerate verlieren ihren Glanz

Dann kam 1968 und der Beginn einer starken Baisse am Aktienmarkt. Konglomerate konnten keine Wunder mehr wirken und ihre Aktien erlitten allen voran einen jähen Sturz, der Tausende von Anlegern unsanft aus ihren Träumen riss. Konglomeratswerte erlitten die schlimmsten Einbussen aller Marktwerte und mindestens eine Gesellschaft, die KDI Corporation, musste liquidiert werden.

Der Preissturz an der Börse erreichte seinen tiefsten Punkt Mitte 1970, dann konnte sich das Kursniveau innerhalb weniger Monate kräftig erholen. Echte Wachstumsgesellschaften wie IBM, und Unternehmen mit wertvollen Vermögenswerten wie die Ölgesellschaften, waren beim Wiederaufschwung führend. Die Konglomerate erholten sich nur mühsam und viele von ihnen machten sich daran, unproduktive Erwerbungen wieder abzustossen.

Das Anlagepublikum war durch diese Entwicklung allgemein ernüchtert. Man sprach von einer «Rückkehr zum Wesentlichen». Die Gesellschaften betonten in ihren Jahresberichten wieder Vorzüge wie Liquidität, Produktivität und einzigartige Wettbewerbsvorteile. Aber obgleich sich der Ton geändert hatte, begannen nur erstaunlich wenige Gesellschaften an Qualität und Aufmachung ihrer Jahresberichte zu sparen. Die meisten der 1970 angefragten Gesellschaften erklärten, dass sie in Zukunft genau so viel oder sogar noch mehr für ihre Geschäftsberichte auszugeben gedachten wie 1969. Die Unternehmen wollten weiter wie Wachstumsgesellschaften aussehen. Und die Anleger setzten ihre Suche nach Wachstumsgesellschaften fort, wenn sie jetzt auch bessere Beweise forderten.

Die Tendenz geht in Richtung klarer Finanzinformation

Zum Glück für die Anleger geht die Tendenz in der Finanzwelt in der Richtung besserer Lesbarkeit, grösserer Klarheit und weitgehenderer Offenbarung von Fakten. Die Textkapitel der Einleitung werden von den Gesellschaften immer kürzer gehalten: der *Westinghouse* Geschäftsbericht für 1969 enthält nur 3500 Worte — halb soviel wie der vorhergehende Bericht.

Die Aufsichtsbehörde für Wertschriften und Börse, sowie andere Regierungsstellen in den Vereinigten Staaten verstärken ihren Druck auf die Gesellschaften, mehr erläuternde finanzielle Daten zu liefern, die jedermann auf gleicher Basis zugänglich sind. So verlangt die SEC zum Beispiel genauere Angaben über die Verkäufe und Erträge, die sich aus den verschiedenen Tätigkeiten oder Produktgruppen der Gesellschaft ergeben. Damit soll verhindert werden, dass ein Unternehmen, das vielleicht einen Grossteil seines Gewinns der Produktion von Kautschuk verdankt, den Eindruck zu erwecken versucht, es sei in Wirklichkeit eine in der Weltraumschiffahrt engagierte Gesellschaft.

Ein etwas weniger direkter Druck, der zu besserer Information für Aktionäre führen soll, kommt noch von einer anderen Seite, nämlich von der Wochenzeitschrift FINANCIAL WORLD, die seit 1941 jährlich Auszeichnungen für Jahresberichte ausrichtet[4] und in den letzten Jahren Gesellschaften vorzieht, die solche Produktgruppen separat aufgliedern.

Der Einfluss, den die FINANCIAL WORLD ausübt, ist bedeutend. Die Zeitschrift beurteilt jedes Jahr an die 5000 Jahresberichte und verleiht mehr als 90 Bronzeauszeichnungen für dritte Plätze (bestehend aus einer einzigen Bücherstütze), ein Dutzend Silbermedaillen für den zweiten Platz und eine Goldauszeichnung für den besten Geschäftsbericht des Jahres. Der goldene Oskar der Industrie für 1970 wurde *Westinghouse Electric* erteilt. Ihr Geschäftsbericht für 1969 gliederte zum ersten Mal die Verkäufe und die Einnahmen separat für die fünf wichtigsten Betriebseinheiten der Gesellschaft, während die Berichte der vorangegangenen Jahre jeweils nur die Prozentanteile der Produktkategorien am Gesamtumsatz aufführten.

Ein sogenannter «Ausschuss für Grundlagen der Berichterstattung» hat ausserdem viele Änderungen vorgeschlagen, um den Anlegern verlässlichere Daten zu bieten. Viele Unternehmen haben auf diese Art Druck reagiert, und veröffentlichten ausführliche und bessere Informationen in ihren Geschäftsberichten.

Auch auf anderen Gebieten machen die Finanzausweise Zugeständnisse an den Trend zu besserer Übersichtlichkeit und eingehenderer Berichterstattung. Seit Jahren müssen die Gesellschaften einen «gesetzlich vorgeschriebenen» Geschäftsbericht unter Verwendung des Formulars 10 K der Regierung unterbreiten. Seit kurzem verlangt die Regierung beträchtlich weitergehende Angaben als im Jahresbericht für die Aktionäre aufgeführt werden müssen. Um diese Ungleichheit zu beseitigen, sind eine wachsende Anzahl Unternehmen dazu übergegangen, in ihrem Jahresbericht für die Aktionäre die gleichen Informationen vorzulegen, wie sie für die 10 K Berichte gefordert werden.

Selbst Fussnoten, traditionell in kleiner Schrift gedruckt und gewöhnlichen Sterblichen, die nicht gerade Bücherexperten sind, im allgemeinen unverständlich, werden langsam aber sicher etwas lesbarer. Es wurde sogar vorgeschlagen, dass sie künftig im gleichen Schriftsatz wie der Rest des Textes gedruckt werden müssen.

Eine andere Richtung will die Fussnote völlig beseitigen und sie dem Bericht selbst einverleiben. *General Electric* bedient sich bereits seit Jahren dieser Praxis und gibt die Fussnoten in den Erläuterungen zu den Finanzausweisen neben Zahlenaufstellungen. Dies macht die Lektüre etwas langweilig, bedeutet aber einen wichtigen Schritt zur Beglaubigung des gesamten finanziellen Textmaterials durch die Kontrollstelle. *J.C. Penney*, die ihren Geschäftsbericht für 1969 nach

---

[4] Die Zeitschrift FINANCIAL WORLD beurteilt jedes Jahr über 5000 Geschäftsberichte. Gegen Ende Juni werden Anerkennungsauszeichnungen an etwa 3000 Unternehmen gesandt, die die Mindestanforderungen erfüllt haben. Dabei beziehen sich 50 Prozent der Beurteilung auf die Berichterstattung für den Aktionär, 25 Prozent auf den Inhalt für den Wertschriftenanalytiker und Berufsanleger, und die restlichen 25 Prozent auf den allgemeinen Eindruck des Heftes. Die bei der Beurteilung als Richter fungierenden Wertschriftenanalytiker haben jedoch im allgemeinen in Bezug auf die graphische Gestaltung einen eher konservativen Geschmack. Ende Oktober werden die Endresultate an einem Bankett bekanntgegeben, an dem bis 1500 Vertreter der Geschäftswelt teilnehmen. An etwa 300 Gesellschaften, die 90 verschiedene Industrien vertreten, werden Auszeichnungen verteilt. Um an dem Wettbewerb teilzunehmen, sollten zwei Exemplare des Jahresberichts bis zum 21. Mai an die folgende Adresse gesandt werden: Director, Annual Report Survey, Financial World, 17 Battery Place, New York, N.Y. 10004.

dem Muster von General Electric aufgezogen haben, hat nicht nur die Fussnoten in die Finanzübersicht eingeschlossen, sondern als weiterer Schritt auch einen Teil der schwerfälligen Prosa eliminiert. Anstatt alle Angaben über gemietete Liegenschaften ausführlich auszuführen, Angaben, die nur einen Berufsanalytiker interessieren, erwähnt Penney in der Finanzübersicht lediglich, dass auf Wunsch ein Memorandum über dieses Thema erhältlich ist.

Alle diese Bemühungen haben die begrüssenswerte Tendenz, aus dem Jahresbericht eine noch zuverlässigere und genauere Informationsquelle zu machen.

Kapitel 3: Wie gestaltet man einen guten Jahresbericht?

Die Darstellung des Unternehmens als Wachstumsgesellschaft führte zu einer Erneuerung der graphischen Gestaltung des Jahresberichtes, die auch eine neuartige Verwendung des Textes bedingte. So entstand die neue Sprache der Unternehmensjournalistik, die sich weitgehend der Methoden der Zeitungen, Magazine und des Fernsehens bediente, der Medien also, die ebenso eifrig um Gunst und Aufmerksamkeit der Leser kämpfen. Es war höchste Zeit, dass die Verfasser von Jahresberichten erkannten, wie notwendig eine interessante Gestaltung ist: wie Alvin Toffler in seinem Buch *Der Zukunfts-Schock* schreibt, wird der Durchschnittsmensch mit einem Vielfachen der 10 000 bis 20 000 gedruckten Worte bombardiert, die er täglich schlucken kann.

Ausserdem konkurrieren die Jahresberichte direkt miteinander: Eine Umfrage der *General Electric* hat gezeigt, dass der durchschnittliche Aktionär der *GE* noch Aktien von 16 weiteren Unternehmen besitzt. Folglich widmet er jedem der Berichte weniger als 10 Minuten. Dieser Kampf um den Leser ist sogar noch schärfer innerhalb einer Industriegruppe, in der eine positive Reaktion der Wertschriftenanalysten beim Vergleich der einzelnen Geschäftsberichte von grösster Wichtigkeit ist.

Der Text Bei einem so harten Konkurrenzkampf braucht man erstklassige Berufstalente, um einen erfolgreichen Geschäftsbericht zu schaffen. So ist es zum Beispiel wichtig, den Text von einem gut ausgebildeten Berufsautor, evtl. in Zusammenarbeit mit einem Redakteur, verfassen zu lassen, wobei es sich entweder um einen aussenstehenden Spezialisten oder einen Mitarbeiter der Gesellschaft handeln kann.

Der grösste und offensichtlichste Wert des Verfassers für die Gesellschaft liegt darin, dass er Material beschafft, Gespräche führt und die oft sehr umfassenden und fernliegenden Themen, die behandelt werden sollen, ordnet, bevor er sie in einem ersten und später einem zweiten Entwurf zusammenfasst. Nach einer immer noch weit verbreiteten, jedoch völlig falschen Auffassung kann kein Aussenstehender genug über eine Gesellschaft in Erfahrung bringen, um über sie zu schreiben. In Wirklichkeit wissen die meisten Eingeweihten so viel über ihre Gesellschaft, dass sie nicht fähig sind, die wichtigen Aspekte herauszustellen. Liegt der Grundtext einmal vor, so kann er von den anderen leitenden Angestellten nach eigenem Ermes-

sen redigiert oder umgeschrieben werden. Das Können und die Erfahrung eines Schriftstellers kann der Geschäftsleitung beim Entwurf des Jahresberichtes viele Stunden ersparen und dürfte ein besser lesbares Manuskript ergeben, das das Wesentliche enthält und Nebensächlichkeiten beiseite lässt.

Der Autor trägt in verschiedener Hinsicht hierzu bei. «Das Schlimmste, was eine Gesellschaft sich antun kann, ist, sich in allzu weissem Licht zu sehen», sagt Dan Lufkin, ehemaliger Wertschriftenanalytiker und Mitbegründer von *Donaldson, Lufkin & Jenrette, Inc.*, einer von Wall Streets erfolgreichsten jungen Firmen. Ein Unternehmen, das Finanzexperten durch falsche Information verleitet, übertrieben optimistische Prognosen für seine Entwicklung zu stellen, zieht sich nur die nachhaltige Feindschaft dieser Fachleute zu, die sich hintergangen fühlen.

Die Aufgabe, eine Gesellschaft der Öffentlichkeit vorzustellen, ist daher sowohl schwierig als auch äusserst delikat. Einerseits soll der Verfasser die Gesellschaft in das bestmögliche Licht rücken; andererseits läuft er Gefahr, ihr durch Übertreibung grossen Schaden zuzufügen.

Ein subtiler aber wichtiger Beitrag des erfahrenen Autors besteht darin, so zu schreiben, dass es «genau richtig klingt». Der Text eines Jahresberichtes sollte an die einfache, klare Darstellung des WALL STREET JOURNAL oder der BUSINESS WEEK erinnern, beides Publikationen, die zur Standardliteratur der amerikanischen Geschäftswelt gehören. Texter aus der Werbebranche versagen häufig bei Geschäftsberichten, einfach, weil ihnen das für Glaubwürdigkeit so notwendige Fingerspitzengefühl für Untertreibung fehlt. Rechtsanwälten und Geschäftsleuten dagegen fällt es oft schwer, einen klaren kurzen Satz hervorzubringen.

Die Photographie Während der Textteil des Jahresberichtes es vermeiden soll, einen allzu rosigen Eindruck des Unternehmens zu vermitteln, soll die graphische Gestaltung alle interessanten Aspekte hervorheben und so eindrücklich wie möglich präsentieren. Erstklassige Aufnahmen bilden einen wichtigen Bestandteil bei der Schaffung des Images einer erfolgreichen Gesellschaft oder eines Wachstumsunternehmens und sind auch Grund für den hohen Aufwand bei der Herstellung des modernen Jahresberichtes.

Die meisten Photographen, die in Grossstädten für die Illustration von Jahresberichten arbeiten, berechnen zwischen $ 300 und $ 700 pro Tag für Aufnahmen an Ort und Stelle. Studiophotographen verlangen unter Umständen $ 1000 pro Tag oder noch mehr. Auslagen für Transport, Unterkunft, Film- und Entwicklungskosten werden extra berechnet.

Die Direktoren finden diese Honorare oft übertrieben. Dennoch wird von den Beantwortern der GRAPHIS-Umfrage «verspätete Lieferung der Aufnahmen» als zweitgrösstes Übel bei der Jahresberichterstellung genannt (das schlimmste und das grösste Problem: die verschiedenen Ansichten der Mitglieder der Geschäftsleitung in Einklang zu bringen). Und gerade hier liegt die Antwort: Spitzenphotographen bieten Zuverlässigkeit, Einfallsreichtum und breites Fachwissen. Sie photographieren nicht nur einen oder mehrere Tage, sondern konferieren auch mit dem Gestalter und orientieren sich über die grundlegende Zielsetzung des Geschäftsberichtes – alles Zeit, die nicht berechnet wird – ein weiterer Grund, warum die Aufnahmen fast immer die gewünschte Wirkung haben. Auch ist es wichtig, einen Photographen zu engagieren, der gewohnt ist, mit leitenden Leuten umzugehen, die berechtigterweise wenig Verständnis für Zweitaufnahmen oder auch nur den leisesten Verdacht von Dilettantismus haben. Wer den ersten besten Photographen engagiert, geht ein Risiko ein in bezug auf den gesamten visuellen Eindruck seines Produktes und gefährdet zudem den Ruf des für die Gestaltung des Geschäftsberichtes verantwortlichen Teams.

Die spezifischen Rechte der Firma an der Berichterstattung des Photographen müssen von Anfang an festgelegt werden. Die Vereinigungen der Berufsphotographen haben einen Kodex aufgestellt, wonach Aufnahmen nur für den Zweck verwendet werden dürfen, für den sie ursprünglich aufgenommen wurden. In der Praxis erhalten die Gesellschaften im allgemeinen das Recht, die Bilder für alle möglichen Nebenzwecke zu benutzen, z. B. in Geschäftspublikationen, für Pressecommuniqués und anderem verkaufsförderndem Material. Für den Einsatz der Aufnahmen in der Werbung ist eine separate Vereinbarung erforderlich. Die Werbeagentur verhandelt mit dem Photographen und zahlt ihm ein zusätzliches Honorar in Höhe der Summe, die gespart wird, weil das Bild nicht neu aufgenommen werden muss.

Die graphische Gestaltung Noch wichtiger für die Gestaltung eines erstklassigen Jahresberichtes ist der Designer (Graphiker/Gestalter), der verstehen muss, welche Botschaft die Gesellschaft übermitteln will; er ist es, der die richtigen Aufnahmen aus einer Fülle von Bildern auswählt, sie richtig beschneiden und möglichst wirkungsvoll einsetzen muss. Bisweilen wird er es vorziehen, nicht Photographien, sondern hochwertige Illustrationen zu verwenden, besonders wenn die Gesellschaft ein Finanzinstitut oder ein anderes Unternehmen ist, das nichts Photogenes aufzuweisen hat. Illustrationen können, richtig ausgedacht und verwendet, immaterielle Eigenschaften einer Firma oft besser veranschaulichen als Photographien. Ein Bergwerksunternehmen beispielsweise wollte seine bedeutenden Investitionen in neuen Minen und Hüttenwerken zeigen. Ein Photograph hätte sich der kaum zu bewältigenden Aufgabe gegenübergesehen, das verwirrende und wenig eindrucksvolle Durcheinander der Minenstollen und die grossangelegten, jedoch graphisch nicht sehr eindrucksvollen Schmelzanlagen

zu knipsen. Der Illustrator dagegen war in der Lage, das Riesenausmass dieser Projekte und ihre Bedeutung für die Gesellschaft vor Augen zu führen.

Auf der Suche nach immer originelleren Wegen, sich der Öffentlichkeit vorzustellen, sprengen die Unternehmen die überlieferte Einstellung zur Illustration. Der *Scovill*-Geschäftsbericht für 1969 zeigt Montagen aus Holz, Glas und anderen Stoffen, die überaus eindrucksvoll die Absatzmärkte der Firma veranschaulichen. Solche Kunstwerke können später als Wandschmuck am Geschäftssitz dienen, vorher aber muss eindeutig festgelegt werden, wer endgültiger Besitzer dieser Originalwerke ist. Neuartig war auch der *Ansul*-Geschäftsbericht für 1969, der drei Faltplakate führender Plakatkünstler enthielt. Die Plakate waren als integrierender Bestandteil des Geschäftsberichtes gedacht und die Ansul-Aktionäre konnten auf Wunsch eine begrenzte Anzahl beziehen.

Die Typographie ist ein Gebiet, für das die Geschäftsleitung selten Verständnis hat und das sie meist nicht gebührend zu würdigen weiss. Oft macht sie jedoch den Unterschied zwischen einer gewöhnlichen, stümperhaften Wirkung und einem vornehm erscheinenden «Qualitätsprodukt». Die Wahl des Schriftbildes für den Geschäftsbericht sollte dem Graphiker überlassen bleiben, denn nur er kennt die subtilen Unterschiede zwischen den Schriftarten.

Genau wie andere Elemente des Jahresberichtes, sind auch die Schriftarten Modeeinflüssen unterworfen. Moderne Grotesk-Schriften sind gegenwärtig sehr en vogue. Die Wahl einer Grotesk-Schrift für die Geschäftsberichte der *General Electric* – die 1961 und 1962 mit Goldmedaillen der FINANCIAL WORLD ausgezeichnet wurden – bestätigte die Lesbarkeit dieser Schriften und trug wesentlich zu ihrer vermehrten Verwendung bei.

Überschriften und andere Lösungen für die Texthervorhebung bilden ebenfalls wichtige graphische Faktoren und können einen konservativen oder modernen Eindruck erwecken oder auch dem Bericht einen technologischen Anhauch verleihen.

Der so wirkungsvolle Einsatz von weissem Raum kann den Geschäftsleitern oft nur schwer verständlich gemacht werden. Geschäftsleute sind an Memoranden und ähnliche, nicht für einen bestimmten Zweck entworfene Mitteilungsträger gewohnt und finden meist, dass alle Flächen mit Worten oder Aufnahmen gefüllt sein sollten. Sie sehen nicht ein, dass der Gebrauch oder Missbrauch des verfügbaren Raums Wirkung und Tragweite des gedruckten Textes entscheidend beeinflusst. Die grosszügige Verwendung von viel weisser Fläche in den *IBM*-Jahresberichten hat diese Art der Gestaltung zu einem Element moderner Berichterstattung gemacht.

Diagramme und Tabellen bieten eine weitere gute Möglichkeit für die graphische Gestaltung und die Betonung der wichtigsten Teile der Aussagen der Gesellschaft. Vor allem ist Einfachheit und Klarheit anzustreben; manche Gesellschaften haben sich zu wahren Experten für einfache Säulen- und Kurvendiagramme entwickelt. Auch Kreisdiagramme werden immer häufiger verwendet, im Zuge des stärkeren Aufschlusses über Verkaufs- und Einnahmeziffern nach Produktgruppen, seitens einer wachsenden Zahl von Unternehmen. Manche Gesellschaften benutzen Tabellen und graphische Darstellungen, um ein gutes Jahr zu illustrieren, und lassen sie weg, wenn sie ein weniger gutes Jahr zu verzeichnen hatten. Diese leicht zu durchschauende Handhabung könnte von Finanzanalytikern dahingehend gedeutet werden, dass die Gesellschaft keinen Aufwärtstrend dieser graphischen Erfolgsindikatoren erwartet.

Das Druckpapier Ein weiterer, leicht zu übersehender, aber wichtiger Faktor ist das Papier, auf dem der Bericht gedruckt wird. Gewicht, Strich und Farbton, charakteristische Merkmale des Papiergrundstoffes, machen den Unterschied im Aussehen und beim Anfühlen des Papieres. *IBM* war führend in der Verwendung von matt gestrichenem Papier, einer Qualität, die in den sechziger Jahren fast allgemein gebraucht wurde. Technische Neuerungen bieten dem Designer von heute eine Vielfalt von Material für die Vermittlung seiner Botschaft. Sie reichen von gestrichenen Hochglanz-Papiersorten, die glänzende Photoreproduktionen ermöglichen, bis zu einem konservativen, fast zarten Aussehen, das oft mit den vielen leicht körnigen Farbpapieren erreicht werden kann. Das Gewicht des gewählten Papiers kann mit dem Unterschied zwischen einem festen und einem schlappen Händedruck verglichen werden. Ein allzu schäbiger Jahresbericht kann den Eindruck von Substanz zunichte machen, den der Text zu erwecken versucht.

Information in Schichten Alle diese graphischen Komponenten können jedoch wenig erreichen, wenn sie nicht als harmonische Begleitung des Textes konzipiert sind. Den grössten Anspruch an die Zusammenarbeit von Redakteur und Graphiker stellt der allgegenwärtige Konsument der Geschäftsliteratur, der flüchtige Leser. In der Zeitspanne, die der durchschnittliche Aktionär der Lektüre des Jahresberichtes widmet, kann man unmöglich viele Einzelheiten über Geschäftstätigkeit und Erfolge des Unternehmens vermitteln. Der Jahresbericht soll deshalb einen haftenden *Eindruck* von der Stärke, der technologischen Fortschrittlichkeit und der Produktionsausweitung des Unternehmens erzeugen – kurz, von all dem, was der Gesellschaft am meisten am Herzen liegt.

Eine Lösung hiefür besteht darin, wichtige Informationen schichtweise zu präsentieren. Es ist eine besonders für flüchtige Leser gedachte Methode, die sich der im Zeitungswesen üblichen Gewohnheit annähert, die aktuellsten Nachrichten in der Überschrift, etwas weniger wichtige Neuigkeiten im nächsten Abschnitt usw. zu bringen. Beim Jahresbericht besteht die erste Schicht eigentlich im Umschlag – er vermittelt den allgemeinsten Eindruck. Der Brief des Präsidenten bildet die zweite Schicht – laut Rundfrage der *General Electric* ist er auch der Teil des Jahresberichtes, der am meisten gelesen wird. Die dritte Schicht – bestimmt für diejenigen Leser, die die zwei ersten interessant genug gefunden haben, um weiter zu lesen – bilden die Aufnahmen und begleitenden Legenden. Der Zwischentitel, der über den Geschäftsverlauf orientiert, bildet wohl die nächste Stufe oder Schicht. Dies besonders dann, wenn sie eigentliche Informationen bieten – wie zum Beispiel «Umsatz um 17 Prozent gestiegen» anstatt nur «Umsatz». Und einleitende Zusammenfassungen, die das Nachfolgende in einem kurzen Absatz geben, sind ebenfalls nützliche, aus dem Zeitungswesen übernommene Darstellungsweisen.

Die letzten Schichten bilden Einzelheiten des Tätigkeitsberichtes, der Finanzausweise und andere für den gründlichen und gut unterrichteten Anleger bestimmte Informationen. Der vollständige Jahresbericht präsentiert die Finanz- und Betriebsdaten, Photos und andere graphische Komponenten in einheitlicher und ansprechender Aufmachung.

Zweiteilige Jahresberichte Einige Gesellschaften gehen genau umgekehrt vor: sie trennen die verschiedenen Informationskategorien völlig voneinander und legen einen zweiteiligen Geschäftsbericht vor. *U. S. Plywood-Champion Paper* sowie *Ralston Purina Co.* haben zweiteilige Jahresberichte herausgegeben. Ein separates, an die innere Umschlagseite angeheftetes, zweifarbiges Heft enthielt eine Mitteilung an die Aktionäre und die Finanzausweise; der illustrierte Teil konnte dann auf der rechten Seite gelesen werden.

Andere Unternehmen gingen so weit, zwei völlig getrennte Schriften zu versenden; ein geradezu selbstvernichtendes Vorgehen. Es ist dann für den wichtigsten Leser, den Wertschriftenanalytiker, allzu verlockend, das Heft mit der Finanzinformation aufzubewahren und den illustrierten Teil wegzuwerfen. Da man aber den Wertschriftenanalytiker an dem Wachstumspotential der Gesellschaft interessieren will und da Text und Photos eine positive Botschaft der Gesellschaft vermitteln wollen, sollte dem Analytiker alles zusammen unterbreitet werden. Der vollständige Geschäftsbericht, zweifellos die wirkungsvollste Art der Präsentation, sollte die Informationen in Schichten darbieten – das Offensichtlichste zuoberst, für den nicht allzu interessierten Aktionär, und darunter die in Einzelheiten gehende nuancierte Information für den Analytiker.

Die Finanzsprache Anleger-Umfragen berichten manchmal besorgt, dass die meisten Aktionäre die in den Jahresberichten verwendete Finanzsprache nicht verstünden, so zum Beispiel Ausdrücke wie «Wandelobligationen» und andere. In Wirklichkeit ist dieses Problem nicht so wichtig. Selbst der Aktionär, der die Finanzsprache versteht, könnte eine aus dem Zusammenhang gerissene finanzielle Angabe kaum vernünftig deuten, da zu viele Möglichkeiten bestehen, diese zu präsentieren. Die Interpretation der Finanzausweise wird am besten dem Berufsanalytiker überlassen, der dann leitende Angestellte der Gesellschaft über ihre genaue Bedeutung befragen kann.

In diesem Zusammenhang besteht gegenwärtig eine Kontroverse, ob Jahresberichte sich hauptsächlich an «Lieschen Müller» bzw. ihr männliches Gegenstück, den Prototyp des kleinen Durchschnittsaktionärs wenden, oder ob sie verfasst werden sollen, um Persönlichkeiten zu informieren, die wichtige Anlageentscheidungen zu treffen haben. Obwohl diese Leute im allgemeinen Berufsanalytiker sind, kann es sich bisweilen auch um einen kleinen Geschäftsmann oder in finanziellen Dingen bewanderten Familienvorstand handeln. Was das Volumen der gehandelten Aktien betrifft, so werden jedoch alle Entscheidungen über Aktienkauf und -verkauf, abgesehen von einem verschwindend kleinen Prozentsatz, von einem beruflichen Finanzexperten entweder getroffen oder wenigstens beeinflusst. Als Leser sind diese Fachleute mindestens 100 mal so einflussreich wie einzelne Kleinaktionäre. Ein wirkungsvoller harmonisch ausgewogener Jahresbericht dürfte jedenfalls sowohl für das kleine «Lieschen Müller» wie auch für den Finanzexperten interessant und so von Bedeutung für ihre Entscheidungen sein.

Die originelle Konzeption Ein gut gegliederter, vollständiger Bericht ist praktisch zur Norm für die Berichterstattung geworden, der eine Gesellschaft entsprechen muss, wenn sie auf dem Finanzmarkt konkurrenzfähig sein will. Doch gelingt es gelegentlich einem Unternehmen, seinen Bericht derart originell und einfallsreich zu gestalten, dass er allgemeine Anerkennung und Publizität erhält. Auf einem Gebiet, wo ungeheurer Mangel an wirklich originellem Denken herrscht, sind die Geschäftsmedien nur zu erpicht, über tatsächlich Neues zu berichten. Leider verwechseln viele Gesellschaften echt Schöpferisches mit kompliziert ausgearbeiteten Graphiken oder Mätzchen, die die Leser vor den Kopf stossen, anstatt sie anzuziehen. Kniffe, wie Drucke mit parfümierter Druckerschwärze oder Mitteilungen via Grammophonplatte, die der Analytiker weder in sein Dossier legen noch eventuell spielen kann, sind in der Finanzwelt durchaus unangebracht.

Immerhin haben gewisse Gesellschaften es fertiggebracht, in ihren Jahresberichten gänzlich neuartige Ideen zu verarbeiten.
• Ein frühes klassisches Beispiel war *Charles Pfizer*, eine Gesellschaft, die ihren Bericht für 1956 als Beilage der Sonntagsausgabe der NEW YORK TIMES, der CHICAGO TRIBUNE und der LOS ANGELES TIMES für deren 3,5 Millionen Leser druckte. Um sicher zu gehen, dass ihr Jahresbericht einen Leserkreis von prominenten Persönlichkeiten erreichte, verteilte Pfizer 200 000 weitere Exemplare an Kongressmitglieder, Staatsgouverneure sowie führende Leute in Verwaltung und Industrie an Orten, wo das Unternehmen Werke unterhielt; an Lehrer, Apotheker, Ärzte, öffentliche Bibliotheken, an den eigenen Mitarbeiterstab ohne Aktienbesitz, Kunden und Lieferanten, Mitglieder der Finanzwelt, Fabrikbesucher sowie an Leute, die Einfluss auf die öffentliche Meinung hatten. Die Associated Press brachte einen Bericht über dieses Ergebnis in über 100 Zeitungen und das Magazin THE NEW YORKER bezeichnete Pfizers Vorgehen als «bahnbrechend». Das Zeitungsbeilage-Programm wurde in den darauffolgenden zwei Jahren wiederholt. Es hatte eine Schlüsselstellung in Pfizers systematischer PR-Kampagne beim Anlagepublikum, einem Programm, das 1954 gestartet wurde, als die Gesellschaft insgesamt 13 000 Aktionäre zählte. Mitte der sechziger Jahre war die Zahl der Pfizer-Aktienbesitzer auf 80 000 gestiegen.
• Um hervorzuheben, dass sich ihr Verkaufsprogramm nicht nur auf Blechdosen beschränkte, versandte die *American Can Company* Anfang der sechziger Jahre ihren Jahresbericht in einer Rolle aus Pappe. Diese Rolle war Bestandteil des neuen, reichhaltigen Produktionsprogrammes für Verpackungsmittel in der Lebensmittelbranche. American Can hat später erfahren, dass weit über 90 Prozent der Empfänger dieses so originell verpackten Geschäftsberichtes ihn auch aus der Umhüllung zogen und ansahen, gegenüber dem gewöhnlichen Prozentsatz von 60 Prozent. Leider verblieb der Bericht in aufgerolltem Zustand und konnte nur unter Schwierigkeiten abgelegt werden, was denn auch zu Beschwerden der Wertschriftenanalytiker führte. Die gute Werbewirkung hatte diesen Nachteil jedoch mehr als aufgewogen.

• «Sehr geehrter Herr: Ich bin 15 Jahre alt und habe etwas Geld gespart, das ich gerne in Aktien irgendeiner Gesellschaft anlegen möchte ... können Sie mir bitte erklären ... was Sie tun und warum ... mit besten Grüssen, Chris Nelson.» Diese Sätze aus einem Brief auf dem Umschlag des Geschäftsberichtes der *Bell & Howell* für 1963 boten dem Unternehmen die beste Einleitung für einen Jahresbericht, der Chris und den zahlreichen jungen Leuten, die «wie Du ein aufrichtiges Interesse an den Geschäftsunternehmen Amerikas haben», gewidmet war. Im weiteren Verlauf ihres Berichtes erklärte die Gesellschaft ihre Leistungen und Tätigkeit in der hochentwickelten Welt der Technologie in einfacher, klarer Sprache — und gewann dadurch auch die dankbare Anerkennung manch erwachsener Aktionäre, die gleichfalls wenig von dem Tätigkeitsbereich der Firma verstanden.
• Im Jahre 1969 beauftragte die *Girard Bank* in Philadelphia den Schriftsteller James Michener und den Maler Andrew Wyeth, eine Broschüre mit dem Titel «Das schöne Leben» zu verfassen. Der das Büchlein begleitende Jahresbericht war verhältnismässig einfach gehalten und nicht kostspielig gewesen. Aber die bedeutsame und aufsehenerregende Botschaft in dem hübsch aufgemachten Büchlein der beiden Einwohner des Staates Pennsylvania erregte beträchtliche Aufmerksamkeit und brachte der Gesellschaft nicht weniger als 5000 Lobesbriefe. Die Bank wiederholte ihren früheren Erfolg im Jahre 1970 mit einem 74 Seiten zählenden Buch, betitelt «Ein Städte-Planet?» (''An Urban Planet?''). Verfasserin war eine bekannte internationale Volkswirtschaftlerin; die Illustrationen stammten von einem Aquarellisten aus Philadelphia.
• Originalität und Kreativität am anderen Ende der literarischen Skala bewies eine kleine Gesellschaft in New Jersey, namens *Cybernatics, Inc.*, mit einem jährlichen Verkaufsvolumen von etwa 6 Millionen Dollar. Ihr Geschäftsbericht für 1969 stiess in ein Gebiet vor, das sonst fast nie betreten wird — er betrachtet die Gesellschaft mit Humor. Der Umschlag lautete: «Lassen Sie sich von acht unparteiischen Beobachtern sagen, wie Cybernatics Inc. 1969 wirklich abgeschnitten hat». Die im Text aufgeführten Gutachten stammen von der Putzfrau — «der Abfall ist bei Cybernatics um 630 % gestiegen», dem Jungen, der die Mittagessen bringt — «Sie bestellten sieben Mal so viel Cheeseburgers wie letztes Jahr» und vom Fensterputzer — «Sie scheinen mehr zu tun zu haben als letztes Jahr».
• *Combustion Engineering* wollte einmal sehen, wie das Unternehmen aus der Sicht eines Aussenseiters aussah. Es engagierte einen 17jährigen Farbigen, dessen Aufnahmen in einem Photowettbewerb preisgekrönt wurden und beauftragte ihn, die Gesellschaft während 20 Tagen zu photographieren. Der junge Photograph reiste für seine Aufnahmen kreuz und quer durch die USA. Jeden Abend nahm er seine Eindrücke vom Tage auf Tonband auf. Die Photos des jungen Mannes wurden in den Jahresbericht aufgenommen und seine Kommentare zu einem wichtigen Bestandteil des Textes gemacht. Was die Firma auf diese Weise zu erreichen versuchte, war ein Brückenschlag zwischen Wirtschaft und Jugend.

Ein ästhetisch ansprechender und originell konzipierter Jahresbericht, der einen positiven Einfluss ausübt, zählt zu den bedeutendsten Beiträgen, die eine Gesellschaft auf dem Gebiet der Geschäftsberichterstattung leisten kann.

Kapitel 4: Die Bestandteile des Jahresberichtes

Im grossen ganzen enthält ein Jahresbericht den Brief an die Aktionäre, einen Überblick über den Geschäftsgang, die Finanzrechnungen, Anmerkungen, eine Liste der Mitglieder des Verwaltungsrates und der Geschäftsleitung und den gesetzlich vorgeschriebenen Bericht der Kontrollstelle. Diese Angaben sind im allgemeinen vom Umschlag bis zur letzten Seite in der gleichen Reihenfolge angeordnet und verursachen daher bei der Gestaltung des Berichtes gewisse Schwierigkeiten, die man aber auch als Ansporn betrachten kann. Aus Konkurrenzgründen enthalten die Geschäftsberichte der grossen Gesellschaften von heute jedoch meist mehr als diese wesentlichen Angaben, um das Charakteristische des Unternehmens zu beschreiben und herauszustellen. In diesem Kapitel wird ein derart erweiterter Jahresbericht beschrieben.

Der Umschlag

Der Umschlag bildet das wichtigste graphische Element des Jahresberichtes. Er soll den Leser zum Öffnen des Berichtes reizen und das Image der Gesellschaft einprägen oder vertiefen. Die meisten Berichte wählen ein interessantes Photo als graphischen Blickfang. Sei es auf dem Umschlag eines Geschäftsberichtes oder auf dem Titelblatt des LIFE Magazines – ein ansprechendes Bild erregt Neugier und veranlasst den Leser, sich den Inhalt anzusehen.

Wenn eine konservative Note angeschlagen werden soll, können andere Faktoren von grösserer Bedeutung sein – zum Beispiel farbiges Papier, Prägungen oder Golddruck. In den letzten Jahren haben einige der waghalsigsten Konglomerate ihre Jahresberichte in höchst konservative Umschläge gehüllt, offenbar in der Absicht, ein besser fundiertes Image zu erwecken.

Wenn ein Jahresbericht einem bestimmten, scharf umrissenen Thema gewidmet ist, so kann es durch den Umschlag wirkungsvoll hervorgehoben und eingeleitet werden. Der Umschlag des Geschäftsberichtes der *Chase Manhattan Bank* für 1967 zeigte ein leicht abstraktes Bild der traditionellen Wolkenkratzer-Silhouette von Manhattan; im Vordergrund sah man den Umriss von Harlem. Die Ansprache des Vorsitzenden des Verwaltungsrates an die Aktionäre begann wie folgt: «Wir halten es für angebracht, dass unser Titelblatt für 1967 die Verschmelzung von New Yorks «anderer» Silhouette mit der gewohnten zeigt ... So vereint, illustrieren die beiden Skylines sowohl die Pracht New Yorks als auch die drohende Gefahr, die ihm aus seinen Elendsvierteln erwächst. Im Jahre 1967 hat sich die Chase Manhattan dafür eingesetzt, die Kluft zwischen diesen so ungleichen Welten zu verringern...»

Da es viele Arten moderner Aktiengesellschaften gibt, besteht auch ein grosser Spielraum für den Umschlagsentwurf. Paul Rand von der *IBM* zum Beispiel findet, der Umschlag solle nicht allzu nüchtern sein: «Wenn wir einfach einen Gegenstand auf dem Umschlag abbilden, so gibt das das Image der Gesellschaft nicht wieder. Benütze ich jedoch eine gegenstandslose, nicht erkennbare, abstruse Photographie – umwittert von einem Hauch von Geheimnis – so kann ich verständlich machen, was für eine Gesellschaft die IBM wirklich ist.» *IBM* und *Xerox* z. B. haben Umschläge mit abstrakten Aufnahmen verwendet.

Wenn der Umschlag den Leser zum Lesen verlocken soll, so sollen die Aufschlagsseiten – die Innenseite des Umschlags und die erste Seite zusammen – ein gewisses Mass an Information, möglichst in Worten, bieten, die das Interesse des Lesers an dem Unternehmen erregt. Ein blosses Inhaltsverzeichnis und eine Titelseite genügen meist nicht, um die mit diesen 2 Seiten gebotene ausgezeichnete Gelegenheit, eine grosse Wirkung zu erzielen, voll auszuschöpfen.

Die Identitäts-Beschreibung

Ein kurzer Text, der das Unternehmen in aussagekräftigen Worten charakterisiert, bildet den wirkungsvollsten Einsatz der Einführungsseiten und wird immer üblicher. Er kann von Produkten oder Märkten handeln oder auch von der Grösse der Gesellschaft oder auf andere Vorzüge hinweisen, die als Fundament für weiteres Wachstum dienen können. Er beschreibt dem Leser kurz und bündig das Wesen der Gesellschaft und ihre Bedeutung.

Der Corporate-Image-Abschnitt im Jahresbericht der United Merchants für 1969, um ein Beispiel zu nennen, lautet wie folgt: «*United Merchants and Manufacturers, Inc.* zählt zu Amerikas bedeutendsten Herstellern modischer Stoffe für Männer-, Frauen- und Kinderbekleidung sowie Dekorationsstoffe. United Merchants produziert und vertreibt auch Glasstoffe und Produkte mit Plastikbelag – darunter die gut eingeführten Con-tact® and Kwick-Kover® Sortiments von Selbstklebeartikeln.

«Dazu kommen kommerzielles Factoring und Finanzierungen sowie die *Robert Hall Clothes*, eine über das ganze Land verbreitete Kette von 118 Bekleidungsgeschäften. Bedeutende ausländische Produktionsstätten und verwandte Betriebe befinden sich in Argentinien, Brasilien, Kolumbien, Uruguay, Venezuela, Kanada, Frankreich und Grossbritannien. *United Merchants* betreibt 49 Fabriken in den Vereinigten Staaten und im Ausland, besitzt Verkaufs- und Verteilerbüros in grösseren Städten und beschäftigt über 36 000 Männer und Frauen.»

Das Inhaltsverzeichnis

Entgegen der Meinung einiger Kritiker der Jahresberichte, ist die Verwendung eines Inhaltsverzeichnisses der freien Wahl überlassen und tatsächlich in vielen Fällen ganz überflüssig. Da nur wenige Berichte mehr als 36 Seiten zählen, kann der Leser das ganze Büchlein leicht durchblättern – ein Vorteil für die Gesellschaft, weil dadurch mehr vom gesamten Inhalt aufgenommen wird. Ein Inhaltsverzeichnis bringt oft nur Unordnung in die einleitenden Seiten, verwässert den Eindruck der Beschreibung der Gesellschaft und trägt mit Ausnahme der Aufführung des Inhalts nichts Positives bei.

Gewisse Gesellschaften haben ein neuartiges Inhaltsverzeichnis eingeführt, das sowohl Information als auch Interesse bietet. So hat der Geschäftsbericht der *First National City Bank* für 1969 ein in acht verschiedene Themen aufgegliedertes Inhaltsverzeichnis, in dem jedes Thema in etwa 6 Zeilen umschriebe und mit verkleinerten Ausschnitten aus den Illustrationen im Text versehen ist.

Der Finanz-Kurzbericht

Hier sind die wichtigsten Finanzdaten für die abgelaufene Geschäftsperiode angeführt – je kürzer, je besser. Der *Aiken Industries* Bericht für 1968 enthielt nur 3 Posten – Nettoverkäufe, Nettoeinkommen und Nettoverdienst pro Aktie. Andere Gesellschaften vergeuden Platz und Aufmerksamkeit des Lesers, indem sie eine ausführliche Zusammenfassung der wichtigsten Finanzinformationen am Anfang drucken, nur um dann den Grossteil dieser Daten in einer statistischen Übersicht für die letzten 5 oder 10 Jahre weiter hinten im Bericht zu wiederholen. Am besten verbindet man eine kurze Übersicht mit einer ausführlichen Zusammenfassung der Entwicklung der letzten 10 Jahre. Die kurze Übersicht kann auf der zweiten Umschlagseite, der ersten Seite oder auch neben das Vorwort an die Aktionäre gestellt werden. Wird sie dem Vorwort gegenübergestellt, so kann sich dieses auf erklärende und beschreibende Belege konzentrieren und nur bei Zahlen auf die Übersicht verweisen. In den letzten zehn Jahren war diese Art der Darstellung vorherrschend.

Das Vorwort an die Aktionäre

Dieses Vorwort, das die Unterschrift des Präsidenten und des Generaldirektors, bisweilen auch noch die des Vorsitzenden des Verwaltungsrates trägt, ist der am meisten gelesene Teil des Jahresberichtes. Das Vorwort sollte kurz und aufschlussreich sein und dem Präsidenten Gelegenheit geben, die Leser direkt über die wichtigsten Ereignisse des Geschäftsjahres zu orientieren. Die Aufnahme eines bestimmten Themas im Vorwort unterstreicht seine Wichtigkeit. Obgleich das Vorwort kurz sein sollte, muss es über die Hauptprodukte, die Absatz-Märkte, finanziellen Entwicklungen und Neuerwerbungen orientieren. Ebenso sollte es über die Zielsetzung des Unternehmens für das kommende Jahr Aufschluss geben, jedoch, von ganz speziellen Fällen abgesehen, niemals genaue Angaben finanzieller Natur über Zukunftsprojekte enthalten.

Das Vorwort ist das geeignete Instrument, um politische Fragen und heikle Probleme der Geschäftspolitik zu erörtern. Eine Gesellschaft hatte im Laufe des Jahres 1970 hart am Problem des Umweltschutzes gearbeitet und eine Anzahl Auszeichnungen auf diesem Gebiet erhalten. Nachdem die Leiter des Unternehmens zuerst erwogen hatten, einen besonderen Teil über den Beitrag der Firma im Kampf gegen die Umweltverschmutzung beizufügen, entschlossen sie sich schliesslich, nur einen Absatz über dieses Thema in das Aktionärsvorwort aufzunehmen. Der wertvollen Arbeit des Unternehmens wurde dadurch der verdiente Prestigeplatz im Jahresbericht eingeräumt, ohne gleichzeitig übertriebene Aufmerksamkeit auf ein unerfreuliches und schwieriges Thema zu lenken.

In bezug auf die Politik kann das Vorwort als eine

Standortbestimmung verwendet werden. Im Jahresbericht der *Philip Morris* für 1969 zum Beispiel wurde in acht Abschnitten des Briefes des Präsidenten die Einstellung der Zigarettenindustrie zur Frage des Rauchens und der Gesundheit dargelegt.

Im übrigen ist es angebracht, den veralteten und schwerfälligen Brauch abzuschaffen, in einem Schlussabsatz allen Mitarbeitern und leitenden Angestellten, Aktionären und Kunden, oft sogar den Lieferanten, Dank und Anerkennung für den Erfolg des Geschäftsjahres auszusprechen. Eine derartige Erklärung klingt einigermassen unaufrichtig, wenn sie Jahr für Jahr neu ausgesprochen wird.

Weiterhin sollte man auf die Aufzählung der Namen der während des Jahres beförderten oder neuernannten Mitarbeiter verzichten. Vom Gesichtspunkt des Lesers ist eine solche Liste einer der uninteressantesten Bestandteile eines Jahresberichtes. Diese Information sollte zwar im Geschäftsbericht aufgeführt werden, jedoch am Ende des Kapitels über den Geschäftsverlauf erscheinen. Neue Mitglieder des Verwaltungsrates sollten hingegen im Vorwort kurz erwähnt werden.

Das Vorwort sollte das Datum des Tages tragen, an dem das endgültige Manuskript an die Druckerei geht – also das Datum, nach dem keinerlei Änderungen irgendwo im Geschäftsbericht mehr angebracht werden können. Das Vorwort kann und soll also alle Ereignisse in der Gesellschaft bis zu diesem Datum einschliessen, anstatt sich auf das Kalenderjahr zu beschränken, das vielleicht schon mehrere Wochen oder Monate früher zu Ende gegangen ist.

Der Titel der Person, die das Vorwort unterschreibt, sollte stets unter die Unterschrift gedruckt werden und sein Name sollte auch in Druckbuchstaben erscheinen. Die Unterschrift der Geschäftsführer von heute ist in vielen Fällen so unleserlich, dass diese zusätzliche Zeile zur Identifizierung des Verfassers unbedingt notwendig geworden ist.

In der Kürze liegt nicht nur die Würze, sondern auch der Weg zur grössten Leserzahl. Umfragen haben ergeben, dass die Leserschaft rapide absinkt, sobald der Brief länger als zwei Seiten ist. Durch Veröffentlichung eines Photos des Unterzeichneten kann die Leserzahl noch erhöht werden.

Spezielle Sonderberichte

Dies sind Elemente, die dem Jahresbericht zusätzlich zu den durch Gesetz oder Gewohnheit vorgeschriebenen Teilen beigefügt werden. Wie bereits in Kapitel 1 erwähnt, können diese Sonderberichte Neuerwerbungen und Beteiligungen, Forschung, besondere Marktmeldungen, Neuigkeiten über Mitarbeiter oder Aussenstehende oder anderes, die Gesellschaft irgendwie Tangierendes, umfassen. Der Geschäftsbericht der *Time Inc.* von 1968 widmete einem Spezialbericht mit dem Titel «Werbung: Ein Verkaufsverfahren» nicht weniger als 28 Seiten. Er brachte dramatische Schwarzweiss-Photos und auf Band aufgenommene Kommentare repräsentativer Mitarbeiter des 350 Köpfe zählenden Werbestabs der Gesellschaft. Zweifellos diente der Bericht diesen Mitgliedern der Verkaufsabteilung im folgenden Jahr als ausgezeichnete Visitenkarte, schilderte er sie doch als wortgewandte, sympathische Menschen.

Die Frage-und-Antwort-Methode

Eine steigende Zahl von Jahresberichten enthält in

der einen oder anderen Form einen Frage- und Antwortteil. Die *Gilette Company* zum Beispiel bringt einen solchen Teil bereits seit über 10 Jahren. In ihrem neuen, vierteljährlich erscheinenden Geschäftsbericht-Magazin bringt die *General Electric* 1969 einen Teil «Anleger stellen Fragen», der allen Aktionären Antworten zugänglich macht, die auf Fragen im Briefwechsel mit Aktionären, an den Generalversammlungen und von professionellen Analytikern erteilt wurden. Die Frage-und-Antwort-Methode hat mehrere wichtige Vorteile. Erstens geht sie auf das Wesentliche ein; der *Olin* Geschäftsbericht für 1968 erteilt eine klare annehmbare Antwort auf die harte Frage: «Werden die Gewinne rapide sinken, sobald das Schiessen in Vietnam zu Ende ist?». Den Frage-und-Antwortteil kann man auch rasch überfliegen: Die Fragen wirken wie Untertitel und ermöglichen es dem Leser, den Text nur zu überfliegen, bis er auf eine Frage stösst, die ihn interessiert. Ausserdem bietet der Frage-und-Antwortteil eine Möglichkeit, Charakter und Persönlichkeit der leitenden Männer wenigstens bis zu einem gewissen Grade kennenzulernen. Malcolm Baldrige, der Präsident von *Scovill*, schrieb im Jahresbericht seiner Gesellschaft für 1965: «Wenn man die sich bietenden Möglichkeiten betrachtet, gibt es so viele Wege, die wir einschlagen könnten, dass ich mir manchmal vorkomme wie ein blinder Hund in einer Metzgerei.» Dies als Antwort auf eine Frage über zukünftige Absatzgebiete und Möglichkeiten.

Der Rückblick auf den Geschäftsverlauf

Dieser Teil variiert von der ausführlichen Behandlung des Themas, wie sie ein einfach aufgebautes kleineres Unternehmen möglich macht, bis zum kurzen Aufzählen der Höhepunkte bei einer grossen, komplexen Gesellschaft. Im allgemeinen sollte die Übersicht über den Geschäftsverlauf einigermassen ausführlich behandeln, was die Gesellschaft im abgelaufenen Geschäftsjahr im Hinblick auf neue Produkte, neue Absatzmärkte, Verkaufsvolumen und Einnahmen erreicht hat – und die Gründe für ihr Vorgehen angeben. Ferner sollte der Rückblick Kapitalinvestitionen behandeln und darauf hinweisen, welche Leistungen für das kommende Jahr von der Gesellschaft erwartet werden. Dieser Teil ist oft mit Betriebsdaten und technischem Jargon vollgestopft und lässt dann die vom Aktionär benötigte Perspektive vermissen: Tatsachen und Trends, die den Gewinn pro Aktie in den nächsten Jahren entscheidend beeinflussen werden.

Die Finanzübersicht

Eine wachsende Anzahl von Gesellschaften fügt diesen wichtigen Teil ihrem Jahresbericht bei. Er befriedigt den immer stärker werdenden Ruf nach mehr Offenheit und bietet einen weitaus besseren Platz für ausführliche Finanzinformationen, als das Vorwort an die Aktionäre, das dadurch zu überladen würde.

Die Finanzübersicht ist für den Wertschriftenfachmann und andere professionelle Anleger bestimmt. Sie erleichtert die Arbeit des Fachmanns durch die Angabe von Verhältniszahlen und anderen Daten, die er sonst mühsam in den Finanzausweisen zusammensuchen müsste. Die Übersicht sollte die Finanzdaten auch interpretieren, d. h. Gründe angeben, warum Erträge gestiegen sind oder das Betriebskapital gesunken ist, oder warum weniger als der volle Steueransatz bezahlt wurde.

Natürlich hängt es von dem Wesen der einzelnen Gesellschaft ab, was genau in der Finanzübersicht enthalten sein sollte. Beispielsweise: Verkäufe, Einkommen, ausserordentliche Posten, cash flow, Fremdwährungen, Bedingungen der Neuerwerbungen, Investitionen, Dividenden, die langfristige Verschuldung, das Betriebskapital, Eigenkapital, Wandelobligationen und Neuausgaben von Aktien sowie Personalunkosten.

Die Finanzausweise

Hier sind Variationen in der Darstellung begrenzt. Die Finanzausweise bestehen gewöhnlich aus einer Gewinn- und Verlustrechnung, einer Abrechnung des Gewinnvortrages (der einbehaltenen Erträge), einer Bilanz oder Aufstellung der Aktiva und Passiva und einer Rechnung über die Herkunft und Verwendung der Mittel.

Die Anmerkungen

Wie bereits in Kapitel 2 erwähnt, werden diese wichtigen Zusätze zu den Finanzdaten in verschiedener Beziehung geändert, um sie vollständiger und lesbarer zu gestalten. Die amerikanische Regierung hat vorgeschlagen, dass die Fussnoten in einer Schriftgrösse von mindestens 10 Punkten gedruckt werden, entsprechend dem Schriftsatz in Zeitschriften. Obwohl die Verwendung dieser Schrift den Geschäftsbericht übermässig in die Länge ziehen könnte, ist der Beweggrund dafür begrüssenswert. Andererseits hat man mit Erfolg versucht, die Fussnoten in die Finanzübersicht einzugliedern.

Bestätigung der Revisionsstelle

Dieser vom Gesetz vorgeschriebene Bericht bescheinigt, dass eine unabhängige und gesetzlich anerkannte Revisionsstelle die Rechnungsabschlüsse geprüft hat, dass die Angaben richtig sind und nach den allgemein anerkannten Grundsätzen der Rechnungslegung gemacht wurden. In einzelnen Fällen enthält dieses Zeugnis einen Einwand, der darauf hindeuten kann, dass etwas mit der Rechnungsablegung der Gesellschaft ganz und gar nicht stimmt. Diese Bescheinigung steht meistens direkt nach den Fussnoten. Der Name der Revisionsstelle sollte in Druckbuchstaben und nicht in Handschrift wiedergegeben sein, letzteres ist veraltet und kann zu Verzögerungen und anderen Schwierigkeiten führen.

Der langfristige Finanzüberblick

Dieser Teil ist, obwohl nicht vorgeschrieben, in den meisten Geschäftsberichten enthalten. Die beliebteste Form ist eine Übersicht über 10 Jahre, während eine Firma, deren Aufbau sich innerhalb einer kurzen Zeit wesentlich verändert hat, im allgemeinen eine Zusammenfassung von 5 Jahren vorzieht. Nur wenige Unternehmen dehnen diesen Bericht auf eine Zeitspanne von 15 Jahren oder mehr aus – bereits Geschichte – in unserem Zeitalter des raschen Wandels.

Diese Informationen können auf die verschiedenste Art dargeboten werden: Eine gute Methode ist es, mit der Ergebnisstatistik anzufangen (grösstenteils Daten aus der Bilanz), dann Ertragsdaten pro Stammaktie, mit Einschluss von Posten wie cash flow, Anzahl der Aktionäre und der Mitarbeiter, zu geben. Für den Wertschriftenfachmann ist es auch sehr wertvoll, eine Kursspanne der Stammaktien in den letzten 10 Jahren vorzufinden sowie gewisse Verhältniszahlen, wie den

Prozentsatz der langfristigen Verschuldung; die Kapitalisierung in Prozenten des Eigenkapitals, das Nettoergebnis in Prozenten der Verkäufe und das Nettoergebnis als Prozentsatz des Eigenkapitals.

Verzeichnis der Geschäftsleiter

Diese Aufstellung ist in allen Jahresberichten, meistens auf der letzten Textseite oder der inneren Umschlagseite enthalten. Es ist wichtig, die anderen Geschäftsverbindungen und Titel der Aufsichtsratsmitglieder zu erwähnen. Das Weglassen dieser Informationen lässt entweder auf einen fast völlig aus betriebseigenen Mitgliedern bestehenden oder auf einen, hauptsächlich aus Pensionierten zusammengesetzten Aufsichtsrat schliessen.

Wichtige Firma-Angaben

Dieser Teil sollte alle Daten umfassen, die den vielen Lesern des Jahresberichtes nützlich sein könnten. Unbedingt erforderlich ist die Adresse des Hauptsitzes; viele Firmen geben auch ihre Telefonnummer an. Auch wen man um weitere Informationen bitten kann, sollte angegeben sein. Datum, genaue Zeit und Ort der jährlichen Aktionärsversammlung sollte erwähnt werden. Im allgemeinen führen die Gesellschaftsdaten auch die Namen der Transfer- und Registrierstellen an und eventuell die der Rechtsberater oder der Revisionsstelle. Ferner sollten die Börsen angegeben werden, an denen die Aktien gehandelt werden – Auslands- und Regionalbörsen inbegriffen. *Indian Head* bringt in diesem Teil ihres Geschäftsberichtes sogar die Zahl der Personen, die eine bestimmte Kategorie ihrer Wertpapiere hält (Stammaktien, zwei Serien Vorzugsaktien, Wandelobligationen, im Range nachgehende Schuldverschreibungen und Bezugsberechtigungsscheine).

Eine Aufzählung der Warenzeichen ist eine wertvolle Ergänzung und rationeller als eine Wiederholung des eingetragenen Symbols neben jeder Erwähnung der Schutzmarke. Im Geschäftsbericht der *Olin Corporation* für 1970 wird folgendermassen vorgegangen: «Kursiv gedruckte Produktionsbezeichnungen in diesem Bericht sind Schutzmarken der Olin Corporation».

In einer immer grösseren Anzahl von Geschäftsberichten wird dem Gestalter und Photographen eine Anerkennungsspalte in oder beim Geschäftsdatenteil gewidmet. Dies ganz besonders dann, wenn «Namen-Talente» beigezogen wurden; man kann diesen Mitarbeitern so seinen Dank aussprechen, was zudem als Ansporn wirkt. Ausserdem erhöht diese Spalte das Prestige der Gesellschaft selbst.

Verzeichnis der Betriebseinheiten

Ein Verzeichnis, in dem die Firma nach Betriebseinheiten aufgegliedert ist, kann nützlich sein, solange sie klein und unkompliziert genug ist, dass die einschlägige Information vollständig auf etwa zwei Seiten untergebracht werden kann. In dem Verzeichnis ist meist die Betriebsabteilung mit ihren Hauptprodukten aufgeführt. Auch sollte möglichst Adresse und Telefonnummer jeder einzelnen Betriebseinheit, einschliesslich des betreffenden Managers, angegeben sein. Diese Einzelheiten können betriebsintern sehr hilfreich sein, besonders wenn kein Telefonverzeichnis der Betriebsstellen zur Hand ist.

Die hintere Umschlagseite

Gewisse Gesellschaften haben eine Vorliebe für eine dekorative hintere Umschlagseite mit einer Aufnahme. Diese Seite wird aber meistens – und vorteilhafter – für Firmennamen und Adresse reserviert. Da der Jahresbericht viel benutzt wird, ist es besser, wenn die Firma mit dem Umschlag sofort identifiziert werden kann.

Die Herstellung des Jahresberichtes

«Vom verlegerischen Standpunkt aus gesehen, ist der Jahresbericht das wohl dilettantischste Produkt der Geschäftsleitung» – stellte einmal der PR-Direktor eines bedeutenden, diversifizierten Unternehmens fest. Das hat seinen Grund in verschiedenen Charakterzügen leitender Persönlichkeiten: «Die Geschäftsführung fordert einen geschraubten Stil; so wird der Jahresbericht zu einem Monument geschäftlichen Kauderwelschs», erklärte ein anderer Geschäftsleiter. «Das Management gibt sich literarisch und selbstbewusst, denkt aber nicht daran, Einzelheiten anzugeben und sagt im Grunde überhaupt nichts», lautet der Kommentar eines Dritten. Die Bewilligung zur Veröffentlichung bestimmter Informationen zu erhalten, ist eine weitere grosse Schwierigkeit. «Den Geschäftsbericht dem Vorstandsausschuss zur Genehmigung vorlegen und ihn dann auch durchbringen, bedeutet soviel wie eine blutige Schlacht gewinnen», erklärte ein Mann mit diesbezüglicher Erfahrung. Und das Schlimmste ist, dass die oberste Geschäftsleitung oft mit dem Endergebnis keineswegs zufrieden ist. Warum erweist sich der Jahresbericht, der so viel Geld und Zeitaufwand erfordert, oft als so enttäuschend? Die häufigsten Gründe sind die folgenden:

1. Der oberste Geschäftsleiter beauftragt mit dem Projekt nicht einen Mann, dem er vertraut. So wird der Beauftragte Opfer aller oft entgegengesetzten Meinungen ranghöherer Leute.

2. Der Geschäftsleiter kümmert sich nicht rechtzeitig genug um die Planung, und zwar dann, wenn seine Ansicht noch Einfluss haben könnte. Stattdessen bringt er oft übereilte und schlecht durchdachte Änderungen im letzten Moment an.

3. Der Verfasser des Jahresberichtes beendet den ersten Entwurf zu spät für eine eingehende und sorgfältige Überprüfung durch die Geschäftsleitung.

4. Der Text wird termingemäss geschrieben, aber der Geschäftsführer und andere leitende Angestellte schieben die Durchsicht so auf, bis die Umstände sie dazu zwingen.

5. Die Buchhaltung liefert die Rechnungsausweise zu spät. Dann ist die Zeitspanne zwischen dem Datum, an dem die Zahlen endlich vorliegen und dem Moment, da der Bericht gedruckt und versandt sein muss, viel zu kurz.

6. Die Gestaltung ist festgelegt und die Druckfahnen liegen bereits vor: nun kommt aber eine ganz neue Gruppe – Anwälte, Direktoren, die verschiedensten Vizedirektoren und vielleicht sogar die Frau des Generaldirektors – die eine ganze Reihe neuer Bemerkungen und Vorschläge unterbreitet, ohne das Grundkonzept, auf dem der Jahresbericht von Anfang an aufgebaut war, zu kennen.

7. Der Generaldirektor verliert im letzten Moment den Kopf. Dies gilt besonders dann, wenn Fall 6 eintritt und plötzlich eine Anzahl neuer Meinungen und Kommentare vorgebracht werden. Meist wird dadurch das Grundthema zerstört – der Text wird in aller Eile umgeschrieben und nur freigegeben, weil Redaktionsschluss droht. Der daraus resultierende Kompromiss ist fast eine Garantie, dass das Endresultat äusserst mittelmässig ausfallen wird.

Die meisten dieser Schwierigkeiten könnten von Anfang an ausgeschaltet werden, wenn man sich bewusst würde, dass ein Jahresbericht eigentlich nur Sprachrohr eines einzigen Menschen sein kann – nämlich des Generaldirektors, oder wie sein Titel als oberster Geschäftsführer auch immer lauten mag. Er muss sich von Anfang an um die Vorbereitungsarbeiten kümmern und die Ausführung jemandem übergeben, der sein volles Vertrauen geniesst und dem er seine ganze Unterstützung gewähren will. Die Erstellung des Jahresberichts wird immer häufiger Werbe- oder Public Relations-Chefs übertragen, die jetzt, mit grösseren Vollmachten versehen, in vielen Gesellschaften ernannt werden. Diese Leute tragen oft den Titel eines Direktors für Presse und PR. Die GRAPHIS-Umfrage hat ergeben, dass bei 75 Prozent der antwortenden Gesellschaften der Direktor für Public Relations die Verantwortung für den Geschäftsbericht trägt; als weitere Verantwortliche wurden zu 17 Prozent der Finanzdirektor und zu 8 Prozent der Sekretär genannt.

Manchmal ist es gut, einen aussenstehenden Berater zuzuziehen, dessen Erfahrung dem in der Firma mit dem Jahresbericht Beauftragten nützlich sein kann. Werbeagenturen lehnen ein solches Mandat oft ab: Es ist eine zu weitgehende und zu schwierige Aufgabe im Vergleich mit dem Honorar, das sie dafür berechnen können. Ausserdem wollen sie nicht riskieren, einen guten Werbekunden eventuell zu verärgern.

Trägt eine erfahrene Persönlichkeit, die das Vertrauen des Generaldirektors geniesst, die Verantwortung für den Jahresbericht, so verfährt man wie folgt:

Festlegung von Zeitplan und Gesamtkonzeption

Wenn es sich um eine grössere Gesellschaft handelt, verstreichen zwischen dem ersten Entwurf und dem Versand des Jahresberichts sechs bis sieben Monate. Ein Unternehmen, dessen Geschäftsjahr am 31. Dezember endet, und das den Versand für März vorgesehen hat, sollte die Vorbereitungsarbeiten im September in Angriff nehmen. Mit gewissen Arbeiten – insbesondere mit den Aufnahmen – sollte wenn möglich noch früher begonnen werden. Oft können nur im Sommer aufgenommene Photographien, vor allem Szenen im Freien, genau die Atmosphäre erzeugen, die die Gesellschaft wünscht.

Der Zeitplan sollte umfassend und realistisch sein. Der diesem Kapitel beigefügte Produktionsplan (Seite 53/54) zeigt die wesentlichen Elemente eines solchen Planes; das beste System müsste sowohl ein Abwicklungsdiagramm als auch einen einfacheren Terminplan enthalten. Ein Jahresbericht kann und soll ähnlich wie eine Zeitung oder Zeitschrift produziert werden, wobei einige Teile frühen, andere späten Redaktionsschluss haben.

Der entscheidende Zeitpunkt für die Festlegung des Drucktermins ist das Datum, an dem die Leute vom Rechnungswesen die Jahresabrechnungen liefern. Ein grosser Teil der schöpferischen Arbeit am Textteil, die Photos und die graphische Gestaltung können vorher erledigt werden. Dann wird das Verfahren beschleunigt und die Teile mit späterem Redaktionsschluss werden vervollständigt, nämlich die Finanzübersicht, der Brief an die Aktionäre und die Finanzausweise. Der Zeitplan ist nun sehr angespannt; jeder Vor- und Nachmittag bedeutet einen wichtigen Schritt vorwärts. Geschäftsführer, die Jahresberichte herausbringen, bezeichnen die «fahrplanmässige Lieferung endgültiger und von der Kontrollstelle beglaubigter Zahlen» als ihr drittgrösstes Problem.

Natürlich müssen die Vorbereitungsarbeiten fertig sein, bevor man die Finanzdaten erhalten kann und die Buchhalter, die diese Zahlen liefern, müssen ihren wichtigen Termin einhalten. Änderungen in der Schlussphase verursachen fast immer kostspielige Extraarbeit im Photostudio und Überstunden in der Druckerei.

Die letzte Frist für die Herausgabe des Jahresberichtes wird von den Börsen festgesetzt – für bei der New York Stock Exchange kotierte Gesellschaften 90 Tage nach Abschluss der Rechenschaftsperiode; für Unternehmen, die an der American Stock Exchange kotiert sind, 120 Tage. Für Gesellschaften, deren Aktien ausserbörslich gehandelt werden, ist keine Frist vorgeschrieben, jedoch sollten auch sie ihre Berichte nicht später als 120 Tage nach ihrem Abschlussdatum veröffentlichen. Läuft eine kotierte Gesellschaft Gefahr, ihre Frist zu überschreiten, so muss sie bei der Börse eine Verlängerung beantragen, ein Vorgehen, das als Zeichen schlechten Managements angesehen wird, und das die meisten Gesellschaften verabscheuen. Der im Zeitplan angegebene Termin sollte daher als bindend angesehen werden. Sollte eine Verzögerung eintreten, so muss er revidiert, darf aber niemals verworfen werden.

Wenn das erste Programm aufgestellt wird, sollten die Winterurlaubspläne der leitenden Angestellten überprüft und entweder der Zeitplan oder der Urlaub entsprechend angepasst werden. Nicht wenige Gesellschaften haben es tief bereut, die letzte Fassung des Jahresberichtes unter Abschluss-Druck nach dem Ferienort des Geschäftsleiters fliegen zu müssen.

Der *Plan* für den Jahresbericht ist nicht mit dem *Zeitplan* zu verwechseln. Der Plan sollte eine Anzahl Ziele enthalten, die sich als Ergebnis betriebsinterner und externer Interviews herauskristallisiert haben. Die internen Gedanken sollten von leitenden Leuten stammen, die in den wichtigsten Punkten den Standpunkt des Generaldirektors teilen. Finanzleute, die mit der Gesellschaft und ihrem Industriesektor vertraut sind, nehmen Stellung vom Standpunkt des Externen her.

Diese Ziele sollten drei grundsätzliche Faktoren herausstellen: die Betonung der Vorteile der Gesellschaft; die Berichtigung falscher Auffassungen und die Lieferung neuer Informationen. Natürlich soll der Bericht auch die Ergebnisse des letzten Geschäftsjahres darlegen.

Die Ziele werden oft ein Thema suggerieren; was schon an sich ein äusserst wünschenswertes Ziel ist. Ein Thema gibt dem Bericht eine Einheit und verstärkt seine Wirkung auf den Leser. Es bildet auch einen Rahmen für die Auswahl von Photos und Text und einen willkommenen Schutz gegen Kritiker, die den Text ändern wollen.

Wenn Plan und Ziele aufgestellt sind, sollte der Entwurf genau nach Seiten aufgegliedert werden, um zu zeigen, wie der Bericht vorbereitet werden soll. Diese Unterlagen sollten dem Präsidenten der Gesellschaft im Laufe des Septembers als Memorandum unterbreitet werden und viele Verfasser von Jahresberichten werden merken, dass die Aufstellung dieses Planes die höchsten intellektuellen Anforderungen des ganzen Entwurfs stellt. Dieser erste Planungsentwurf ist jedoch immer lohnend, denn in einem gut organisierten Unternehmen führt die erste Besprechung mit dem Generaldirektor zu einem Aktionsplan, der in grossen Zügen unverändert bleiben sollte. Auch ist es nicht wichtig, ob der leitende Mann den ersten Plan so genehmigt, wie er unterbreitet wird, ob er bedeutende Änderungen anbringt oder eine völlig andere Konzeption verlangt. Wichtig ist, dass er seit dem ersten Entwurf an einen festgelegten Plan gebunden ist, den er gegen jegliche von seiten seiner Angestellten im letzten Moment vorgebrachte Kritik verteidigen wird.

Zusammenstellung der kreativen Bestandteile – Photographie, graphische Gestaltung und Text

Diese Arbeiten, die parallel und gleichzeitig durchgeführt werden, nehmen normalerweise drei Monate in Anspruch. Für die visuellen Elemente wählen die Unternehmen immer mehr einen professionellen Gestalter, der dann selbst einen geeigneten Photographen wählt. Die zunehmende Neigung, einen einzigen Photographen für den ganzen Bericht zu engagieren, hat ausgesprochene Vorteile: Der Photograph kennt Ziele und Thema und macht die Aufnahmen entsprechend. Manchmal können so auch gewisse Einsparungen erzielt werden, besonders wenn das Vorgehen bis ins einzelne im voraus geplant wird.

Unzureichende Planung und Vorbereitung der Aufnahmen sind verantwortlich für die schlimmste Geldverschwendung und den grössten Ärger bei der Erstellung des Jahresberichtes. Der Photograph muss sein Thema genau kennen, bevor er seine Reise durch das Land oder vielleicht rund um die Welt antritt. Ist er einmal am Ziel, so sollte ihn jemand begleiten, ihm bei der Beschaffung von Ausrüstungen behilflich sein und ihm Türen öffnen, die einem Aussenstehenden sonst verschlossen sind. Bei dem heute üblichen Tagessatz von 500 oder 600 Dollar kann ein Unternehmen viel Geld zum Fenster hinauswerfen, wenn der Photograph warten muss, bis er photographieren darf.

Im Zusammenhang mit der Photographie erhebt sich auch die Frage – die oft in letzter Minute von Anwälten angeschnitten wird – ob die Gesellschaft das Einverständnis der Personen einholen muss, deren Bilder im Jahresbericht erscheinen. Obgleich es für den Photographen eine empfehlenswerte Vorsichtsmassnahme wäre, diese Einverständnisse zu erhalten, ist die Gefahr einer Klage vor Gericht gering. Ein New Yorker Anwaltsbüro hat 1969 gründliche Nachforschungen auf diesem Gebiet unternommen und dabei festgestellt, dass noch nie jemand eine Gesellschaft verklagt hat, weil sein Bild in ihrem Jahresbericht erschienen ist. Selbst wenn einmal ein solcher Prozess angestrengt werden sollte, würde dem Betreffenden wahrscheinlich nicht viel Schadenersatz zugesprochen werden. Es würde ihm schwerfallen, Unannehmlichkeiten nachzuweisen; ausserdem wird der Geschäftsbericht nicht für kommerzielle Zwecke verwendet, sondern gratis verteilt.

Die Hauptarbeit des Gestalters beginnt natürlich, sobald die Aufnahmen geliefert sind und er bestimmte Photos, den Umschlag inbegriffen, ausgewählt hat. In unserem Musterzeitplan erhält der Photograph seine Anweisungen am 25. September und einen Termin für die Ablieferung der Aufnahmen am 16. November, also etwa zwei Monate später. Der Gestalter benützt diese Zeitspanne, um jedem Teil des Berichts den benötigten Platz zuzuteilen und einen groben Entwurf zu machen.

Inzwischen nimmt der Verfasser des Textes Kontakt mit den Direktoren der verschiedenen Abteilungen auf. Das bestärkt diese Herren in dem Gefühl, aktiv an der Erstellung des Jahresberichts mitzuarbeiten und erhöht ausserdem die Genauigkeit der technischen Angaben. Eine solche Besprechung sollte folgende Themen behandeln:

• Welche Resultate erzielte die Abteilung bezüglich Umsatz und Ertrag im Laufe des Geschäftsjahres? Welche wichtigen Faktoren beeinflussten dieses Resultat?

• Welches waren die hauptsächlichen Kapitalaufwendungen dieser Abteilung im vergangenen Jahr? Welche Kapitalaufwendungen sind für das kommende Jahr geplant? Wie werden sich diese Ausgaben auf die Gewinnaussichten der Abteilung auswirken?

• Welche neuen Produkte oder Dienstleistungen hat die Abteilung im Laufe des Jahres eingeführt? Welche sind für die nächsten Jahre vorgesehen?

• Bestehen soziale oder wirtschaftliche Tendenzen, die die Ergebnisse der Abteilung, entweder negativ oder positiv, beeinflussen?

Sobald diese Informationen vorliegen, sollten sie in einem ersten Entwurf verarbeitet und dem Abteilungsdirektor unterbreitet werden. Jeder dieser Direktoren sollte nur die Unterlagen sehen, die seine eigene Abteilung betreffen. Es ist in diesem Zusammenhang wichtig, darauf zu bestehen, dass diese Unterlagen termingerecht retourniert werden. So kann ein revidierter Entwurf für den Generaldirektor ohne Verzögerung erstellt werden.

Einholen von Druckofferten

Es empfiehlt sich, erste Offerten der Druckereien auf Grund des vorjährigen Geschäftsberichts schon vor den Vorbereitungsarbeiten am Entwurf (Dummy) einzuholen. Die Offerten können und sollen dann überprüft werden, sobald der Generaldirektor den Dummy genehmigt hat (siehe unten), womit die endgültige Wahl der Druckerei getroffen werden kann. Die Wahl der Druckerei ist gar nicht so einfach und die Meinung des Gestalters – ob Mitarbeiter des Unternehmens oder Aussenstehender – sollte ausschlaggebend bei der Vergebung sein. Es ist wichtig, bei den Konkurrenzangeboten die Offerten von Druckereien ähnlicher Qualität und Leistungsfähigkeit zu vergleichen. Die billigste Offerte mag ganz einfach von der qualitativ schlechtesten Druckerei stammen. Andererseits kann eine ausgezeichnete Druckerei eine höhere Offerte als ihre Konkurrenten unterbreiten, da sie sich routinemässig stark einsetzt, um dem Kunden Überstunden und andere Extraausgaben soweit wie möglich zu ersparen. Eine Druckerei diesen Kalibers sollte man genau so energisch zu finden trachten, wie man ihr Gegenteil, die Druckerei, die von den Unzulänglichkeiten und Fehlern ihres Kunden profitiert, vermeiden muss.

Um eine möglichst genaue Offerte zu erhalten, sollte man sich vorher einigen, wieviel Tage der Druckerei zum Drucken zur Verfügung stehen – meist sind es neun bis fünfzehn Arbeitstage – und diese Tage genau festlegen. So wird betont, welche Bedeutung der Entwicklung eines Zeit- und Arbeitsplanes von Anfang an zukommt. Eine Offerte mit unrealistisch niedrigen Preisen könnte auch darauf zurückzuführen sein, dass die Druckerei mehr Arbeitstage vorgesehen hat, als der Zeitplan der Gesellschaft erlaubt.

Bei der Entscheidung, wieviele Exemplare des Jahresberichtes gedruckt werden sollen, muss folgendes erwogen werden: wieviele Exemplare für die im Adressenverzeichnis der Gesellschaft aufgeführten Aktionäre gebraucht werden; wieviele Exemplare an Börsenmakler für die bei ihnen deponierten Aktien gehen; wieviele Exemplare schliesslich für Aktionäre neuerworbener Unternehmen und Mitarbeiter gebraucht werden, die den Jahresbericht im Zusammenhang mit einem Aktienbeteiligungsplan erhalten sollen. Es muss auch festgelegt werden, ob ein Spezialversand an Wertschriftenanalytiker geplant ist oder ein Zeitungsinserat für Zustellung des Jahresberichtes auf Wunsch erscheinen soll. Zum Ergebnis kommen noch die Exemplare, die voraussichtlich für allgemeine Geschäftszwecke gebraucht werden. Die meisten Gesellschaften drucken zwei- bis dreimal mehr Jahresberichte, als sie an Aktionäre verteilen. Eine zu kleine Auflage erweist sich stets als höchst unbequemer und kostspieliger Fehler: Unter Umständen kann der Nachdruck von ein paar tausend Exemplaren fünfmal soviel kosten wie der Originaldruck. Beim Erhalt der Druckereiofferten soll immer nach den Kosten für weitere tausend Exemplare gefragt werden, falls man sich in letzter Minute für eine höhere Auflage entscheidet.

Hier eine Anmerkung zum Thema Druckerei-Rechnungen: Es ist normaler, berufsethischer Brauch der Druckereien, 10 Prozent mehr oder weniger Exemplare als im Kontrakt vorgesehen zu drucken, und die Rechnung dann der tatsächlichen Anzahl anzupassen. In der Praxis druckt eine gute Druckerei selten weniger als vereinbart und überschreitet die festgesetzte Zahl im allgemeinen nicht um mehr als fünf Prozent. Trotzdem kann die Zusatzberechnung zu Missverständnissen führen.

Vorlegen von Entwurf und Text

Der Entwurf (Dummy) sollte Photos sowie getippte Legenden und Überschriften am richtigen Platz enthalten. Der Schreibmaschinentext sollte das vollständige Manuskript umfassen, ausgenommen die Teile, die wegen ihrer Abhängigkeit von den Schlusszahlen der Buchhalter späteren Redaktionsschluss haben. Die Teile mit frühem Redaktionsschluss sind die Übersicht über den Geschäftsverlauf oder irgendwelche Sonderartikel, den Corporate Image oder «Identitäts-Beschreibung»-Teil, das Inhaltsverzeichnis und alle weiteren Angaben über die Gesellschaft, die nicht von erst später erhältlichen Zahlen abhängen. Es ist gut, dem Generaldirektor den Entwurf mit dem Text vorzulegen, denn so kann er sich vorstellen, wo die Informationen hinkommen und wieviel Platz sie beanspruchen. Auch kann er sich dann ein Bild vom Zusammenspiel von Text und visuellen Elementen machen. In unserem Musterfahrplan ist diese Besprechung mit dem Generaldirektor auf den 10. Dezember eingesetzt. Zu diesem Zeitpunkt kann der Präsident oder Generaldirektor einige seiner Berater zuziehen – vielleicht den Direktor der Finanzabteilung, einen der Hauptdirektoren oder den Vorsitzenden des Aufsichtsrates. Die Rolle des Präsidenten oder Generaldirektors ist ebenso entscheidend wie auch heikel, da er mit dem ursprünglichen Konzept vertraut ist. Er hat jetzt Anwalt des Projektes gegenüber Beratern zu sein, die es nicht kennen. Wenn er es nicht verteidigen will oder kann, so muss das Team der Gestalter höchstwahrscheinlich wieder von vorne anfangen.

Druckerei, Kuvert, Verteilung

Das mit der Verteilung des Jahresberichtes verbundene Durcheinander sowie der daraus resultierende Ärger, können durch Vorausplanung vermieden werden. Während der Vorbereitung von Entwurf und Manuskript sollte die Druckerei eine Liste der Verteilerstellen für den fertigen Jahresbericht erhalten, mit Angabe, in welcher Reihenfolge abgeliefert werden soll.

Eine anscheinend so einfache Sache wie Kuverts kann Ärger machen, weil man sie entweder ganz vergisst oder die diesbezügliche Entscheidung auf die letzte Minute verschiebt. Hier muss die Auswahl des Papiers, die Ausführung und die Wahl einer Druckerei beachtet werden. Wird der Jahresbericht von einem professionellen Gestalter betreut, so soll er auch ein angemessenes, ansprechendes Kuvert entwerfen. Die Kuverts sollten lange vorher gedruckt und zwei Wochen vor Lieferung der Jahresberichte an das Versandhaus verschickt werden, damit sie vor Empfang der Berichte adressiert werden können.

Immer mehr Unternehmen verzichten auf ein Kuvert und versenden den Jahresbericht mit der Adresse auf dem Umschlag. Ein grosser Vorteil dieser Art des Versandes besteht darin, dass der Aktionär den Bericht eher beachten wird, weil er ihn nicht erst aus dem Kuvert nehmen muss. Der Verzicht auf Kuverts kann auch als ein Zeichen von Sparsamkeit gedeutet werden; ein Eindruck, den man vielfach erzielen will, wenn Aktionäre den Werbeaufwand oder andere Unkosten kritisiert haben.

Ein bei der Auswahl der Kuverts und Festlegung des Zeitplanes in den letzten Stadien zu beachtender Faktor ist die Art der Postzustellung. Posttaxen sind bereits sehr hoch und werden ständig weiter erhöht und der Unterschied zwischen Briefpost und Drucksache kann ohne weiteres 20 bis 40 Cents pro Bericht ausmachen. Bei 10 000 Exemplaren beläuft sich das auf einen Betrag von 2000 bis 4000 Dollar. Briefpost sollte überhaupt nur dann gewählt werden, wenn die Buchhalter ihre Angaben zu spät geliefert haben. Sollen die Jahresberichte als Drucksache befördert werden, so müssen sie sechs Wochen (auf keinen Fall weniger als fünf Wochen) vor der Generalversammlung an die Aktionäre versandt werden.

Farbdiapositive gehen an die Druckerei

Sobald der Entwurf vom Generaldirektor genehmigt ist, werden die Diapositive verschickt, damit Farbauszüge hergestellt werden können. Genug Zeit für den richtigen Farbauszug, seine Verbesserung und Anpassung zur Verfügung zu stellen, ist eines der wichtigsten Elemente bei jedem Druckprojekt. Druckereien in New York brauchen mindestens drei Wochen für den Farbauszug und eventuelle Änderungen beanspruchen zwei weitere Wochen; man muss also insgesamt fünf Wochen vorsehen.

Satz und Druckvorlagen für Teile mit frühem Redaktionsschluss

Das Absetzen dieses ersten Textes und der Umbruch sollte ohne Schwierigkeiten für die Druckerei erfolgen, nachdem alle wichtigen Leute den Inhalt genehmigt haben. Ausserdem wurden diese Teile absichtlich unabhängig von Finanzinformationen der letzten Minute verfasst.

Auch der Umschlag sollte zu diesem Zeitpunkt für den Druck freigegeben werden – man kann ihn in einem separaten Druckverfahren im voraus herstellen. Bei der Gestaltung des Jahresberichts sollte der Finanz-Kurzbericht nicht für die Innenseite des Umschlages vorgesehen werden. Eine solche Anordnung würde ein Warten auf spät eintreffende Zahlen erfordern und den Druck des Umschlages verzögern.

Vorbereitung der Teile mit spätem Redaktionsschluss

Mit dem Verfassen dieser Texte – Vorwort des Präsidenten, Finanz-Kurzbericht und Finanzübersicht – kann angefangen werden, während die Druckvorlagen für die Teile mit früherem Redaktionsschluss fertiggestellt werden. Das Vorwort des Präsidenten an die Aktionäre ist der heikelste Teil des Jahresberichtes und er wird ihm die meiste Zeit widmen müssen. Er sollte im Entwurf verfasst und dem Generaldirektor so bald wie möglich unterbreitet werden. Am besten in den Weihnachtsfeiertagen, die ihm Zeit lassen, den Entwurf zu prüfen. Natürlich wird der Brief später – sobald die letzten Zahlen vorliegen – weiter ausgearbeitet und auf den letzten Stand gebracht.

Buchhaltung liefert die Jahresabrechnung – Projekt geht in die Schlussphase

Die Zahlen für die Finanzinformation sollten zur Verfügung stehen, wenn der Generaldirektor den Entwurf bearbeitet bzw. bis zu dem Tag, an dem der endgültige Entwurf zum Absetzen herausgeht. Die gleiche Zeitplanung gilt für die Finanzübersicht, wobei dieser Teil eventuell vom Direktor für Finanzen anstatt vom Generaldirektor genehmigt werden kann. Sowohl die Finanzübersicht als das Vorwort an die Aktionäre sollten bis zum Eintreffen der Rechnungsausweise in endgültiger Fassung getippt zurückgehalten werden. Die Zahlen können dann nach Bedarf eingesetzt werden und alles wird dann zusammen an die Druckerei zum Absetzen geschickt.

Von diesem Moment an darf nichts die Lieferung des gesamten Jahresberichtes an die Druckerei aufhalten. Ausgenommen die Zeit, die für den Versand und die Korrektur der Druckfahnen, die Anforderung von Repro-Abzügen, Fertigstellung und Überprüfung der Druckvorlagen und die Zusammenstellung aller Unterlagen für die Druckerei benötigt wird. Zwei Wochen sollten hierfür vorgesehen werden, wenn einmal die Finanzausweise von den Buchhaltern geliefert worden sind. Unter Druck kann diese Arbeit in gewissen Fällen aber auch in einer Woche bewältigt werden.

Haben die Buchhalter ihre Unterlagen fristgemäss abgeliefert und sind die Texte von allen zuständigen Stellen endgültig genehmigt und freigegeben worden, so kann der Zeitplan ohne Störung eingehalten werden. Sollten aber bestimmte Teile des Jahresberichtes bis zu diesem Augenblick nicht vorliegen und dann in letzter Minute eintreffen, so kann es in der Schlussphase zu ausserordentlich kostspieligen Krisen kommen.

Änderungen im bereits gesetzten Text, die sogenannten Autorenkorrekturen, sollten bei der Herstellung des Jahresberichtes am ehesten vermieden werden – denn sie sind sehr kostspielig. Die Satzkosten sind in den letzten Jahren rapide gestiegen und werden voraussichtlich weiter steigen. Nicht selten bezahlt eine Gesellschaft 2000 Dollars für den ursprünglichen Satz eines Geschäftsberichtes und später weitere 10 000 oder sogar 15 000 Dollars für verschiedene Änderungen im letzten Moment, was ganz einfach mangelndes Vertrauen in die bereits geleistete Arbeit bedeutet.

In dieser Phase wird deutlich, wie wichtig es ist, dass eine einzige Person für den gesamten Jahresbericht verantwortlich zeichnet und dass der Betreffende dem Vorstandspräsidenten direkt untersteht. In sehr grossen Unternehmen delegiert der Vorsitzende seine eigene Funktion in bezug auf den Geschäftsbericht oft an einen Top Manager. Diese beiden Männer sollten die einzigen sein, die berechtigt sind, Änderungen im Stil des Berichtes anzubringen. Die so kostspieligen Änderungen sind oft auf eine individuelle Vorliebe für eine bestimmte Ausdrucksweise zurückzuführen, und der Text erfährt selten eine Verbesserung. Ganz im Gegenteil, er wird durch die resultierende Unausgeglichenheit des Stils meistens nur verschlechtert werden.

Manche Gesellschaften zählen verhinderte Redakteure zu ihren Mitarbeitern, die von Komma- und anderen Interpunktionsfragen besessen sind. Ein solcher Manager kann es durch seinen Versuch, den Bericht seinem eigenen Sprachgebrauch anzupassen, möglicherweise ahnungslos fertigbringen, dass das Ganze neu gesetzt werden muss. Ein anderer Komma-Besessener in der Gesellschaft, mit anderen Grammatikkenntnissen, wird dann den Text wieder in die Originalversion zurückverwandeln. Indem man im getippten Text alle Änderungen der Stellen, die konsultiert werden müssen, zusammenfasst, kann später unendlich viel Geld eingespart werden.

Die Verteilung von Fahnenabzügen an die verschiedenen Geschäftsführer ist ebenfalls eine Gefahrenquelle. In gewissen Fällen werden Abzüge bis zu einem Dutzend mal verteilt, und zwar jedes Mal eine andere Version. Manchmal wartet ein Geschäftsführer, bis die von allen anderen Korrektoren vorgeschlagenen Änderungen angebracht sind. Erst dann prüft er den Abzug sorgfältig und bringt eine ganze Reihe neuer Änderungen an – ein kostspieliges Vorgehen! Es ist wichtig, die Phasen der Text-Genehmigung zu beschränken und jedem ein genau festgelegtes Abschlussdatum vorzuschreiben, nach dem seine Kommentare nicht mehr berücksichtigt werden. Die Rechtskonsulenten sollen sich auf Rechtsfragen und die Mitglieder des Rechnungswesens auf Finanzinformationen beschränken. Der Generaldirektor ist derjenige, der mit dem Bericht zufrieden sein muss, und die anderen Manager sollten ihre Beiträge auf Fakten und gelegentlich auf Auslegungen beschränken.

Druckvorlagen gehen zum Drucker

Sobald alle Druckvorlagen komplett sind und jedes Element seinen richtigen Platz gefunden hat, werden sie der Druckerei überbracht. Zwei oder drei Tage später werden diese Unterlagen in Form einer Blaupause retourniert. Dieser Abzug des Jahresberichtes wird nach einer Filmvorlage hergestellt und ist das Stadium kurz vor der Plattenherstellung im Offset-Verfahren. Er zeigt jeden Elementteil genau an der Stelle, wo er gedruckt wird und kann nicht nur, sondern sollte auch auf Genauigkeit geprüft werden. Besonders wichtig ist es, die Blaupausen in bezug auf Richtigkeit der Tabellen und die Anordnung und genaue Position der Photographien und Legenden zu kontrollieren.

Drucküberwachung

Das Heft kommt jetzt in den Druckprozess – der insgesamt zwischen neun und fünfzehn Tage beanspruchen wird. Viele Geschäftsführer verstehen nicht, warum das Drucken und das Ausrüsten so viel Zeit in Anspruch nimmt. Ein Hauptgrund ist, dass mindestens drei Viertel aller Jahresberichte während der arbeitsreichen «Jahresbericht-Saison» im Februar und März gedruckt werden, und dass die meisten guten Druckereien mit derartigen Aufträgen voll ausgelastet sind. Sie versuchen daher in ihren Terminen ein Zeitpolster einzubauen, um bei eventuellen unerwarteten Schwierigkeiten bei gewissen Jahresberichten nicht unbedingt Überstunden machen zu müssen.

Qualitätsdruckereien sind genau so interessiert, ein erstklassiges Produkt herzustellen wie ihre Kunden. Sie wissen nur zu genau, dass es ausser Leistungsfähigkeit keine Abkürzung des Weges zum guten Druckerzeugnis gibt. Die verschiedenen Schritte bei der Plattenherstellung, das Drucken auf beiden Seiten der Pressbogen, das Ausrüsten und Schneiden sowie die Vorbereitungen für den Versand müssen sorgfältig gemacht werden. Fehlt es hier an Sorgfalt, so kann das Ergebnis der konzentrierten Arbeit von sechs oder sieben Monaten völlig zunichte gemacht werden. Die Finanzleute erteilen ihr endgültiges O. K. im allgemeinen in der Blaupausen-Phase und sehen den Bericht erst wieder, wenn er bereits vollständig gedruckt ist. Der Graphiker sollte die Pressbogen überprüfen, um sich zu vergewissern, dass die Farben wie vorgesehen zur Geltung kommen. Die Gesellschaft erhält normalerweise ein oder zwei von Hand geheftete, aus Pressbogen gefaltete Vorlieferungsabzüge.

Sie werden an den mit der Erstellung des Jahresberichtes Beauftragten adressiert, der sie üblicherweise dem Präsidenten oder Generaldirektor, falls dieser erreichbar ist, vorlegt. Der Hauptsitz erhält meist die ersten 100 Exemplare, die aus der Ausrüstungsabteilung der Druckerei kommen. Die Arbeit an dem Bericht hat jetzt sechs bis sieben Monate gedauert und man ist allgemein gespannt auf das Ergebnis. Es ist Pflicht des Verantwortlichen, dafür zu sorgen, dass alle Beteiligten so bald wie möglich ein Exemplar erhalten. Wenn er gescheit ist, nimmt er jede Kopie kurz in die Hand, um offensichtliche Irrtümer der Druckerei, wie zum Beispiel einen verkehrt gebundenen Umschlag, sofort zu entdecken.

Der Jahresbericht wird abgeliefert und versandt

Die fertigen Hefte werden von der Ausrüstungsabteilung an die Versandstelle geliefert; in vielen Fällen dient eine Bank als Übermittlungsstelle. Sind die Vorkehrungen richtig getroffen worden, so kann die durchschnittliche Versandstelle 20 000 bis 25 000 Jahresberichte pro Tag verschicken, grössere Versandstellen bewältigen sogar noch mehr.

Bisweilen entdeckt man, trotz vorheriger schärfster Kontrollen, dass der Jahresbericht irgendeinen Fehler aufweist. Wie man sich dazu verhält, hängt von zwei

Faktoren ab: Der Bedeutung des Fehlers und dem Zeitpunkt in bezug auf die Versandfrist, an dem er entdeckt wird. Überall im Verlagswesen verlieren Fehler mit dem Näherrücken des Abschlusstermins an Wichtigkeit. Das Drucken einer Zeitung wird nie unterbrochen, um einen Fehler zu verbessern, ausser er sei katastrophal oder bedeute soviel wie eine Verleumdung mit möglichen gerichtlichen Folgen. Aber als Amateurverleger haben die Geschäftsunternehmen eine panische Angst vor Fehlern. Eine Angst, die so weit geht, dass die Geschäftsführung jedes Urteil über die relative Bedeutung eines Fehlers verliert. Die Wichtigkeit einer falschen Zahl beim Ertrag pro Aktie wird der eines falsch gesetzten Kommas, das den Sinn überhaupt nicht ändert, gleichgesetzt.

Natürlich ist Genauigkeit bei der Jahresberichterstellung wichtig und kommt auf jeder Herstellungsstufe zuerst. In den allerletzten Phasen sollten unwichtige Fehler nicht beachtet werden. Ein Unternehmen entdeckte, nachdem der Umschlag bereits gedruckt war, in der Adressenspalte ein Komma an falscher Stelle und beschloss, den vollfarbigen Umschlag völlig neu drucken zu lassen. Die Kosten betrugen Tausende von Dollars. Die allgemein übliche und empfehlenswerte Lösung, wenn sachliche Fehler nach vollendeter Drucklegung, aber vor dem Versand entdeckt werden, ist das Fehlerverzeichnis oder die Korrigenda. Das kleine Stück Papier kann schnell gedruckt und an die Innenseite des Umschlages oder die betreffende Seite angeheftet werden. Das Problem ist auf diese Weise mit geringem Kostenaufwand gelöst. Doch selbst im Falle eines fehlerfrei gedruckten Jahresberichtes erfährt die Reaktion der obersten Geschäftsleitung meist einen gewissen Aufschub. Der Präsident und andere Top Management Leute suchen meist erst Kritik und Stellungnahme von Freunden, Kollegen und Mitgliedern der Finanzwelt, ehe sie sich entscheiden können, wie ihnen der neue Jahresbericht gefällt. Diese Verzögerung der Reaktion ist eine starke Belastung für den verantwortlichen Geschäftsführer, der gerade sechs Monate intensiver Beschäftigung mit dem Projekt hinter sich hat.

Eine Besprechung mit dem schöpferischen Team, dem Gestalter, dem Autor und anderer eng mit dem Projekt verbundenen Personen ist eine positive Tätigkeit während dieser Wartezeit, die manchmal wochenlang dauert. Mit der Erfahrung noch frisch im Gedächtnis, sollten alle bei dieser Konferenz Anwesenden besprechen, was daneben und was gut gegangen ist und Vorschläge für den nächsten Jahresbericht unterbreiten. Mit Rücksicht auf die Art des Themas und die Zeit, die so eine Diskussion beansprucht, ist es empfehlenswert, diese Zusammenkunft in einem erstklassigen Restaurant abzuhalten, und zwar an einem Freitagabend, wenn kein zwingender Grund besteht, nach den Feierlichkeiten ins Büro zurückzukehren.

Le phénomène du changement

La science et la technique modernes ont suscité à une vitesse fantastique, une incroyable évolution. Il y a actuellement presqu'autant de savants en pleine activité qu'il y en a eu en deux mille ans. La moitié de l'énergie consommée par l'homme au cours des vingt derniers siècles l'a été ces cent dernières années. Et la production totale de biens et de services double tous les quinze ans dans les pays industrialisés.

Aux Etats-Unis, le superboom industriel date vraiment du milieu des années 1950 lorsque les ordinateurs ont commencé à engendrer une technologie nouvelle, que les cours des actions se sont mis à monter en flèche et que l'économie en général a pris de la vitesse. Le produit national brut, qui était de 364 milliards de dollars en 1954, a augmenté à une vitesse vertigineuse pour atteindre le seuil de 1 billion de dollars en 1971, alors que les compagnies américaines traversaient des phases de croissance et de changement de plus en plus rapides. Considérons, à titre d'exemples, ce qui est arrivé à trois entreprises depuis 1954.

W.R. Grace & Co., dont les ventes se chiffraient à 413 millions de dollars en 1954, était essentiellement une compagnie de transports maritimes et de commerce en Amérique latine. En 1970, ses ventes avaient atteint 1,9 milliard de dollars et la société s'était presque entièrement transformée: le département «transports maritimes» avait été vendu, les activités en Amérique latine considérablement réduites et Grace était devenue la cinquième entreprise de produits chimiques des Etats-Unis.

Litton Industries – l'une des sociétés industrielles américaines les plus évolutives – a été fondée en 1954. En 1967, elle réalisait déjà un chiffre d'affaires de 1 milliard de dollars, preuve de son succès dans des domaines aussi divers que les machines de bureau, la construction navale, le papier, l'édition, l'électronique, la radioscopie. En 1970, ses ventes s'élevaient à 2,4 milliards de dollars.

International Business Machines (IBM) réalisait en 1954, au début de l'âge de l'ordinateur, un bénéfice impressionnant de 46,5 millions de dollars, avec ses machines de bureau. En 1970, la société était la première productrice d'ordinateurs du monde et son bénéfice se montait à 1 milliard de dollars.

Il n'est donc pas étonnant qu'au cours de ces dernières vingt années un nouveau type de rapport annuel ait vu le jour.

Le rapport annuel d'IBM en offre l'illustration la plus frappante. En 1954, il avait pour ainsi dire le même aspect que tous ceux qui avaient paru depuis la fondation de l'entreprise, 42 ans auparavant: une couverture rigide en papier brun, 20 pages sobres à l'intérieur, couvertes d'informations financières – aucune photographie ou aucune recherche artistique.

L'année suivante, IBM décidait de moderniser son rapport annuel; depuis lors, celui-ci est à la pointe du progrès tant en ce qui concerne la maquette que l'intérêt et la qualité des textes. Cette innovation a inspiré rapidement quelques autres sociétés importantes et, dès les années 1960, la plupart des grandes compagnies américaines suivaient le mouvement et publiaient des rapports annuels enfin conçus pour le public auquel ils étaient destinés.

Le rapport annuel, clé de voûte des communications de l'Entreprise

La transformation des sociétés était tellement rapide que le rapport annuel, faute de mieux, est devenu le principal et souvent l'unique moyen de rendre compte aux actionnaires de leur croissance souvent stupéfiante – à croire que chaque année ils se trouvaient en présence d'une nouvelle société.

En bref, les entreprises expérimentaient peut-être sans s'en rendre compte cette notion de «l'éternel provisoire» et du «changement permanent» qu'évoque magistralement Alvin Toffler dans son bestseller: *Choc de Future*. Tous éléments normaux d'information, films, plaquettes ou dépliants étant souvent dépassés lors de leur utilisation, les présidents sont incités à profiter de la tenue rapide des assemblées générales pour expliquer leurs résultats et définir leur avenir à leurs actionnaires.

D'où ce souci de présenter un rapport aussi «accrochant» que possible et leur accord pour un budget correspondant? Elles engagent donc les graphistes et les photographes les plus talentueux pour «visualiser» leur rapport annuel, et utilisent du papier et une impression de qualité supérieure.

Ces Sociétés constituent ensemble un «marché» du rapport annuel de plusieurs millions de dollars. Plus de 50 000 sociétés américaines sont, en effet, cotées en Bourse et celle qui compte le plus grand nombre d'actionnaires (3 100 000): *American Telephone and Telegraph*, publie environ quatre millions d'exemplaires de son rapport annuel, ce qui lui revient à environ 575 000 dollars.

Il ressort de l'enquête de GRAPHIS[1] sur les rapports annuels des 1000 plus grandes entreprises américaines que la plupart d'entre elles – à l'exception de celles qui procèdent à de très forts tirages – dépensent 1 dollar ou davantage par exemplaire pour la réalisation de ceux-ci. Les grandes sociétés (300 000 à 4 millions d'exemplaires) dépensent 33 cents par exemplaire, les compagnies moyennes (55 000 à 63 000 exemplaires) 96 cents et les petites entreprises 1,19 dollar en moyenne.

Même au prix de 2 dollars l'exemplaire lors d'un tirage de 5000, par exemple, le rapport annuel est d'ordinaire un bon investissement pour les petites sociétés nouvelles car il revêt pour elles une impor-

[1] Les données inédites figurant dans le présent ouvrage proviennent d'une enquête minutieuse à laquelle s'est livrée la Corporate Communications Report auprès des 1000 plus importantes sociétés des Etats-Unis pour le compte des Editions Graphis. Les résultats de cette enquête Graphis sur les rapports annuels, que nous croyons être la plus importante du genre réalisée à ce jour, sont incorporés dans le texte qui suit.

tance toute particulière. Les grandes sociétés jouissent de relations solidement établies avec leurs actionnaires, leurs fournisseurs et leurs clients et ont d'habitude des relations publiques actives et des programmes de publicité, alors que, pour de nombreuses petites entreprises, le rapport annuel est le seul moyen de communication efficace.

Si les rapports annuels exercent une influence favorable sur les opérations permettant de nouveaux investissements, ils ont pour toutes les sociétés une valeur encore bien plus spécifique. Au cas où l'intérêt d'un rapport annuel et la manière dont il est diffusé contribuent à faire monter, ne fût-ce que d'un point, le Price/Earnings-ratio (cf. chapitre 2) d'une entreprise de taille moyenne telle que *Joy Manufacturing* (chiffre d'affaires de 273 millions de dollars en 1970), cela équivaut à une augmentation de la valeur totale des actions de l'ordre de 10 millions de dollars. Pour AT & T, l'augmentation serait d'environ 2 milliards de dollars.

Afin d'accentuer l'attrait de leurs rapports annuels, un nombre croissant de sociétés y incluent, au début, une sorte de carte d'identité de l'entreprise. Cette présentation écrite de la compagnie, mise à jour chaque année, et utilisable à beaucoup d'autres fins permet d'économiser à tous les échelons de la hiérarchie des heures d'un temps très précieux.

Plusieurs raisons contribuent à assurer au rapport annuel une incontestable primauté : son honnêteté n'est pas mise en doute, le président le signe, les commissaires aux comptes contrôlent l'exactitude et la validité des opérations financières et les organismes officiels de contrôle ont toute latitude pour faire de même.

Le rapport annuel est souvent le document d'information que préfère la direction de l'entreprise parce qu'elle a pris une part plus personnelle à sa mise au point qu'à celle de tels ou tels prospectus rédigés par des juristes ou d'autres chefs de services. Le fait que les sociétés font souvent imprimer deux ou trois fois plus de rapports qu'elles n'ont d'actionnaires souligne les nombreux usages que la Direction veut en faire. En effet, outre l'information des actionnaires, le rapport annuel est utilisé régulièrement à d'autres fins : recrutement du personnel, climat à créer ou à maintenir avec la clientèle et, dans une mesure croissante, comme «carte de visite» de l'entreprise lorsqu'elle traite avec des hommes d'affaires étrangers.

La *Westinghouse Electric Corporation*, par exemple, a fait imprimer 400 000 exemplaires de son rapport annuel 1969. Elle en a distribué 166 000 à ses actionnaires nominatifs et 33 000 à des actionnaires au porteur (dont les actions sont entre les mains d'agents de change, de Banques ou de gérants de fortune). En outre, la société a, pour la première fois envoyé un rapport à chacun de ses employés, soit 142 000 au total. Elle a réservé 12 000 rapports pour la formation et le recrutement, 3 500 pour les analystes financiers, les banques, les universités et les bibliothèques et 3 700 pour les relations publiques. Enfin elle a gardé les derniers 4 000 exemplaires pour des fins générales.

La parution régulière et la distribution systématique du rapport annuel, et le fait qu'il est classé chaque année dans les dossiers de tous les milieux de Banque, de Bourse et d'Epargne lui donnent le caractère d'une institution. Le rapport annuel est une tranche d'histoire, un document d'archives, une information complète de base de l'entreprise embrassant tous les domaines.

Le rapport annuel révèle souvent pour la première fois l'orientation nouvelle de la politique de l'entreprise, soit par une déclaration directe sur ses prochaines intentions, soit en mettant l'accent sur telle ou telle préoccupation.

Ainsi, le rapport annuel 1969 de *l'American Can Company*, dont la première page présentait la photographie grand format d'une jeune consommatrice séduisante, voulait souligner l'importance croissante que la société attachait aux réactions du consommateur. Faut-il ajouter que les cadres sont particulièrement intéressés par la lecture du rapport qui leur permet de mieux comprendre les orientations de la société et d'adapter leur propre plan de travail.

Le rapport annuel sert également de catalyseur pour donner une forme à différentes situations dans une compagnie qui change rapidement. En effet, bon nombre d'importantes décisions de la direction sont hâtées par l'approche de la publication du rapport annuel. Le nom du chef d'un certain groupe peut manquer dans un graphique d'organisation; souvent, le cadre sera nommé lorsque le délai approche. Il arrive fréquemment que des titres de personnes et des fonctions d'unités d'opération soient précisés plus rapidement à cause de la parution du rapport annuel.

Le rapport annuel, en raison de l'importance qu'il prend dans la vie de l'entreprise, sert bien souvent de support à une action encore plus large d'information technique, commerciale ou humaine. Voici quelques exemples :

• *L'Ethyl Corporation*, devant l'insistance croissante pour l'élimination des vapeurs de plomb dans l'essence (mesure contre la pollution de l'atmosphère), a encarté dans son rapport annuel 1969 un opuscule spécial proposant une solution «maison».

• Le rapport annuel 1968 de la *Fidelity Corporation* était particulièrement conçu pour souligner l'intérêt de sa politique de prises de participation. Il était donc divisé en deux parties principales : un dialogue entre les deux directeurs généraux sur le caractère bénéfique de cet objectif et une série de témoignages de directeurs de sociétés absorbées sur leurs contacts avec la Fidelity Corporation et leur épanouissement en son sein.

• Le rapport annuel 1967 de la *J.C. Penney Co.* avait comme objectif particulier de recruter de jeunes cadres en démontrant que, contrairement à ce que l'on pouvait croire, la société offrait un grand avenir à de jeunes ambitieux de valeur. Le rapport publiait donc les photographies et les noms de ses jeunes cadres, en précisant leurs fonctions et en insistant sur le fait que Penney offrait aux jeunes universitaires un large éventail de pistes intéressantes.

• *Litton Industries* a fait imprimer en russe 3 000 exemplaires de son rapport annuel 1963 et les a envoyés à des ambassadeurs soviétiques et américains dans le monde entier, ainsi qu'à des lecteurs de choix en URSS. Le but de cette mesure était de se rappeler au souvenir de certaines ambassades américaines et des milieux bancaires britanniques, étape préliminaire d'un programme d'expansion à l'étranger que Litton a lancé l'année suivante.

• Le rapport annuel 1969 de la société *US Industries* voulait ajouter au prestige des cadres supérieurs des

130 compagnies absorbées, agissant désormais au sein de l'USI comme directeurs autonomes. Pour cette raison, ce rapport comprenait plusieurs pages de photographies de groupes de ces dirigeants, avec légendes correspondantes.

Les milieux d'affaires sont confrontés aux Etats-Unis aujourd'hui, avec une situation sans précédent. Des jeunes gens, des prêtres, des actionnaires dont le nombre va croissant, sensibilisés par les problèmes raciaux, la pauvreté, la pollution et l'importance des industries d'armes mettent en cause le droit d'existence de la puissante industrie américaine. Les chefs d'entreprise doivent donc, à l'heure actuelle, défendre ce qui est juste dans le capitalisme américain et assurer au public qu'ils s'emploient à corriger ce qui y est erroné. Cette préoccupation est d'ailleurs évoquée dans certains rapports annuels. *Crown Zellerbach* a encarté dans son rapport annuel 1968 douze pages sur la responsabilité sociale de l'entreprise. La *Southern California Edison* a joint à son rapport annuel 1969 une publication spéciale de 16 pages «Edison et la crise de l'environnement». La *Bank of America*, la plus grande des Etats-Unis, a publié son rapport annuel 1970 sur du papier «régénéré», épargnant ainsi 600 à 1 000 arbres, alors que *l'Outboard Marine* a publié un essai intitulé «The Quality of Life... and what we are doing about it» (La qualité de la vie... et ce que nous faisons pour elle).

Le rapport annuel doit faire état des facteurs de croissance

Si le rapport annuel peut être un support efficace pour certaines informations particulières, n'oublions pas que son premier but doit être de présenter avec les activités de l'entreprise, les facteurs qui en font la force et le succès et en déterminent la croissance future. Ce message est évidemment destiné en premier lieu aux actionnaires actuels ou potentiels, mais il s'adresse également aux Banquiers et aux Brokers, au personnel, aux fournisseurs et aux clients, ainsi qu'aux hommes d'affaires et aux autorités administratives. Rappelons ci-dessous les facteurs essentiels de croissance que les entreprises doivent s'efforcer de mettre en lumière dans leur rapport annuel.

Technologie Dans un monde en permanente transformation, il est essentiel qu'une entreprise soit toujours à la pointe des techniques avancées. *Weyerhaeuser* a donné dans son rapport 1968 un aperçu de sa haute technologie par deux pages d'impressionnantes microphotographies et un texte prônant la recherche: «Une idée de laboratoire peut permettre demain une industrie nouvelle. Chez Weyerhaeuser, nous agissons ainsi. La moitié de nos ventes de cette année correspondent à des fabrications ignorées il y a quinze ans.»

Puissance financière Le fait que des sociétés aussi importantes que *Penn Central Railroad*, *Lockheed Aircraft* et *Ling-Temco-Vought* ont rendu publique la gravité de leurs difficultés financières a détruit l'illusion que les grandes sociétés étaient «automatiquement» des sociétés riches. Les entreprises qui ont une réelle solidité financière ont saisi tout l'intérêt du rapport annuel pour la souligner. En règle générale, on y consacre plusieurs paragraphes. Précisons toutefois que la *Tishman Realty & Construction Co.* n'a

pas hésité à présenter sur deux pages un graphique saisissant des actifs qui justifient l'importance de son cash-flow.

Productivité La croissance des années 1960 n'a été possible qu'en raison de l'accroissement de la productivité dû à l'automation et à d'autres investissements de capitaux. Dans les années 70, il sera plus difficile d'augmenter encore le taux de productivité qui, pourtant, demeure un élément décisif dans le calcul des bénéfices. Lorsqu'elles le peuvent, les sociétés utilisent le rapport annuel pour montrer leur capacité d'accroître la productivité.

Recherche En mettant l'accent sur les recherches de pointe poursuivies dans ses usines, le rapport annuel 1969 de *Squibb Beach-Nut* sensibilisait ses lecteurs sur ses possibilités techniques pour la mise au point de nouveaux produits pharmaceutiques, rappelant indirectement au public et au gouvernement que le coût élevé de celle-ci justifiait le prix de détail correspondant.

Marchés étrangers Les marchés d'outre-mer se développant plus vite que les marchés nationaux, un nombre croissant d'entreprises mettent actuellement l'accent sur leurs fortes positions à l'étranger. Ainsi, la *First National City Bank* a souligné l'importance de ses opérations à l'étranger en faisant imprimer son rapport annuel 1970 en trois langues, l'anglais et les deux langues principales de ses marchés d'outre-mer, le français, et l'espagnol.

Absorptions En 1967, le rapport annuel de la *SCM Corporation* s'est étendu notamment sur la rapide acquisition de la *Glidden Company*, grande productrice de colorants et de produits chimiques, opération qui doublait la taille de l'entreprise mais en diluait l'image prestigieuse dans le domaine des machines à copier. En consacrant quatre pages à un dialogue intitulé «Ce que signifie l'opération Glidden: un forum SCM», la société a permis à neuf cadres supérieurs des deux compagnies d'expliquer pourquoi et comment ils pensaient qu'une fusion renforcerait la position de la SCM. La presse financière a repris leurs arguments et les a largement commentés.

Marchés Pour s'imposer à l'attention des analystes financiers et à d'autres professionnels de la Bourse, il est important pour une compagnie d'indiquer clairement les marchés où elle est présente, en particulier lorsque leurs possibilités de croissance sont supérieures à la moyenne.

Dans son rapport 1967, la *Berkey Photo* consacre tout un chapitre au marché de l'audiovision et du cinéma, définissant en suite sa position dans ce domaine. Faisant preuve de beaucoup d'imagination, la *Motorola* expose sur neuf pages de son rapport annuel (1965) les importants services rendus à la ville de Jan Jose en Californie, démontrant de manière impressionnante que «Motorola peut affecter la vie de tout un chacun, d'une manière ou d'une autre».

Gestion La plupart des professionnels de l'investissement estiment que le facteur numéro un de la réussite d'une entreprise est la qualité de sa direction générale. Il n'est donc pas surprenant que les rapports annuels s'appliquent d'une manière conséquente à présenter ses dirigeants sous le meilleur jour possible. Le rapport annuel lui-même donne dans bien des cas un aperçu de ces personnalités. En effet, au lieu des portraits officiels, la tendance dans les rapports annuels modernes est aux photographies prises sur le vif permettant de mieux «sentir ceux qui gouvernent».

Mais, même la période de 12 mois qui s'écoule d'un rapport annuel au suivant est parfois trop longue en cette époque de transformations constantes. Les entreprises américaines ont donc envisagé des communications nouvelles qui leur permettent des mises à jour plus fréquentes. *General Electric*, qui innove constamment en matière de rapports annuels, a divisé son rapport en quatre fascicules trimestriels renseignant les actionnaires de façon approfondie à intervalles rapprochés. *Pan American World Airways*, soucieux du moral de ses employés au beau milieu des problèmes financiers qui affectent l'exploitation des lignes régulières, a créé à l'usage du personnel un service téléphonique d'informations qui maintient l'esprit adéquat sous forme de messages enregistrés du Président. Une autre importante société envisage d'installer pareil système téléphonique à l'intention de ses actionnaires.

De nouveaux média vont entraîner la mise au point de nouveaux types de messages. Dans un proche avenir, la vidéocassette, par exemple, permettra des possibilités intéressantes de diffusion périodique d'informations sur les sociétés cotées en Bourse.

Mais les sociétés savent que le rapport annuel demeurera le document de base indispensable pour l'activité de toute entreprise. En tant que tel, il continuera à être utilisé pour la réalisation de multiples objectifs par les dirigeants d'entreprises qui éprouvent un besoin impérieux, au sein d'un monde en constante gestation, d'identifier avec précision aux yeux du public la société dont ils ont la responsabilité.

Cependant, beaucoup de présidents ne se rendent pas encore totalement compte de l'importance et de la diversité d'utilisation du rapport annuel de leur société. Demandez à un responsable d'entreprise — dans le secret de son bureau — quel profit il entend retirer de la publication d'un rapport annuel : il vous répondra tout simplement qu'il en escompte un intérêt accru du public à investir des capitaux dans sa compagnie. La magie qui s'attache à la faveur d'un investisseur est discutée au chapitre suivant.

Le phénomène de croissance

Si la fonction primordiale d'un rapport annuel est d'établir la communication avec les investisseurs, le message capital à leur communiquer est celui-ci: «Achetez nos actions.» Depuis le milieu des années 1950, une nouvelle catégorie d'actionnaires américains a fait son apparition qui, encouragée par la publication des rapports annuels de style moderne, s'est mise à acheter sur leurs recommandations et a ainsi créé le phénomène de l'entreprise à croissance rapide.

Objectif numéro 1: la croissance du capital

Il y avait an 1954 de 6 à 7 millions d'actionnaires aux Etats-Unis — des hommes d'affaires chevronnés, des gens qui pouvaient s'entourer de conseillers en investissement, réputés et efficaces. Aujourd'hui, quelque 30 millions d'actionnaires détiennent directement des parts de capital social, et une centaine de millions d'Américains sont devenus propriétaires d'actions par le biais de mutuelles ou de caisses de retraite. Les actionnaires d'aujourd'hui ont une tendance marquée à être plus jeunes, moins bien installés dans la vie, moins calculateurs et plus impatients de voir leurs investissements porter leurs fruits. Jusqu'aux années 50, les actionnaires s'intéressaient en premier lieu au rendement de leur capital sous forme de dividendes et moins à la valeur absolue de leurs actions. Depuis le milieu des années 1950, et dans une mesure plus large au cours de la décennie écoulée, la croissance du capital investi est devenue le souci primordial de la plupart des investisseurs, et les portefeuilles traditionnels en placements familiaux à dividendes fixes ont beaucoup perdu de leur attrait.

Et pour cause. Fin 1961, un capitaliste en herbe pouvait revendre à 158 dollars une action *IBM* qui lui avait coûté 100 dollars au début de la même année. La même opération avec des actions *Litton Industries* lui rapportait même un bénéfice de 100%, le cours étant passé de 17 à 33 dollars. Cette chance de doubler leur mise laissait les actionnaires indifférents quant aux dividendes.

C'est ainsi que les détenteurs de capitaux se mirent en quête d'entreprises à croissance rapide. Les entreprises, de leur côté, s'efforcèrent avec autant d'empressement à être considérées comme telles. Dans le cadre de l'enquête GRAPHIS, les dirigeants de 146 des 1000 sociétés les plus importantes des USA furent appelés à indiquer l'adjectif qui, selon eux, caractérisait le mieux l'impression que le public devait retirer de la lecture du rapport annuel. On nota une forte majorité en faveur de «growth-oriented» (en pleine croissance), suivi de «honnête» (20 réponses). Un seul président de société avança «blue chip» (solide comme roc). Cette préférence marquée pour l'image d'une entreprise en pleine expansion explique pourquoi les sociétés américaines sont tellement prodigues de leurs deniers et de leur temps pour la réalisation de leur rapport annuel.

Importance de l'image de l'entreprise à croissance rapide

La ferveur avec laquelle les sociétés essaient de s'identifier à des entreprises en pleine croissance ne se comprend cependant pleinement qu'en tenant compte de cette pierre de touche décisive qu'est le multiplicateur cours-bénéfice ou multiplicateur P/E (de l'anglais «price/earnings»).

Le multiplicateur P/E est le nombre par lequel on multiplie les profits d'une entreprise pour obtenir le prix théorique de vente de ses actions. Les cours de clôture varient journellement en Bourse, alors que l'application du P/E permet d'établir la fourchette des prix de vente pour une durée plus longue. Les multiplicateurs sont déterminés de façon assez mystérieuse par les analystes financiers et autres spécialistes du marché des valeurs. En règle générale, ils sont basés sur le taux de croissance résultant des profits escomptés pour l'exercice en cours d'une société donnée.

C'est ainsi qu'une société papetière peut, aux yeux des professionnels de l'investissement, ne présenter qu'un intérêt moyen en raison de ses espérances de croissance: on lui attribuera par exemple un P/E de 10 seulement. Une entreprise d'électronique, par contre, qui se spécialise dans un domaine technologique nouveau et riche de promesses, se verra assigner un P/E de 50 en raison de l'extraordinaire potentiel de croissance qu'on lui reconnaît. Mettons à présent que pour les deux entreprises, les profits s'établissent à 1 dollar par action; le multiplicateur intervenant, les actions papetières se vendront à 10 dollars, les électroniques à 50 dollars. Dès que les bénéfices passent à 2 dollars par action, la valeur boursière de l'action papetière grimpe à 20 dollars, tandis que celle de l'électronique passe à 100 dollars.

Le secret de la croissance des conglomérats

C'est au début des années 60 que certaines sociétés ont appris le secret de la mobilisation de multiplicateurs importants au profit de la croissance des conglomérats. Cela se passe de la façon suivante:

La société d'électronique A, dont deux millions d'actions sont en circulation, fait état de 4 millions de profits, soit 2 dollars par action. Ses actions sont achetées à 100 dollars pièce en vertu du multiplicateur, qui est de 50. La société d'électronique A approche alors la société papetière B pour lui proposer une fusion. La société B déclare les mêmes profits, mais n'a qu'un P/E de 10, ce qui fait que ses actions se vendent à 20 dollars. La société A rachète la société B au prix de dix fois ses profits, soit 40 millions de dollars. Toutefois, la société A ne paie pas en espèces, mais en parts de son capital à 100 dollars pièce. Cela nécessite l'émission de 400000 actions qui seront attribuées aux propriétaires de la société B. Résultat de l'opération: la société A a maintenant 2400000 actions en circulation, ses profits s'élèvent à

8 millions de dollars ou 3,33 dollars par action. L'application du multiplicateur 50 à ces nouveaux profits fait monter le cours des actions de la société A de 100 à 166,50 dollars.

L'image de la société à croissance rapide

Toutes les sociétés n'ont évidemment pas recours à des fusions pour réaliser leurs objectifs de croissance ou imposer des P/E élevés. Trois des entreprises qui ont eu le taux de croissance le plus élevé au cours de la décennie écoulée – *IBM*, *Xerox* et *Polaroid*, chacune dominant un secteur technologique en pleine expansion – l'ont atteint par leurs propres moyens. Ce sont précisément ces trois groupes industriels, et en particulier IBM, qui ont créé le style de l'entreprise à croissance rapide qui est si manifeste dans les rapports annuels d'aujourd'hui.

Thomas Watson, Jr., qui accéda à la présidence d'IBM en 1951, fit appel à Paul Rand pour la réalisation d'un nouveau programme de design. Rand, l'un des meilleurs artistes graphiques au plan international, a conçu tous les rapports annuels d'IBM depuis 1957. Citons parmi les innovations qu'on lui doit: le papier (aux vieilles feuilles de papier blanc tirant sur le bleu utilisées dans l'impression typographique, il substitua du beau papier vergé mat); des caractères d'une grande beauté au dessin recherché; des formats différant du format standard de 21,60 × 28 cm; ainsi que bien d'autres trouvailles subtiles améliorant la présentation. Sa contribution la plus importante fut toutefois l'illustration photographique du rapport annuel. Rand fit appel à quelques grands noms internationaux du reportage photographique (Erich Hartman et Ernst Haas, de *Magnum*, entre autres) pour lancer un genre nouveau, impressionniste et quelque peu mystérieux de la photo industrielle exprimant à merveille la technologie spécifique où s'est engagé IBM – photographies en couleurs, évidemment très accrochantes, alliées à une très large répartition des blancs et d'autres éléments visuels – et qui a concouru à créer le style du rapport annuel de sociétés en pleine expansion.

Autre pionnier dans ce domaine de l'innovation graphique, *General Dynamics* a produit grâce à Erik Nitsche un rapport qui en 1958 constituait le néo plus ultra de l'époque. De belles photos noir et blanc d'avions de fusées et de sous-marins y alternaient avec des demi-pages où s'étalaient des photos couleur, pour la plupart des motifs abstraits de caractère industriel. Trois procédés d'impression avait été mis en œuvre: l'hélio pour le noir et blanc, la typo pour la couleur et la litho pour la couverture et le texte (voir les ill. 394, 401–403).

Malheureusement, trois ans après ce prestigieux rapport, General Dynamics essuyait la plus grande perte dans l'histoire des sociétés anonymes américaines, 143 millions de dollars, après l'échec de son incursion sur le marché de l'avion à réaction commercial. Cela conduisit à une présentation «spartiate» du rapport annuel et la société dut renoncer pour quelques années à son rôle de leader dans le domaine des rapports annuels novateurs.

Entre-temps, ceux-ci avaient commencé d'attirer l'attention des milieux graphiques, et les expositions d'art graphique lui faisaient désormais une place qui alla grandissant. A cet égard, l'Exposition Internationale de Rapports Annuels de la *Mead Library of Ideas*[2] mérite une mention spéciale. Inaugurée en 1956 par la *Mead Paper Co.*, cette exposition se présente aujourd'hui sous la forme de cinq expositions itinérantes qui touchent plus de 100 villes aux Etats-Unis et au Canada. Les envois sont soumis à l'appréciation d'un jury composé de designers et de publicitaires de renom.

La voie qu'a suivie la *General Electric Co.* pour se forger une image d'entreprise à croissance rapide ne doit pas tout à l'excellence du design de ses rapports annuels. GE y est arrivée également par le biais d'une présentation rédactionnelle très étudiée, très méthodique, très logique. Au milieu des années 50, la GE avait reconnu l'importance du concept de croissance et en fit dès lors l'un des grands sujets traités dans ses publications. Le succès fut tel que malgré un taux annuel de croissance assez moyen de 4% tout au long des années 60, la société réussit à se faire attribuer un P/E vigoureux et jouit toujours dans le public de la réputation d'un groupe industriel en pleine expansion.

Les rapports annuels de GE ont été mis au point de façon scientifique en tenant compte de nombreuses innovations que suggéraient au fil des années les enquêtes auprès des lecteurs organisées régulièrement dès 1953. Ces sondages révélèrent par exemple que la Lettre du Président serait lue in extenso par un nombre de lecteurs bien plus considérable à condition d'en réduire le texte à une seule page et de présenter une photo du Président. Autre découverte: un rapport illustré de photos en couleur tout au long du texte avait plus de chances d'être lu en entier.

Toutefois, la contribution majeure de la General Electric à l'évolution des rapports annuels a été la présentation très visuelle de sujets particuliers, traités dans le corps même du rapport, en harmonisant le texte, les titres, les photos et les légendes. Au début des années 60, par exemple, le rapport GE mit en vedette le haut degré de compétence du groupe dans la mise au point de systèmes intégrés, ce qui, à l'époque, était synonyme d'aptitude à la croissance accélérée. Un nombre toujours grandissant de sociétés cherchant à faire de leurs rapports annuels une plate-forme pour la communication d'idées concrètes, la technique GE pourrait bien constituer l'un des éléments les plus durables de la modernisation du rapport annuel.

Le rapport annuel de prestige

Si *IBM* ouvrit la voie au design de qualité et *General Electric* mobilisa la recherche scientifique pour réaliser de grands rapports annuels, *Litton Industries* fait également figure de pionnier grâce au prestige de ses rapports. Société de création récente, il lui manquait la réputation attachée au nom de General Electric dans le domaine de la fabrication de produits de consommation. Conglomérat d'entreprises aux activités fort diverses, Litton Industries ne pouvait offrir au public la pureté du profil technologique qui caractérise IBM et ses ordinateurs, *Xerox* et ses polycopieurs ou *Polaroid* et ses appareils de photo à

[2]L'Exposition Internationale de Rapports Annuels de la Mead Library of Ideas regroupe tous les ans le meilleur de la création graphique dans ce domaine. En avril, les graphistes sont invités à faire parvenir leurs travaux au jury, la date limite étant le 31 juillet. Normalement, c'est en août que les cinq experts qui composent le jury opèrent leur choix. L'exposition a lieu à New York en septembre ou en octobre, avant d'alimenter des expositions itinérantes. L'adresse de la Mead Library of Ideas est 200 Park Avenue, New York, N.Y. 10017.

développement instantané. Il fallut dès le début donner l'image d'un groupe affirmant une volonté inflexible de croissance. Peu de temps après sa fondation, en 1954, Litton Industries projetait déjà sur la scène économique américaine la physionomie du groupe industriel réalisant un milliard de chiffres d'affaires que son fondateur, Tex Thornton, avait en vue.

C'est ainsi que Litton adopta pour ses rapports annuels une stratégie double: des thèmes rédactionnels très étudiés, combinés avec une présentation graphique spectaculaire. Crosby Kelly, qui fut jusqu'en 1965 le directeur des relations avec les investisseurs de l'entreprise et le fer de lance de la politique Litton en matière de rapports annuels, nous dit à ce sujet: «Il fallait en fait dire au public: 'Nous sommes en route, nous y arriverons.' Le but principal du rapport annuel est de constituer un capital de confiance et de foi en la société.»

Tant auprès du personnel qu'auprès des actionnaires. «Je suis convaincu que toute société a besoin de quelque chose qui symbolise son effort, quelque chose qui ressemble à un drapeau. L'un des problèmes que rencontre l'industrie, c'est l'absence de symboles qui pourraient servir de signes de ralliement. Comment faire pour gagner votre confiance absolue? Il faut vous montrer un drapeau à suivre. Ce drapeau, ç'a été notre rapport annuel.»

En effet, Litton projetait une vision de l'avenir de la société qui n'était encore qu'en projet au temps présent, technique qui eut par la suite beaucoup d'imitateurs. Pour la réalisation des premiers rapports annuels, Kelly fit équipe avec Robert Miles Runyan dont le style graphique brillant et flamboyant fit merveille pour la mise au point de la série de rapports annuels la plus passionnante et la plus imaginative qui ait jamais vu le jour.

Le rapport Litton pour 1959, le premier à renfermer des éléments graphiques sortant de l'ordinaire et à présenter un thème délimité, comportait trois double pages illustrées de photos statiques accompagnées de textes introduisant le thème du rapport. La première présentait des instruments scientifiques anciens, faisait entendre que Litton se situait à la pointe du progrès technologique et affirmait que l'industrie américaine devait opposer à la concurrence étrangère «une productivité supérieure, une meilleure qualité, une intelligence plus déliée et un esprit d'invention aux ressources inépuisables pour la conception et le développement de produits nouveaux». La deuxième double page, illustrée d'un canon miniature, d'armes historiques et d'un exemplaire de la Déclaration de l'Indépendance, déclarait que «notre pays doit continuer à s'assurer une puissante défense nationale» et traçait de Litton le portrait d'«un grand industriel qui sert utilement les besoins de la défense nationale de son Pays». Sur la troisième figuraient un vieux coffre fort ainsi que quelques titres d'actions Litton. Le texte assurait les actionnaires du soin qu'apportait Litton à une saine gestion financière - garantissant entre autres «un profit adéquat sur le chiffre d'affaires réalisé afin d'assurer à l'actionnaire un rendement intéressant du capital investi».

Ce rapport fut parmi les premiers à brosser le «grand tableau» des réalités économiques et sociales de l'époque et à situer ensuite l'action de l'entreprise sur cette impressionnante toile de fond. «Il ne suffit pas d'énumérer les faits,» dit Kelly, «il est de votre responsabilité de vous assurer que les lecteurs n'en tirent pas des conclusions erronées.» Le même Kelly admet ne pas trop s'être soucié de fournir des explications précises sur le fonctionnement de la société. Il préférait susciter assez de curiosité de la part des analystes financiers pour les inciter à venir apprendre l'histoire complète au siège de Litton Industries à Los Angeles. Il interprète comme un compliment cette remarque que lui fit un analyste: «Crosby, j'ai lu ton rapport annuel en entier avant de m'apercevoir que tu ne m'avais au fond absolument rien dit.»

D'année en année, les rapports *Litton* visèrent de plus en plus haut. C'est ainsi que la couverture du rapport '62 était ornée d'une superbe photo de l'Acropole d'Athènes et le rapport tout entier consacré à l'idée de Liberté, «au jour où l'humanité tout entière aura sauté par dessus le Mur». La partie illustrative du rapport relatait les épisodes historiques de l'homme à la poursuite de la liberté. Le halo mystique entourant cet esprit de croisade planétaire n'étant cependant rien en comparaison de la force mystérieuse qui faisait grimper les cours des actions Litton toujours plus haut, au grand dépit de la concurrence.

Bientôt la stratégie du conglomérat adoptée par Litton Industries fit tache d'huile, et nombreux furent les cadres supérieurs de Litton même qui mirent à profit la technique acquise pour fonder leurs propres entreprises, les doter d'un P/E élevé et appliquer ce dernier aux petites sociétés rachetées tous azimuts. Ainsi naquirent *City Investing*, *Walter Kidde*, *Teledyne* et la *KDI Corporation*.

Fidèle à son style agressif, Robert Miles Runyan n'hésita pas à s'assurer la clientèle de ces nouveaux venus, qu'il réunissait sous le terme générique de LIDOS (Litton Industries Drop-Outs, les transfuges de Litton). Il sut insuffler à leurs rapports au milieu des années 60 le même caractère missionnaire et mystique qui avait fait le succès des rapports Litton.

Ce genre de rapports subordonnait souvent, s'il ne le sacrifiait pas entièrement, le texte au design. Un superbe rapport Teledyne faisait ressortir des photos en couleurs de sujets technologiques abstraits sur un aplat gris foncé, le texte noir ne se détachant guère de ce même fond gris. Le rapport de City Investing pour 1968 se présentait sous forme d'un album de photos dépourvues de légendes. Même les photos et une chronique des événements de l'année dans le monde qui figuraient au haut des pages ne parvenaient pas à donner à ce document, par ailleurs prestigieux, un véritable caractère informatif.

D'autres conglomérats, non-LIDOS cette fois-ci, adoptèrent le même style missionnaire et mystique dans la conception de leurs rapports annuels. *Gulf and Western Industries*, *A-T-O* et *Ling-Temco-Vought (LTV)* furent du nombre. Le rapport LTV pour 1965, classique d'apparence, ne l'est pas au sens où l'entendait la direction de l'entreprise. Les colonnes grecques blanches gaufrées se détachent joliment du fond noir de la couverture, et le rapport est plein de réminiscences grecques en images, avec cette déclaration pompeuse: «Nous avons donc fait surgir du passé l'Age d'Or des Héllènes pour illustrer l'objectif de notre société et le thème du présent rapport, 'construire des valeurs durables'.» Mais il ne s'agit en somme que d'une imitation du style Litton, avec le flair en moins, et le résultat a un fâcheux arrière-goût de nouveaux riches.

Perte de vitesse des conglomérats

Puis vint 1968 et la baisse inopinée des valeurs qui fit même justice de la magie attachée aux opérations des conglomérats. Leurs actions furent perdantes comme les autres et même les premières à dégringoler, anéantissant par-là les espoirs de milliers d'actionnaires. Au creux de la vague, un conglomérat dut même déposer son bilan, la *KDI Corporation*.

La baisse se poursuivit jusqu'au milieu de l'année 1970, puis le redressement s'amorça dans l'espace de quelques mois. Les sociétés à croissance réelle telle *IBM* et celles qui disposaient de ressources considérables telles les compagnies pétrolières repartirent en flèche. Les conglomérats suivirent tant bien que mal, beaucoup s'évertuant à vendre celles de leurs sociétés qui ne faisaient plus de profits.

Les détenteurs de capitaux n'en menaient pas large. Il était beaucoup question de la nécessité d'un retour aux sources, aux valeurs sûres. Les entreprises se mirent alors à souligner dans leurs rapports annuels les vertus de la liquidité et de la productivité et les avantages concurrentiels particuliers dont elles prouvaient se targuer. Si le langage était nouveau, la présentation n'avait guère changé, et peu d'entreprises se montrèrent disposées à faire marche arrière pour la qualité graphique de leurs rapports. La grande majorité des sociétés étudiées en 1970 comptait dépenser autant, sinon davantage, pour leurs rapports annuels que ce qu'elles y avaient consacré l'année précédente. Elles avaient l'intention ferme de maintenir intacte leur image d'entreprises en pleine croissance. Les capitalistes, au fond, étaient toujours en quête, eux aussi, de firmes en expansion, tout en exigeant des preuves plus concrètes de celles-ci.

La tendance est à l'information financière complète

Par bonheur pour les détenteurs de capitaux, une tendance marquée se fait jour dans le monde financier en faveur d'une plus grande clarté d'exposition et d'une information plus complète. Les sociétés abrègent les textes figurant en tête des rapports annuels tout en les rendant plus intelligibles. C'est ainsi que le rapport 1969 de *Westinghouse* ne compte plus que 3500 mots, 50% de moins que l'année précédente.

La Securities and Exchange Commission, tout comme les autres autorités de contrôle du marché des valeurs, fait pression sur les sociétés pour qu'elles donnent au public un plus grand nombre d'informations financières se prêtant à l'analyse et qu'elles mettent celles-ci à la portée de tout détenteur de capitaux. Pour prendre un exemple : la SEC désire que les entreprises publient un état circonstancié du chiffre d'affaires et du bénéfice par départements ou groupes de produits. On entend ainsi éviter qu'une société réalisant la majeure partie de ses bénéfices sur le caoutchouc émette des prétentions à être classées dans l'industrie aérospatiale.

Une pression subtile s'exerce dans une mesure bien plus importante de la part du grand hebdomadaire financier FINANCIAL WORLD. Depuis 1941, ce journal décerne des prix annuels pour les meilleurs rapports.[3] Ces dernières années, préférence a été donnée aux sociétés qui fournissent au public des statistiques précises par groupes de produits.

Le FINANCIAL WORLD exerce une influence considérable du fait qu'il passe chaque année au crible quelque 5000 rapports annuels représentant plus de 90 branches de l'Economie et distribue des trophées en bronze (chaque prix consistant en un serre-livres), une douzaine de médailles d'argent pour les grands secteurs de l'industrie et récompense d'une médaille en or le meilleur rapport de l'année. En 1970, l'Oscar de l'Industrie a été décerné à Westinghouse Electric dont le rapport pour 1969 a fourni pour la première fois le détail des ventes et profits pour chacune de ses cinq grandes unités opérationnelles. Les rapports précédents du même groupe ne faisaient état que de pourcentages globaux des ventes par grandes catégories de produits.

L'Accounting Principles Board, cette autorité de contrôle comptable, a également publié une série de recommandations visant à fournir à l'actionnaire un plus grand nombre de données valables qui lui permettent d'analyser la situation d'une entreprise. Les sociétés en tiennent compte — en multipliant et améliorant l'information contenue dans leurs rapports.

L'Etat veille lui aussi à ce que les résumés financiers des résultats d'un exercice soient présentés avec le maximum de clarté et de détails. Les sociétés sont tenues de soumettre aux autorités fédérales un rapport annuel dit légal sur formule idoine, la 10 K. Or, le gouvernement vient d'augmenter considérablement le nombre de données à lui fournir sur l'état financier d'une société. Pour éviter d'avoir à préparer des rapports annuels de volume différent pour l'Etat et pour les actionnaires, les sociétés commencent à inclure dans leurs rapports destinés aux actionnaires tous les éléments d'information figurant dans la 10 K.

On constate que même les notes en bas de page imprimées en petits caractères et traditionnellement accessibles aux seuls spécialistes de la comptabilité sont désormais rédigées avec plus de clarté. On a même proposé de ne plus les distinguer du texte en adoptant le même corps pour les lettres qui les composent.

Une autre tendance vise à éliminer entièrement les notes en bas de page et d'en incorporer les éléments dans le texte même. *General Electric*, qui a adopté cette présentation il y a quelques années, les regroupe tous dans une sorte de commentaire face aux tableaux financiers. La lecture alors de ces pages peut paraître plus fastidieuse, mais cette manière de faire présente un énorme avantage : Ces commentaires seront désormais également certifiés par les commissaires aux comptes au même titre que les données chiffrées. *J. C. Penney* est allé encore plus loin dans cette voie en éliminant de son rapport les textes trop techniques n'intéressant que les spécialistes et en renvoyant ces derniers à un document séparé, à demander à la direction de l'entreprise.

Tous ces efforts vont dans un même sens très louable; ils visent en effet à faire du rapport annuel tout entier une source documentaire encore plus précise et plus sûre.

---

[3]La revue FINANCIAL WORLD examine chaque année plus de 5000 rapports annuels. Fin juin, des distinctions appelées Merit Award Certificates sont décernées aux quelque 2000 sociétés qui ont satisfait aux normes minimales. Sont appréciées successivement: l'information donnée aux actionnaires, celle qui intéresse l'analyste financier et le professionnel de l'investissement, la présentation générale. A noter que les analystes financiers qui constituent le jury ont des goûts plutôt conservateurs en matière de design. En octobre, les résultats du concours sont annoncés à l'occasion d'un banquet qui réunit jusqu'à 1500 dirigeants de sociétés. Des prix sont décernés à près de 300 sociétés représentant 90 branches de l'industrie. Les sociétés désirant participer à ce concours font tenir deux exemplaires de leur rapport annuel avant le 31 mai à l'adresse suivante: Director, Annual Report Survey, Financial World, 17 Battery Place, New York, N.Y. 10004.

Chapitre 3: La création d'un rapport annuel de qualité

Le new look graphique introduit par les entreprises à croissance rapide dans les rapports annuels comportait des éléments exaltants qui ne manquèrent pas d'en influencer la conception et de donner naissance à un nouveau style rédactionnel empruntant largement aux techniques de communication des journaux, magazines et programmes de télévision. Il était grand temps que le rapport annuel découvrît les techniques propres à accrocher l'attention du public, saturé par le flot d'informations qui l'assaille.

En outre les rapports annuels se concurrencent eux-mêmes. Un sondage de *General Electric* a révélé que l'actionnaire GE moyen possède des parts dans 16 entreprises différentes, ce qui limite à 10 minutes le temps de lecture qu'il peut consacrer à chacun des 16 rapports annuels. Cela est encore plus vrai lorsque l'on compare, comme le font les analystes financiers, plusieurs rapports annuels émanant de sociétés ayant le même genre d'activités.

La rédaction Face à une concurrence aussi vive, seul un spécialiste de premier ordre est capable d'assumer avec succès la rédaction d'un rapport annuel. On s'assurera donc les services d'un écrivain et d'un rédacteur professionnel que l'on choisira soit au sein de l'entreprise, soit à l'extérieur.

Ce rédacteur a pour tâche essentielle de rassembler la masse des faits, souvent disparates, à évoquer dans le rapport annuel, d'interviewer les responsables, d'établir un plan et, avec tous les éléments recueillis, de procéder à une première, puis à une seconde rédaction. C'est une erreur assez commune de penser qu'une personne étrangère à l'entreprise ne saurait assez en pénétrer les problèmes pour être capable de publier une analyse de ses activités. La plupart des cadres d'une entreprise disposent de trop d'informations pour être en mesure de dégager les faits qui comptent véritablement. Il est évident que le rapport mis au point par le rédacteur extérieur à l'entreprise doit ensuite être soumis au président qui le remanie comme il l'entend. Toutefois, le travail préliminaire du rédacteur, de même que sa compétence et son expérience, sont très précieux pour l'entreprise. Ils lui évitent d'immobiliser un ou plusieurs de ses cadres pendant des centaines d'heures et lui fournissent un manuscrit lisible, centré sur l'essentiel et débarrassé de toute phraséologie initiale.

«Le plus mauvais service qu'une société puisse se rendre à elle-même, c'est de se présenter dans son rapport annuel de manière trop élogieuse», dit Dan Lufkin, ancien analyste financier et cofondateur de *Donaldson, Lufkin & Jenrette, Inc.*, un nouveau venu particulièrement prometteur à Wall Street. L'entreprise qui induit en erreur les analystes financiers en leur donnant des informations exagérément optimistes risque de se mettre à dos pour le reste de son existence les spécialistes de l'investissement qu'elle aura leurrés. On voit par là combien la tâche du rédacteur d'un rapport annuel est délicate. Il doit bien entendu présenter l'entreprise sous le meilleur jour possible mais constamment veiller à être prudent et à ne pas aller au-delà de la vérité.

Le rédacteur a une tâche plus subtile, mais aussi importante à assumer lors de la mise en forme d'un rapport annuel: il faut qu'il puisse se mettre au diapason du style qu'emploient le WALL STREET JOURNAL ou BUSINESS WEEK pour écrire d'une manière qui sonne juste aux oreilles des lecteurs de ces deux journaux qui sont imbattables en matière de présentation experte de faits financiers et d'informations sur le monde des affaires. Les rédacteurs venant de la publicité font souvent fausse route lorsqu'ils se hasardent à rédiger un rapport annuel dont la prétention de sérieux et de véridicité réclame un style discret alors qu'ils ne sont guère habitués à mettre une sourdine à leurs déclarations. Quant aux hommes de loi et aux hommes d'affaires, ils ne sont guère experts dans l'expression de constats en phrases courtes, simples, directes.

La photographie Nous avons vu que le texte d'un rapport annuel doit éviter de donner une impression euphorique éloignée de la réalité. Quant aux graphiques à y inclure, ils peuvent au contraire fort bien mettre en relief les atouts majeurs de l'entreprise. La photographie de grande qualité a été l'un des éléments essentiels de l'image d'une entreprise en pleine expansion, en même temps qu'elle accroissait sensiblement le coût de production d'un rapport annuel. La plupart des photographes spécialisés dans l'illustration de rapports annuels prennent de 300 à 700 dollars par jour pour un reportage dans les grandes villes. Un photographe opérant en studio peut demander jusqu'à 1000 dollars ou plus par jour. S'y ajoutent les frais de transport, de logement, de matériel et de développement.

Les dirigeants d'entreprises trouvent ces honoraires souvent exagérés, et pourtant l'enquête GRAPHIS a révélé que la seconde grande source de déception, pour les cadres interrogés, était la difficulté «d'obtenir à temps de bonnes photos» (la première source de déception étant la difficulté de mettre en harmonie les points de vue des principaux responsables). La solution du problème est évidemment que les grands photographes attelés à la tâche fassent leur travail avec compétence, un sens créateur en éveil et un respect absolu des délais impartis. Préalablement, ils doivent s'entretenir avec le designer et situer avec précision les grandes lignes du rapport annuel, sans facturer le temps qu'ils y consacrent. Seule la connaissance intime des objectifs du rapport à illustrer leur permet de fournir des documents parfaits.

On recrutera un photographe habitué à discuter d'un projet avec un PDG pour arrondir les angles lors des explications inévitables entre professionnels de deux bords différents. Les sociétés qui font appel au premier photographe disponible font courir des risques sérieux à la qualité du produit tout comme à la réputation de l'équipe chargé de la production du rapport annuel.

Il importe de bien préciser dès le début les droits de l'entreprise sur les documents photographiques dont elle passe commande. Les associations professionnelles de photographes ont mis au point un code qui restreint l'utilisation d'une photo à la seule fin prévue lors de la commande. Dans la pratique, toutefois, la société jouit généralement du droit d'utiliser une photo pour des usages annexes — dans la revue d'entreprise, les communiqués de presse et autres publications promotionnelles. La publicité est exclue de cet accord de principe. L'agence désirant illustrer une campagne publicitaire doit négocier avec le photographe des honoraires supplémentaires représentant généralement l'économie réalisée du fait que la photo existe déjà et dispense l'utilisateur d'une nouvelle commande de reportage.

Design Un facteur encore plus important pour la création d'un rapport annuel de qualité est la personnalité du designer. On lui demande d'assimiler la politique de communication de l'entreprise et ses objectifs, de sélectionner avec goût, à-propos et cohérence les meilleures illustrations et d'en faire une utilisation optima. Il renoncera parfois à la photographie pour illustrer de dessins et gravures de grande qualité les rapports de sociétés financières ou autres pour lesquelles il serait difficile de trouver un sujet de reportage-photo. Des illustrations de ce genre, bien conçues, peuvent visualiser des sujets abstraits d'une manière souvent plus frappante que des photos. Dans son rapport pour 1967, la *St.Joe Minerals Corporation* désirait mettre en lumière les capitaux importants qu'elle venait d'investir dans des exploitations minières et des fonderies. Un photographe se serait heurté à la difficulté qu'il y a à tirer des effets sensationnels d'une galerie de mine ou d'une fonderie certes impressionnante par ses dimensions, mais peu photogénique. L'illustrateur, par contre, réussit à évoquer valablement l'ampleur de ces projets et à sensibiliser le public sur l'importance qu'ils revêtaient pour la St.Joe.

Certaines sociétés cherchent à sortir des habitudes traditionnelles. C'est ainsi que le rapport 1967 de *Scovill* est illustré de compositions de bois, de verre et d'autres matériaux, évocation figurative des marchés où s'exerçait l'activité de la société. Ce genre de création peut ensuite servir à donner une note de modernisme à la décoration du siège social, à condition, une fois de plus, de déterminer clairement les droits respectifs de la société et du créateur. Autre innovation : les trois affiches encartées dans le rapport pour 1967 de *l'Ansul Co.* étaient dues à des graphistes de renom et considérées comme faisant partie intégrante du rapport. L'entreprise en offrait un tirage limité aux actionnaires, sur simple demande.

Typographie Un élément rarement compris ou apprécié à sa juste valeur par les dirigeants d'une entreprise, est la typographie. Et pourtant, c'est bien elle qui fait souvent toute la différence entre une présentation grossière, à peine décantée et qui frise l'amateurisme, et une image de distinction et de qualité. Le choix du caractère pour un rapport annuel

donné devrait être laissé au designer qui est seul capable de saisir toutes les nuances subtiles et sophistiquées qui peuvent exister entre les familles de caractères disponibles dans les imprimeries.

En matière de caractères typographiques, il faut tenir compte de modes tout comme pour les autres éléments d'un rapport annuel. Les gothiques modernes connaissent actuellement une certaine vogue et sont parfaitement lisibles, comme le prouve l'exemple des rapports *General Electric* qui ont remporté la médaille d'or de FINANCIAL WORLD en 1961 et 1962, ce qui a évidemment concouru à la diffusion de ces caractères.

Les manchettes, titres, sous-titres et autres éléments typographiques de mise en relief ont aussi leur importance et peuvent contribuer à la création d'une image conservatrice, moderniste ou technologique.

L'emploi judicieux et efficace des blancs est souvent difficile à expliquer et à justifier aux yeux d'un homme d'affaires peu familiarisé avec ces problèmes. Il ne sera pas aisé de lui faire admettre que la présence ou l'absence de blancs est pour beaucoup dans l'impression générale qui se dégage d'un texte imprimé. Par bonheur, *IBM* fait un si large emploi de blancs que les rapports annuels se voulant modernes ont fini par les accepter comme éléments de style.

Tableaux et graphiques Une autre occasion d'aérer la page tout en développant des passages essentiels du texte est fournie par l'emploi de tableaux et de graphiques. Le mot d'ordre le plus valable ici, c'est la simplicité. Certaines sociétés sont devenues expertes dans l'art de la visualisation. Les graphiques par secteurs se multiplient au fur et à mesure que les sociétés fournissent le détail de leurs ventes et de leurs bénéfices par groupes de produits. Certaines sociétés illustrent par de superbes graphiques les résultats des bonnes années et n'en donnent pas pour les mauvaises. Mais cette pratique discutable est vite percée à jour par les analystes.

Le papier Autre élément de réussite des rapports, le papier, son poids, son apprêt, sa couleur dans l'effet global de la page, revêtent une particulière importance. C'est à *IBM* que l'on doit l'innovation du papier couché mat qui devint la norme au cours de la décennie écoulée. Le progrès technique met aujourd'hui à la disposition du designer une très grande diversité de papiers pour reproduire son message : papiers couchés brillants, supports idéals pour la photographie, papiers-couleur à la fine contexture, etc.... Le poids d'un papier n'est pas négligeable puisqu'il introduit la distinction qui existe entre une poignée de main faible ou virile. Un rapport imprimé sur du papier trop léger, trop inconsistant, peut nuire à l'impression de solidité et de sécurité que l'on souhaite donner au lecteur.

Informations en «bandeaux» Tous ces éléments graphiques ne représenteraient pas grand-chose dans un rapport annuel s'ils n'étaient pas conçus de manière à coller exactement à son contenu. Le plus gros problème à résoudre dans la rédaction et l'illustration d'un rapport, c'est l'omniprésence du lecteur rapide habitué à lire en diagonale. L'actionnaire consacre souvent au déchiffrage d'un rapport annuel un laps de temps ridicule par rapport au nombre d'informations que l'on voudrait lui communiquer. Il faut donc s'assurer avant tout que chaque page du rapport donne la même *impression* de puissance, de solidité, de progrès technique et d'avenir, quel que soit le message essentiel sur lequel l'entreprise entend mettre l'accent.

Pour y parvenir, un moyen fréquemment employé consiste à donner les informations importantes en «bandeaux». Dans la presse, cette technique est utilisée à l'intention de ceux qui se contentent de parcourir rapidement les informations essentielles dans les titres, les suivantes dans le premier alinéa, et ainsi de suite. Dans un rapport annuel, c'est d'abord la couverture dont «l'accroche» est essentielle. C'est ensuite la lettre du président, qui, selon les tests de la General Electric, est la partie du rapport la plus lue. Puis, pour les lecteurs qui ont trouvé les deux premières suffisamment intéressantes pour continuer, ce sont les images et les légendes qui les accompagnent. De nombreuses personnes ne lisent une légende que lorsque l'image est assez captivante. De même pour les sous-titres, lorsque ceux-ci constituent en eux-même de véritables informations, par exemple, «Augmentation des ventes de 17 pour cent», au lieu de simplement «Ventes».

Enfin, pour le lecteur spécialisé ou disposant de plus de temps, les résultats financiers.

En bref, le rapport annuel «intégré» présente à la fois les données financières, une revue des activités, des illustrations photographiques et graphiques dans un ensemble attrayant.

Le rapport annuel bipartite Certaines sociétés choisissent la méthode inverse, séparant complètement ces types d'informations, et publient leurs rapports annuels en deux parties. C'est ce qu'ont fait la *U.S. Plywood-Champion Paper* et la *Ralston Purina Co.* en agrafant au début du rapport proprement dit, réduit à une série d'illustrations commentées, un encart en deux couleurs contenant un message aux actionnaires ainsi que l'analyse financière.

D'autres sociétés ont publié deux plaquettes distinctes, ce qui leur a porté tort. En effet, les principaux intéressés, les analystes financiers, ont classé le document financier et ignoré l'autre. L'objectif étant d'éveiller l'intérêt de tous les lecteurs sur le potentiel de croissance de l'entreprise grâce aux textes et aux illustrations, les destinataires devraient recevoir un seul document. Le rapport annuel complet est donc certainement le plus efficace.

La terminologie financière Les enquêtes auprès des actionnaires révèlent parfois que la plupart de ceux-ci ne comprennent pas le langage financier utilisé dans les rapports annuels, même de simples expressions telles «obligation convertible». Un problème est ainsi posé.

On discute indéfiniment sur le point de savoir si le rapport annuel doit être écrit en priorité pour intéresser «tante Jeanne», symbole du petit actionnaire, ou pour informer le professionnel qui décide d'un investissement, mais qui peut être également un petit homme d'affaires ou un chef de famille timoré sur le plan financier. En bref on peut dire que la plupart des décisions d'acheter des actions sont prises ou influencées par des professionnels. En tant qu'audience, les professionnels sont au moins cent fois plus importants que les petits actionnaires individuels. Quoi qu'il en soit, un rapport, pour être efficace devra convenir aussi bien à tante Jeanne qu'aux professionnels.

L'esprit d'invention Le rapport annuel bien conçu est devenu virtuellement le standard auquel une compagnie doit répondre si elle veut être compétitive sur le marché financier. Cependant, de temps à autre, une entreprise a une idée si créatrice et si innovatrice qu'elle suscite l'admiration générale. Dans un domaine où les idées vraiment originales sont extrêmement rares, la presse spécialisée s'empresse de le souligner.

Malheureusement, de nombreuses sociétés confondent la créativité authentique avec une présentation graphique sophistiquée qui déçoit le lecteur au lieu de l'attirer. Imprimer le rapport avec de l'encre parfumée ou mettre le message sur un disque que l'analyste ne peut pas classer, voilà des exemples de méthodes fort peu adéquates dans le domaine des communications d'entreprise.

Cependant, plusieurs compagnies ont trouvé des moyens vraiment originaux de présenter leurs rapports annuels.

• La *Charles Pfizer's* a publié son rapport annuel 1965 comme supplément de l'édition du dimanche du New York Times, de la Chicago Tribune et du Los Angeles Times représentant 3 500 000 lecteurs. En outre, pour renforcer cette initiative, plus de 200 000 autres exemplaires ont été adressés individuellement aux parlementaires, aux gouverneurs, aux fonctionnaires des Etats où elle avait des installations, aux éditeurs, aux pharmaciens, aux médecins, etc. Un article d'Associated Press consacré à l'événement a été repris par plus de cent journaux et la revue The New Yorker a qualifié Pfizer de «pionnier». La formule du supplément de journal, que Pfizer a reprise les deux années suivantes, a eu vraiment d'importantes répercussions sur le public: en 1954, la société comptait 13 000 actionnaires; au milieu de la décennie suivante, elle en avait plus de 80 000.

• Pour souligner qu'elle était plus qu'un simple fabricant de boîtes de conserve, l'*American Can Company* a expédié son rapport annuel au début des années 1960 dans un tube de carton. Le tube faisait partie d'une nouvelle gamme de matériel d'emballage de la compagnie destiné aux denrées alimentaires. Résultat: plus de 90 pour cent des destinataires ont ouvert le rapport annuel cette année-là, au lieu de quelque 60 pour cent les autres années. Malheureusement, le rapport annuel est resté ondulé et il a été difficile à classer, d'où protestations de certains analystes, mais les résultats obtenus n'en n'ont pas moins été excellents.

• «Messieurs, j'ai quinze ans et quelques économies que j'aimerais placer dans les actions d'une entreprise… Auriez-vous l'obligeance de m'expliquer… ce que vous faites et pourquoi… Avec mes salutations distinguées, Chris Nelson.» Ces phrases, tirées d'une lettre reproduite sur la couverture du rapport annuel 1963 de la *Bell & Howell Company*, ont fourni une parfaite accroche à cette société, qui a dédié son rapport à Chris et «aux nombreux jeunes gens qui, comme lui, portent aux entreprises américaines un intérêt aussi authentique». Elle a ensuite expliqué ses activités hautement technologiques en termes très simples, ce qui a été fort apprécié par de nombreux actionnaires adultes qui ne comprenaient pas non plus ce que faisait l'entreprise.

• En 1969, la *Banque Girard* de Philadelphie a chargé l'auteur James Michener et l'artiste Andrew Wyeth de réaliser un petit livre «Quality of Living». Le rapport annuel accompagnant l'ouvrage était plutôt simple et peu coûteux. Cependant, le message pertinent et frappant contenu dans l'opuscule joliment présenté par les deux auteurs a suscité de nombreuses et excellentes réactions dont 5000 lettres laudatives. La Banque est restée sur la voie du succès en publiant l'année suivante un livre de 64 pages intitulé «An Urban Planet?», de la plume de Barbara Ward, économiste de renom international, avec des illustrations d'un aquarelliste de Philadelphie.

• *Cybernatics, Inc.*, petite entreprise de New Jersey, avec des ventes d'environ 6 millions de dollars par année, a fait également preuve de créativité, mais de toute autre manière. Son rapport annuel 1970 a présenté la société sous un aspect humoristique. Sa couverture : «Huit observateurs impartiaux vous disent comment Cybernatics, Inc. a *vraiment* marché en 1969.» Les témoignages réunis à l'intérieur émanaient de la femme de ménage — «Les déchets chez Cybernatics ont augmenté de 63%», du garçon qui sert le lunch — «Ils ont commandé sept fois plus de sandwiches au fromage que l'année précédente», et du laveur de carreaux — «Ils ont l'air plus affairés que l'année dernière».

• En 1970, selon M. Robert Amen, vice-président pour les relations publiques, la *Combustion Engineering* «voulait savoir quel visage aurait la compagnie présentée par quelqu'un qui la regarderait d'un œil neuf». Aussi M. Amen a-t-il décidé de charger un jeune noir de 17 ans, dont il avait remarqué le talent dans un concours de photographie, de prendre des photos de l'entreprise pendant vingt jours. Le jeune homme, Stewart Jackson, prit des photos dans toute l'Amérique, y compris celles d'installations pétrolières dans le golfe du Mexique, vues d'un hélicoptère; en outre il enregistra tous les soirs ses impressions sur ce qu'il avait vu et fait. Les photographies de l'adolescent ont été publiées dans le rapport annuel et ses commentaires ont constitué une grande partie du texte. Ce que la Combustion Engineering a réalisé de cette manière fort simple a constitué un lien entre les générations d'une part et entre le monde des affaires et la jeunesse d'autre part.

Une des plus grandes contributions qu'une entreprise puisse fournir dans le domaine du rapport annuel consiste à publier un rapport original et de bon goût qui ait un effet positif.

L'essentiel d'un rapport annuel tient en six éléments : l'allocution du Président, le survol des activités au cours de l'exercice, les résultats financiers, les commentaires correspondants et le rapport des commissaires aux comptes et la composition du Conseil d'administration et de la Direction. Ces éléments sont généralement toujours disposés dans le même ordre, ce qui ne facilite pas la tâche du designer dans le domaine de l'innovation. Toutefois, les rapports annuels modernes, surtout ceux des grandes sociétés, lui offrent un certain nombre de possibilités d'expression qui, s'il en fait bon usage, contribueront à donner au rapport l'intérêt et l'attrait souhaités. Ce chapitre a pour but de mettre en lumière les possibilités et la manière de s'en servir valablement.

La couverture

La couverture est indiscutablement l'élément graphique le plus important d'un rapport annuel. Elle a pour mission de piquer la curiosité du lecteur, de l'inciter à ouvrir le rapport et à en commencer la lecture. Elle constitue un support capital à l'image de marque de l'entreprise. Il y a plusieurs moyens pour réaliser une bonne couverture, mais l'un des plus efficaces est d'utiliser une photo-choc qui — peu importe qu'on la rencontre sur la couverture d'un rapport annuel ou du magazine LIFE —, entraînera inévitablement le lecteur à prendre connaissance du contenu de la publication.

Lorsqu'il paraît préférable de souligner la respectabilité d'une entreprise, on peut agir différemment et envisager par exemple un luxueux papier de couleur, un gaufrage, ou un timbrage au fer à dorer. La décennie écoulée a vu les entreprises les plus en flèche donner à leurs rapports annuels des couvertures très traditionnelles qui, dans l'esprit de leurs dirigeants, devaient créer une impression de sociétés très assises.

Si un rapport annuel est axé sur un thème particulièrement important, la couverture peut très bien s'en inspirer. Le rapport de la *Chase Manhattan Bank* pour 1967 présentait en couverture une photo un peu abstraite de la silhouette familière de Manhattan et de ses gratte-ciel, avec, en surimpression, celle d'Harlem. Le message du Président débutait par ces mots : «Nous estimons opportun de montrer sur la couverture de notre rapport deux aspects opposés de New York, le traditionnel et «l'autre»… pour rappeler aussi bien la majesté de notre ville que la menace que fait peser sur elle l'existence des bidonvilles. Tout au long de l'année 1967, notre banque a œuvré pour combler le fossé qui sépare encore beaucoup trop ces deux modes de vie si terriblement différents !»

Les structures très diverses des sociétés d'aujourd'hui justifient la grande variété que l'on constate dans la conception des couvertures. Paul Rand, *d'IBM*, est par exemple convaincu qu'une couverture ne doit pas être trop réaliste : «Nous n'arriverons pas à donner une impression correcte des activités de notre société en reproduisant simplement une pièce d'équipement en page de couverture. C'est seulement par le truchement d'une photo non figurative, impossible à identifier, obscure voire mystérieuse que j'arrive à suggérer ce qu'IBM représente vraiment.» Les thèmes photographiques abstraits sont devenus le signe distinctif des couvertures *IBM* et *Xerox*.

La couverture doit accrocher le lecteur, soit. Mais dès la première double page — formée par la page deux de couverture et la première page de texte —, il faut relancer son intérêt par des éléments rédactionnels. Un simple sommaire et une page de titre constituent une piètre amorce; en adoptant ce genre de présentation, ne risque-t-on pas de gâcher une excellente occasion de sensibiliser à nouveau le lecteur ?

Définition de l'entreprise

La première double page peut bien servir de support à la présentation résumée de l'entreprise, sorte de brève fiche d'identité. C'est ce que font un nombre croissant de sociétés en donnant un aperçu de leurs activités et de leur rôle dans la vie économique.

Voici un exemple de définition de l'entreprise, emprunté au rapport annuel pour 1969 de United Merchants : *«United Merchants and Manufacturers, Inc.* est l'un des plus grands fournisseurs américains de tissus mode pour les industries du vêtement et de l'ameublement. United Merchants fabrique aussi des tissus en fibres de verre, des films plastiques et la gamme réputée de produits adhésifs Con-tact et Kwick-Kover.

Le groupe s'efforce de se diversifier le plus possible même dans le domaine des opérations financières et de marketing. C'est ainsi qu'il a acquis la chaîne nationale des 418 magasins de confection *Robert Hall Clothes*. Il possède aussi d'importantes unités de production en Argentine, au Brésil, en Colombie, en Uruguay, au Venezuela, au Canada, en France et en Grande-Bretagne. United Merchants dispose de 49 fabriques aux Etats-Unis et à l'étranger, entretient des bureaux commerciaux dans toutes les grandes villes et emploie plus de 36 000 personnes.»

Le sommaire

Contrairement à ce qu'en pensent certains critiques, le sommaire n'est pas un élément indispensable du rapport annuel. Souvent même, il est superflu, la plupart des rapports n'excédant pas 36 pages.

Faute de sommaire, le lecteur est bien obligé de parcourir le rapport tout entier, ce qui l'amène à prendre connaissance du message global. Un sommaire occupe souvent une place que l'on peut mettre à profit pour identifier l'entreprise aux yeux du lecteur, comme nous l'avons montré plus haut.

Certaines sociétés savent aménager le sommaire de manière à stimuler l'intérêt du lecteur. C'est ainsi que le sommaire du rapport 1969 de la *First National City*

Bank est divisé en huit paragraphes agrémentés chacun d'un petit commentaire d'une demi-douzaine de lignes et d'une reproduction miniature d'une illustration figurant dans le corps du rapport.

Les chiffres-clés du bilan

Il s'agit d'une présentation succinte et très claire des principaux résultats de l'exercice. Sa brièveté en renforcera encore l'intérêt. Exemple : le rapport 1968 d'*Aiken Industries* ne présentait que trois chiffres : produit net des ventes, bénéfice net, bénéfice net par action. On veillera à ne pas faire figurer des chiffres détaillés qui, de toute façon, seront repris dans le tableau final des cinq ou dix derniers exercices.

Ce «panorama» de l'exercice peut figurer en page deux de couverture, ou à la page une du texte, ou encore en page de gauche, face à l'allocution du Président, ce qui permet à ce dernier de dominer son sujet en donnant une vue d'ensemble de la marche de la société et de son évolution future. Une telle tendance commence à s'imposer depuis une dizaine d'années.

L'allocution du Président

Ce message est un terrain de choix pour évoquer la politique suivie, les options prises et la solution des problèmes délicats. Le Président d'une entreprise qui avait été l'objet d'une série de mises en demeure en 1970 en raison de la pollution dont elle était responsable préféra à la réflexion exposer dans son allocution les faits et les efforts pour pallier ces graves inconvénients plutôt que de les évoquer dans le corps du rapport. Ainsi, il entendait donner au «sinistre» et à ses remèdes l'importance qu'ils méritaient sans entrer dans trop de détails.

Les prises de position abondent dans les allocutions présidentielles. Le Président de *Philip Morris*, dans son allocution pour l'exercice 1969, a consacré par exemple huit alinéas à montrer la position des fabricants de cigarettes face aux problèmes de santé des fumeurs.

Par ailleurs, on ne mentionnera dans l'allocution que le nom des nouveaux administrateurs, ceux des nouveaux membres de la Direction figurant globalement à la page prévue à cet effet.

Pour éviter toute confusion, il importe de dater l'allocution du jour où le manuscrit part à l'impression, aucune modification ne devant intervenir après cette date tant dans son texte que dans celui du rapport annuel. Bien entendu, ce message évoquera également tous les événements importants intervenus entre le jour de la clôture de l'exercice et la date du dernier bon à tirer.

Une signature étant en règle générale peu lisible, on fera figurer au-dessous de celle-ci, le nom et la qualité de l'auteur du message.

Plus cette allocution sera brève, plus elle aura de chances d'être lue en entier, et par un grand nombre de lecteurs. Les sondages d'opinion recommandent de limiter la longueur du message à deux pages au maximum. La photographie du signataire devrait figurer, car elle constitue un attrait non négligeable.

Exposés spéciaux

Ceux-ci ne sont pas coutumier, mais il ne faut pas hésiter à les évoquer (rachats, recherches, marchés spéciaux, etc...) si on le juge nécessaire. Le rapport pour 1968 de *Time Inc*. a consacré 28 pages au démarchage publicitaire sous le titre : «La Publicité-presse : comment la vendre». On y trouvait des commentaires très directs sur ce problème-clé, avec de saisissantes photographies en noir et blanc des représentants les plus valables des 350 courtiers en publicité qu'occupe l'entreprise. C'était là, au fond, une excellente carte de visite qui dut profiter l'année suivante à ces mêmes démarcheurs que l'on présentait sous un jour très vivant et très humain.

Questions et réponses

Un nombre croissant de rapports annuels comportent une section de questions et réponses (Q & R) sous une forme évidemment variable. Depuis plus d'une décennie, la *Gillette Co*. est fidèle à sa Q & R, tandis que *General Electric* a inclus dans son rapport nouveau style pour 1969, au format d'une revue trimestrielle, un courrier des actionnaires intitulé «Les actionnaires nous posent des questions». On y trouve, à l'usage de tous les actionnaires, les réponses à diverses questions posées soit par lettres, soit lors d'assemblées générales, soit par des analystes financiers désireux de démonter les mécanismes de la société. La Q & R présente des avantages évidents. Elle va droit à l'essentiel. Le rapport d'*Olin* pour 1968 donnait une réponse raisonnable à la question incisive : «Est-ce que les profits vont être cassés net par la fin des hostilités au Vietnam ?» Une Q & R est facile à éplucher, chaque question faisant fonction d'un sous-titre et point de repère pour l'actionnaire pressé d'en venir à ce qui l'intéresse. La Q & R est aussi un moyen de donner vie à la personnalité du directeur qui rédige la réponse. Dans le rapport de *Scovill* pour 1965, le président de la société, Malcolm Baldridge, ne mâchait pas ses mots en déclarant au sujet des perspectives d'avenir dont s'inquiétait un actionnaire : «Quand je passe en revue les choix possibles, j'ai parfois l'impression d'être un chien aveugle dans une boucherie, ne sachant plus quelle route prendre parmi tant d'alléchantes.»

Rapport sur les activités

Le rapport proprement dit, très fouillé dans le cas d'une petite ou moyenne entreprise dont l'organisation est simple, devra, pour un groupe industriel aux multiples ramifications, se limiter à l'exposé des faits saillants. En règle générale, le rapport de gestion rend compte par le détail de ce que la société a accompli l'année précédente dans le domaine de ses fabrications, des nouveaux marchés, de ses ventes et des bénéfices, en commentant les résultats et précisant comment ils ont été obtenus. Sont également exposés les investissements en capital et les perspectives de développement pour l'exercice en cours.

Ce chapitre est hélas trop souvent bourré de détails opérationnels inutiles et rédigé en un jargon technique rébarbatif, alors que l'actionnaire désire tout simplement connaître les faits et les tendances qui influenceront les bénéfices qu'il entend retirer de ses actions au cours des années à venir.

Aperçu financier

Les sociétés consacrent de plus en plus une large place à la présentation de leur rapport et à l'analyse des comptes. C'est que ce chapitre important répond aux exigences des actionnaires qui veulent être mieux renseignés. Il regroupe sous une forme aérée les données qui ne trouvent pas leur place dans l'allocution du Président.

L'analyse des comptes intéresse aussi le spécialiste financier et les autres professionnels de l'investissement. Elle facilite leur travail en les renseignant sur le pourquoi du résultat net. Pourquoi les bénéfices ont-ils augmenté? Pourquoi les capitaux investis sont-ils en baisse? Pourquoi les impôts n'ont-ils pas été acquittés dans leur totalité?, etc... Elle leur évite ainsi toutes recherches fastidieuses.

Quant aux données à incorporer dans l'analyse des comptes, elles peuvent varier d'une entreprise à l'autre, mais comprennent généralement: le chiffre d'affaires brut, le résultat brut, le cash flow, les capitaux étrangers, les actifs immobilisés, les dividendes, les dettes à long terme, les capitaux propres, le rendement des capitaux investis, les valeurs réalisables à court terme, les charges fixes, en particulier les dépenses et charges salariales, etc...

Présentation du bilan

Par nécessité, la forme du bilan varie peu. On y trouve généralement le résultat brut, le bénéfice non distribué, la balance des soldes des comptes d'actifs et de passifs, un bilan résumé d'inventaire, l'origine et l'emploi du capital de l'entreprise.

Les notes en bas de page

Comme nous l'avons vu au chapitre deux, la présentation de ces notes qui complètent utilement le rapport financier, mais sont difficilement lisibles, est en train d'évoluer. Le Gouvernement a proposé qu'elles soient composées dans un caractère plus gros, ce qui permettra une meilleure lecture mais augmentera sensiblement la surface imprimée. Cela aurait évidemment pour effet de grossir encore le volume du rapport annuel, mais l'avantage serait indéniable. Une autre tendance très appréciée et plus souhaitable consiste à incorporer ces notes tout simplement dans le chapitre financier lui-même, ce qui le rendrait plus homogène et plus complet.

Rapport des commissaires aux comptes

Ce rapport, exigé par la loi, certifie qu'un commissaire aux comptes agréé par l'Etat — donc indépendant — a examiné tous les comptes et éléments financiers de la société, et en trouve la présentation correcte et conforme aux usages comptables de la profession. Le commissaire aux comptes a le droit absolu, pour dégager sa responsabilité, de signaler dans son rapport son désaccord avec telle ou telle interprétation ou indication du rapport financier présenté par le Président. Le rapport du commissaire aux comptes vient en principe toujours après le rapport financier. Ajoutons que le nom du commissaire aux comptes devrait être reproduit en caractères d'imprimerie plutôt que sous forme de signature car cette coutume ancienne peut causer certaines difficultés.

La statistique financière quinquennale ou décennale

D'autres renseignements, bien que facultatifs, figurent de plus en plus souvent en fin de rapport. Il s'agit de la présentation résumée des principaux chiffres des dix derniers exercices. Toutefois, cette présentation est fréquemment réduite à cinq ans.

Il existe plusieurs manières de présenter ces chiffres. En voici une qui a fait ses preuves: sont cités en tête les résultats bruts, puis les données des bilans successifs. On indique ensuite les chiffres rapportés à l'action (rendement net, dividendes en espèces, valeur comptable, etc...). Puis d'autres données telles que le cash flow, le nombre d'actionnaires et les effectifs. Il sera également très utile pour l'analyste financier de trouver parmi celles-ci l'évolution du cours des actions durant les cinq ou dix années écoulées et un certain nombre de ratios: capitalisation/dettes à long terme et bénéfice net/capitaux propres.

Composition du Conseil et de la Direction

Les membres du Conseil d'Administration et de la Direction figurent nommément en dernière page ou en troisième page de couverture. Il est utile de faire état de tous les titres et fonctions des administrateurs, ceci afin de bien donner à entendre que le Conseil comprend surtout des personnalités en pleine activité, donc capables de rendre à la société le maximum de services.

Renseignements généraux

Ce chapitre du rapport annuel donne toutes sortes de renseignements et adresses utiles à l'usage des différentes catégories de lecteurs: siège social (adresse et numéros de téléphone), nom du responsable de l'information, lieu, date et heure de l'Assemblée Générale, nom et adresse du Banquier de la société, nom et adresse du commissaire aux comptes, nom et adresse des avocats et conseils de la société, Bourse où sont cotées les actions de la société. *Indian Head* indique même le nombre d'actionnaires ou obligataires par catégorie.

Un tableau des marques déposées de l'entreprise est un renseignement général utile qui dispense de faire figurer derrière chaque nom de produit déposé le symbole de protection. Le rapport d'Olin pour 1970 résout le problème en déclarant: «Les noms de produits imprimés en italiques sont des marques déposées de l'*Olin Corporation*.»

On trouve de plus en plus, au chapitre des renseignements généraux, mention du designer et du photographe, en particulier lorsqu'il s'agit d'artistes en renom, ce qui ajoute au prestige de l'entreprise, tout en rendant un hommage mérité aux responsables de la présentation du rapport.

Structure de l'entreprise

Un tableau détaillé de la structure de l'entreprise a son utilité lorsque l'organigramme n'est pas trop complexe et que sa présentation peut tenir en une double page. On y énumère les principaux départements et leurs produits-clés, avec si possible les noms de leurs directeurs respectifs et toutes autres indications professionnelles pouvant faciliter leur approche.

La quatrième page de couverture

Certaines entreprises affectionnent les belles photos décoratives en dernière page de couverture. Toutefois, le meilleur usage qu'on puisse faire de cette page, est d'y imprimer la raison sociale et le siège social. Les principaux intéressés ont tant de rapports entre les mains qu'ils apprécient de pouvoir les identifier de l'extérieur, au recto comme au verso.

La production du rapport annuel

«Pour un spécialiste de l'édition, le rapport annuel se présente trop souvent comme un travail d'amateur et est certainement l'une des tâches dont les dirigeants de l'entreprise s'acquittent le plus mal.» C'est le directeur des relations publiques d'un groupe aux multiples ramifications qui parle. A qui la faute? Aux dirigeants eux-mêmes et à leur mentalité particulière. «Les cadres supérieurs sont infatués de beau langage pompeux», nous confie un autre responsable; «le résultat en est un monument de verbalisme creux. L'emphase et la vanité s'y ramassent à la pelle, mais d'information, de détail, point.» Autre obstacle majeur quant au contenu du rapport annuel: la diversité d'opinions au sein de la direction générale. «Faire accepter le rapport annuel au comité de direction d'une grande entreprise équivaut à livrer un combat sanglant où tout le monde laisse des plumes», assure un vétéran de la question. Qui pis est, le résultat ne satisfait trop souvent personne, et on voit les membres de la direction bouder leur propre création.

Pourquoi un rapport annuel qui est le fruit de tant d'efforts finit-il par sombrer dans l'indifférence et faire regretter le temps passé et l'argent dépensé? Il y a à cela un certain nombre de raisons; voici les plus fréquentes:

1° Le directeur général n'estime pas utile que la confection du rapport soit confiée à un de ses proches collaborateurs. Faute de jouir de la confiance du patron, le rédacteur du rapport est en butte à toutes les vexations imaginables de la part de personnes plus haut placées, aux idées contradictoires.

2° Le directeur général n'intervient pas dans la rédaction du rapport dès la première ébauche, alors qu'il pourrait donner une orientation décisive au document. Par contre, il multiplie les modifications hâtives et souvent pas assez réfléchies lorsque les textes sont prêts à partir à l'impression.

3° L'auteur du rapport n'achève pas son premier projet dans les délais prescrits, et la direction générale n'a pas le temps matériel d'examiner le texte à la loupe.

4° La rédaction est prête à temps, mais le directeur général et ses proches collaborateurs en remettent la lecture jusqu'à ce qu'il soit pratiquement trop tard.

5° La comptabilité n'établit pas à temps les comptes définitifs et surtout le consolidé, et la rédaction du rapport s'achève dans une précipitation extrême, préjudiciable à sa cohérence et à son impact.

6° Au stade des premières épreuves et de la maquette, toute une série de personnes, avocats-conseils, administrateurs, vice-présidents, peut-être même la femme du P.D.G., se mettent à proposer diverses additions et modifications en contradiction avec l'esprit du rapport annuel et la conception initiale.

7° Le directeur général s'inquiète au dernier moment, surtout en raison de ces critiques. Le thème choisi est alors remis en cause, le texte récrit à la hâte

et publié tant bien que mal, plutôt mal que bien, l'échéance arrivée. Fruit d'un compromis, le rapport annuel est alors d'une inévitable médiocrité.

La plupart de ces problèmes ne se poseraient même pas si l'on admettait au départ qu'un rapport annuel ne peut exprimer que la pensée d'un seul homme: le Président-Directeur-Général. Celui-ci doit s'intéresser au projet de très près, dès le début, et en charger une personne en qui il a une confiance absolue et qu'il est prêt à soutenir contre vents et marées. Cette personne, c'est de plus en plus un type nouveau de responsable doté de pouvoirs étendus et ayant souvent le titre de Vice-Président chargé des relations extérieures. D'après l'enquête réalisée par GRAPHIS, le rapport annuel est du ressort du directeur des relations extérieures dans 75% des cas, de celui du vice-président responsable des finances dans 17% des entreprises. Enfin, dans 8% des cas, les rapports annuels sont rédigés par le secrétaire général de la société.

Il est parfois préférable de faire appel à un conseiller étranger à l'entreprise, dont l'expérience peut compléter utilement celle du responsable. Les agences publicitaires ne montrent pas beaucoup d'empressement à accepter une semblable tâche car il s'agit d'un travail laborieux, comportant beaucoup de détails et qui n'enrichit pas son auteur. Entreprise peu rentable donc, et de surcroît un peu dangereuse pour une agence tenant à conserver ses clients. Or, nous avons vu les oppositions et les heurts que peut susciter la rédaction d'un rapport.

Si le projet est mis entre les mains d'un homme averti, jouissant de l'entière confiance du P.D.G., la marche à suivre pour la préparation d'un rapport annuel réussi est tout indiquée.

Plan et délais

Dans une grande société, il faut compter de six à sept mois entre la mise en route du rapport annuel et sa diffusion. Pour une entreprise dont l'année fiscale se termine le 31 décembre, on devrait commencer à penser au rapport en septembre en vue de le sortir en mars. Certains éléments peuvent même être recueillis bien avant, les illustrations par exemple. Ce sont souvent en effet des photographies prises l'été, surtout pour les extérieurs, qui expriment le mieux l'image que l'entreprise entend donner d'elle-même et de ses activités.

La prévision des délais doit être complète et réaliste. Le planning de production illustrant ce chapitre (p. 77/78) renferme les éléments essentiels sur lesquels doit porter cette prévision. Un rapport annuel peut et devrait être réalisé à la manière d'un journal ou magazine, en deux temps: les opérations de préparation normale et les opérations de dernière heure, celles-ci risquant parfois de bousculer celles-là.

La date qui détermine celle du tirage est le jour où les comptables remettent le bilan. Préalablement, la majeure partie des éléments créateurs (illustrations, graphiques, maquette) de même que les textes auront été préparés. Passé cette date, il faut mettre rapidement au point les chapitres correspondant à ce travail de «dernière heure»: présentation et analyse des comptes, allocution du président, rapport des commissaires aux comptes. Enfin, on reverra rapidement l'ensemble de la maquette pour s'assurer de son harmonie définitive. A ce moment-là, chaque demi-journée compte et les difficultés fréquemment éprouvées pour obtenir à temps les données financières dûment contrôlées doivent être surmontées coûte que coûte. Faut-il rappeler que toute modification intervenant à un stade avancé se traduit par des heures supplémentaires au studio et à l'imprimerie avec toutes les augmentations de prix en découlant.

La date limite de publication d'un rapport annuel est fixée par la Bourse, 90 jours après la fin de l'année fiscale pour les sociétés cotées à la Bourse de New York, 120 jours pour celles qui sont cotées à l'American Stock Exchange. Les sociétés non inscrites à la cote ont intérêt à publier leur rapport dans les 120 jours. Une société cotée qui n'arrive pas à assurer la publication de son rapport à la date prévue doit présenter une demande de prolongation à la direction de la Bourse, ce qui lui vaut un certain discrédit et une réputation de mauvaise gestion. La date limite de publication doit donc être considérée comme irrévocable et en cas de retard interne, il convient de simplifier la présentation pour le rattraper afin, quoi qu'il arrive et quoi qu'il en coûte, de sortir dans les délais.

Lors de l'élaboration des prévisions de délais, il importe de tenir compte des vacances d'hiver des dirigeants de l'entreprise. En effet, on a vu souvent une société adresser aux Bahamas le texte définitif du rapport annuel pour ultime relecture afin que puissent être respectés les délais d'impression.

Le plan du rapport est indépendant des prévisions dans le temps. Il est établi sur la base d'objectifs déterminés après enquête au sein et à l'extérieur de l'entreprise: auprès des cadres dirigeants partageant les vues d'ensemble du Président, mais aussi auprès d'analystes financiers connaissant l'entreprise et le secteur industriel auquel elle appartient.

Les objectifs énumérés dans le plan doivent être conformes à trois orientations fondamentales de la politique de communication: rappeler en l'explicitant l'ampleur et la puissance de l'entreprise, dissiper toutes interprétations erronées la concernant, donner des informations encore inédites.

Les objectifs fixés constituent souvent un thème, un but idéal vers lequel peuvent converger les activités de l'entreprise. Un tel thème donne son unité au message et accroît l'effet que celui-ci produit sur le lecteur. Il fournit aussi le cadre des illustrations et du texte et trace en quelque sorte une ligne de défense contre ceux qui, souvent sans raison, veulent sans cesse tout changer.

Une fois le plan et les objectifs précisés, un feutre d'ensemble prévoyant déjà le nombre de pages idéal et l'importance respective des chapitres avec emplacement souhaité des illustrations est présenté au Président au cours du mois de septembre. Ce premier avant-projet détaillé, qui représente un grand effort intellectuel, porte toujours ses fruits. En effet, les décisions prises par le Président au vu de ce document constituent une base de travail qui, dans une entreprise bien gérée, demeurera inchangée dans ses grandes lignes, quoiqu'il advienne. Bien sûr, le Président modifiera ce plan détaillé. Peut-être même le remaniera-t-il de fond en comble. Qu'importe, une fois ses décisions connues, on pourra vraiment s'attaquer au projet définitif avec l'assurance que le Président le défendra contre toutes interventions de dernière heure de ses pairs ou de ses proches collaborateurs.

Illustrations, design et textes

Le travail simultané sur ces trois plans occupe raisonnablement un trimestre entier. Pour la maquette, les sociétés ont recours à un designer auquel elles laissent le soin de s'assurer les services d'un photographe, la tendance étant au photographe unique, qui, ayant une vue d'ensemble du projet, peut donner à son reportage une unité de bon aloi. A noter aussi que le fait de prendre un seul photographe, surtout lorsque son travail est bien préparé préalablement, permet une réelle économie.

En effet, faute d'un planning précis et d'une bonne préparation des prises de vues, le reportage risque de décevoir et des sommes importantes d'être dépensées inutilement. Le photographe ne doit donc pas partir à l'aveuglette faire le tour du monde ou des Etats-Unis. Il faut l'orienter, lui fournir sur place tout ce dont il a besoin. Au tarif journalier de 500 à 600 dollars, on imagine l'argent que perd une société en condamnant à l'oisiveté un photographe incomplètement informé ou privé de guide.

Un problème se pose souvent au dernier moment: faut-il ou non obtenir l'autorisation des personnes dont la photographie est publiée dans le rapport annuel? Il est évidemment plus sage de le faire, et le photographe y veillera. Toutefois, comme l'a indiqué un groupe d'avocats newyorkais qui s'est penché sur la question en 1969, il n'y a jamais eu d'action intentée à ce sujet. De toute façon, il serait difficile d'obtenir des dommages-intérêts vu que la publication du rapport annuel ne sert pas à des fins commerciales, et ne peut à priori léser ceux dont la photographie y figure.

Le vrai travail du designer commence à la réception des photographies. Au préalable, il a réparti l'espace disponible et mis au point une première maquette. Dans notre exemple, le photographe reçoit ses instructions le 25 septembre et livre ses photos le 16 novembre. Le designer se met à l'œuvre et sélectionne les meilleures illustrations, tant pour l'intérieur que pour la couverture.

Entre-temps, le rédacteur désigné aura interrogé chacun des vice-présidents responsables d'une grande division opérationnelle sur les points suivants:
• Résultats obtenus au cours de l'exercice en terme de chiffre d'affaires et des profits. Facteurs essentiels de cette réussite.
• Investissements de l'année, investissements envisagés pour l'an prochain, incidence escomptée de ceux-ci sur les futurs profits.
• Fabrications ou services nouveaux en cours d'année. Qu'envisage-t-on pour le prochain exercice?
• Tendances sociales ou économiques susceptibles de bien ou de moins bien influencer l'évolution de la situation actuelle.

Ces renseignements permettent une première rédaction qui est soumise à l'appréciation de chaque vice-président mais seulement pour la partie concernant sa division. Il faut veiller à obtenir l'accord ou les modifications de chaque vice-président dans des délais impérativement fixés, afin de commencer sans retard la rédaction d'ensemble à soumettre au Président.

Contact avec les imprimeurs

Dès avant la préparation de la maquette, on s'enquiert du coût de l'impression auprès de diverses imprimeries, sur la base des offres faites l'année précédente. L'accord du Président obtenu pour la maquette (voir ci-dessous), on passe commande ferme à un imprimeur après avis du designer, qu'il appartienne à la société ou qu'il soit indépendant, car il sera particulièrement à même d'en apprécier la qualité et le sérieux.

Il importe évidemment de ne comparer entre elles que des offres assurant la même qualité et les mêmes capacités d'impression. L'offre la moins chère peut émaner d'un imprimeur incapable de faire face à ses engagements. Une imprimerie de premier ordre peut proposer des prix élevés incluant d'expérience le travail supplémentaire de dernière heure et diverses charges spéciales. On cherchera à s'assurer les services d'un tel imprimeur avec autant d'énergie qu'on en mettra à repousser ceux qui entendraient profiter d'un éventuel manque de technicité de leurs clients.

L'appel d'offres doit préciser le délai d'impression, généralement de 9 à 15 jours ouvrables, et le situer dans le temps. D'où l'importance de mettre au point dès le début la prévision des délais et le plan général. A quoi bon payer moins, si l'imprimeur n'est pas capable de faire le travail dans le temps voulu!

On détermine l'importance du tirage en tenant compte des facteurs suivants: nombre d'actionnaires nominatifs; nombre d'actionnaires dont les actions sont déposées dans les Banques ou chez des agents de change ou des gérants de fortune; nombre d'actionnaires des entreprises absorbées; nombre des employés admis à la participation. On décidera si l'on inclut les analystes financiers dans la liste d'adresses ou si l'on préfère publier des annonces offrant le rapport à ceux qui en feront la demande. On ajoute au total ainsi obtenu le nombre d'exemplaires destinés à l'usage interne. La plupart des entreprises commandent bien souvent un nombre d'exemplaires de deux à trois fois supérieur à celui des actionnaires. C'est en effet une grave erreur, coûteuse de surcroît, de faire faire un trop faible tirage. On risque alors de payer ensuite jusqu'à cinq fois le prix des quelques milliers d'exemplaires supplémentaires. C'est pourquoi il est recommandé de faire inclure dans le devis de l'imprimeur, le prix d'un tirage supplémentaire de mille, deux mille... exemplaires.

Ajoutons que les usages de la profession — admis par les Tribunaux — permettent à l'imprimeur une passe pouvant aller jusqu'à 10% en plus ou en moins du nombre d'exemplaires commandés. Dans un cas comme dans l'autre, c'est le prix de l'exemplaire en plus qui sert de base au calcul de la majoration ou de la minoration. Dans la pratique, les bons imprimeurs sont fidèles à leur contrat en livrant la quantité convenue, et les dépassements n'atteignent pas plus de 5%. Néanmoins, des malentendus peuvent surgir si le client n'est pas au courant de cette pratique.

Présentation au Président de la maquette et des textes

La maquette soumise au Président doit être complète, c'est-à-dire, outre la couverture, comprendre les illustrations photographiques et leurs légendes, les graphiques, les titres composés des chapitres à leur vraie place indiquant ainsi l'emplacement des textes prévus. Parallèlement, tous les textes — sauf la partie de «dernière heure» — seront présentés dactylographiés. Ces textes comprendront le sommaire, la fiche d'identité de la société, le rapport d'activité ou un exposé sur un thème particulier (la recherche par exemple), tous les chiffres ne dépendant pas des dernières données comptables, la liste des administrateurs et des directeurs, etc... C'est un grand avantage que de pouvoir présenter au Président la maquette en même temps que le texte. Il se rend compte ainsi de la place réservée à l'information et de son volume et constate comment vont s'imbriquer rédaction, chiffres et illustrations. Notre exemple prévoit cette réunion avec le Président à la date du 10 décembre.

Le Président demande souvent à certains de ses proches collaborateurs de participer à cette réunion, par exemple le vice-président responsable des finances, le vice-président-directeur général adjoint. Le rôle du Président est à la fois capital et délicat, puisqu'il connaît le projet initial, auquel il a même collaboré. Il doit maintenant en défendre la conception devant ses collaborateurs directs. S'il n'y réussissait pas, l'équipe créatrice n'aurait plus qu'à se remettre au travail, et la tâche de trois mois aurait été inutile!

Impression, enveloppes, diffusion

Le climat de confusion et d'irritation dans lequel se fait souvent l'expédition du rapport annuel ne peut s'expliquer que par un manque de prévision et de planning. Parallèlement à la préparation de la maquette et du texte, il faut veiller à fournir à l'imprimeur une liste des points de distribution et à lui indiquer l'ordre dans lequel seront faites les expéditions.

Les enveloppes ne paraissent pas poser de problème. En réalité, leur oubli ou leur livraison tardive sont souvent cause de gros soucis. Pourtant, il suffit de choisir un papier, une présentation et un imprimeur. Si le rapport annuel est entre les mains d'un designer expert, il apparentera la présentation de l'enveloppe à celle du rapport, de manière à accrocher l'attention. L'entreprise chargée de l'expédition doit être en possession des enveloppes imprimées au plus tard deux semaines avant réception des rapports, ce qui permet de les faire passer à l'adressographe.

Un nombre croissant d'entreprises renoncent à l'enveloppe en utilisant un rapport pouvant être expédié «tel quel». L'avantage est évident: l'actionnaire n'a plus besoin d'extraire le rapport de son enveloppe et ne peut donc l'ignorer. L'absence d'enveloppes peut aussi être interprétée comme un souci d'économie, particulièrement bienvenu lorsque les budgets publicitaires ou autres de l'entreprise sont sujets à critique.

Le choix des enveloppes et la prévision des délais d'expédition sont influencés par le mode d'envoi, lettre ou imprimé. Les tarifs postaux sont en augmentation constante, et la différence entre les tarifs lettres et imprimés peut atteindre 20 à 40 cents par rapport, soit 2000 à 4000 dollars pour 10000 exemplaires. Pourtant, il faut parfois utiliser le tarif lettres pour rattraper le retard des comptables lors de la préparation du bilan. Au tarif des imprimés, l'expédition devrait être achevée six semaines et à l'extrême rigueur, cinq semaines avant l'assemblée générale.

Remise des diapositives couleurs à l'imprimeur

Dès que la maquette a été approuvée par le directeur général, les ozalides sont remis à l'imprimeur pour sélection. La qualité de la reproduction ne sera assurée que si on lui laisse le temps matériel de mener à bien cette sélection et les corrections consécutives. Les imprimeurs établis dans la région de New York demandent un minimum de trois semaines pour les opérations de sélection, plus quinze jours pour les modifications éventuelles, ce qui fait cinq semaines en tout.

Sections rédactionnelles avancées; composition et maquette d'impression

La composition des premiers chapitres et la préparation du bon à tirer devraient se faire sans accrocs, puisque le texte a été vu par tous les responsables et conçu indépendamment des informations financières de dernière heure.

C'est à ce moment également que l'on devrait passer commande de la couverture à l'imprimeur, travail indépendant de l'impression du rapport proprement dit et qui peut être fait à l'avance. Ceci implique évidemment que l'on renonce à faire figurer les chiffres-clé du bilan en deuxième page de couverture. Dans la négative, la réalisation de la couverture devrait être repoussée jusqu'à la remise des comptes définitifs.

Chapitre de «dernière heure»

Tandis que l'on commence la rédaction de cette partie du texte, qui comprend l'allocution du Président, les chiffres-clé du bilan, l'analyse de ce dernier et des comptes, et le rapport des commissaires aux comptes, le bon à tirer des premiers textes sera établi. L'allocution du Président doit être particulièrement réfléchie. Une première version devrait être fournie au Président avant la fin de l'année, si possible pour les vacances de Noël. On peut être assuré que c'est le texte auquel il attachera le plus d'attention. Il doit donc disposer du temps nécessaire à son examen. Le message sera mis à jour et complété lorsque les résultats seront connus.

Réception des éléments comptables – le projet est en voie d'achèvement

Les comptes de l'exercice devraient être donnés au rédacteur un peu avant que le projet définitif de ceux-ci, après contrôle ultime du chef comptable, parte à la frappe. De même en ce qui concerne le rapport financier – qui aura été approuvé par le vice-président responsable au lieu et place du Président – et l'allocution du Président. Il s'agira d'une frappe définitive. Toutefois, ces chapitres ne partiront en composition que lorsque le rapport des commissaires aux comptes sera lui aussi terminé et pourra leur être joint.

Rien ne devrait donc plus retarder l'imprimeur dans sa tâche, sauf le minimum de temps nécessaire à la relecture et à la correction des épreuves, à la commande des films d'épreuves de reproduction et au contrôle général du bon à tirer. Pour toutes ces opérations, deux semaines sont nécessaires. Mais quelquefois, on réussit à raccourcir ce délai.

A condition que les comptables aient fait leur travail dans les délais prévus et que tous les responsables aient approuvé le texte de façon définitive, le rapport s'achemine sans heurts vers l'impression.

Les modifications apportées au texte déjà composé, sont considérées comme «corrections d'auteur», et sont très onéreuses. En effet, les frais de composition augmentent d'année en année, et il n'est pas rare qu'une entreprise dépensant normalement 2000 dollars pour la composition de son rapport annuel voie le coût global de celui-ci augmenter de 10000 à 15000 dollars du fait des nombreux changements de dernière heure, dus à l'indécision des responsables, contraignant à la réimpression d'un certain nombre de feuillets, ce qui aurait certainement pu être évité.

C'est ici qu'apparaît clairement l'importance d'un responsable unique, placé sous l'autorité directe du Président. Dans les très grandes entreprises, ce dernier délègue souvent ses responsabilités en matière de rapport annuel à l'un de ses proches collaborateurs. Ces deux personnalités devraient se réserver l'exclusivité de toutes modifications. Car la plupart des changements introduits au dernier moment concernent le style et expriment des préférences très personnelles de tel ou tel vice-président qui n'ajoutent guère à la qualité du rapport, occasionnent des frais élevés et créent une impression disparate.

On trouve dans certaines entreprises des rédacteurs en mal de puissance qui font montre d'une véritable obsession en matière de ponctuation. S'ils s'y prennent trop tard, ils risquent de faire recomposer le texte entier pour la satisfaction de corriger des virgules et changer des signes de ponctuation qu'un autre «maniaque de l'orthographe», assumant également des responsabilités dans l'entreprise, peut fort bien rejeter ensuite en bloc. Il s'agit donc de consulter à temps tous ceux qui ont leur mot à dire dans la présentation du texte et de tenir compte des suggestions dès la version dactylographiée.

La remise d'épreuves à relire aux différents membres de la direction est une autre source inévitable d'ennuis si l'on ne limite pas strictement le nombre de personnes consultées et si l'on n'exige pas le respect absolu de la date limite au-delà de laquelle aucune observation ne sera retenue. Il est inconcevable qu'un membre de la direction attende les secondes épreuves pour remanier le texte de fond en comble, alors que celui-ci contient déjà les suggestions de ses collègues. Les conseils de la société doivent se limiter aux corrections de nature juridique, les comptables à celles des données financières, les autres membres de la direction à redresser des faits ou à suggérer des interprétations différentes. Seul le Président et son délégué devraient recevoir l'ensemble.

Remise de la maquette à l'imprimeur

Une fois ces dernières corrections intervenues, l'imprimeur prépare un ozalide par l'intermédiaire d'un film en l'espace de deux à trois jours. C'est la dernière occasion de contrôle de la mise en pages, en particulier de l'emplacement des tableaux et graphiques ainsi que des illustrations et leurs légendes.

Contrôle de l'impression

Le processus final d'impression est alors mis en route. Avec le façonnage, il faut compter de 9 à

15 jours ouvrables. Nombreux sont, hélas, les dirigeants d'entreprises qui ne conçoivent pas la nécessité d'un tel délai, car ils oublient que les bons imprimeurs ont leur carnet de commande rempli au maximum pendant les deux mois où se réalisent des rapports annuels. Il est donc sage de prévoir une marge pour faire face à tout incident imprévu sans être astreint à travailler en heures supplémentaires.

D'un autre côté, les imprimeurs sont aussi soucieux de la qualité de ce qu'ils sortent que leurs clients. Il s'ensuit qu'ils doivent consacrer le temps qu'il faut à la fabrication des clichés, à l'impression, au contrôle et au brochage, enfin à la préparation de la diffusion et à l'expédition. Toute improvisation hâtive, dans ces domaines, peut réduire à néant six ou sept mois de travail acharné.

Les responsables du bilan donnent généralement leur bon à tirer au vu des ozalids. Le designer doit vérifier sur machine la qualité de la couleur. Le responsable du rapport annuel reçoit généralement un ou deux exemplaires agrafés à la main dès que les feuilles imprimées sont sèches et prêtes à façonner, ceci à l'intention du Président. Les cent premiers exemplaires brochés sont distribués aux cadres supérieurs qui sont généralement impatients de connaître le résultat d'un labeur qui a duré six ou sept mois et a mis tous les nerfs à l'épreuve. Il appartient au responsable du rapport de s'assurer que chaque membre de la direction reçoit l'exemplaire auquel il a droit et que cet exemplaire ne comporte pas de fautes d'impression trop visibles ou la couverture brochée à l'envers, par exemple.

Livraison aux routeurs et diffusion

Les plaquettes terminées sont livrées aux routeurs qui les expédient à raison de 20 000 à 25 000 par jour si toutes les dispositions nécessaires ont été prises à temps.

Il arrive parfois qu'une erreur ait échappé au contrôle le plus minutieux. Il importe alors de déterminer s'il s'agit d'une erreur grave et, si tel est le cas, si elle peut encore être réparée avant le délai prévu pour l'expédition. Dans toute publication, les erreurs découvertes au dernier moment sont généralement les moins importantes. L'impression d'un journal n'est jamais retardée pour correction d'erreurs, à moins qu'il ne s'agisse d'une coquille ou d'une phrase susceptible de valoir un procès à la direction. Les entreprises sont toutefois assez tâtillonnes, du fait qu'elles n'ont pas une grande expérience de l'édition, et on voit des directeurs généraux s'affoler à la découverte de coquilles insignifiantes, alors qu'ils ne devraient s'alarmer que de chiffres mal placés.

L'exactitude reste évidemment l'un des objectifs essentiels du rapport annuel à tous les stades de sa réalisation. Mais lorsque le projet entre dans sa phase d'achèvement, il vaut mieux ignorer les erreurs de détail. Une entreprise qui avait relevé une virgule mal placée dans l'indication du siège social, sur la couverture en couleurs, fit réimprimer celle-ci à grands frais, solution évidemment discutable! On recommande dans des cas similaires d'insérer dans le rapport un petit papillon à la page deux de couverture ou a telle autre page nécessaire, sur laquelle la rectification sera évoquée.

Un rapport même parfait à tous points de vue n'est pas toujours apprécié dès sa publication, le président et les autres membres de la direction désirant connaître d'abord la réaction de leurs amis, de leurs associés et d'analystes et banquiers importants avant de formuler leur jugement. Le responsable de la publication se trouve désarmé devant ces atermoiements. Force lui est de les accepter. Il peut toutefois occuper cette attente, qui peut durer plusieurs semaines, à réunir l'équipe créatrice pour un échange de vues critique. Le designer, le rédacteur et les autres responsables pourront exposer leurs idées quant aux erreurs commises, aux résultats acquis et à la leçon à retenir pour le rapport de l'année à venir.

Etant donné la nature du sujet et le délai enfin très large pour cette prise de conscience, il y a intérêt à la situer dans le cadre d'un très bon restaurant, un vendredi soir, alors que l'on sera certain de ne pas devoir retourner au bureau pour un travail urgent.

Plann

Veuillez ouvrir

Le pla
s'est avé
préparati
délais im
ning se c
les lignes
les cercle
Lorsqu'u
on rempli
feutre co
tion suiva
avant qu
Tous les
datés et
logique,
le temps
annuel. [
les délais

Les ba
principale
ration d'u
productio
suivi des
rations re
l'expéditi
rieure. La
inférieure

Ce sys
d'œil l'ét
le nombr
cles vide
tableau d
combant
l'équipe.

Le gra
version s
l'auteur
réseau d'
agrandi
mettant
détaillées

The Cover

Der Umschlag

La couverture

Covers/Umschläge
Couvertures

DESIGNER:

1–5: Paul Rand
6: Robert S. Nemser
7: Dale K. Johnston
8: Saul Bass & Associates

PHOTOGRAPHER:

1: Arthur d'Arazien
2, 3, 5: Erich Hartmann
4: Cornell Capa
6: Allen Vogel
7: William Garnett
8: Max Yavno

ART DIRECTOR:

1–5: Paul Rand
6: Robert S. Nemser
7: Richard D. Frybarger

STUDIO – AGENCY:

6: Corporate Annual Reports, Inc.
8: Saul Bass & Associates

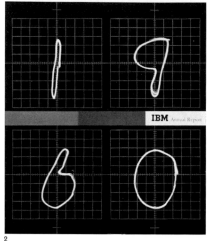

1–5: Covers for annual reports of *International Business Machines Corporation,* one of the most influential style-setters of modern annual report design. 1) Magnified electronic devices are used as graphic elements. 2) The scrawled numbers 1, 9, 6 and 0 as they appear on instruments *IBM* scientists are using in the development of machines that can read handwritten characters. 3) Pattern formed by circuit modules to be fed into testing devices. 4) A burst of light being emitted by an experimental *IBM* data storage system. 5) An *IBM* sales office in Rome framed by the centuries-old Bernini fountain. (USA)
6: *The American Can Company* used a white-in-white product photo as cover subject. (USA)
7: Aerial view of a California rice field forms the design of this cover for the annual report of *Deere & Company,* makers of agricultural equipment. (USA)
8: Close-up of filled shopping bag in full color. *Hunt Foods and Industries, Inc.* (USA)

1–5: Umschläge von Berichten der *IBM,* einer Gesellschaft, die auf dem Gebiet moderner Jahres-berichtgestaltung Pionierdienste geleistet hat. 1) Vergrösserung elektronischer Anlagen. 2) So er-scheinen hingekritzelte Zahlen (1, 9, 6 und 0) auf Instrumenten für die Entwicklung eines Com-puters, der handschriftliche Zeichen lesen kann. 3) Kreisförmig angeordnete Schaltkreis-Moduln, die automatisch in die Endprüfungsanlagen gelangen. 4) Von einem Versuchs-Speichersystem ausgestrahltes Lichtbündel. 5) *IBM*-Verkaufslokal in Rom mit Bernini-Brunnen. (USA)
6: Umschlag des Jahresberichtes eines Behälterfabrikations-Konzerns. Ton-in-Ton-Photo. (USA)
7: Flugaufnahme eines kalifornischen Reisfeldes. Umschlag des Jahresberichtes für ein Unter-nehmen, das Landwirtschaftsmaschinen herstellt. (USA)
8: Nahaufnahme einer gefüllten Einkaufstasche. Mehrfarbiges Titelblatt des Jahresberichtes einer Nahrungsmittelfirma. (USA)

1–5: Couvertures de rapports annuels de l'*IBM;* leur conception et leur style ont beaucoup contribué à orienter les recherches du design contemporain en cette matière. 1) Motif obtenu par agrandisse-ment de circuits électroniques. 2) Ces formes sont celles des chiffres 1, 9, 6, 0 tels que soumis par les expérimentateurs à des modèles de machines à lire. 3) Cette structure circulaire est constituée par des modules destinés à équiper des mémoires d'ordinateur. 4) Jet de lumière émis par un dis-positif expérimental appliqué au stockage des informations. 5) A Rome, les larges baies du bureau de vente *IBM* voisinent avec une vénérable fontaine. (USA)
6: Couverture illustrant, ton sur ton, des produits d'une entreprise de conditionnement. (USA)
7: Rizière vue d'avion – frontispice du rapport d'une société d'équipements agricoles. (USA)
8: Gros plan d'un sac à provision, comme emblème d'une firme de produits alimentaires. (USA)

4

5

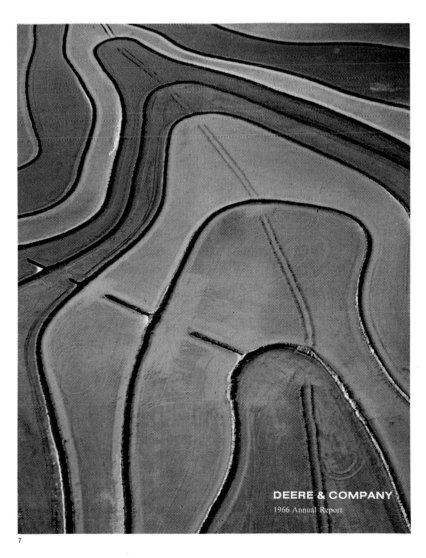

7

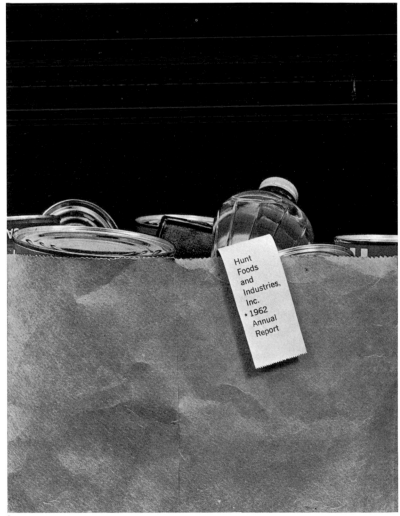

8

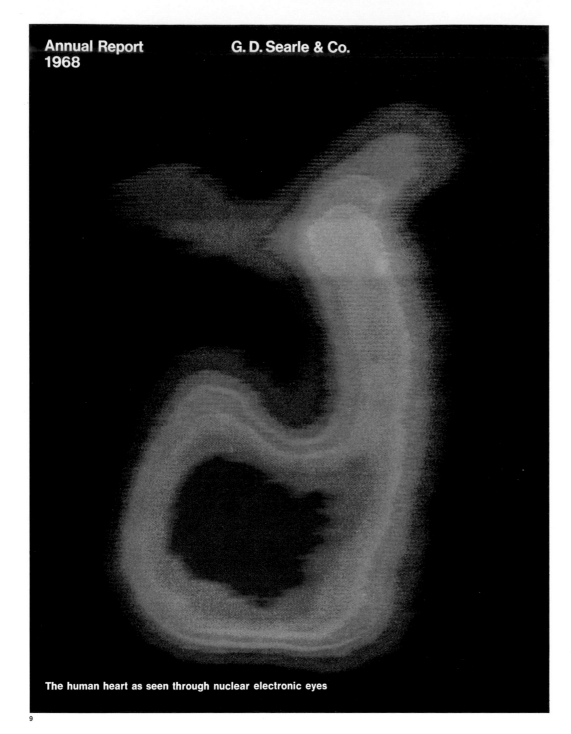

Annual Report 1968

G. D. Searle & Co.

The human heart as seen through nuclear electronic eyes

9

10

1963 Annual Report

13

United Illuminating   Annual Report 1967

16

DESIGNER:

9: W. Wayne Webb
10: Schechter & Luth, Inc.
11: William Field/John Lees
12: Rudi Wolff
13: George Tscherny
14: Irwin Goldberg
15: Ken Parkhurst
16: Roger Cook/Don Shanosky
17: Robert Nemser
18: Herman and Lees

PHOTOGRAPHER:

9: Evan Evans
10: William E. Cornelia
11: John Hill
12: Rudi Wolff
14: Henry Sandebank
15: Todd Walker
16: JonPaul Photography
17: Simpson Kalisher
18: Ted Polumbaum

ART DIRECTOR:

9: W. Wayne Webb
10: Norman Rosfeld/Herbick & Held Printing Co.
11: William Field
13: George Tscherny
14: Irwin Goldberg
15: Robert L. Steinle
16: Roger Cook/Don Shanosky
17: Robert Nemser
18: S. Herman

STUDIO – AGENCY:

9: Robert Vogele, Inc.
10: Town Studios
11: Herman, Lees Associates
12: Rudi Wolff, Inc.
13: George Tscherny, Inc.
14: Nadler & Larimer
15: Advertising Designers Inc.
16: Cook and Shanosky Associates, Inc.
17: Corporate Annual Reports, Inc.
18: Herman and Lees

POLAROID Annual Report 1966

11

International Basic Economy Corporation
1968 Annual Report

12

Continental Can Company, Inc.
Annual Report 1966

14

Monterey Oil Company annual report 1956

15

9: Gamma-ray photograph of the human heart symbolizing *G.D.Searle & Co.'s* research in the service of mankind. (USA)
10: The globe in the trademark implies that *H.J.Heinz Company* is a worldwide enterprise. Full color on white. (USA)
11: A research technician in the stereoscopic cage, a test area used in *Polaroid Corporation's* continuing investigation of three-dimensional phenomena. Full color. (USA)
12: The *International Basic Economy Corporation* initiates and operates corporate ventures responsive to basic human needs and the economies of developing nations. (USA)
13: *Burlington Industries, Inc.,* a leading producer of textiles, shows the firm's name in green on blue fabric. (USA)
14: Paper, plastic and metal, basic packaging materials, take the form of *Continental Can Company's* trademark. (USA)
15: Cover for a report of the *Monterey Oil Company.* (USA)
16: The extensive construction program of *United Illuminating,* aimed at meeting tomorrow's demands for electricity, inspired this photographic cover design. (USA)
17: Meshing gears—symbol of *Condec Corporation's* application of advanced technologies to achieve growth. (USA)
18: Wide-angle photo of a power station being built by a new subsidiary of the *Raytheon Company.* (USA)

9: Von Gamma-Strahlen durchleuchtetes Herz als Symbol für die im Dienst der Menschheit geleisteten Forschungsarbeiten eines pharmazeutischen Unternehmens. (USA)
10: Welt mit Firmenzeichen zur Illustration der weltweiten Verbreitung der *Heinz*-Produkte. Mehrfarbig. (USA)
11: Aufnahme einer Laborantin der *Polaroid* in einem experimentellen stereoskopischen Raum. Mehrfarbig. (USA)
12: Jahresbericht eines Wirtschafts- und Sozialhilfswerks für Gemeinschaftsaktionen in Entwicklungsländern. (USA)
13: Mit Grün in blauen Stoff eingewobener Firmenname einer Textilfabrik. (USA)
14: Darstellung der Initialen «C» einer Verpackungsfirma in Karton, Plastik und Metall, den meistgebrauchten Verpackungsmaterialien. (USA)
15: Umschlag des Jahresberichtes einer Ölgesellschaft. (USA)
16: Das Titelbild symbolisiert das ausgedehnte, den zukünftigen Anforderungen angepasste Konstruktionsprogramm. Jahresbericht einer Stromversorgungsgesellschaft. (USA)
17: Ineinandergreifende Zahnräder illustrieren das auf moderner Technik gründende Wachstum einer Maschinenfabrik. (USA)
18: Ein mit einem Weitwinkelobjektiv aufgenommenes Elektrizitätswerk im Bau. (USA)

9: Photo aux rayons gamma d'un cœur, symbolisant l'œuvre de recherche d'une société pharmaceutique. (USA)
10: La mappemonde superposée à la marque de la société *Heinz* en évoque l'envergure mondiale. Polychrome. (USA)
11: Rapport d'une société d'instruments d'optique: Une technicienne dans une «cage stéréoscopique» servant à l'étude des phénomènes de vision en trois dimensions. (USA)
12: Couverture du rapport annuel d'une société assurant la coordination d'actions économiques et sociales dans les pays en voie de développement. (USA)
13: Le nom de cette firme textile est tissé en vert sur fond d'étoffe bleue. (USA)
14: Trois «C» majuscules, dessinés par trois rouleaux de carton, de plastique et de métal, forment les initiales d'une société fabriquant des matériaux d'emballage. (USA)
15: Chemise du rapport d'une compagnie pétrolière. (USA)
16: Rapport annuel d'une compagnie d'électricité. (USA)
17: Ces roues dentées prêtes à s'engrener symbolisent l'effort créateur d'une société de constructions mécaniques. (USA)
18: L'objectif grand-angle a capté une image impressionnante d'un des chantiers d'une compagnie électrique. (USA)

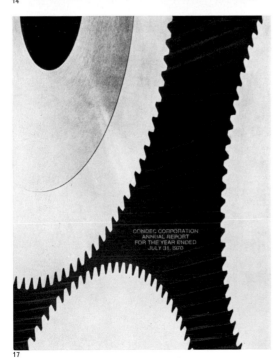

CONDEC CORPORATION
ANNUAL REPORT
FOR THE YEAR ENDED
JULY 31, 1970

17

Raytheon Annual Report 1969

18

Covers/Umschläge/Couvertures

19

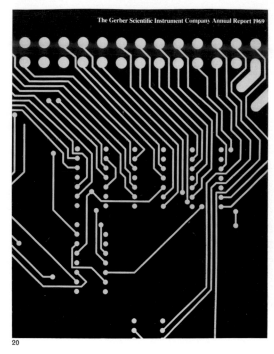

20

19: The design suggests the market *Westinghouse Electric Corporation* sees for 1971—serving the whole world. (USA)
20: The design of *The Gerber Scientific Instrument Company* report cover is based on a master used for the manufacture of printed circuit boards. Silver on black. (USA)
21: Cover for *Clairtone Sound Corporation Limited* annual report. Blue and purple on white, black lettering. (CAN)
22: Design in dark green, red, orange and black on white for the *Allen Electric and Equipment Company*. (USA)
23: Blind-embossed pattern. For *Oceanarium Inc., Marineland of the Pacific*, a giant aquarium. (USA)
24: Cover of an annual report of *Baifield Industries, Inc.* Arrows in five different colors. (USA)
25: Blind-embossed shapes representing the major markets of *Abbott Laboratories*. Lettering grey and black. (USA)
26: Embossed cover for the 1960 annual report of the *International Minerals & Chemical Corporation*. Black, brown and green on white. (USA)
27: The *VSI Corporation* embellished its report cover with a clear plastic enclosure containing rivets used for aircraft and a poker chip made with a *VSI* mold base. The box can be removed for filing purposes. (USA)
28: Cover for *John Labatt Limited*. Gray and red. (CAN)

19: «Im Dienst des Menschen» – das Umschlagsujet zeigt die neuen Marktbestrebungen von *Westinghouse*. (USA)
20: Vorlage für die Einrichtung von Drucktastensystemen als Titelbild des Berichtes einer Firma für wissenschaftliche Instrumente. Silber auf Schwarz. (USA)
21: Jahresbericht eines Herstellers von elektronischen Einichtungen. Blau und violett auf Weiss. (CAN)
22: Sujet in Dunkelgrün, Rot, Orange und Schwarz. Jahresbericht einer Firma für elektrische Anlagen. (USA)
23: Blindgeprägter Umschlag des Jahresberichtes über den Betrieb eines Riesenaquariums an der Pazifik-Küste. (USA)
24: Titelbild für den Jahresbericht eines Industriekonzerns. Pfeile in fünf Farben. (USA)
25: Blindgeprägte Darstellung der Absatzmärkte einer Firma für pharmazeutische Produkte. (USA)
26: Umschlag mit Prägedruck für den Jahresbericht einer chemischen Fabrik. Schwarz, braun, grün. (USA)
27: In einem an den Umschlag gehefteten Plastikbehälter finden sich zwei Nieten für den Flugzeugbau, sowie ein aus einer *VSI*-Form gegossener Poker-Chip. (USA)
28: Umschlag für den Bericht eines Unternehmens der Getränke- und Lebensmittelbranche. Grau und rot. (CAN)

19: Le sujet de cette couverture traduit la volonté d'universalité d'une grande compagnie d'électricité. (USA)
20: Le graphisme ornant la couverture de ce rapport d'une fabrique d'instruments scientifiques reproduit un schéma de montage de circuits électroniques. (USA)
21: Couverture du rapport d'une société d'équipements électroniques. Bleu et violet sur fond blanc. (CAN)
22: Ce quadruple diagramme (vert, rouge, orange et noir) sert d'emblème à une société d'appareillage électrique. (USA)
23: Décor gaufré de la couverture d'un rapport publié par l'administration d'un aquarium géant. (USA)
24: Les cinq doigts de cette main émettent autant de flèches multicolores. D'une société industrielle. (USA)
25: Figuration en relief des principales branches de production d'une société pharmaceutique. (USA)
26: Couverture du rapport 1960 d'une société minérale et chimique. Motifs gaufrés. (USA)
27: Le boîtier et son contenu (rivets et jeton de poker moulé dans une forme *VSI*) sont réels. Encastré dans la couverture, cet ornement protubérant est amovible. (USA)
28: Rapport de *John Labatt Limitée*. Gris et rouge. (CAN)

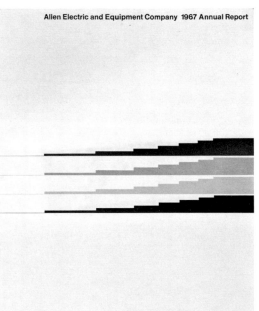

22

23

26

27

Clairtone Sound Corporation Limited
Annual Report/1966

clairtone

21

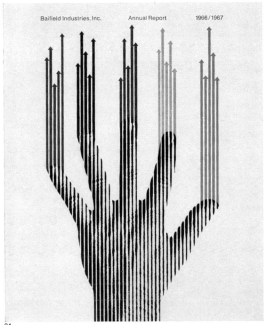

Baifield Industries, Inc.   Annual Report   1966/1967

24

Abbott Laboratories   Annual Report 1963

25

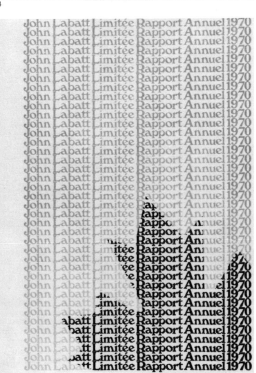

28

ART DIRECTOR:

19: Paul Rand
21: Burton Kramer
22: Edward Hughes
24: Advertising Designers/Lou Frimkes
25: Charles A.Walz
26: Morton Goldsholl
27: Keith Bright
28: Al Pollock/Southam Murray Press

STUDIO – AGENCY:

20: Cook and Shanosky Associates
22: Edward Hughes Design
23: Cal Art & Associates
24: Advertising Designers, Inc.
25: Norman Perman Design
26: Morton Goldsholl Design Associates
27: Keith Bright & Associates
28: Southam Murray Press

Covers
Umschläge
Couvertures

29

30

31

32

DESIGNER:

29, 32: Roger Cook/Don Shanosky
30: Thomas Geismar
31: Dominic Arbitrio
33, 34: Sheldon Seidler

PHOTOGRAPHER:

29: Jon Silla
30: Carl Fischer
31: Arthur d'Arazien
32: Roger Cook/Don Shanosky
33, 34: Erich Hartmann (Magnum)

ART DIRECTOR:

29, 32: Roger Cook/Don Shanosky
30: Thomas Geismar
31: Dominic Arbitrio

STUDIO – AGENCY:

29, 32: Cook and Shanosky Associates
30: Chermayeff & Geismar
  Associates Inc.
31: Page, Arbitrio & Resen
33, 34: Sheldon Seidler Design

29: The cigarette being snuffed out on the cover of the *American Cancer Society's* annual report symbolizes a major achievement of 1968, when cigarette consumption declined for the first time since 1964, year of the Surgeon General's report. Black and white with red insignia. (USA)
30: Full-color photograph of yarns merging into a braid. Cover for the report of *Burlington Industries,* a major textile manufacturer. (USA)
31: Gas turbine compressor blades form the pattern on *General Electric's* cover. Full-color photograph. (USA)
32: The raw material—a log, and the manufactured product—a roll of paper, are the design elements of this cover for the *Brown Company,* a producer of paper, paper products, plywood and wood cellulose. (USA)
33, 34: A photograph of liquid crystals glowing under reflected lights illustrates a research breakthrough of major importance—electronic control of light through liquid crystals. Cover of an *RCA* annual report. (USA)

29: Das Titelbild des Jahresberichtes der amerikanischen Liga für Krebs-bekämpfung symbolisiert den Erfolg – den Rückgang des Zigarettenkon-sums –, den der Bericht des Gesundheitsministeriums über die Zusammen-hänge zwischen Zigarettenrauchen und Lungenkrebs zeitigte. (USA)
30: Aufnahme farbiger Wollgarnfäden, die zu einem Zopf geflochten werden. Umschlag des Jahresberichtes einer Textilfabrik. (USA)
31: Die mehrfarbige Illustration des Umschlags für den Jahresbericht der *General Electric* zeigt die Verdichterschaufeln einer Gasturbine. (USA)
32: Das Rohmaterial – Holz – und das Fertigprodukt – Papier – wurden als Sujets für den Jahresbericht einer Papierfabrik gewählt, die auch Sperrholz und Holzzellulose herstellt. (USA)
33, 34: Diese Lichtwiderspiegelung flüssiger Kristalle soll ein wichtiges Forschungsergebnis illustrieren – die elektronische Steuerung des Lichts durch flüssige Kristalle. Umschlag des *RCA*-Jahresberichtes. (USA)

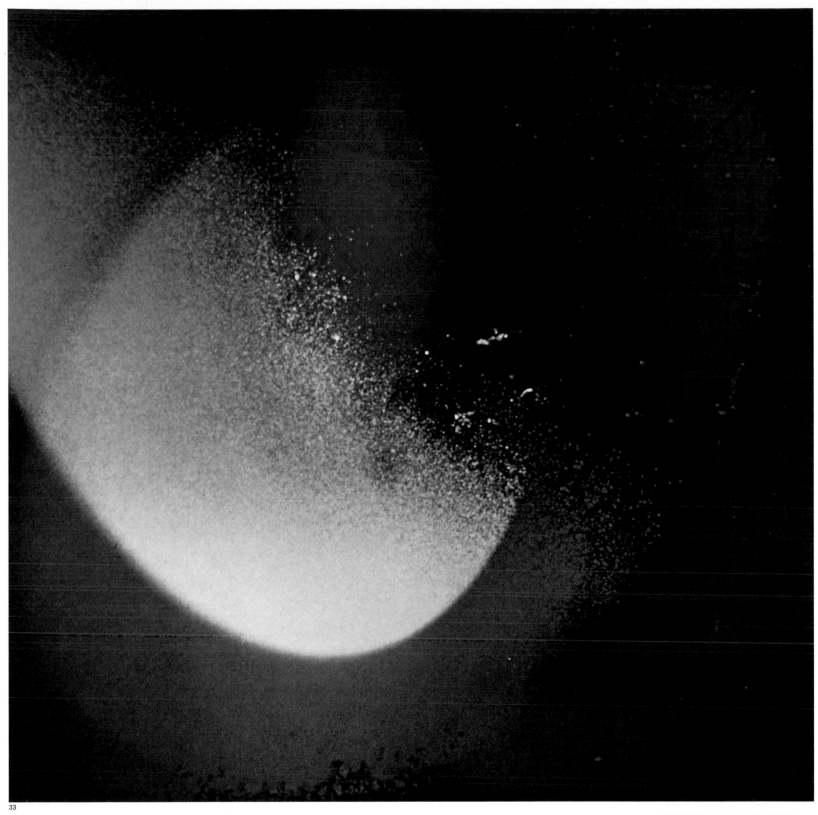

33

29: En 1969, à la suite de la publication d'une importante étude de l'autorité sanitaire sur l'étiologie du cancer du poumon, la consommation de cigarettes, jusqu'alors croissante, a significativement diminué aux Etats-Unis. C'est cet événement que célèbre, en couverture d'un rapport de la Ligue américaine contre le cancer, le geste éloquent de cette main. (USA)
30: Tressage de filés de laine. Photographie en couleurs en couverture de l'un des rapports annuels d'une grande fabrique textile. (USA)
31: Le décor graphique de ce rapport de la *General Electric* est fourni par une photographie en couleurs de l'intérieur d'une turbine à gaz. (USA)
32: Matière première (bois d'œuvre) et produit (papier-journal): ce parallèle résume l'activité d'une fabrique de papier et cellulose. (USA)
33, 34: Cristaux liquides réfléchissant un flux de lumière: cette photo en couverture d'un rapport annuel de la *RCA* illustre un important développement récent des techniques de signalisation optique. (USA)

34

35

36

DESIGNER:

35, 36: Concept
37: Peter Misteli
38: Arnold Saks/Tomas Nittner
39: Brownjohn, Chermayeff & Geismar Assoc.
40: Horst Bachmann
41: Ingo Scharrenbroich/Arnold Saks
42: J. Bradbury Thompson

ART DIRECTOR:

35, 36: Duncan McAllan
38: Arnold Saks
39: Robert Brownjohn
42: J. Bradbury Thompson

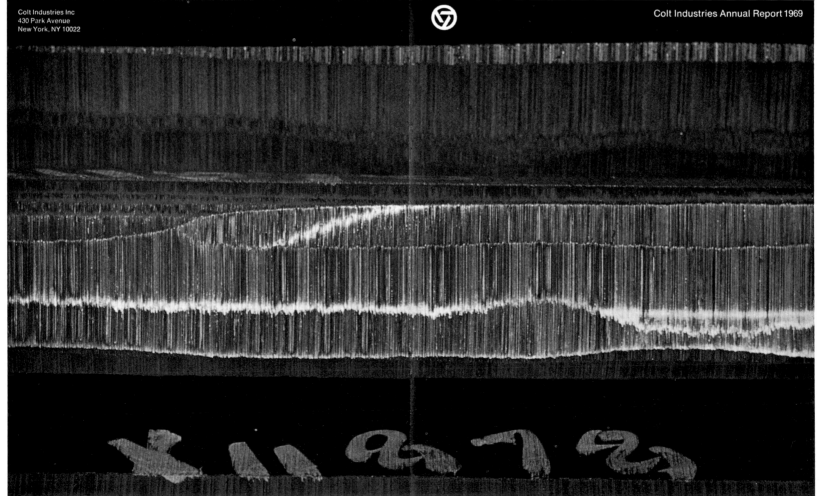

Colt Industries Inc
430 Park Avenue
New York, NY 10022

Colt Industries Annual Report 1969

38

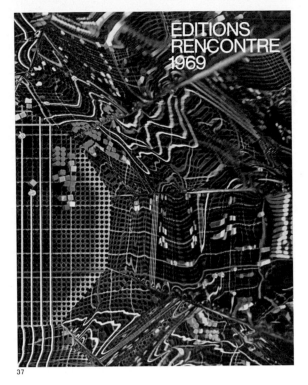

37

35, 36: Annual report cover for the *Overseas Telecommunications Commission*. (AUL)
37: A kaleidoscopic photograph of a pegboard production plan section yielded this abstract cover design for the annual report of a publishing company. Printed in full color. (SWI)
38: Close-up of stainless steel billets, which will be rolled into bars, rods and wire for a variety of uses in industry. Four-color printing. For *Colt Industries*. (USA)
39: Stacked bottle caps show increasing sales figures on the *Pepsi-Cola Company* cover. (USA)
40: Front and back of the report cover of a real estate fund. Blue background. (SWI)
41: Photo of speeding electronic "tape", reporting the latest stock exchange transactions, extends over the front and back of the *Merrill Lynch, Pierce, Fenner & Smith Inc.* report. (USA)
42: Members of the marketing organization department staff posed for the cover picture of the *West Virginia Pulp and Paper Company* annual report. Full color. (USA)

35, 36: Umschlag des Berichtes der Kommission für überseeische Fernverbindungen. (AUL)
37: Durch die kaleidoskopische Aufnahme des Produktionsplanes eines Verlags wurde ein abstraktes Muster für den Umschlag dieses Jahresberichtes erzielt. (SWI)
38: Nahaufnahme von Barren aus rostfreiem Stahl, die zu Stäben, Stangen und Draht verarbeitet werden. Für den Jahresbericht einer Maschinenfabrik. (USA)
39: Aufgetürmte *Pepsi-Cola*-Deckel zeigen die steigenden Verkaufsziffern dieser Firma. (USA)
40: Geöffneter Umschlag des Jahresberichtes der *Uto-Fonds AG*. Blauer Hintergrund. (SWI)
41: Die Aufnahme der elektronisch durchgegebenen Meldungen über die neusten Börsenkurse läuft über die Vorder- und Rückseite des Jahresberichtes eines Finanzinstituts. (USA)
42: Eine Gruppe aus dem Stab der Marktforschungsabteilung einer Papierfabrik posierte für die Aufnahme des Umschlages. Mehrfarbig. (USA)

35, 36: Couverture d'un rapport de la Commission des télécommunications d'outre-mer. (AUL)
37: Le graphisme apparemment abstrait de la couverture de ce rapport des *Editions Rencontre* n'est autre qu'une vue kaléidoscopique d'un plan de production. Photo en couleurs. (SWI)
38: Gros plan de barres d'acier inoxydable brut. Rapport d'une fabrique de machines. (USA)
39: L'ascension pyramidale de ces piles de capsules de bouteille illustre la progression des ventes d'une marque de boisson sans alcool. (USA)
40: Recto et verso du rapport d'un fonds de placements immobiliers. (SWI)
41: Photo de télex boursier courant sur les deux faces du rapport d'un institut financier. (USA)
42: Une fabrique de papier a fait figurer, en couverture de l'un de ses rapports, un régiment de membres de son service de prospection des ventes. (USA)

PHOTOGRAPHER:

35, 36: Stewart Emery
37: Eugène Mihaesco
38: Jay Maisel
39: Brownjohn, Chermayeff & Geismar Assoc. Inc.
41: Burk Uzzle
42: Herman Lanshoff

STUDIO – AGENCY:

35, 36: Berry Currie Advertising Pty. Ltd.
37: Editions Rencontre S.A.
38: Arnold Saks, Inc.
39: Brownjohn, Chermayeff & Geismar Assoc.
41: Arnold Saks, Inc.

39

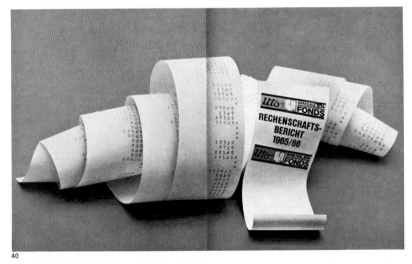

40

41

42

43: *Western Union International, Inc.*, 1968 report cover. Design in green, blue and ocher. Lettering black. (USA)
44: *Colt Industries* 1968 annual report. Pattern in olive, blue, carmine and black on silver. (USA)
45: Stacked on the cover are shapes symbolizing what salesmen from TIME, LIFE, SPORTS ILLUSTRATED and FORTUNE, the four *Time Incorporated* magazines, have to sell—space. (USA)
46: Typographic design for the cover of *Chicago Bridge & Iron Company's* report. Black and grey on white. (USA)
47–49: The cover shows the blurred image of *Canadian Pacific's* color scheme and multimark (48) on a moving diesel locomotive. Fig. 49 shows the entire cover. (CAN)
50: Cover in blue and red for *Esso Standard;* the design is based on the company's logotype. (FRA)
51–53: Three panels of a six-sided cover folder containing the report of *Electronic Memories, Inc.* The wrapper symbolizes the major product of each of the six company divisions. (USA)

43: Umschlag eines Jahresberichtes für ein privates Telegraphenamt. Illustration in Grün, Blau und Ocker. (USA)
44: Jahresbericht einer Maschinenfabrik. Graphische Darstellung des Firmenzeichens: olive, blau, aubergine, schwarz. (USA)
45: Was die Vertreter von TIME, LIFE, SPORTS ILLUSTRATED und FORTUNE verkaufen, wird durch die übereinanderliegenden Formen symbolisiert – nämlich Anzeigenraum. (USA)
46: Typographische Gestaltung des Umschlages für den Bericht eines Unternehmens für Stahlkonstruktionen. (USA)
47–49: Aufnahme des Firmenzeichens (48) auf der vorbeisausenden Diesellokomotive eines Transportunternehmens. (CAN)
50: Die Schutzmarke von *Esso* bildet das Grundelement für die Gestaltung dieses Umschlags. Rot und blau. (FRA)
51–53: Drei Seiten einer Schutzmappe für den Jahresbericht einer Computerfirma. Die graphischen Darstellungen symbolisieren Produkte verschiedener Abteilungen. (USA)

43: Rapport d'une compagnie télégraphique. Les trois faisceaux sont respectivement vert, bleu et ocre. Lettres noires. (USA)
44: Rapport d'une société de constructions mécaniques. Vert olive, bleu, carmin et noir sur argent. (USA)
45: Ces quatre empilements de plans de différents formats doivent représenter le choix des espaces publicitaires mis à la disposition des annonceurs par quatre grands périodiques. (USA)
46: Couverture du rapport d'une société de charpentes métalliques. Décor purement typographique noir et gris sur blanc. (USA)
47–49: Image, déformée par la vitesse, de l'emblème (48) d'une compagnie ferroviaire peinte sur le flanc d'une locomotive. (CAN)
50: Le logotype bien connu d'une compagnie pétrolière se profile sur la couverture de son rapport 1968. (FRA)
51–53: Trois éléments d'un portefeuille à six pans contenant le rapport d'une société constructrice d'ordinateurs. Le graphisme s'inspire des appareillages créés et montés dans les différents départements. (USA)

DESIGNER:

43: James S. Ward
44, 45: Arnold Saks
46: Henry Robertz
47, 49: Frank Lipari
50: Michel Rohmer
51–53: Jim Odgers/
Roger Marshutz/Ken Parkhurst

PHOTOGRAPHER:

47, 49: Albert Krafczyk

ART DIRECTOR:

43: James S. Ward
44, 45: Arnold Saks
46: E. Zapalik
47, 49: Frank Lipari
50: Jean-Benoît Bruant
51–53: Ken Parkhurst

STUDIO – AGENCY:

43: James S. Ward, Inc.
44, 45: Arnold Saks, Inc.
46: Henry Robertz Design
47, 49: Gazette Printing Co. Ltd.
51–53: Ken Parkhurst & Assoc.

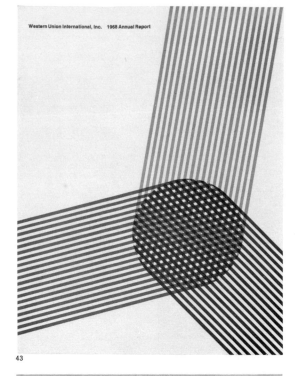

Western Union International, Inc.   1968 Annual Report

43

Colt Industries   Annual Report 1968

44

Time Incorporated   1968 Annual Report

45

"...our only true resources are people." These words ended last year's message to our shareholders, but they are even more appropriate as a beginning to this **Annual Report for 1969**. Our customers do not do business with a company. They do business with people. So this report is the story of people and what they create for customers of **Chicago Bridge & Iron Company**.

46

esso **standard** s.a.f. rapport annuel   1968

50

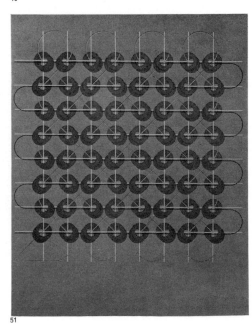

51

47

48

1968

Canadian Pacific   Annual Report
49

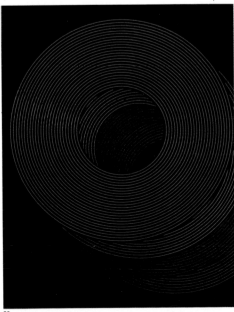
52

53

Covers
Umschläge
Couvertures

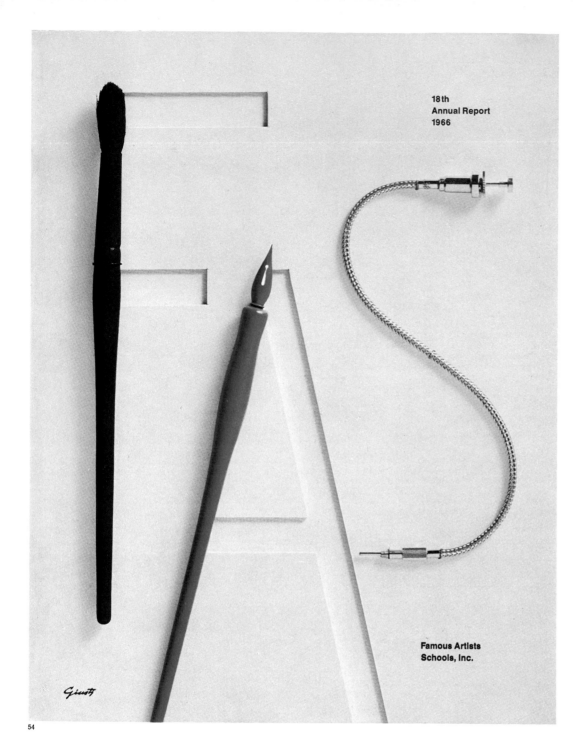

18th
Annual Report
1966

Famous Artists
Schools, Inc.

54

Inter City Papers Limited   Annual Report   1961

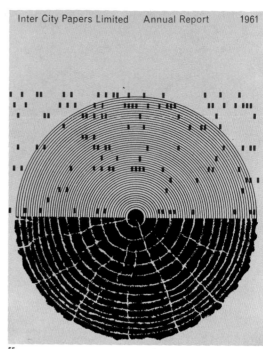

55

RoyFund Ltd. Annual Report 1969   RoyFund Ltée Rapport Annuel 1969

58

78th Annual Report 1965   The New Brunswick Telephone Company, Limited

DESIGNER:

54: George Giusti
55, 56, 58: Rolf Harder
57: James S. Ward
59: Paul Rand
60: John Massey
61: Ernst Roch
62: Joe Weston/David Pacheco
63: John Rieben/William J. Lloyd

ART DIRECTOR:

54: Harold L. Rogers
55, 56, 58: Rolf Harder
59: Paul Rand
60, 63: John Massey
61: Ernst Roch
92: Joe Weston

STUDIO – AGENCY:

55, 56, 58, 61: Design Collaborative Montreal Ltd.
57: James S. Ward, Inc.
62: Robert L. Steinle

61

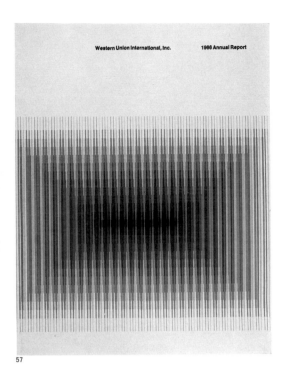

56

57

59

Container Corporation of America

Annual Report   1965

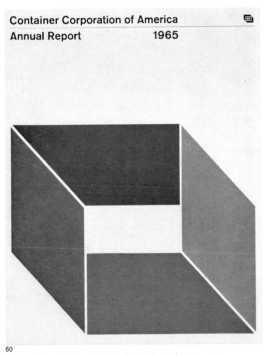

60

CYPRUS MINES CORPORATION   1963 ANNUAL REPORT

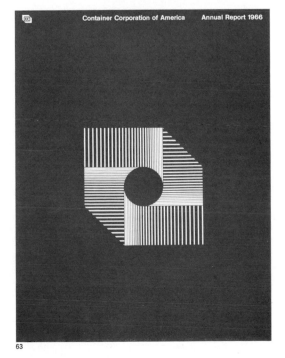

62

Container Corporation of America   Annual Report 1966

63

54: *Famous Artists Schools, Inc.*, offers correspondence courses in commercial art, writing and photography. The report uses tools of those trades as cover subjects. (USA)
55, 56: Two annual report covers for *Inter City Papers Limited*; 6×9 inches in size, they are printed in two colors on special papers made by the company. Colored stock is used for the inside pages. (CAN)
57: Annual report of *Western Union International* for 1966. Blue shades, yellow and green. (USA)
58: The *Roy Fund Ltd.* 1969 annual report introduces on its cover the newly created symbol of the fund. (CAN)
59: *Cummins Engine Company* chose a typographical design for its 1969 report cover. Black and tan. (USA)
60: The cover design of this *Container Corporation of America* report is based on the company's trademark. Rust shades and ocher on white. Lettering black. (USA)
61: The new symbol of *The New Brunswick Telephone Company* is introduced on the cover of this report. (CAN)
62: Annual report for 1963 of the *Cyprus Mines Corporation*. Multi-colored shovel, blind-embossed lines. (USA)
63: *Container Corporation*'s 1966 report uses a graphic design in the shape of its trademark. Blue-gray. (USA)

54: Die *Famous Artists Schools, Inc.* organisiert Fernkurse für Illustratoren, Schriftsteller und Photographen. Das Titelbild zeigt dafür benötigte Werkzeuge. (USA)
55, 56: Zweifarbige Umschläge auf Spezialpapier von zwei kleinformatigen Jahresberichten einer Papierfabrik. Die Innenseiten wurden auf farbigem Papier gedruckt. (CAN)
57: Umschlag des Jahresberichtes 1966 einer Telephon- und Telegraphengesellschaft. Blautöne, Gelb und Grün. (USA)
58: Das Titelbild des Berichtes einer Investitionsgesellschaft stellt das neue Firmensignet vor. (CAN)
59: Typographisch gelöste Umschlaggestaltung für den Bericht einer Maschinenfabrik. Schwarz, braun, weiss. (USA)
60: Die Gestaltung des Umschlagsujets für den Bericht einer Verpackungsfirma basiert auf deren Signet. Rostrot und ocker auf Weiss. Schwarze Schrift. (USA)
61: Dieser Jahresbericht einer Telephon- und Telegraphengesellschaft führt das neue Firmenzeichen ein. (CAN)
62: Mehrfarbige Schaufel als Umschlagsujet des Berichts einer Bergbaufirma; blindgeprägte Linien. (USA)
63: Auch bei diesem Bericht einer Verpackungsfirma wurde als graphisches Grundelement das Firmensignet verwendet. Blau-grauer Hintergrund. (USA)

54: Pinceau, plume et raccord souple, qui composent ici le sigle d'un cours par correspondance, figurent les principaux domaines (art, littérature, photographie) auxquels s'étend son enseignement. (USA)
55, 56: Présentation de deux rapports d'une papeterie. Impression extérieure sur papiers spéciaux de la maison, intérieure sur papiers de couleur. (CAN)
57: Rapport annuel d'une compagnie privée de télégraphie. Plusieurs bleus avec jaune et vert. (USA)
58: En frontispice de son rapport 1969: le nouvel emblème adopté depuis peu par un institut financier. (CAN)
59: Décor exclusivement typographique (noir et ocre) de la couverture du rapport d'une fabrique de moteurs. (USA)
60: Une structure optique dérivée de sa marque de fabrique caractérise le rapport d'une fabrique d'emballages. (USA)
61: Nouveau symbole d'une compagnie téléphonique privée, en couverture de l'un de ses rapports annuels. (CAN)
62: Couverture du rapport 1963 d'une compagnie minière d'outre-mer. Pelle polychrome. Nervures gaufrées. (USA)
63: Autre interprétation, l'année suivante, de la marque de la société d'emballages précitée (ill. 60). (USA)

64: *Aspen Institute for Humanistic Studies,* design in black and white. (USA)
65: Wrap-around cover for *Ansul Company's* 1957 annual report. The woodcut technique was also used for the inside illustrations (see figs.252, 253). (USA)
66: Workers erect a home using factory-built components provided by an acquisition of *Olin Corporation.* Photo in full color. (USA)
67: Photograph of printed circuits, transistors, etc., was used as background for this *Toronto Stock Exchange* report. Blue, violet, black. (CAN)
68: The cover design depicts the ever-expanding operations of *Sammons Enterprises, Inc.,* a diversified operating company in the services industry. Multicolored shapes on blue background. (USA)
69: Annual report attached to a four-flapped mailing carton. On opening, an expanse of timberland is revealed, suggesting the natural resources of the *Fibreboard Corporation.* Printed in two shades of green. (USA)
70: Five separate annual reports by member banks of *Financial Management Associates* are presented in one cardboard slipcase. The uniting theme of all five reports is "Helping the Community Grow". (USA)
71: Cover in red, green and black for *Canadian National Railways.* (CAN)

64: Bericht eines Instituts für humanistische Studien. Schwarzweiss. (USA)
65: Holzschnitt auf der Vorder- und Rückseite und Klappe des Berichtes einer chemischen Fabrik. Für die Innenseiten siehe Abb. 252, 253. (USA)
66: Dieses im Bau befindliche Haus wird aus Fertigelementen, die von einem Mischkonzern fabriziert werden, zusammengestellt. (USA)
67: Eine Aufnahme von Drucktastensystemen, Transistoren etc. dient als Hintergrund für den Umschlag des Berichtes der Börse von Toronto. (CAN)
68: Die Illustration symbolisiert das sich ständig ausdehnende Tätigkeitsfeld eines Mischkonzerns. Mehrfarbig auf blauem Grund. (USA)
69: Versandkarton mit vier Klappen und aufgeklebtem Bericht einer Papier- und Holzverarbeitungsfabrik. Beim Öffnen zeigt sich eine Waldlandschaft als Symbol für Naturschätze. Zwei Grüntöne. (USA)
70: Fünf separate Jahresberichte affiliierter Banken eines Finanzinstituts, in einem Schieber präsentiert. Die ganze Serie steht unter dem Thema «Förderung des wirtschaftlichen Wachstums der Gemeinde». (USA)
71: Umschlag des Berichtes der kanadischen Staatsbahnen. (CAN)

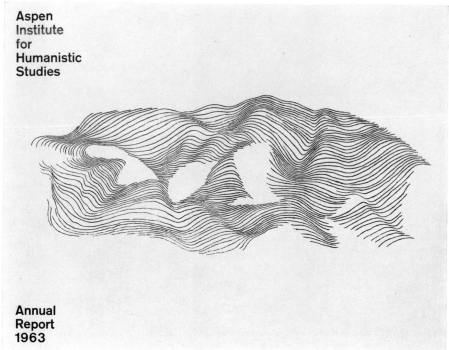

Aspen
Institute
for
Humanistic
Studies

Annual
Report
1963

64

66

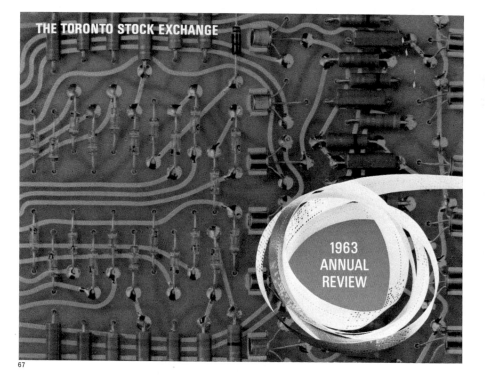

67

64: D'un institut d'études sociales: dessin en noir et blanc. (USA)
65: Dépliant enveloppant le rapport d'une société chimique. Gravure sur bois, comme les illustrations des pages intérieures (v. 252, 253). (USA)
66: Bâtisseurs montant des éléments préfabriqués distribués par un consortium à branches d'activité multiples. Photo en couleurs. (USA)
67: Le titre de ce rapport de la Bourse de Toronto se détache sur un arrière-plan photographique de circuits électroniques, transistors, etc. (CAN)
68: Le dessin de couverture du rapport d'une société assumant de multiples fonctions dans le domaine des services symbolise l'extension et la diversification continues de ses activités. Formes multicolores sur fond bleu. (USA)
69: Rapport fixé dans un carton d'expédition à quatre rabattants qui, ouvert, révèle une vaste étendue de forêts – évocation des ressources naturelles à la base des produits de la société (carton, emballages, etc.). (USA)
70: Les rapports annuels individuels de cinq établissements bancaires groupés au sein d'un consortium financier sont présentés ensemble, dans un emboîtage cartonné. Ils traitent de l'aide aux collectivités locales. (USA)
71: Rapport de la Société des chemins de fer canadiens. Rouge, vert, noir. (CAN)

69

65

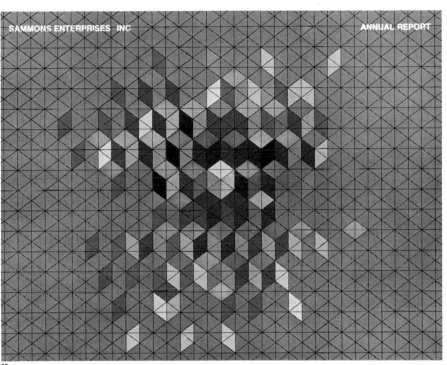

68

DESIGNER:

64: Herbert Bayer
65: Donald Marvine
66: Leslie A. Segal
67: Verne Lilley
68: Jerry Herring
69: Ronald Rampley/
     Stan Sollid
70: Jim Lienhart
71: James Valkus

ARTIST – PHOTOGRAPHER:

65: Antonio Frasconi
66: Burt Glinn
68: Jerry Herring

ART DIRECTOR:

65: Robert Vogele
66: Leslie A. Segal
67: Verne Lilley
68: Jerry Herring
69: Ronald Rampley
70: Jim Lienhart

STUDIO – AGENCY:

65, 70: RVI Corporation
        (formerly Robert Vogele, Inc.)
66: Corporate Annual Reports, Inc.
68: Gleen Advertising/
    Stan Richards & Associates
69: Logan, Carey & Rehag
71: James Valkus, Inc.

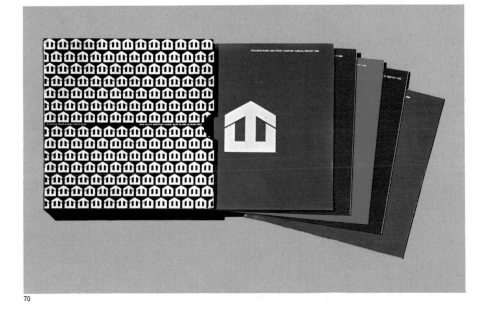

70

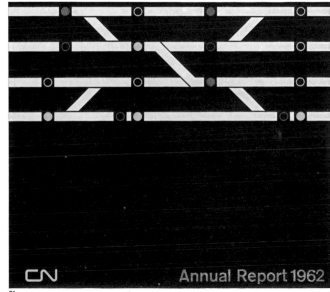

71

Covers
Umschläge
Couvertures

DESIGNER:

72–76: Saul Bass & Associates
77, 78: Johnson-Simpson
79: Leonard Fury

PHOTOGRAPHER:

77, 78: Bill Witt
79: Phil Marco

ART DIRECTOR:

77, 78: Milt Simpson
79: Leonard Fury

STUDIO – AGENCY:

72–76: Saul Bass & Associates
79: Corporate Annual Reports, Inc.

77

72

78

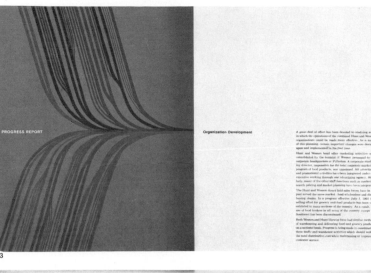

73

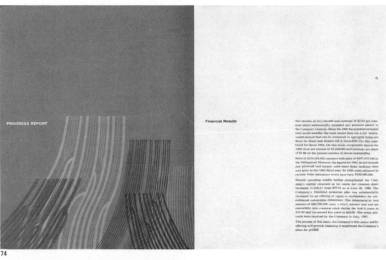

74

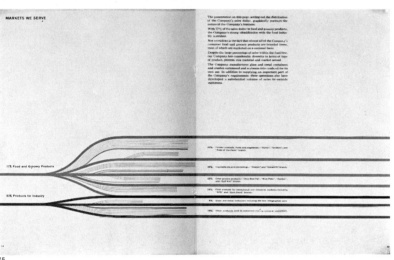

75

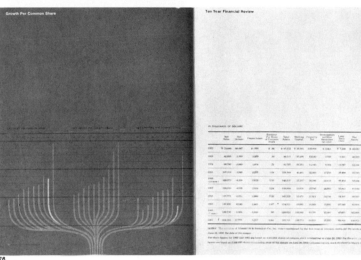

76

79

72–76: Cover and inside spreads from the 1961 annual report of *Hunt Foods and Industries, Inc*. The design theme, patterns based on charts, has been used throughout the report. Blue, green and ocher shades set the color scheme. (USA)
77, 78: The *Singer Company*, a diversified enterprise serving various markets internationally, shows on its 1966 annual report cover a ''synthetic'' multi-national flag, photographed with a zoom lens, combining all the countries the company does business with. (USA)
79: Full-color photographic illustration, incorporating a company product and extending over a four-panel fold-out cover for the 1970 *Sterling Drug Inc*. annual report. The section on the second panel from the right is the actual cover picture before unfolding. (USA)

72–76: Couverture et pages intérieures du rapport 1961 d'une société de produits alimentaires. Tous les motifs graphiques sont dérivés de schémas et diagrammes, traités dans des teintes bleues, vertes et ocre. (USA)
77, 78: La couverture du rapport 1966 d'un consortium industriel à vocation internationale s'orne de l'image photographique (obtenue par objectif zoom) d'un drapeau symbolique, synthétisant les couleurs de l'ensemble des pays auxquels s'étend l'activité. (USA)
79: Chemise dépliante à quatre volets contenant le rapport 1970 d'une société de produits chimiques. C'est le volet avec l'image de l'enfant qui constitue la couverture proprement dite, le visage de la mère et la reproduction du produit cité apparaissant après ouverture. (USA)

72–76: Umschlag und Innenseiten des Jahresberichtes 1961 eines Nahrungsmittelkonzerns. Als durchgehendes graphisches Thema wurden diagrammähnliche Linienkompositionen verwendet. Blau-, Grün- und Ockertöne bilden das Farbschema. (USA)
77, 78: Das Titelbild des Jahresberichtes eines Mischkonzerns mit internationalen Beziehungen zeigt eine multinationale Flagge (mit Zoom-Objektiv photographiert), die alle Länder vereinigt, die von dieser Firma beliefert werden. (USA)
79: Mehrfarbige Aufnahme mit Abbildung eines Produktes auf dem vierseitigen Umschlag des Jahresberichtes einer chemischen Fabrik. Die zweite Seite von rechts bildet die eigentliche Titelseite des Jahresberichtes. (USA)

Overall Design

Die Gesamtgestaltung

La conception générale

The President's Letter
Vorwort der Geschäftsleitung
Avant-propos du président

The Letter, signed by the company's top executive, is the best read section of the annual report. To be effective, it should not bog down in complicated details. Rather it should hit the high points, telling what's important and why. The Letter should discuss bad news in a candid, straightforward manner. And, most important, the Letter — like a crystal ball — should give the reader a glimpse of the future, the direction of the company, the source of growth. The best read Letters are brief, one or two pages, and include a photo of the man who signs the Letter. Below, we show six different examples of Letters from chief executives to the shareholders of their corporations.

DESIGNER:

80: Sheldon Seidler/Irene Liberman/Laurie Logan
81: Don Jim
82: James S. Ward
83: Michael C. Kaiser
84: George Tscherny
85: John Massey/Center for Advanced Research in Design

PHOTOGRAPHER:

80: Erich Hartmann (Magnum)
81: Will Martin
82: Robert Isear
83: Marvin Lyons/George Meinzinger
84: Bill Farrell
85: Harry Gehlert

ART DIRECTOR:

80: Sheldon Seidler
81: Will Martin
82: James S. Ward
83: Robert Miles Runyan
84: George Tscherny
85: Maxwell Ewing/Atlantic Richfield Co.

STUDIO – AGENCY:

80: Sheldon Seidler Associates, Inc.
81: Martin/Collins
82: James S. Ward, Inc.
83: Robert Miles Runyan and Associates, Inc.
84: George Tscherny, Inc.
85: Center for Advanced Research in Design

80

83

80: Financial highlights, letter to shareholders and portrait of chief executive in one spread. Sculpture in portrait connotes the chairman's interest in the arts. *RCA* 1969 report. (USA)
81: Portrait of chairman and president rendered in an ink-and-wash technique. Black and white on gray stock. 1968 report of *Western Bancorporation*. (USA)
82: The chairman and the president of *Gulf & Western Industries*, a conglomerate, photographed as they addressed the annual meeting of shareholders. In full color. (USA)
83: Black-and-white photo accompanying chief executive's letter. *Republic Corporation*. (USA)
84: Formal portrait in color of the chairman and president of *North American Rockwell*. (USA)
85: *Atlantic Richfield Company's* letter to the shareholders is juxtaposed with a black-and-white photograph of its signers, the chairman of the board and the president. (USA)

Das Vorwort, von der obersten Geschäftsleitung unterschrieben, ist sicher der meistgelesene Teil des Jahresberichtes. Um seine Wirkung nicht zu verfehlen, sollte es sich nicht in Details verlieren, sondern direkt auf die wichtigsten Punkte hinzielen. Schlechte Nachrichten sollten offen diskutiert werden. Und – der wichtigste Punkt – das Vorwort sollte einen kurzen Abriss geben über die zukünftige Geschäftspolitik und die weitere Entwicklung. Die meistgelesenen Vorworte sind kurz, über eine, höchstens zwei Seiten, und zeigen eine Aufnahme des Unterzeichners. Wir zeigen hier sechs Beispiele von verschiedenen Präsentationen solcher Vorworte zu Jahresberichten.

La lettre, signée par le dirigeant le plus responsable de la société, est le texte le plus largement lu du rapport annuel. Pour être efficace, elle doit s'en tenir aux points essentiels, en montrant le pourquoi de leur importance. Elle doit exposer sans détours les faits négatifs, sur le ton de la plus entière franchise. Surtout elle doit, telle une boule de cristal, permettre au lecteur de deviner l'avenir, de distinguer l'orientation générale de la société, de situer ses chances de croissance. Les lettres les mieux lues sont brèves – une ou deux pages – et présentent la photo du signataire. Nous reproduisons ci-dessous six exemples de différentes lettres des dirigeants adressées aux actionnaires.

81

82

84

85

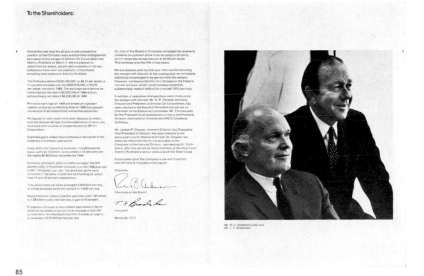

80: Überblick über Finanzlage, Vorwort an Aktionäre und Portrait des Generaldirektors. Die Plastik im Hintergrund zeigt, dass sich der Direktor für Kunst interessiert. *RCA*-Bericht. (USA)
81: Lavierte Tuschzeichnung der beiden obersten Geschäftsführer einer Grossbank. Schwarzweiss auf grauem Papier. Aus dem Bericht 1968. (USA)
82: Mehrfarbige Aufnahme des Generaldirektors und des Verwaltungsratspräsidenten bei der Ansprache an die Aktionäre während der Generalversammlung. Bericht eines Mischkonzerns. (USA)
83: Schwarzweiss-Aufnahme mit Brief des Generaldirektors. Bericht eines Mischkonzerns. (USA)
84: Aufnahme der beiden obersten Geschäftsleiter eines Industriekonzerns. (USA)
85: Vorwort an die Aktionäre mit Schwarzweiss-Aufnahme der Unterzeichner – Generaldirektor und Verwaltungsratspräsident. Aus dem Bericht eines petrochemischen Konzerns. (USA)

80: Rapport 1969 de la *RCA*: présentation sur une double page de quelques chiffres essentiels, de la lettre aux actionnaires et du portrait de son auteur (avec, à l'arrière-plan, une sculpture qui suggère l'intérêt personnel que porte celui-ci aux arts contemporains). (USA)
81: Dessin à la plume au lavis représentant les deux principaux responsables d'une société bancaire (extrait du rapport annuel 1968). Impression en noir et blanc sur papier gris. (USA)
82: Reproduction en couleurs d'un instantané photographique montrant le directeur général et le président d'un consortium industriel au cours de l'assemblée annuelle des actionnaires. (USA)
83: Rapport d'un consortium: lettre aux actionnaires et photo en noir/blanc de l'auteur. (USA)
84: Portrait photographique en couleurs des deux chefs d'un consortium industriel. (USA)
85: D'une compagnie pétrolière: lettre aux actionnaires; photo des signataires. (USA)

Presenting the Management
Direktoren-Portraits
Portraits de directeurs

86, 87: The 1969 annual report of *Squibb Beech-Nut, Inc.*, featured a 22-page special section on the corporation's research and development from which two spreads are shown here. Full-color photographs illustrate various aspects of these activities, and the directors are portrayed and introduced in small insets. (USA)

88, 89: In the "Review of Operations" section of *Combustion Engineering's* 1967 report the key executives and managers are photographed in their professional habitat. In full color. (USA)

90–93: *Olin,* a diversified industrial and chemical company, devoted a double spread to each corporate division. Each spread showed full-page color photomontages of the division chief's portrait and a scene symbolizing his group. (USA)

94: Photograph in full color of an *Incentive AB* member company's managing director. He is shown with a patented product manufactured by his firm. From the 1967 annual report. (SWE)

86, 87: Der Jahresbericht einer Firma für Pharmaka und Nahrungsmittel gibt einen Überblick über die Forschungstätigkeit und die Entwicklung des Unternehmens. Jede Doppelseite beleuchtet einen Aspekt aus dem Aufgabenkreis der verschiedenen Abteilungen und zeigt ein Portrait des jeweiligen Abteilungschefs. (USA)

88, 89: Die Aufnahmen im Bericht einer Kesselbaufirma zeigen im «Überblick über die Geschäftstätigkeit» die Direktoren und Abteilungschefs in ihrer beruflichen Umgebung. (USA)

90–93: Die verschiedenen Abteilungen einer chemischen Fabrik sind in deren Bericht je mit einer Doppelseite vertreten. Ganzseitige Photomontagen zeigen die Abteilungschefs mit symbolisierenden Illustrationen über ihr Tätigkeitsfeld. (USA)

94: Die mehrfarbige Aufnahme zeigt den Direktor einer Tochtergesellschaft eines Mischkonzerns mit einem von seiner Firma hergestellten Produkt. (SWE)

86, 87: Dans le rapport 1969 d'une société de produits pharmaceutiques et diététiques, une large place était faite à son effort de recherche. Les pages reproduites ici sont extraites de ce chapitre, où des photographies en couleurs évoquant successivement diverses branches d'activité font pendant à des textes illustrés d'un portrait du responsable de chaque division. (USA)

88, 89: Dans le rapport 1967 d'une fabrique de chaudières figuraient des photographies en couleurs des principaux dirigeants de l'entreprise, représentés dans leur cadre professionnel. (USA)

90–93: Les différents secteurs d'une entreprise de produits chimiques sont représentés par une suite de doubles pages illustrées d'un photo-montage où le chef de division apparaît dans un cadre dont les éléments symbolisent son domaine d'activité. (USA)

94: Rapport 1967 d'un consortium: photographie en couleurs du directeur de l'une des entreprises affiliées, dont il présente l'un des produits. (SWE)

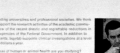

86

87

90

91

88

89

92

93

94

DESIGNER:

86, 87: Arnold Saks/Ingo Scharrenbroich
88–93: Leslie A. Segal
94: Karl Erik Lindgren

PHOTOGRAPHER:

86, 87: Simpson Kalisher
88–93: Burt Glinn

ART DIRECTOR:

86, 87: Arnold Saks
88–93: Leslie A. Segal

STUDIO – AGENCY:

86, 87: Arnold Saks Inc.
88–93: Corporate Annual Reports, Inc.
94: Sivert Ahringer AB

Design
Gestaltung
Conception

DESIGNER:

95, 96: Jay Novak
97—101: Lou Dorfsman/Ted Andresakes
Joel Azerrad

PHOTOGRAPHER:

95, 96: Marvin Silver
97: NASA Photo
98: Elliot Landy/Don Hunstein
99: Harvey Lloyd/Burt Schovitz
Black Star Photo
100: Ben Rose/Garry Winogrand
101: Pix, Inc./Rapho Guillemette/Alpha Photos
Fundamental Photo, Inc./Ted Andresakes

ART DIRECTOR:

95, 96: James Cross
97—101: Lou Dorfsman

STUDIO – AGENCY:

95, 96: James Cross Design Office, Inc.
97—101: CBS/Broadcast Group

95

95, 96: Center gatefold, closed (95) and opened (96), from the 1968 report of *Fluor Corporation Ltd.*, an oil and petrochemicals company. The full-color photographs depict major energy needs and resources of our planet. (USA)

97—101: Five spreads from the 1968 annual report of *Columbia Broadcasting System, Inc.* (CBS). This major company in the field of communications has expanded into other fields besides broadcasting through numerous acquisitions. These pages illustrate highlights of the various group activities. 97) Photo of earth as seen from moon accompanying the report to the shareholders. 98) Musicians recording on the *Columbia* label are pictured on this double page. 99) The report on the Broadcast Group concludes with this color page. 100) Comtec Group's function is in communications technology. Featured here is a new system of video recording, developed by *CBS*. 101) This spread illustrates aspects of the Holt Group's achievements, a division engaged in publishing and educational enterprises. (USA)

97

99

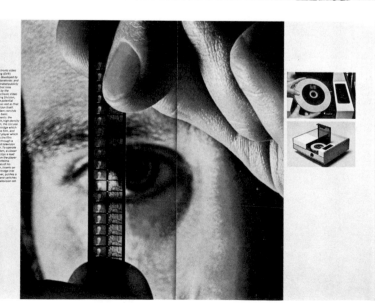

98

100

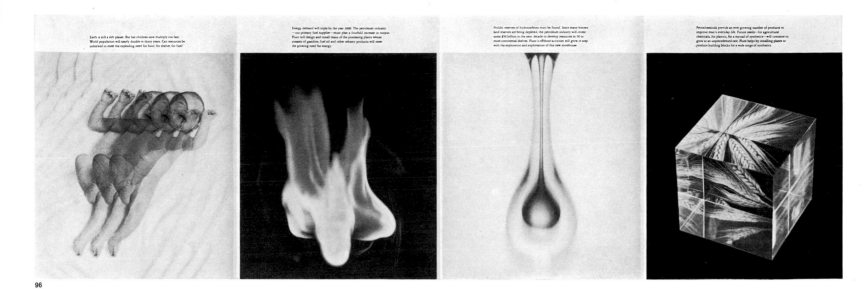

96

95, 96: Doppelseite (95) und Ausklappseiten (96) aus dem Bericht einer petrochemischen Fabrik. Die Innenseiten behandeln Energiebedarf und Naturschätze unseres Planeten. (USA)
97–101: Doppelseiten aus dem CBS-Jahresbericht. Im Laufe der letzten Jahre hat sich die Tätigkeit dieser Firma in Rundfunk und Fernsehen durch Neuerwerbungen auf andere Gebiete der Massenkommunikation ausgedehnt. Die Seiten illustrieren kurz den Aufgabenkreis der verschiedenen Gruppen. 97) Aufnahme der Erde vom Mond aus gesehen mit nebenstehendem Bericht an die Aktionäre. 98) Band bei Plattenaufnahmen im CBS-Studio. 99) Mit dieser Doppelseite schliesst der Bericht der Rundfunkabteilung. 100) Die Aktivität der Comtec-Gruppe erstreckt sich auf die Kommunikations-Technologie; die Abbildungen zeigen ein von der CBS entwickeltes System für Fernseh-Kassetten. 101) Diese Seite beleuchtet einige Aspekte aus dem Tätigkeitsfeld der Holt-Gruppe, die sich an wissenschaftlichen Publikationen beteiligt und aktiv an Bildungs-Programmen mitarbeitet. (USA)

95, 96: Dépliant à deux rabattants, montré fermé (95) et ouvert (96), extrait du rapport annuel 1968 d'une compagnie du secteur de la pétrochimie. Les photographies en couleurs évoquent les besoins et les ressources en énergie de la planète. (USA)
97–101: Cinq doubles pages tirées du rapport 1968 d'une grande chaîne radiophonique (CBS) qui, au cours de ces dernières années, a étendu son champ d'action à maints autres domaines connexes, en procédant à de nombreuses acquisitions et en se dotant de multiples branches décentralisées. 97) Cette photographie de la Terre vue de la Lune accompagne le rapport aux actionnaires. 98) Musiciens enregistrant pour la marque Columbia. 99) Page terminale, en couleurs, du chapitre consacré à la section «radio-diffusion». 100) Au sujet de la branche chargée du développement des techniques de télécommunications: la photographie reproduite illustre un nouveau système d'enregistrement vidéo. 101) Pages illustrant divers aspects des activités déployées par la société dans le domaine des publications et de l'éducation. (USA)

101

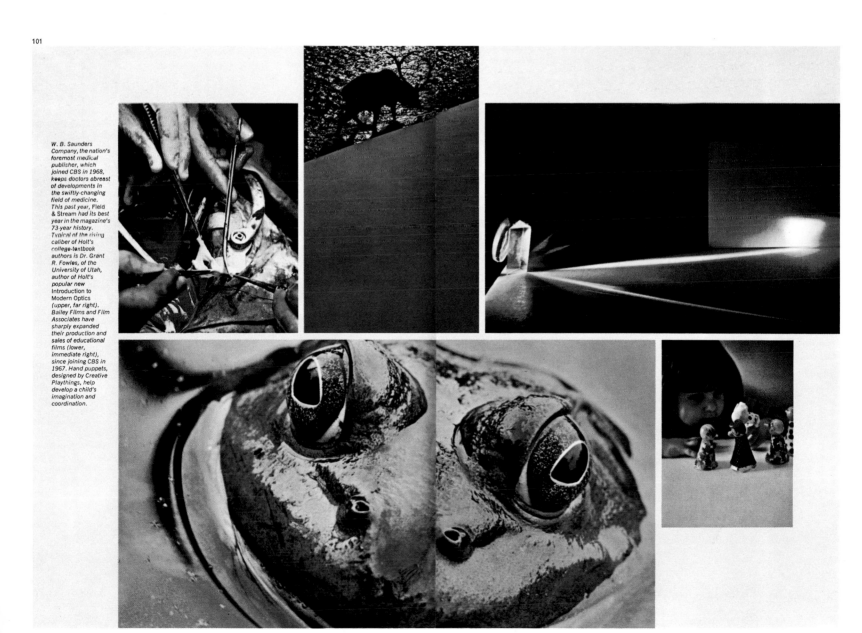

W. B. Saunders Company, the nation's foremost medical publisher, which joined CBS in 1968, keeps doctors abreast of developments in the swiftly-changing field of medicine. This past year, Field & Stream had its best year in the magazine's 73-year history. Typical of the rising caliber of Holt's college-textbook authors is Dr. Grant R. Fowles, of the University of Utah, author of Holt's popular new Introduction to Modern Optics (upper, far right). Bailey Films and Film Associates have sharply expanded their production and sales of educational films (lower, immediate right), since joining CBS in 1967. Hand puppets, designed by Creative Playthings, help develop a child's imagination and coordination.

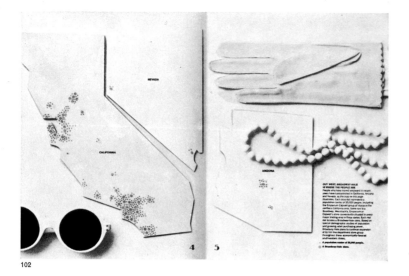

102

102: Double page from the 1967 report of *Broadway-Hale Stores, Inc.* A stylized map shows the main population centers and locations of stores in three Western states. (USA)

103, 104: *Herman Miller, Inc.*, wanted an annual report which would break the traditional methods of financial reporting and, at the same time, adhere to certain standards expected by financial analysts. A poster was designed and constructed in such a way that the financial report can be removed from the poster and folded for filing purposes (103). The poster can then be framed and exhibited without any reference to the company. (USA)

105: Spread from a report of the *Ogden Corporation* on a company division organized to implement plans for participation in the development of large-scale real estate projects. (USA)

106: A double page from an anniversary report of an employees' health insurance company. The text highlights company achievements; the pictures on this spread show scenes from food processing plants, whose employees the company insures. Full-color photographs. (SWI)

107, 108: *Norton Simon Inc.*, a corporation involved in consumer-related products and service fields, devoted a double page to each of their five major business areas. Shown are the spreads on packaging systems and graphic systems. Printed in black on white. (USA)

109, 110: Cover and view of partly opened folder containing the financial report of *Data Dynamics Inc.* Attached to this folder is a 12-page booklet titled "Capabilities", describing the organization's services in data management. Booklet printed on colored stock. (USA)

111, 112: Preceding the financial section of the *Colt Industries* 1968 annual report, a 16-page booklet of two-thirds page width shows full-colour reproductions of photos depicting scenes from various plant sites. Fig.111 shows a double page from that booklet. (USA)

DESIGNER:

102, 107, 108: Maurice Yanez
103, 104: R. Joseph Hutchcroft/
Center for Advanced Research
in Design
105: Jay Tribich
106: Elso Schiavo
109, 110: William A. Di Meo
111, 112: Arnold Saks

ARTIST–PHOTOGRAPHER:

104: R. Joseph Hutchcroft/
Center for Advanced Research
in Design
106: Herbert Michel
107, 108: Birgitta Forsman
111, 112: Jay Maisel

ART DIRECTOR:

102, 107, 108: Robert Miles Runyan
103, 104: John Massey
105: William R. Tobias
106: Elso Schiavo
109, 110: William A. Di Meo
111, 112: Arnold Saks

STUDIO–AGENCY:

102, 105, 107, 108: Robert Miles
Runyan & Associates
103, 104: Center for Advanced
Research in Design
106: Werbeagentur Ben Plüss
109, 110: Allen, Dorsey & Hatfield,
Inc.
111, 112: Arnold Saks, Inc.

103

104

109

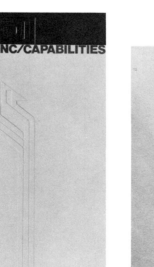

110

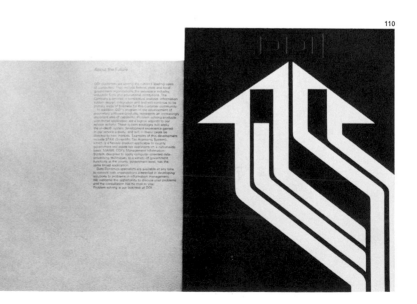

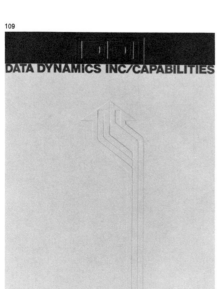

**Design
Gestaltung
Conception**

105

106

107

108

102: Doppelseite aus dem Bericht einer Warenhauskette. Auf einer stilisierten Karte von drei West-staaten wurden die grössten Siedlungszentren mit Läden dieser Firma eingezeichnet. (USA)

103, 104: Eine Firma für Büroplanung und -einrichtungen stellte die Bedingung, dass ihr Finanzbericht mit der Tradition der herkömmlich gestalteten Berichte breche, gleichzeitig aber den von Finanz-experten gestellten Erwartungen entspreche. Ein Poster ohne Firmenbezeichnung könnte vom Jahresbericht abgetrennt (103) und später eingerahmt und aufgehangt werden. (USA)

105: Doppelseite aus dem Bericht eines Industriekonzerns über die Tätigkeit einer affiliierten Gesell-schaft, die Beteiligungsprogramme für grossangelegte Bauprojekte ausarbeitet. (USA)

106: Bericht zum 25jährigen Bestehen der *Schweizerischen Betriebskrankenkasse*, mit kurzem Überblick über den Aufbau und die Entwicklung der Gesellschaft. Die mehrfarbigen Abbildungen zeigen Angestellte einer Nahrungsmittelfirma, die bei dieser Kasse versichert sind. (SWI)

107, 108: Ein Unternehmen der Konsumgüter- und Dienstleistungsbranche widmete den fünf Haupt-produktionszweigen je eine Doppelseite. Die hier gezeigten Seiten betreffen die Abteilungen für Verpackungen und für drucktechnische Einrichtungen. Schwarzweiss. (USA)

109, 110: Umschlag und Doppelseite aus dem Jahresbericht einer Computer-Firma. Dem Finanz-bericht wurde eine 12seitige Broschüre beigeheftet, die verschiedene Aspekte der von dieser Firma auf dem Gebiet der Datenverarbeitung geleisteten Dienste beleuchtet. Diese Broschüre wurde auf farbigem Papier gedruckt. (USA)

111, 112: Der Jahresbericht 1968 eines Industriekonzerns enthält einen 16seitigen Teil, der mit mehr-farbigen Photos (zweidrittelseitig) Ausschnitte aus der Tätigkeit der verschiedenen Abteilungen illustriert. Abb.111 zeigt eine Doppelseite aus diesem Beihefter. (USA)

102: Double page du rapport annuel 1967 d'une chaîne de grands magasins. Dans la carte géogra-phique stylisée sont indiqués les principaux centres de population et l'implantation de la société sur la côte Ouest. (USA)

103, 104: Soucieuse de sortir des sentiers battus tout en respectant les exigences pratiques de l'in-formation financière, une fabrique de meubles a eu recours à cette solution originale: le rapport annuel proprement dit constitue le soubassement d'une affiche, dont il peut être séparé: plié, il se présente alors sous la forme d'un fascicule d'aspect et de format usuels (103), tandis que l'affiche, où le nom de la firme n'est pas mentionné, peut être encadrée et exposée telle quelle. (USA)

105: D'un rapport annuel d'une société financière: pages évoquant le concours apporté à la réalisa-tion d'importants projets de constructions immobilières. (USA)

106: Les photos en couleurs illustrent ces pages d'un rapport d'une caisse-maladie montrent des scènes prises dans les établissements dont le personnel est assuré par ses soins. (SWI)

107, 108: Deux des cinq doubles pages consacrées à ses principales branches d'activité, dans l'un de ses rapports annuels, par une entreprise fournissant au public tout à la fois des produits et des services. Ici: emballages (107) et travaux graphiques (108). (USA)

109, 110: Couverture et vue après déploiement d'un volet, du portefeuille contenant le rapport finan-cier d'une société spécialisée dans le traitement de l'information. Un fascicule annexe, imprimé sur papier de couleur, décrit les services qu'elle offre au public. (USA)

111, 112: Un fascicule de photographies en couleurs, d'un format plus étroit que celui de la publication elle-même, précède le compte rendu financier dans le rapport 1968 d'un groupe indus-triel. On y voit des scènes prises sur les lieux de fabrication. (USA)

111

112

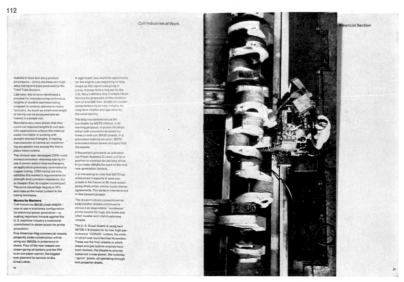

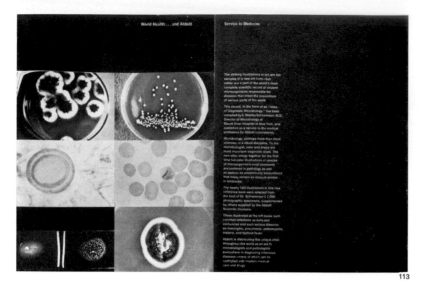

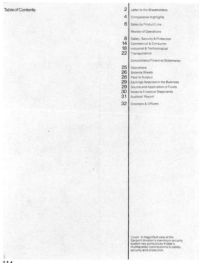

113

114

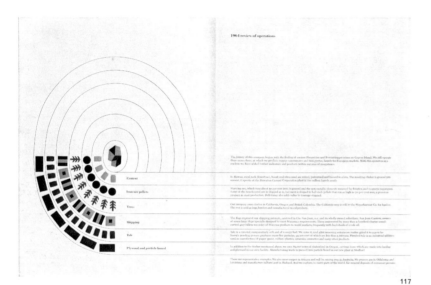

117

118

113: Stapled into the centerfold of the *Abbott Laboratories* 1965 report is a 20-page picture section illuminating the international scope of medical problems and the corporation's role in solving those problems. Reproduced here is the center spread with the last page of the booklet. It shows in full color six virulent microorganisms. (USA)

114–116: Table of contents and two double-page spreads from the 1969 report of *Walter Kidde & Company*, whose main business lies in security and protection products and services. The vertical line was used as a unifying graphic element. Bar charts in blue and black. (USA)

117: Title spread for the Review of Operations section of the *Cyprus Mines Corporation* 1964 annual report. Typography black and white, graphic symbols in shades of blue. (USA)

118–120: Cover and two double pages from the 1969 annual report of *Esterline Corporation*, manufacturers of scientific instruments and apparatus. The horizontal double line in the upper half of the page runs through the entire report. Printed in one color. (USA)

121: The *RCA* 1968 report included a 55½'' long accordion fold-out, showing silhouetted and in full color about 600 *RCA* products and services. (See also figs.143–145). (USA)

122–124: The 1968 annual report of the *Education Development Center* is a 94-page book of which only eight pages are used for financial accounting. The rest informs of the activities of the center. The initials EDC, which form the graphic theme of the report, are shown in numerous variations throughout the book. Cover printed red and black on yellow stock. (USA)

DESIGNER:

113: Norman Perman
114–116: Robert Pellegrini
117: Joe Weston
118–120: Elena Bloomfield
121: Sheldon Seidler
122–124: Dietmar Winkler

PHOTOGRAPHER:

113: S. Stanley Schneierson, M.D.
118, 120: Wolf von dem Bussche
121: Erich Hartmann (Magnum)

ART DIRECTOR:

113: Charles Walz, Jr.
114–116, 118–120: William R. Tobias
117: Advertising Designers, Inc./R. L. Steinle
121: Sheldon Seidler

122

121

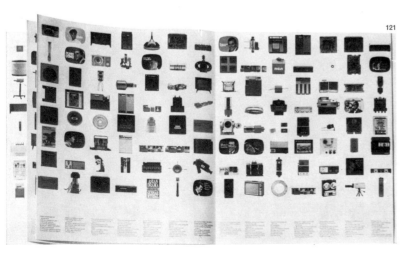

STUDIO – AGENCY:

113: Norman Perman, Design
114–116, 118–120: Robert Miles Runyan
    & Associates
117: Advertising Designers, Inc.
121: Sheldon Seidler Design

**Design/Gestaltung
Conception**

113: Zum Jahresbericht einer chemischen Fabrik gehört ein 20seitiger illustrierter Beihefter, der eine Übersicht über medizinische Probleme auf internationaler Ebene vermittelt und gleichzeitig die von dieser Firma gemachten Anstrengungen zur Lösung dieser Probleme beschreibt. Die mehrfarbige Illustration zeigt sechs schädliche Mikroorganismen. (USA)

114–116: Aus dem Bericht eines Unternehmens für Sicherheits- und Schutzvorrichtungen. Die vertikale Linie wurde im ganzen Bericht einheitlich als graphisches Grundelement verwendet. Schematische Darstellung (116) in Dunkel- und Hellblau. (USA)

117: Diese Doppelseite gibt einen Überblick über die verschiedenen Zweige einer Bergbaufirma. Schwarze Schrift, graphische Symbole in Blautönen. (USA)

118–120: Umschlag und Doppelseite aus dem Jahresbericht 1969 eines Unternehmens für wissenschaftliche Instrumente und Apparaturen. Die horizontale Doppellinie in der oberen Hälfte der Seite zieht sich durch den ganzen Bericht. Schwarzweiss. (USA)

121: Der Jahresbericht 1968 der *RCA* enthält einen 130 cm langen Leporello-Beihefter mit mehrfarbigen Abbildungen von rund 600 Produkten. (S. auch Abb.143–145) (USA)

122–124: Der Jahresbericht eines Bildungszentrums umfasst 94 Seiten, wovon nur 8 für den finanziellen Überblick verwendet wurden; der Rest informiert über die Tätigkeit des Zentrums. Die Initialen EDC, die das graphische Grundelement dieses Berichtes bilden, erscheinen immer wieder in abgewandelter Form. Umschlag in Rot und Schwarz auf gelbem Karton. (USA)

113: Le rapport 1963 d'une fabrique de produits chimiques contenait un encart illustré de 20 pages, agrafé au centre de la brochure. Consacré aux grands problèmes médicaux qui se posent dans le monde, il mettait en relief l'effort déployé par la firme pour contribuer à leur solution. La dernière page, telle qu'elle apparaît ici, représentait six microorganismes virulents. (USA)

114–116: Rapport 1969 d'une société fournissant des dispositifs et services de sécurité. Les traits verticaux qu'on remarque sur ces trois doubles feuilles se retrouvent tout au long du fascicule, dont ils constituent ainsi l'élément graphique dominant. Les diagrammes (116) sont en bleu et noir. (USA)

117: Cette double page du rapport 1964 d'une compagnie minière introduit le compte rendu de ses activités productives. Textes imprimés en noir, motifs graphiques en bleu. (USA)

118–120: Couverture et pages extraites du rapport 1969 d'une fabrique d'instruments scientifiques. Le double filet horizontal barrant la partie supérieure des pages court d'un bout à l'autre du rapport. Impression en noir et blanc. (USA)

121: Ce rapport de la *RCA* comprend un dépliant en accordéon, long de 130 cm, représentant (en couleurs) quelque 600 produits et services fournis par la société. (Voir aussi fig.143–145.) (USA)

122–124: Fort de 94 pages, le rapport 1968 d'un centre d'action pédagogique n'en consacrait pas plus de huit au compte rendu financier, tout le reste étant réservé à la documentation vivante. Le sigle de l'institution (EDC), interprété sous de multiples formes, constitue le thème graphique caractéristique de l'ensemble. Couverture imprimée en rouge et noir sur carton jaune. (USA)

125

126

127

125–127: *Time Incorporated* published a two-part annual report in 1966: a 24-page report to stock-holders, with a plain cover in russet (125) and a 48-page booklet "The Year in Review" (126), whose cover photo was also in russet tones. 127) Spread from "Review" section. (USA)
128–130: *Polaroid Corporation's* 1967 annual report (128) was accompanied by a separate booklet, titled "The Useful Image" (129), which presented a portfolio of *Polaroid* industrial and scientific photography. 130) Two full-color photographs from that portfolio. (USA)
131, 132: The 1969 annual report of the *Hongkong and Shanghai Banking Corporation* consists of a cardboard folder with pockets into which are tucked the financial report on one side and an inter-national survey on the other. 131) Cover of folder. 132) Folder opened. (HKG)
133–135: *SCM Corporation*, a diversified manufacturing company, featured a 24-page survey on the company's activities as part of its 1969 report. The back cover of this section contained the finan-cial report in a pocket (133). 134,135) Two spreads from the latter. Full color. (USA)

125–127: *Time, Inc.* publizierte 1966 einen 2teiligen Bericht: einen 24seitigen Bericht für die Aktionäre mit ockerfarbenem Umschlag (125) und eine 48seitige Broschüre «Jahresrückblick» (126), deren Umschlagphoto ebenfalls in Ockertönen gehalten ist. 127) Doppelseite mit mehrfarbiger Aufnahme aus dem «Jahresrückblick». (USA)
128–130: Der Jahresbericht einer Firma für optische Geräte (128) enthielt eine separate Broschüre (129) mit Aufnahmen aus Industrie und Wissenschaft. 130) Doppelseite aus dieser Broschüre mit zwei mehrfarbigen Aufnahmen. (USA)
131, 132: Eine Kartonhülle mit zwei Einsteckklappen enthält den Finanzbericht und einen Überblick über die internationale Tätigkeit einer Grossbank. (HKG)
133–135: Der Jahresbericht 1969 eines Mischkonzerns brachte eine 24seitige Übersicht über die Tätigkeit der Firma, mit Einsteckklappe für den Finanzbericht auf der dritten Umschlagseite (133). 134, 135) Doppelseiten mit mehrfarbigen Abbildungen aus diesem Bericht. (USA)

125–127: En 1966, le rapport de la société éditrice de *Time* se présentait sous la double forme d'un compte rendu de 24 pages (125), adressé aux actionnaires, et d'une brochure de 48 pages (126, couverture) destinée au public; 127) double page illustrée en couleurs. (USA)
128–130: Le rapport 1969 d'une société d'instruments optiques (128) contenait une brochure séparée (129) composée d'une suite de photographies industrielles et scientifiques, telles que celles qui figurent sur cette double page (130) et qui sont en couleurs. (USA)
131, 132: A l'intérieur de ce portefeuille cartonné (131), deux poches latérales contiennent, d'une part, le rapport financier, d'autre part, le compte rendu des activités internationales d'une société bancaire ayant son siège en Extrême-Orient. (HKG)
133–135: Dans le rapport 1969 d'un consortium industriel, le compte rendu financier (134,135: doubles pages polychromes tirées de celui-ci) était inséré, sous la forme d'élément séparé, dans une poche aménagée à l'intérieur de la couverture (133) (USA)

ART DIRECTOR:

125–127: Arnold Saks
128–130: William Field, Herbert Rogalski
133–135: Leslie A. Segal

STUDIO – AGENCY:

125–127: Arnold Saks, Inc.
131, 132: Graphic Communication Limited
133–135: Corporate Annual Reports, Inc.

133

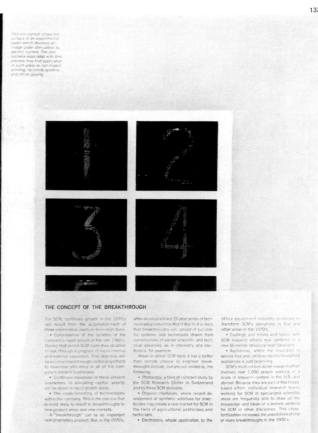

**Design
Gestaltung
Conception**

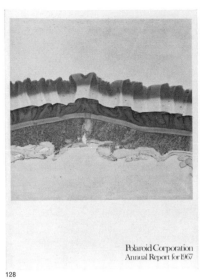

Polaroid Corporation
Annual Report for 1967

The Useful Image

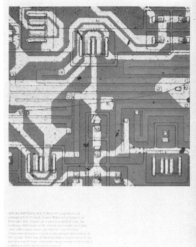

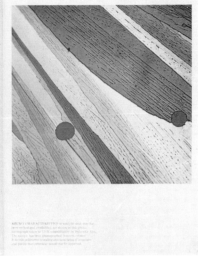

128

129

130

DESIGNER:

125–127: Arnold Saks
128–130: Herbert Rogalski
131, 132: Henry Steiner
133–135: Leslie A. Segal

PHOTOGRAPHER:

126: Brian Brake
127: Larry Burrows
128–130: Polaroid Corporation
131, 132: F. Fischbeck
133–135: Simpson Kalisher

The Hongkong and Shanghai
Banking Corporation
Annual Report 1969
The Chairman's International Survey

131

132

134

135

Office Equipment
and Related Products

Appliances

The office equipment industry, excluding computers, expanded in 1969 at a 13 percent annual rate. New businesses are being formed at a rate of over 225,000 a year, increasing the demand for ways to record, assemble, copy and communicate data.

Recognizing the increased sophistication that will characterize the industry in the 1970's, SCM's Smith-Corona Marchant Division broadly increased its research and engineering capabilities. This was accomplished both internally, through the establishment of a semiconductor laboratory at Marchant Electronics; and externally, through the acquisition by SCM of Metabo (see section 7 of this Report). A review of operations by major product category follows.

The office copier industry is expected to grow at a rate of 15 percent a year well into the 1970's. Smith-Corona Marchant continued research and development work on extending its wide range of electrostatic office copiers, as well as its research into new copying techniques. The division offers high-speed console and desktop copiers.

In 1969, Smith-Corona Marchant increased production of coated paper

This co-ed is one of seven million students returning to college this fall. Countless term papers will be typed on Smith-Corona portables—not all of them in airports.

Nearly a million new American families are formed and an estimated 1.5 million private-dwelling units are built and furnished each year. These facts account in part for the growth of the market for small electric house wares, already over $1.4 billion in annual sales.

Sales of Proctor-Silex appliances continued to improve in 1969. As noted in the Letter to Shareholders, however, there was a decrease in the overall profit of the division because of declines in Topflame products and Canadian operations. The latter should be improved by the cessation of strike costs and the fact that Canadian manufacture of Sheffield and Proctor-Silex products has been combined in a single plant at Picton, Ontario. Sales administration has also been consolidating in Canada under the brand name Proctor-Silex. All appliance and floor care operations have been consolidated.

During the year, Proctor-Silex closed an older plant in Chicago and consolidated the production of motor-driven appliances in a new factory in Altoona, Pa. The 160,000 sq. ft. facility was built and staffed in record time with production lines operating

Millions of busy housewives depend on Proctor-Silex appliances throughout the day. Small electric housewares constitute a growing $1.4 billion market for U.S. manufacturers.

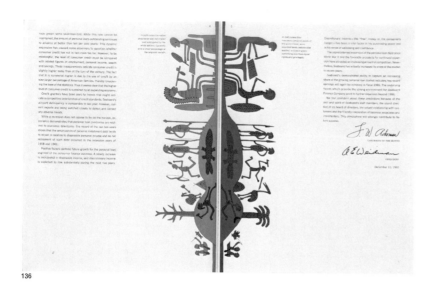

136

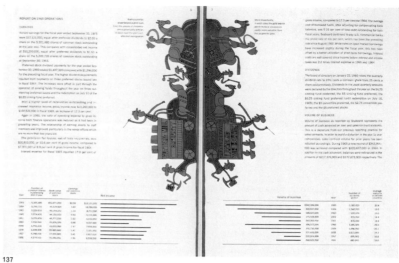

137

140

DESIGNER:

136, 137: Marvin Rubin
138, 139: Eisenman & Enock, Inc.
140: Gaylord Adams/Don Flock
141, 142: Sheldon Seidler/Irene Liberman
143–145: Sheldon Seidler

ARTIST – PHOTOGRAPHER:

136, 137: Marvin Rubin
138, 139: Simpson Kalisher
140: Ralph Marshall/Gaylord Adams
141, 142: Leigh Weiner
143–145: Erich Hartmann (Magnum)

ART DIRECTOR:

136, 137: Advertising Designers, Inc./R. L. Steinle
138, 139: Stanley Eisenman
140: Gaylord Adams/Don Flock
141–145: Sheldon Seidler

STUDIO – AGENCY:

136, 137: Advertising Designers, Inc.
138, 139: Eisenman & Enock, Inc.
140: Adams & Sturman, Inc.
141–145: Sheldon Seidler Inc.

143

136, 137: Graphic interpretation of parallels between Australia and the United States form the theme of the 1965 annual report of *Seaboard Finance Company*. (USA)
138, 139: Spreads with full-color photographs and descriptions of products and achievements of two *PepsiCo* divisions. From the 1965 annual report. (USA)
140: Double page from *Eaton Yale & Towne's* 1969 report. The international involvement of this diversified manufacturing company is highlighted throughout the report. Photos in color. (USA)
141, 142: Double-page layouts from the 1969 report of *Fairchild Camera and Instrument Corp*. Production of semiconductor devices, research and development are the subjects. (USA)
143–145: Pictures of manufacturing stages of electronic parts, publishing activities, educational communications systems and of experiments and tests conducted by a technical planning group illustrate these three spreads from *RCA's* 1968 report. (See also fig.121) (USA)

136, 137: Das Hauptthema des Berichtes 1965 eines Konsumentenkreditinstitutes bilden graphisch interpretierte Darstellungen der Parallelen zwischen Australien und Amerika. (USA)
138, 139: Doppelseiten aus dem Bericht 1965 mit mehrfarbigen Aufnahmen und Beschreibungen von Produkten und Neuerungen zweier Tochtergesellschaften der *PepsiCo*. (USA)
140: Doppelseite aus dem Bericht eines Mischkonzerns, dessen weltweite Geschäftsbeziehungen das Hauptthema dieses Berichtes bilden. Mehrfarbige Aufnahmen. (USA)
141, 142: Aus dem Bericht einer Firma für optische und elektronische Geräte. Die Aufnahmen beziehen sich auf die Produktion von Halbleitern und auf Forschung und Weiterentwicklung. (USA)
143–145: Die Doppelseiten illustrieren verschiedene Produktionszweige der *RCA*: Herstellung elektronischer Geräte, Publikationswesen, Entwicklung von Geräten für Sprachlabors, sowie die von einer technischen Planungsgruppe durchgeführten Experimente. (S.Abb.121) (USA)

136, 137: L'interprétation graphique de parallèles relevées entre la situation en Australie et la situation aux Etats-Unis constituait le thème du rapport 1969 d'un établissement de crédit. (USA)
138, 139: Doubles pages du rapport 1965 de deux entreprises rattachées à une société productrice de boissons sans alcool. En couleurs. (USA)
140: Double page du rapport 1969 d'une société industrielle aux activités multiples, dont il s'attache à mettre en évidence l'extension internationale. Photographies en couleurs. (USA)
141, 142: Du rapport 1969 d'une fabrique d'instruments optiques et électroniques. Les photographies reproduites illustrent la fabrication des semi-conducteurs et l'activité de recherche. (USA)
143–145: Trois doubles pages du rapport 1968 de la *RCA*. Les illustrations évoquent différents domaines de l'activité de la société: fabrication d'instruments électroniques; publications; matériels éducatifs; recherches d'un groupe de planification technique. (Voir aussi fig.121) (USA)

Page Layout/Seitengestaltung/Mise en page

144

138

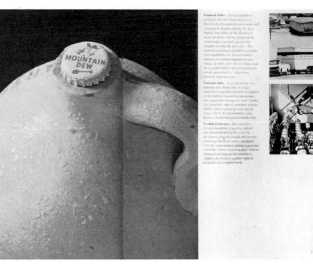
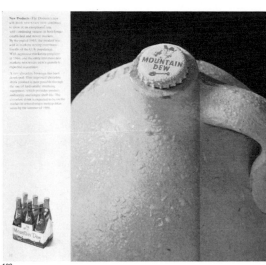

139

141

142

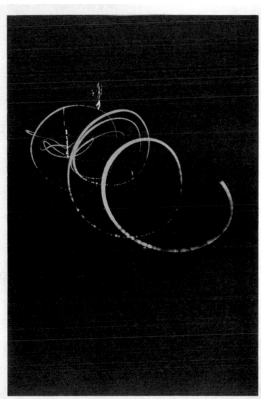

out the promise that infrared laser light signals someday would replace electric signals in the control and operation of computers.

Investigations were carried on in such areas as materials, materials processing, electronic device development, millimeter and submillimeter wave generation, and new bases for consumer electronic systems.

Advanced Technical Planning

Research is not automatically transformed into profitable products. Close coordination is required among corporate research, marketing, and product divisions. To improve this coordination, an Advanced Technical Planning Group was established late in 1968. It has functional responsibility for the advanced development activities of the RCA product divisions, tying them more closely to the company's research, product engineering, and corporate marketing programs.

Left: A new method of coating magnetic disks for use in computer memories undergoes experimental tests at the David Sarnoff Research Center in Princeton, N.J. Right: An RCA research scientist slices a whirling pattern of light through the darkness as he waves the brightest solid-state injection laser ever developed.

145

Design
Gestaltung
Conception

146

149

150

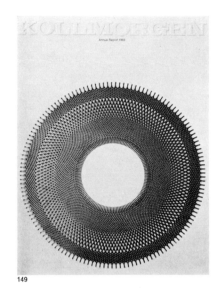

151

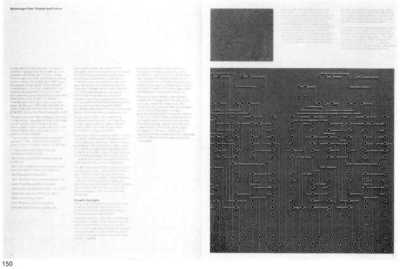

152

146–148: The 1969 annual report of *The Canada Council* was a book of 170 pages, all typographic. Shown here are three spreads from different sections. Black on white. (CAN)
149, 150: *Kollmorgen* 1969 report. The cover design (149) depicts a rotor disc for an electric servo motor manufactured by a company division. The spread shown (150) describes the corporation and illustrates a new patented process developed by their research engineers. (USA)
151, 152: The cover design of the *American Can Company* 1966 report symbolizes the corporation's areas of business: containers and packaging, consumer and service products, and chemicals. The double page reproduced here (152) is devoted to the container division. (USA)
153: Layout of a double-page spread from the *Teledyne* 1965 annual report. Text and photos deal with newly developed electronic instruments used in aviation. Black and white. (USA)
154: Typographic layout for a ten-year financial history of the *General Dynamics Corporation*. From its 1965 annual report. Printed in black, olive and blue on white. (USA)
155: Double-page spread showing the consolidated balance sheets from *Litton Industries* 1970 annual report. Black and olive print on greenish-grey tinted stock. (USA)
156: Spread from the 1970 report of *IBM* giving a ten-year comparative statement of operations. Printed in black on white. Typeface: Garamond. (USA)
157: Table of growth trends over the past five years from the 1969 annual report of *Atlantic Richfield Company*. Printed black on white paper. (USA)

153

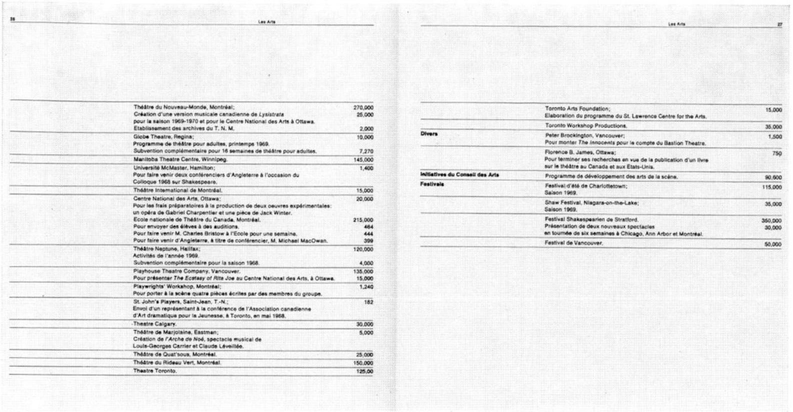

147

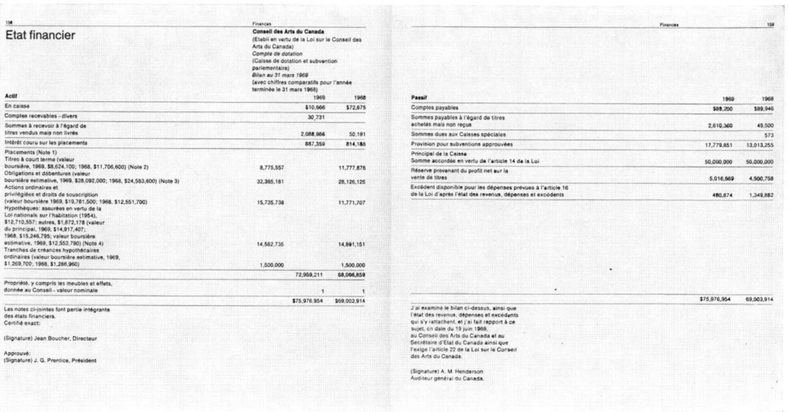

148

146–148: Doppelseite aus dem Jahresbericht des *Canada Council*. (CAN)
149, 150: Bericht eines diversifizierten Industriekonzerns. Rotorscheibe eines Servomotors als Umschlagsujet (149). Die Doppelseite (150) gibt einen Überblick über die Tätigkeit des Unternehmens und beschreibt ein von der Forschungsequipe entwickeltes patentiertes Verfahren. (USA)
151, 152: Die graphische Gestaltung auf dem Umschlag des Berichtes einer Verpackungsfirma symbolisiert die verschiedenen Produktionszweige: Behälter, Verpackungen, Konsumgüter und Chemikalien. Diese Doppelseite befasst sich mit der Behälter-Abteilung. Mehrfarbig. (USA)
153: Doppelseite aus dem Bericht einer Firma für elektronische Anlagen. Die Illustrationen und der Text beschreiben ein neu entwickeltes elektronisches Instrument für Flugzeuge. (USA)
154: Typographisch gelöste Gestaltung des Finanzrückblicks über die letzten 10 Jahre aus dem Jahresbericht eines Mischkonzerns. Blau, oliv und schwarz auf Weiss. (USA)
155: Doppelseite mit Schlussbilanz aus dem Bericht eines Unternehmens für elektronische Anlagen und Einrichtungen. Schrift: schwarz und oliv auf graugrünem Papier. (USA)
156: Doppelseite aus dem Jahresbericht der *IBM* mit einem Zehnjahres-Rückblick über die Finanzlage des Unternehmens. Schwarzweiss. Schrifttyp: Garamond. (USA)
157: Tabelle über Wachstum und Entwicklung eines Industriekonzerns während der vergangenen fünf Jahre. Aus dem Jahresbericht 1969. Schwarzweiss. (USA)

146–148: Pages extraites d'un rapport annuel du Conseil des arts du Canada – volume fort de 170 pages, tout en texte. Impression en noir sur blanc. (CAN)
149, 150: Rapport annuel d'un consortium industriel. En couverture (149), rotor de moteur électrique. Dans les pages reproduites (150), il est question de l'organisation et des buts de la société et d'un procédé nouvellement mis au point par ses ingénieurs. (USA)
151, 152: La couverture de ce rapport annuel d'une fabrique d'emballages attire l'attention sur l'ampleur de ses activités, qui s'étendent à la fabrication de biens de consommation et aux produits chimiques. Les deux pages intérieures reproduites concernent spécifiquement l'emballage. (USA)
153: Pages extraites du rapport 1965 d'une fabrique d'appareils électriques (description d'instruments nouveaux destinés à l'aviation). Impression en noir sur blanc. (USA)
154: Le rapport 1965 d'une société industrielle contenait un historique de son évolution financière au cours des dix années écoulées. Impression en noir, olive et bleu sur blanc. (USA)
155: Bilan d'une fabrique d'appareillage électrique. Noir et olive sur papier gris-vert. (USA)
156: Du rapport 1970 d'*IBM*: vue rétrospective et comparative de la situation financière de la société. Impression en noir sur blanc, en caractères Garamond. (USA)
157: Tableau synoptique mettant en évidence le développement d'un consortium industriel de 1964 à 1969, année du rapport. Impression en noir sur blanc. (USA)

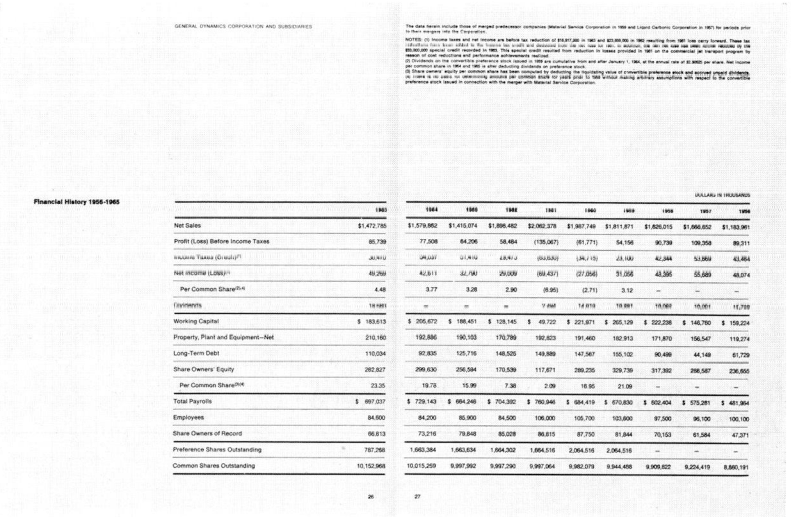

154

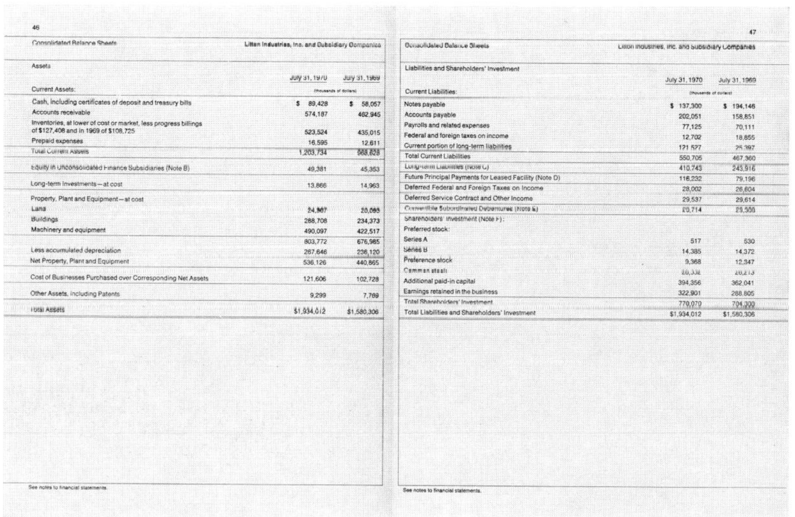

155

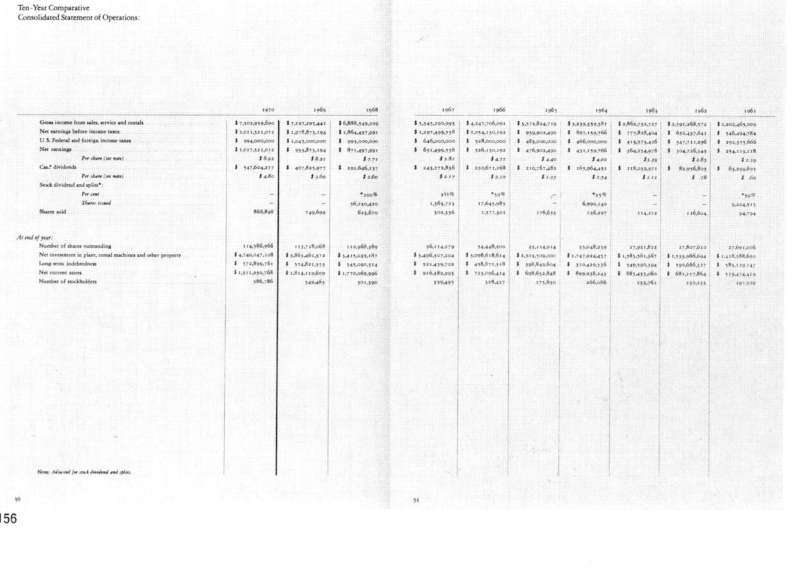

156

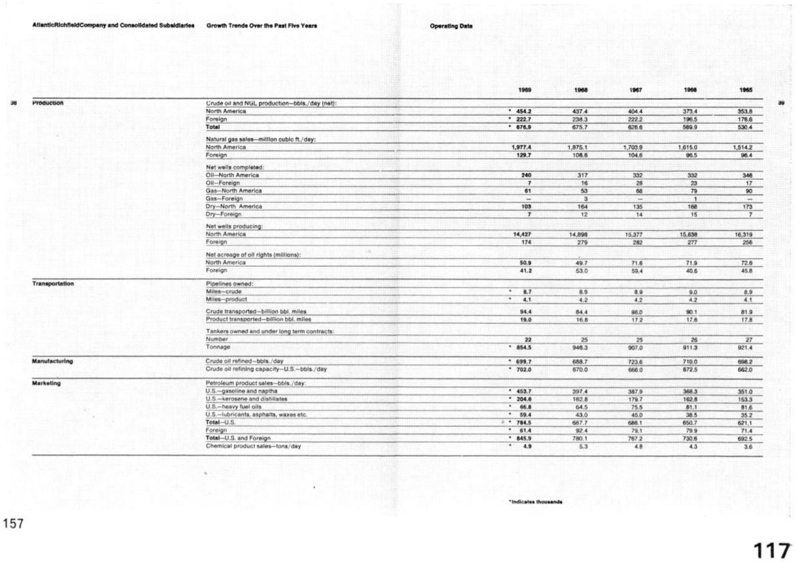

157

Charts and Graphs

Diagramme und Tabellen

Diagrammes et graphiques

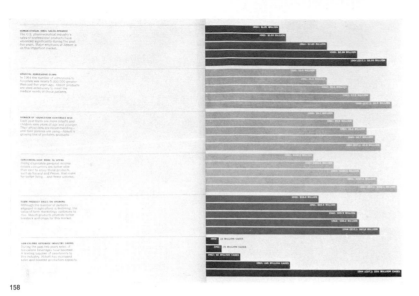

158

159

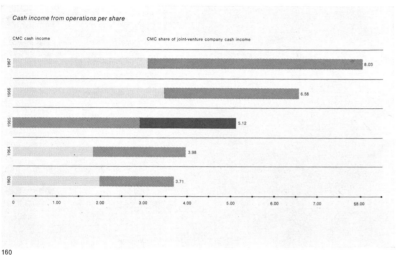

Cash income from operations per share

160

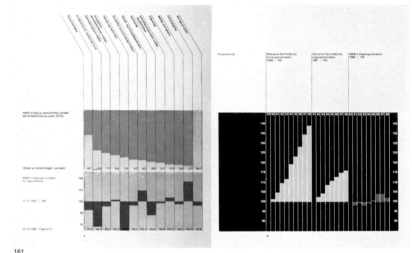

161

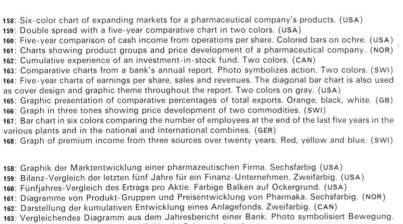

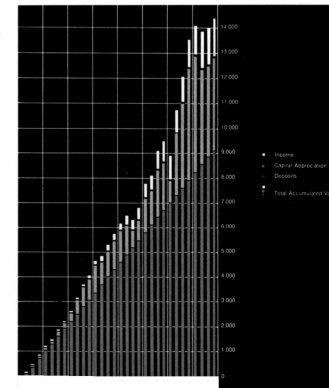

162

158: Six-color chart of expanding markets for a pharmaceutical company's products. (USA)
159: Double spread with a five-year comparative chart in two colors. (USA)
160: Five-year comparison of cash income from operations per share. Colored bars on ochre. (USA)
161: Charts showing product groups and price development of a pharmaceutical company. (NOR)
162: Cumulative experience of an investment-in-stock fund. Two colors. (CAN)
163: Comparative charts from a bank's annual report. Photo symbolizes action. Two colors. (SWI)
164: Five-year charts of earnings per share, sales and revenues. The diagonal bar chart is also used as cover design and graphic theme throughout the report. Two colors on gray. (USA)
165: Graphic presentation of comparative percentages of total exports. Orange, black, white. (GB)
166: Graph in three tones showing price development of two commodities. (SWI)
167: Bar chart in six colors comparing the number of employees at the end of the last five years in the various plants and in the national and international combines. (GER)
168: Graph of premium income from three sources over twenty years. Red, yellow and blue. (SWI)

158: Graphik der Marktentwicklung einer pharmazeutischen Firma. Sechsfarbig (USA)
159: Bilanz-Vergleich der letzten fünf Jahre für ein Finanz-Unternehmen. Zweifarbig. (USA)
160: Fünfjahres-Vergleich des Ertrags pro Aktie. Farbige Balken auf Ockergrund. (USA)
161: Diagramme von Produkt-Gruppen und Preisentwicklung von Pharmaka. Sechsfarbig. (NOR)
162: Darstellung der kumulativen Entwicklung eines Anlagefonds. Zweifarbig. (CAN)
163: Vergleichendes Diagramm aus dem Jahresbericht einer Bank. Photo symbolisiert Bewegung. Balken in Grün, Photo, Linien und Zahlen in Schwarz. (SWI)
164: Fünfjahres-Vergleich des Ertrags pro Aktie und der Einnahmen. Ocker und rot auf Grau. (USA)
165: Graphische Darstellung der prozentualen Aufteilung des Totalexportes. Orange, schwarz. (GB)
166: Kurvendiagramm der Preisentwicklung von Zucker und Kakao. (SWI)
167: Vergleich des Standes der Belegschaft in Werken und Konzernen. Sechsfarbig. (GER)
168: Statistik des Zuwachses von Prämieneinnahmen während zwanzig Jahren. Balken in Orange, Gelb und Blau, Linien und Zahlen in Schwarz. (SWI)

158: Evolution du marché d'une firme de produits pharmaceutiques. Six couleurs. (USA)
159: Comparaison des cinq derniers bilans d'une société financière. Deux couleurs. (USA)
160: Comparaison sur cinq ans des revenus par action. Barres colorées sur fond ocre. (USA)
161: Diagrammes de groupes de produits pharmaceutiques et du développement de leurs prix. (NOR)
162: Evolution globale d'un programme de fonds de placement. Deux couleurs. (CAN)
163: Graphiques tirés du rapport annuel d'une banque. Photo symbolisant le mouvement. (SWI)
164: Comparaisons sur cinq ans du bénéfice par action et des recettes. Ocre et rouge sur gris. (USA)
165: Répartition en pour-cent des exportations globales. Orange sur noir. (GB)
166: Diagramme de l'évolution des prix du sucre et du cacao. (SWI)
167: Comparaison des effectifs occupés dans divers groupes et usines. Six couleurs. (GER)
168: Statistique sur 20 ans de l'accroissement des recettes de primes. Rouge, jaune, bleu. (SWI)

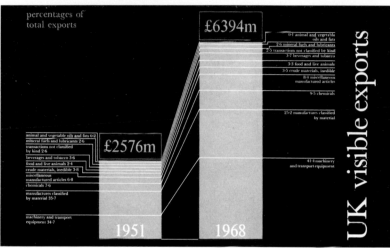

163

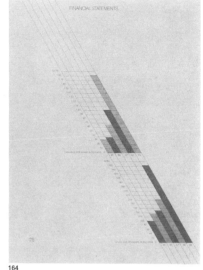

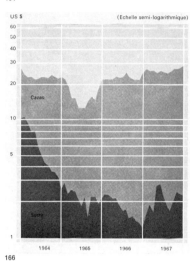

164

DESIGNER:

158: Norman Perman
159: Carl Seltzer
160: Detlef Hallerbach
161: Bruno Oldani
162: Jacques Charette
163: Willi Kunz (Photo Michel Zumbrunn)
164: Jay Tribich
165: Kenn Waplington/Tom Bund
166: Atelier Wicky
167: Volkswagenwerk Aktiengesellschaft
168: Hans Hartmann

ART DIRECTOR:

158: Charles Walz, Jr.
159: Advertising Designers, Inc.
160: R. L. Steinle/
    Advertising Designers, Inc.
162: Jacques Charette
163: Rolf Ziegelbauer
164: William R. Tobias
165: Richard Negus
166: Atelier Wicky

STUDIO – AGENCY:

158: Norman Perman
159, 160: Advertising Designers, Inc.
162: J. E. Charette Designers Inc.
163: Atelier für Werbung & Grafik
164: Robert Miles Runyan Associates
165: Negus & Negus
166: Atelier Wicky
167: Volkswagenwerk Aktiengesellschaft

percentages of total exports

£6394m

£2576m

1951   1968

UK visible exports

165

166

COMPANY:

158: Abbott Laboratories
159: Financial Federation, Inc.
160: Cyprus Mines Corp.
161: NMD Norsk Medisinaldepot
162: Sun Life Assurance Co. of Canada
163: Bank Rohner & Co. AG
164: City Investing Company
165: British National Export Council
166: Suchard Holding S.A.
167: Volkswagenwerk Aktiengesellschaft
168: Schweiz. Mobiliar-Versicherungs-
    gesellschaft

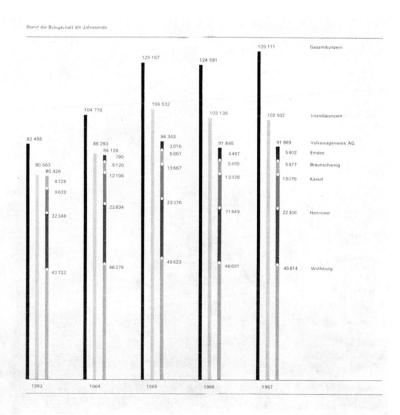

167

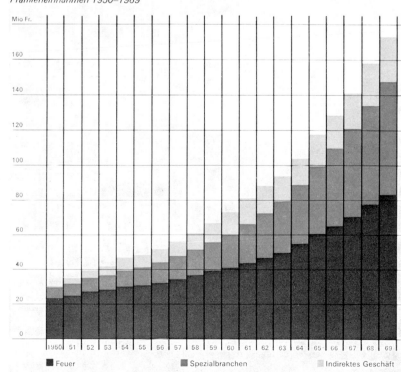

Prämieneinnahmen 1950–1969

■ Feuer   ■ Spezialbranchen   ▪ Indirektes Geschäft

168

Charts & Graphs
Diagramme, Tabellen
Diagrammes et graphiques

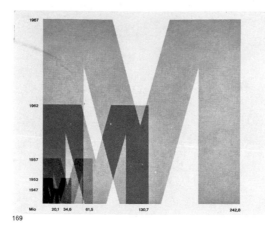

169

170

DESIGNER:

169: Jürg Spahr
170: Samuel Antupit
171: Leslie A. Segal
172: Erik Nitsche
173: Roger Cook/Don Shanosky
174: Peter Wehr
175: Eugen & Max Lenz
176: Eskil Ohlsson
177: Norman Perman
178: Gottfried Prölss

ART DIRECTOR:

169: Jürg Spahr
170: Samuel Antupit
171: Leslie A. Segal
172: Erik Nitsche
173: Roger Cook/Don Shanosky
175: Eugen & Max Lenz
176: Eskil Ohlsson
177: Neal Ball

STUDIO – AGENCY:

170: Hess and/or Antupit
171: Corporate Annual Reports, Inc.
173: Cook & Shanosky Associates, Inc.
175: Atelier Eugen & Max Lenz
176: Mc David, Richmond & Rudd

COMPANY:

169: Genossenschaft Migros Basel
170: Mead Corporation
171: W. R. Grace & Co.
172: General Dynamics Corp.
173: Brown Company
174: Martin Brinkmann AG
175: Swissair Schweizer. Luftverkehr AG
176: Grow Chemical Corp.
177: American Hospital Supply Corporation
178: Energie-Versorgung Schwaben AG

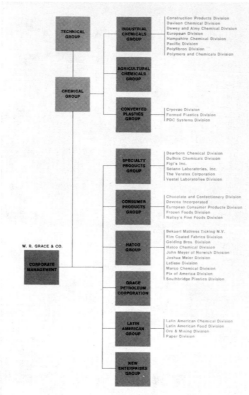

171

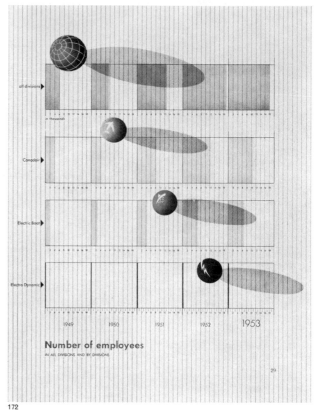

172

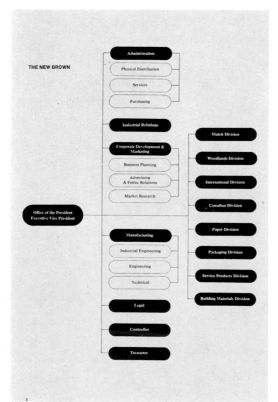

173

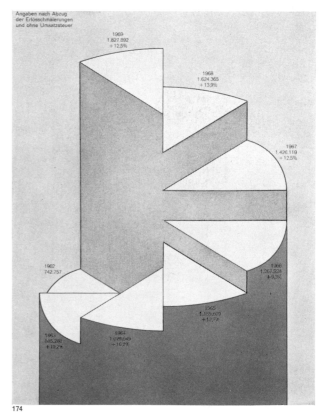

174

122

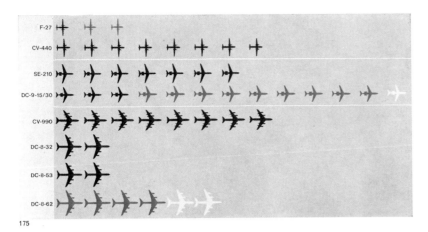

175

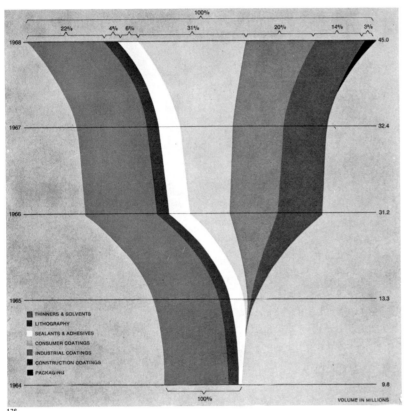

176

169: Sales development of a supermarket chain over twenty years. The company's trade mark, the "M", is used as the graphic element of this chart. Orange and black. (SWI)
170: Graphic presentation in the form of a game showing the company's growth potential. (USA)
171: Corporate structure chart of a diversified company. Colors: rust, ochre, brown and red. (USA)
172: Graph comparing the number of employees by divisions. Full color. (From 1953 report). (USA)
173: Chart of organizational structure of the company. Dark blue on tinted stock. (USA)
174: Spiral-stair chart showing yearly increases in net receipts. Brown, orange, pink on yellow. (GER)
175: Composition of an airline's commercial fleet. Red, blue and white on gray. Red: in service, blue: on order, white: optional. (SWI)
176: Five-year growth chart from the annual report of a chemical company. The colors are from left to right: brown, red, white, lavender, blue, green and black on buff ground. (USA)
177: Growth performance over five years, represented in tree form in shades of red-brown. (USA)
178: Graph of social and salary expenditures and number of employees. In six colors. (GER)

169: Graphische Darstellung der Umsatzentwicklung der letzten zwanzig Jahre. Anwendung des Firmensignets « M » als graphisches Element. Schwarz und orange. (SWI)
170: Illustration des potentiellen Wachstums der Firma in der Form eines Würfelspieles. (USA)
171: Schema der Struktur eines Handels- und Industriekonzerns. Rost, ocker, braun und rot. (USA)
172: Vergleich des Belegschafts-Bestandes verschiedener Abteilungen. (Jahresbericht 1953). (USA)
173: Organisationsstruktur-Schema der Gesellschaft. Dunkelblau auf getöntem Papier. (USA)
174: Jährlicher Zuwachs der Netto-Umsatzerlöse, dargestellt in Wendeltreppenform. Braun, orange und rosa auf gelbem Grund. Linien und Schrift in Schwarz. (GER)
175: Zusammensetzung der kommerziellen Flotte einer Luftverkehrs-Gesellschaft. (SWI)
176: Darstellung des Wachstums der Firma während fünf Jahren. Sechs Farben auf Beige. (USA)
177: Fünfjahres-Vergleich der Zunahme des Ertrages für Aktionäre. In rot-braunen Tönen. (USA)
178: Diagramm des Personalaufwandes und der Zahl der Mitarbeiter. Sechsfarbig. (GER)

169: Evolution sur 20 ans des ventes d'une chaîne de supermarchés. « M », le sigle de l'entreprise, est utilisé comme élément graphique. Orange et noir. (SWI)
170: Potentiel de croissance d'une entreprise, représenté sous forme d'un jeu. (USA)
171: Structure d'une société aux activités diversifiées. Couleurs: roux, ocre, brun et rouge. (USA)
172: Effectifs des employés par division. Multicolore. (Rapport de 1953). (USA)
173: Organigramme d'une société. Bleu foncé sur papier teint. (USA)
174: Graphique en colimaçon: accroissement annuel des recettes nettes. Quatre couleurs. (GER)
175: Composition d'une flotte aérienne commerciale. Rouge, bleu et blanc sur gris. (SWI)
176: Croissance sur cinq ans, graphique tiré du rapport d'une entreprise chimique. Les couleurs sont, de gauche à droite: brun, rouge, blanc, lavande, bleu, vert et noir sur fond chamois. (USA)
177: Croissance sur cinq ans, graphique en forme d'arbre, nuances brun-rouge. (USA)
178: Graphique des charges sociales et salariales et du nombre d'employés. Six couleurs. (GER)

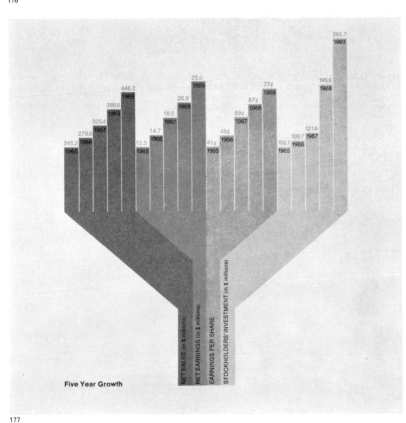

177

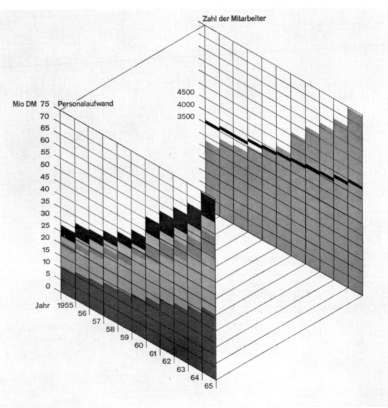

178

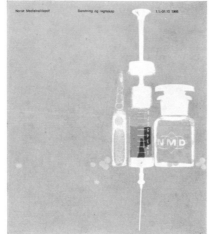

179

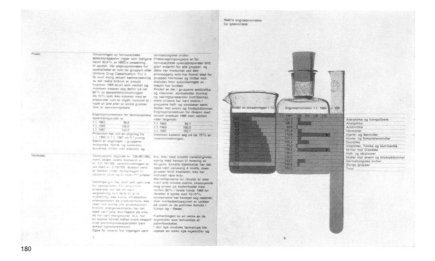

180

DESIGNER:

179–183: Bruno Oldani
184–187: Gottfried Prölss
187–188: Elso Schiavo

ART DIRECTOR:

188: Elso Schiavo

STUDIO – AGENCY:

188: Werbeagentur Ben Plüss

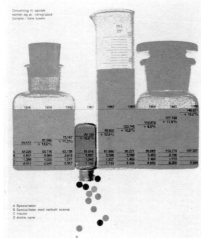

181

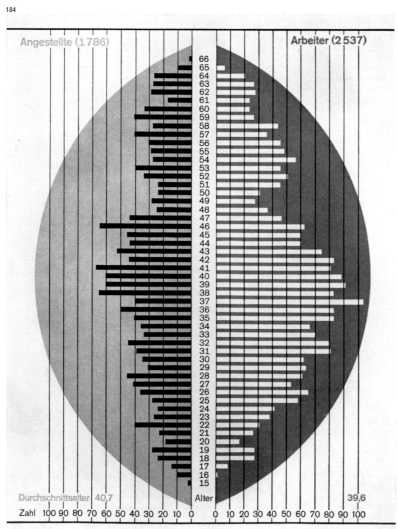

182

184

185

179–183: Annual report of a pharmaceutical company, using photographically derived illustrations as graphic theme: 179) Cover, red background; 180–183) examples of the incorporation of the photographic illustrations into spreads, charts and graphs. All in full color. (NOR)
184–187: Charts and graphs from annual reports of a public utility company: 184) Graph showing age structure of employees; 185) comparison of power-line length and electricity consumption; 186, 187) charts of power production and supply. Three to five colors. (GER)
188: Pie chart of a health insurance company's assets. Identical chart for liabilities. (SWI)

179–183: Jahresbericht einer pharmazeutischen Firma. Die graphischen Motive sind in Kornmanier umgesetzte Photos. 179) Titelseite, auf rotem Grund; 180–183) Anwendungsbeispiele der photographischen Illustrationen in Verbindung mit Diagrammen und Tabellen. Alle mehrfarbig. (NOR)
184–187: Statistische Diagramme aus Geschäftsberichten einer Gesellschaft für Energieversorgung: 184) Altersaufbau der Belegschaft; 185) Vergleich von Leitungslängen und Stromverbrauch; 186, 187) Diagramme von Strombeschaffung und Stromlieferung. Drei- bis fünffarbig. (GER)
188: Kreisdiagramm der Aufteilung der Aktiven im Geschäftsbericht einer Krankenkasse. Die Passiven wurden anhand eines gleichen Diagramms gezeigt. (SWI)

179–183: Rapport annuel d'une firme de produits pharmaceutiques. Illustrations graphiques tirées de photographies: 179) Couverture, fond rouge; 180–183) exemples d'illustrations photographiques en combinaison avec des graphiques et diagrammes. Polychrome. (NOR)
184–187: Graphiques tirés de rapports annuels d'une compagnie d'électricité: 184) Structure d'âge de l'effectif ouvrier; 185) longueur des lignes comparée avec la consommation de courant; 186, 187) graphiques de la production et des livraisons de courant. De trois à cinq couleurs. (GER)
188: Diagramme circulaire montrant la composition des actifs d'une caisse-maladie. (SWI)

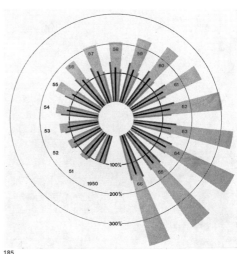

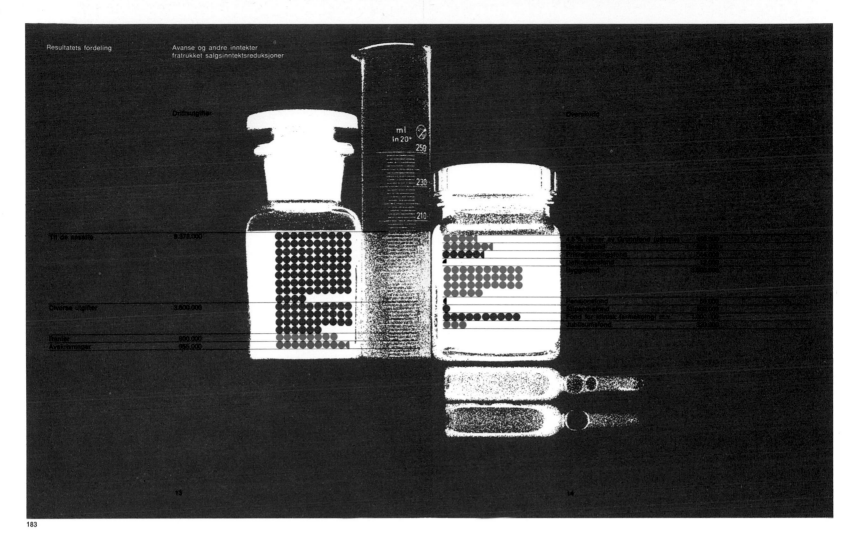

183

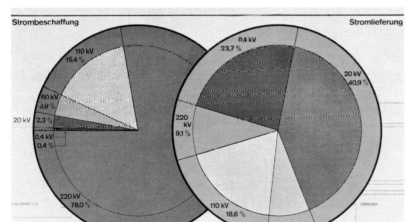

186

COMPANY:

179–183: Norsk Medisinaldepot
184–187: Energie-Versorgung Schwaben AG
188: Schweiz. Betriebskrankenkasse

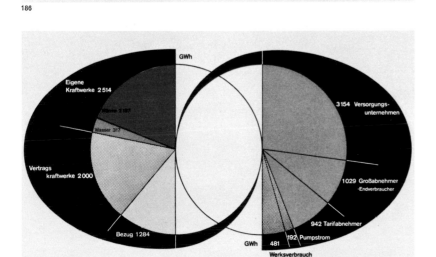

187

188

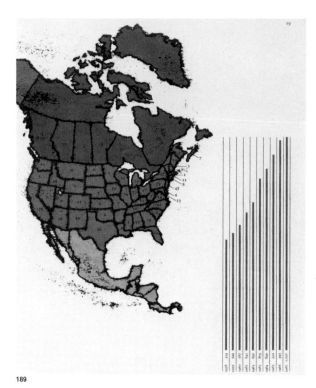

189

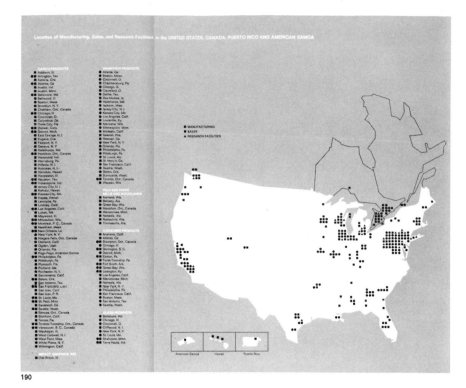

190

189: Map and graph showing distribution and increase of a finance company's branch offices. Ochre, blue, olive and black. (USA)
190: Location map of the company's facilities. Two colors. (USA)
191: Map of rail, air and maritime services, location of hotels owned by the company. Double spread. (CAN)
192–194: Cover and details from the annual report of a bank. The maps show the countries in which it has branches or affiliates. (FRA)

DESIGNER:

189: Carl Seltzer
190: George Tscherny
191: Peter Hablützel
192–194: Georges Lemoine

ART DIRECTOR:

189: Advertising Designers, Inc.
190: George Tscherny
191: Frank Lipary
192–194: Georges Lemoine

STUDIO – AGENCY:

189: Advertising Designers, Inc.
190: George Tscherny, Inc.
191: Gazette Printing Co. Ltd.
192–194: Delpire-Advico S.A.

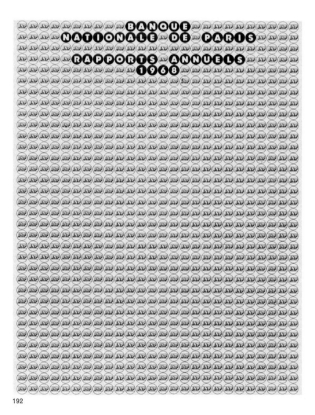

192

189: Karte und Diagramm der Verteilung und der Zunahme von Zweigstellen eines Darlehens-Instituts. Ocker, blau, oliv und schwarz. (USA)
190: Karte der Fabrikations-, Verkaufs- und Forschungsanlagen. (USA)
191: Karte des Bahn-, Luft- und Schiffverkehrsnetzes und Lage von gesellschaftseigenen Hotels. Doppelseite. (CAN)
192–194: Titelblatt, Seite und Detail aus dem Jahresbericht einer Bank. Die Karten zeigen die Länder, in denen sich Filialen befinden. (FRA)

189: Carte et diagramme montrant l'implantation et l'expansion des filiales d'un établissement financier. Ocre, bleu, olive et noir. (USA)
190: Carte des centres de fabrication, de vente et de recherche. (USA)
191: Carte des lignes de chemins de fer, aériennes et maritimes, ainsi que des situations des propres hôtels de la société. Double page. (CAN)
192–194: Rapport annuel d'une banque: couverture et détails. Sur les cartes, pays où elle possède des succursales ou des filiales. (FRA)

193

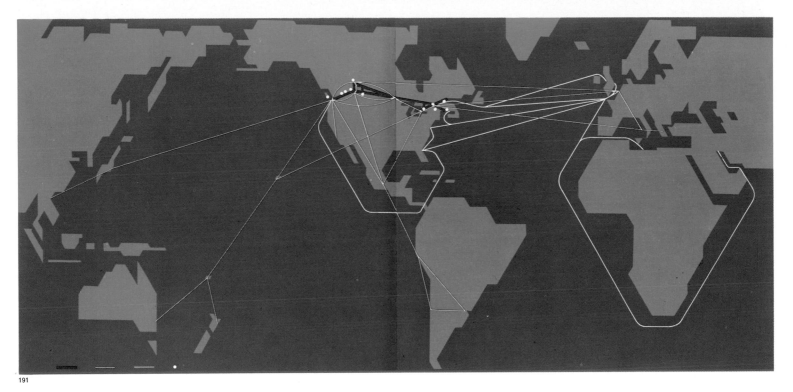

191

COMPANY:

189: Seaboard Finance Co.
190: American Can Company
191: Canadian Pacific
192–194: Banque Nationale de Paris

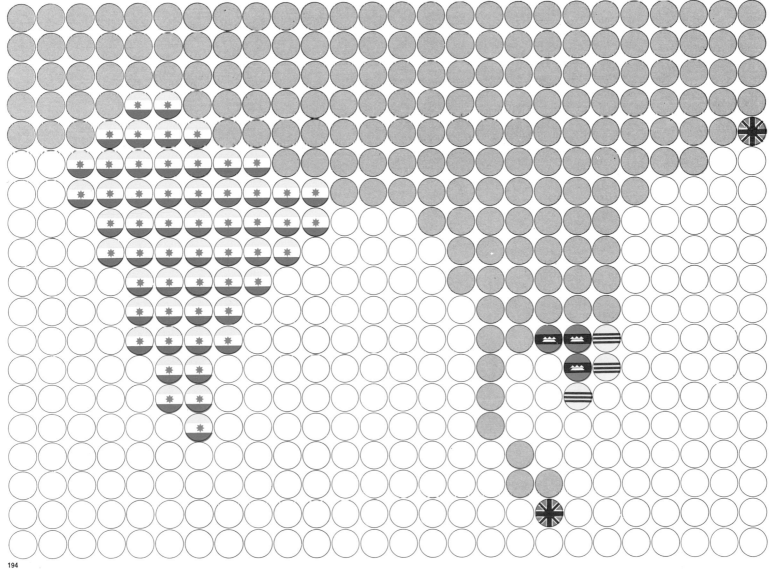

194

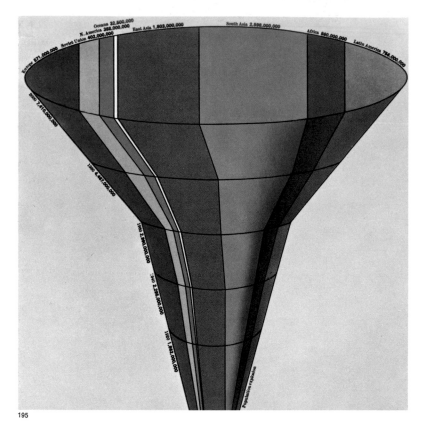

Oceans 22,600,000
N. America 399,000,000
Soviet Union 402,000,000
East Asia 1,903,000,000
South Asia 2,598,000,000
Africa 860,000,000
Latin America 784,000,000
Europe 671,000,000

2000 7,410,000,000
1980 4,467,000,000
1940 2,295,000,000
1900 1,682,000,000

Population explosion

195

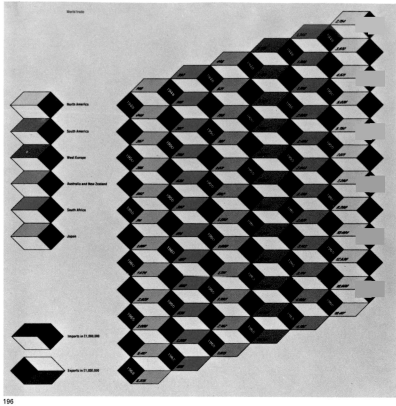

World trade

North America
South America
West Europe
Australia and New Zealand
South Africa
Japan

Imports in £1,000,000
Exports in £1,000,000

196

U CENTRES OF HIGHER EDUCATION   O OIL REFINERIES   C COAL   R MOBILE OIL RIGS   O OIL CONCESSIONS   S SHEEP

F FISHING   M MANUFACTURING AND INDUSTRIAL AREAS   A AGRICULTURAL AREAS   H HYDRO ELECTRIC POWER STATIONS   N NUCLEAR POWER STATIONS   F FISH FREEZING PLANTS

197

DESIGNER:

195–203: Crosby/Fletcher/Forbes
(Charts by Anna Pugh)

STUDIO – AGENCY:

195–203: Crosby/Fletcher/Forbes

COMPANY:

195–203: Inbucon Limited

198

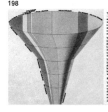

199

128

200

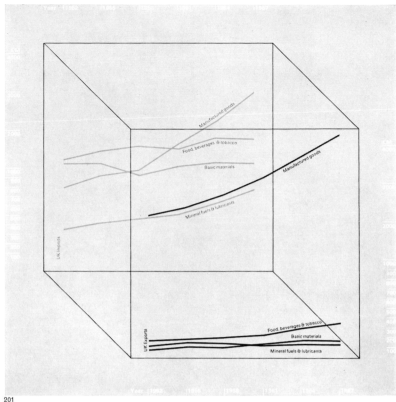

201

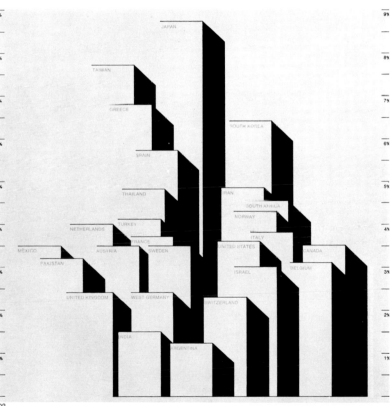

202

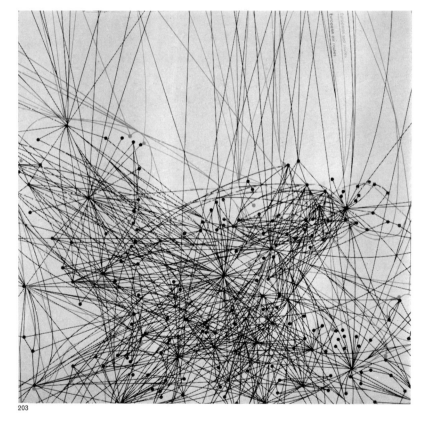

203

195–203: Maps, charts and graphs from the report of a management consultant service organization. The charts illustrate some of the more important factors shaping the international economy: 195, 198) Projection of the population explosion to the year 2000; 196) chart containing data on world trade; 197) typographical map showing the resources of the United Kingdom—the top and bottom lines contain the key; 199, 200) chart of the production of raw materials, the columns representing the continents (full color); 201) graph plotting UK import and export figures, with imports in blue, exports in red, on gray background; 202) graphic presentation of the average annual rise in real GNP per capita, 1962–67, with black verticals, red horizontals on gray; 203) network of European air and sea routes , with air in red, sea in blue on gray ground. (GB)

195–203: Cartes et graphiques tirés du rapport annuel d'une organisation de conseil en management. Les graphiques illustrent quelques-uns des principaux facteurs qui influencent l'économie mondiale: 195, 198) Projection de l'expansion démographique jusqu'en l'an 2000; 196) diagramme avec données sur le commerce mondial; 197) carte typographique des ressources du Royaume-Uni. Les lignes en haut et en bas de la page donnent les explications nécessaires; 199, 200) production de matières premières, les colonnes représentant les continents. Multicolore; 201) diagramme illustrant le développement des importations et exportations du Royaume-Uni. Importations: bleu, exportations: rouge; 202) augmentation annuelle moyenne du Produit National Brut par habitant, de 1962 à 1967; 203) carte du réseau aérien et maritime européen. Lignes aériennes: rouge, lignes maritimes: bleu. (GB)

195–203: Diagramme und Karten aus dem Geschäftsbericht einer Management-Beratungsorganisation. Die graphischen Darstellungen illustrieren einige der wichtigeren Faktoren, welche die internationale Wirtschaft beeinflussen: 195, 198) Projektion der Bevölkerungs-Explosion auf das Jahr 2000. 196) Diagramm mit Daten über Welthandel; 197) typographische Karte der Wirtschaftsquellen von Grossbritannien. Die oberste und unterste Linie enthalten den Schlüssel; 199, 200) Produktion von Rohmaterialien. Jede Säule stellt einen Erdteil dar. Mehrfarbig; 201) Kurvendiagramm der Import- und Exportentwicklung. Importe Blau, Exporte Rot; 202) graphische Darstellung des durchschnittlichen jährlichen Anstiegs des Bruttosozialproduktes pro Kopf von 1962 bis 1967. 203) Europäisches Schiff- und Luftverkehrsnetz. Rot und blau, auf grauem Grund. (GB)

**Charts & Graphs/Diagramme, Tabellen
Diagrammes et graphiques**

129

Graphic Illustration

Die graphische Illustration

L'illustration graphique

204

205

206

204, 205: Illustration and spread from a report of the *National Boulevard Bank of Chicago*. (USA)
206—208: Cover in full color, spread and illustration in black and white from an annual report of the *Perfect Film & Chemical Corporation*, a company with enterprises in the photofinishing, publishing and mail-order fields. (USA)
209—211: Spread and two illustrations from the 1968 annual report of *Sterling Drug, Inc.* The illustrations, each representing a product group, are printed on semi-transparent paper permitting the following page with a list of product names to show through. (USA)

204, 205: Zweifarbige Illustration und Doppelseite aus dem Geschäftsbericht einer Bank. (USA)
206—208: Farbiges Titelblatt, Doppelseite und Illustration in Schwarzweiss aus dem Jahresbericht einer Firma, die sich im Photolabor-, Verlags- und Postversandgeschäft betätigt. (USA)
209—211: Doppelseite und zwei Illustrationen aus dem Jahresbericht eines chemisch-pharmazeutischen Unternehmens. Die Illustrationen sind auf halbtransparentes Papier gedruckt, durch das die darunterliegende Seite mit einer Liste von Produktnamen sichtbar ist. (USA)

204, 205: Illustration en deux couleurs et page double d'un compte rendu d'une banque. (USA)
206—208: Couverture polychrome, page double et illustration en noir et blanc du rapport annuel d'une compagnie entretenant des laboratoires photo, des maisons d'édition et des services d'expédition postale. (USA)
209—211: Page double et deux illustrations extraites du rapport annuel 1968 d'une entreprise de produits chimiques et pharmaceutiques. Les illustrations, représentant chacune un groupe de produits, sont imprimées sur papier semi-transparent faisant transparaître ainsi la page suivante qui contient une liste des produits en question. (USA)

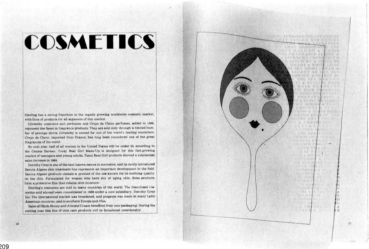

209

DESIGNER:

204, 205: Pitt Group
206—208: Hess and/or Antupit
209—211: Leonard Fury

ILLUSTRATOR:

204, 205: Don Trousdell
206—208: David Wilcox
209—211: Arnold Varga

ART DIRECTOR:

206—208: Frank Zachary
209—211: Leonard Fury

STUDIO – AGENCY:

206—208: Hess and/or Antupit
209—211: Corporate Annual Reports, Inc.

Graphic Illustrations
Graphische Illustrationen
Illustrations graphiques

Perfect Film & Chemical Corporation: 1968

207

208

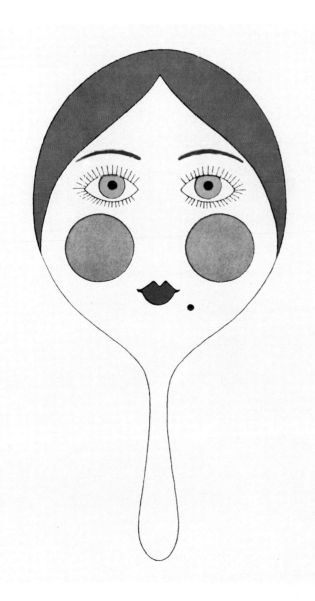

210

211

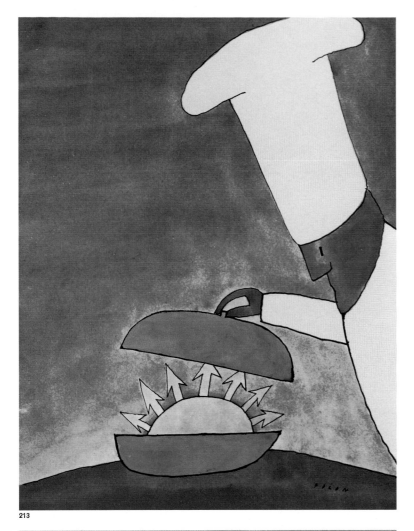

213

214

215

216

212–216: Cover, illustrations and spread from the 1969 annual report of *Restaurant Associates Industries, Inc.* **212, 216**) Full-page illustration and spread introducing the restaurant division of the firm. **213, 215**) Cover detail and complete cover. Illustration on black background. **214**) Illustration facing the report on the Treadway Inns division, a chain of highway motor inns operated by this company. (USA)

212–216: Titelblatt, Illustrationen und Doppelseite aus dem Geschäftsbericht einer Firma der Verpflegungs- und Motelbranche. **212, 216**) Ganzseitige Illustration und Doppelseite, die den Bericht über die Restaurationsbetriebe der Firma enthält. **213, 215**) Titelseite: Illustration und ganze Umschlagseite. Bild auf schwarzem Grund. **214**) Illustration zur Einleitung des Berichtes über die Motel-Abteilung der Gesellschaft. (USA)

212–216: Couverture, illustrations et page double tirées du rapport annuel '69 d'une entreprise spécialisée dans le service du ravitaillement et de l'entretien de motels. **212, 216**) Illustrations sur page entière et page double présentant le compte rendu de restaurants appartenant à cette société. **213, 215**) Couverture: détail et couverture complète; illustration en couleurs sur fond noir. **214**) Illustration introduisant le compte rendu de la chaîne de motels. (USA)

DESIGNER:
212–216: Hess and/or Antupit

ILLUSTRATOR:
212–216: Jean Michel Folon

ART DIRECTOR:
212–216: Richard Hess

STUDIO – AGENCY:
212–216: Hess and/or Antupit

**Graphic Illustrations
Graphische Illustrationen
Illustrations graphiques**

Intergalactic Mining and Manufacturing Company, Incorporated

218
1998 Annual Report

219

DESIGNER:

217–221: Seymour Chwast

ILLUSTRATOR:

217–221: Seymour Chwast

ART DIRECTOR:

217–221: Jack Feldman

STUDIO – AGENCY:

217–221: Brewer, Jones & Feldman, Inc.

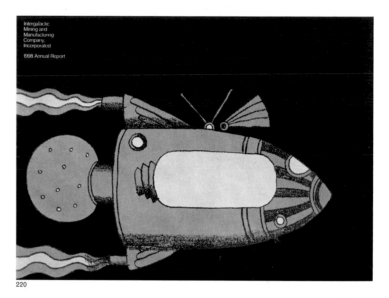

Intergalactic
Mining and
Manufacturing
Company,
Incorporated

1998 Annual Report

220

221

217–221: This double spread shows illustrations from the fictitious 1998 annual report of the *Intergalactic Mining and Manufacturing Company,* a non-existent corporation. The report was produced as part of a sample kit for a paper company, promoting different kinds of paper. The illustrator's aim was to create a spoof rather than a parody. He adopted a childish style, as children are fascinated by outer space. He also wanted to do the opposite of the usual slick photos seen in annual reports. We include this spread as a possible inspiration to designers. 218) Cover; 220) envelope. (USA)

217–221: Diese Doppelseite zeigt Titelblatt (218), Kuvert (220) und Illustrationen aus dem fiktiven Jahresbericht 1998 einer nicht bestehenden «intergalaktischen» Bergbaufirma. Der Bericht war Bestandteil der Mustersendung einer Papierfabrik und war als Scherz konzipiert. Der Illustrator imitierte mit Absicht einen kindlichen Stil, weil Kinder grosses Interesse am Weltraum zeigen. Er suchte bewusst ein Gegengewicht zu den in Geschäftsberichten üblichen raffinierten Photos. Wir zeigen diese Illustrationen als mögliche Inspiration für Gestalter. (USA)

217–221: Couverture (218), enveloppe (220) et illustrations tirées d'un rapport annuel fictif d'une entreprise minière «intergalactique». Ce rapport d'une papeterie faisait partie d'une collection d'échantillons pour introduire de nouveaux papiers. Il a été conçu comme annexe facétieuse et comique. L'illustrateur a intentionnellement imité le style des dessins d'enfants, car l'espace intéresse énormément ceux-ci. Il voulait marquer le pendant des rapports illustrés de photos raffinées. Nous reproduisons quelques exemples qui pourraient servir de source d'inspiration. (USA)

222

223

224

225

226

227

DESIGNER:

222, 223: Robert K. Rafn
224–227: David A. Lizotte/Bill Clark
228: Henry Robertz
229: Robert Saabye/Horton,
      Church & Goff, Inc.

ILLUSTRATOR:

222, 223: Merv Corning
224–227: Charles Saxon
228: Franklin McMahon
229: Jerry Pinkney

ART DIRECTOR:

222, 223: Robert K. Rafn
224–227: Bill Clark
228: E. Zapalik
229: Robert Saabye

STUDIO – AGENCY:

222, 223: Studio Artists
224–227: K & E/Gunn Associates
228: Henry Robertz Design, Chicago
229: Horton, Church & Goff, Inc.

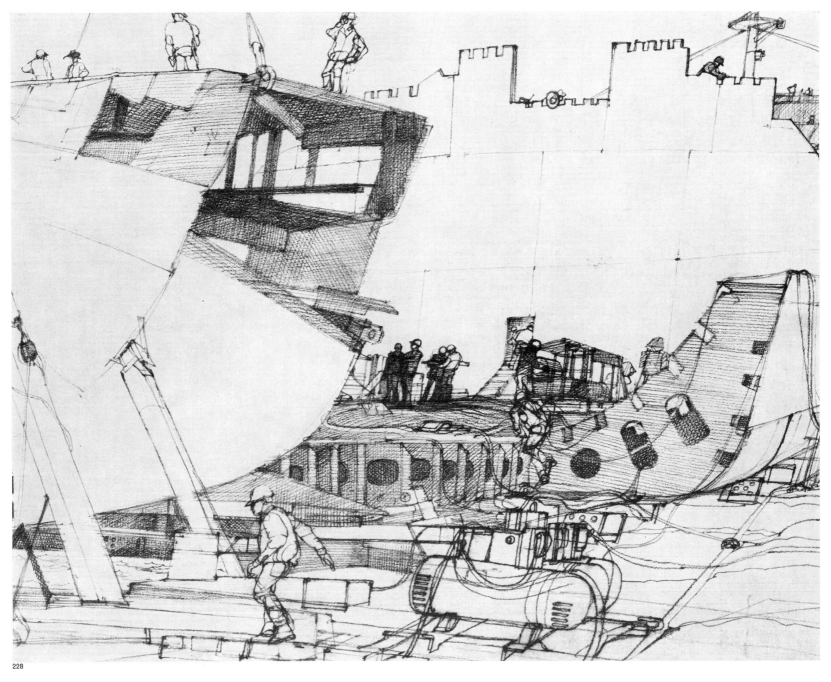

228

222, 223: Paintings from the 1969 annual report of the *Planning Research Corporation*, commissioned to describe the corporation's qualifications for finding practical solutions to social, economic and technical problems arising from the world's urban conditions. (USA)
224–227: "Saxon's Boston" is the theme of the 1969 annual report of the *New England Merchants National Bank*. The illustrator was asked to visit Boston and record his impressions of a changing city in a year of change. (USA)
228: The 1967 annual report of the *Chicago Bridge & Iron Company* features the work and comments of a freelance artist/reporter. "So we might see ourselves as others see us." Shown here is a pencil sketch of a company shipyard scene. (USA)
229: In the 1967 annual report of the *Manufacturers Mutual Fire Insurance Company* Aesop's fables dramatize the need for effective human engineering in establishing and maintaining a successful property conservation program. (USA)

222, 223: Illustrationen aus dem Jahresbericht einer Gesellschaft für Planung und Forschung, die die Fähigkeiten der Firma, soziale, wirtschaftliche und technische Umweltprobleme zu lösen, mit praktischen Beispielen belegen. Vierfarbendruck. (USA)
224–227: «Saxon's Boston» ist das graphische Thema des Geschäftsberichtes einer Bank. Der Künstler wurde nach Boston eingeladen mit dem Auftrag, seine Eindrücke von dieser Stadt in einem Jahr des raschen Wandels zu glossieren. Einfarbig. (USA)
228: Eine Brücken- und Eisenbaufirma beauftragte einen Künstler-Reporter, für ihren Geschäftsbericht ihre Werke und Baustellen zu zeichnen und seine Eindrücke zu beschreiben. (USA)
229: Aesops Fabeln dienen diesem Bericht einer Feuerversicherungs-Gesellschaft als Thema zur Dramatisierung der Notwendigkeit wirksamer menschlicher Leitsätze in der Planung und Durchführung von Eigentumsschutz-Programmen. Vierfarbendruck. (USA)

222, 223: Illustrations du rapport annuel 1969 d'une société de planification et de recherche, symbolisant les efforts de cette société à résoudre les problèmes sociaux, économiques et techniques que posent la condition urbaine de par le monde. (USA)
224–227: «Boston vue par Saxon» est le thème du rapport annuel '69 d'une banque ayant invité l'artiste de ce nom à esquisser ses impressions de la ville pendant que celle-ci subit de grands changements. (USA)
228: Un artiste-reporter fut chargé de l'illustration des chantiers et du commentaire, pour que cette entreprise de construction de ponts «se voie par les yeux d'autrui». (USA)
229: Les fables d'Esope constituent le thème du rapport annuel d'une assurance incendie devant démontrer de manière dramatique la nécessité de principes efficaces pour élaborer et améliorer un programme de protection de la propriété. (USA)

229

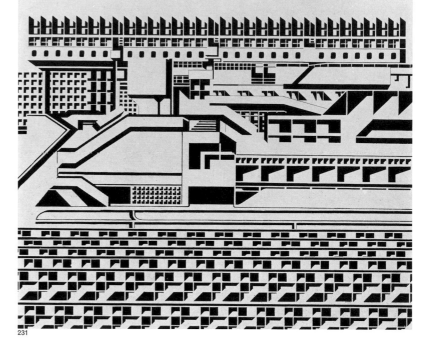

230

Cumbernauld New Town

This complex piece of concrete geometry is at the heart of the world's most stimulating experiment in urban living. It is part of the Town Centre of the New Town of Cumbernauld, which is being built midway between Glasgow and Stirling. By mid-1967, when an artist from the Royal College of Art visited it, the first one-fifth of the Centre had been completed and most of that section had already been occupied by shops, banks, offices, library, hotel, and pub. Another four-fifths will gradually take shape as the town grows to its planned size.

Cumbernauld is unique. Its Centre is as different from an old market town High Street as a 60-seater bus is from a stage coach. It is the first town planned for the motor age. Even when there are 1·4 cars per family, traffic will always be able to flow freely, and yet every house is within walking distance of the weatherproof Town Centre with its shopping, entertainments, and social services. It is a town densely built, but with green open spaces for enjoyment, where children may play safely, and with sun, privacy, and quiet for every house.

231

The Group in 1968

A farm in Denbighshire receives a delivery of tractor fuel. Every day thousands of deliveries of Group products are made in every part of Britain and Ireland to many different types of customer—service stations, farms, factories, ships, aircraft, transport undertakings, road builders, and many others. In the following pages we describe, and our student friends illustrate, some of the ways in which we were improving our service in 1968.

The Retail Petrol Market

Three factors dominate the retail petrol market today. Each must have an impact on the methods an oil company uses to make its service to the motoring public as complete as possible. These factors are :
1. The effect of inflation on petrol retailers' costs.
2. The much wider ownership of motor cars.
3. The continually increasing tax on petrol, which has now reached a record 4s 3.7d per gallon, or over 70 per cent of the price (of ordinary grade petrol).

The first of these factors compels any oil company to try constantly to cut both its own costs and those of the retailers which it supplies. This can be achieved both by providing up-to-date equipment, permitting more effective use of labour, and by improving sales at individual outlets. Shell-Mex and B.P. has tackled both these aspects of the problem energetically and has taken into account at the same time the need, deriving from the second factor of wider car ownership, to develop a more flexible approach to methods of service.

Self-service is an example of the installation of new equipment which both reduces labour costs and provides a facility which is increasingly popular with motorists. In 1968 a new Shell self-service station at Leicester sold well over one million gallons of petrol. At this site the motorist parks his car at one of a large number of pumps, serves himself, and steps over to a kiosk to pay the bill which is already waiting for him. The whole operation can be completed very speedily. There were 25 Shell petrol stations of this type at the end of 1968, with a high and increasing throughput.

National has installed at a filling station at Purley, Surrey, the first multi-note acceptor unit for self-service, which enables the motorist to obtain up to £2-worth of petrol from the nearby pump. In addition National has more than 100 petrol stations with the coin-operated pumps.
By the end of 1968 BP had 100 £1-note-acceptor self-service sites in operation, and plans to have 300 by 1971. Note-acceptor units and coin-operated pumps enable the motorist to obtain petrol 24 hours a day, seven days a week, and this is being increasingly

appreciated by motorists.
All three brands are developing shops for motorists at petrol stations. By the end of 1968 there were some 800 shops in the Shell, National and BP networks.
It is now an established practice at large garages in the United Kingdom to provide diagnostic inspection centres for cars. These centres meet the growing demand from the motorist for an efficient check on the safety and performance of his car. This has indeed become a necessary service in the light of stricter Ministry of Transport regulations on.

232

140

Graphic Illustrations
Graphische Illustrationen
Illustrations graphiques

DESIGNER:

230, 231: Les Seabrook

ILLUSTRATOR:

230: Les Seabrook
231, 233: Michael Cook
232: Michael Bradshaw
234: Jim Haldane

ART DIRECTOR:

232-234: David Tuhill

STUDIO – AGENCY:

230–234: Royal College of Art

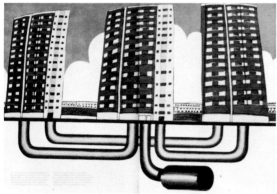

233

230–234: The annual report of the *Shell-Mex and B.P. Group* is published under the title *Book of the Year*. In 1967 they invited a team of students from the Graphic Design School of the Royal College of Art to design, illustrate and art edit the whole book. The experiment was a great success and was repeated in 1968 and 1969. The work is undertaken on fully professional terms and is carried out in a professional way. 230) Cover of the 1967 yearbook. Photographically derived pattern formed by pipes. In black and white. Lettering gold. 231) Graphic interpretation in black and white of a new town built for the motor age and featured in the 1967 yearbook. 232) Double-page illustration in full color showing a tank truck delivering tractor fuel to a farm. 233) Full-color spread dramatizing advances made in community heating. The system illustrated here provides heat in the form of hot water from a central oil-fired station. 234) Illustration from a special 18-page section entitled "Portrait of Wales" in which, among other things, a newly-built tire manufacturing plant in Wales is described. The artist's rendition depicts a bunker structure located in this factory. (GB)

230–234: Titelblatt und Illustrationen aus Jahrbüchern eines Benzin- und Öl-Konzerns. Im Jahre 1967 hat diese Firma ein Studententeam der Graphikabteilung des Royal College of Art eingeladen, das Jahrbuch zu gestalten und zu illustrieren. Das Experiment war ein grosser Erfolg und wurde in den Jahren 1968 und 1969 wiederholt. Die Arbeit wurde gemäss den geltenden beruflichen Bestimmungen übernommen und ausgeführt. 230) Titelblatt des 1967 Jahrbuches. Photographisch erzieltes Muster von gestapelten Röhrenstücken, in Schwarz auf Weiss. Schrift in Gold. 231) Graphische Interpretation in Schwarz und Weiss einer neuen, für das Zeitalter des Automobils gebauten Stadt, der ein Artikel gewidmet ist im Jahrbuch 1967. 232) Doppelseite mit farbiger Illustration, die eine Lieferung von Traktorbrennstoff an einen landwirtschaftlichen Betrieb zeigt. 233) Doppelseitige Illustration, die ein neues Fernheizsystem dramatisiert, das Gebäudekomplexe aus einer zentralen, ölgefeuerten Heizung speist. 234) Illustration aus einem 18seitigen Bericht «Portrait von Wales», in welchem unter anderem eine neue Reifenfabrik in Wales beschrieben wird. Das Bild zeigt einen Silo in dieser Fabrik. (GB)

230–234: Couverture et illustrations extraites de différents annuaires d'une compagnie pétrolière. En 1967 cette compagnie avait chargé une équipe d'étudiants à l'Ecole de Design du Royal College of Art de l'illustration et du design pour son annuaire. L'expérience eut un tel succès qu'elle fut répétée en 1968 et 1969. Il s'agit d'un travail réalisé dans des conditions professionnelles. 230) Couverture de l'annuaire de 1967. Dessin de tuyaux en noir et blanc réalisé par moyens photographiques. Texte en or. 231) Conception d'une ville nouvelle, construite pour l'âge de l'automobile. 232) Page double avec illustration en couleurs représentant la livraison de mazout pour une ferme. 233) Page double illustrant dramatiquement les progrès accomplis dans l'aménagement de chauffages collectifs: ici d'un chauffage central à mazout distribuant l'eau chaude. 234) Soute dans une fabrique de pneus. Illustration tirée du chapitre «Portrait du pays de Galles» traitant de cette nouvelle fabrique. (GB)

234

235

Graphic Illustrations
Graphische Illustrationen
Illustrations graphiques

235–237: The 1969 annual report of the *Scovill Manufacturing Company* features collage-assemblage-type illustrations to underscore their involvement in housing, consumer, industrial and automotive markets. Each illustration represents one of these markets and incorporates in its assemblage some of its major products and the corresponding percentage of total sales it occupies. Shown here is the actual-size illustration devoted to the housing market (235) and two spreads representing the consumer (236) and the automotive (237) markets respectively. A partial list of the products manufactured for those markets accompanies the illustrations. (USA)

235–237: Illustrationen in Collage-Assemblage-Technik aus dem Jahresbericht eines Fabrikationsunternehmens. Jede Illustration stellt einen Produktionszweig dar – Wohnbedarf, Konsumgüter, Industrieprodukte, Autozubehör – mit den verschiedensten dazugehörigen Einzelprodukten und zeigt den prozentualen Anteil des entsprechenden Produktionszweiges am Gesamtverkauf. Die Illustration in Originalgrösse zeigt die für den Wohnbedarf hergestellten Produkte (235), die beiden Doppelseiten illustrieren Artikel der Branchen Konsumgüter (236) und Autozubehörteile (237); im Begleittext sind weitere Angaben über die wichtigsten Produkte der einzelnen Produktionszweige enthalten. (USA)

235–237: Du rapport annuel 1969 d'une société manufacturière: Illustrations réalisées par collage-assemblage. Chacune évoque l'un des grands marchés sur lesquels s'exerce l'activité de la société – aménagement, biens de consommation, automobile, industrie –, chaque image mettant en évidence, avec un ou plusieurs produits types, le pourcentage des ventes réalisées (sur le montant des ventes globales) dans le secteur considéré. L'illustration reproduite en grandeur nature concerne l'aménagement, et les deux doubles pages figurées à droite en format réduit, le marché des biens de consommation et celui de l'automobile. Les textes en regard énumèrent les principaux produits de chaque catégorie. (USA)

236

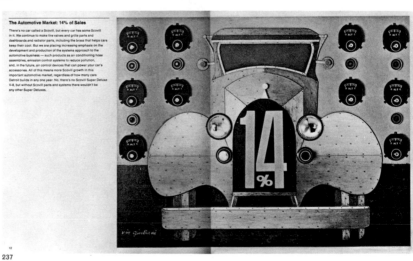

237

DESIGNER:

235–237: Leslie Segal / Corporate Annual Reports, Inc.

ILLUSTRATOR:

235–237: Vin Giuliani

Graphic Illustrations
Graphische Illustrationen
Illustrations graphiques

238–241: Das graphische Thema dieses Jahresberichtes eines landwirtschaftlichen Grossbetriebes behandelt die angebauten und verkauften Produkte. 238) 240) Diese Doppelseite illustriert und beschreibt einen neu-eingeführten Versandbetrieb von Erdbeeren aus Mexico. 239)) Heidelbeeren-pflücker bei der Arbeit, mit Textüberdruck aus dem Bericht des Präsidenten. 241) Graphische Inter-pretation einer erfolgreichen Tomatenernte in Florida. (USA)
242: Ganzseitige Illustration aus dem Geschäftsbericht eines Unternehmens, das unter anderem Nieten für Flugzeug- und Raketenbau fabriziert. (USA)
243: Bleistiftzeichnungen kombiniert mit Photo-Collagen zum Thema Chile, mit einem Portrait des neugewählten Präsidenten Eduardo Frei; aus dem Jahresbericht eines Mischkonzerns. (USA)
244, 245: Detail und Doppelseite aus dem Bericht einer Finanzgesellschaft. Die Vignetten stellen Szenen aus der Kolonialgeschichte der Nordküste Südamerikas dar. (USA)

238–241: *American Foods, Inc.*, in its 1967 annual report, used as graphic theme the products the company grows and sells. 238, 240) This spread illustrates and describes the launching of a straw-berry shipping operation from Mexico. 239) The center spread of the report shows blueberry pickers at work, part of the president's statement being superimposed on the illustration. 241) Full-page visualization of a successful tomato crop in Florida. (USA)
242: This page highlights the *VSI Corporation's* involvement in the aero-space industry. (USA)
243: Pencil and photo-collage illustration on the theme "Chile", with a portrait of its newly elected President, Eduardo Frei. From the 1964 annual report of *Litton Industries*, a 48-page book inter-spersed with this type of illustrations and photographs. (USA)
244, 245: Detail and spread from a *Seaboard Finance Company* annual report. The vignettes depict scenes from the Spanish Main, a seaboard of historic interest. (USA)

238–241: La figuration des récoltes réalisées dans ses domaines a fourni le thème graphique du rapport 1967 d'une société propriétaire de grandes exploitations agricoles. 238, 240) Page double célébrant la création d'un service d'exportation pour fraises au Mexique. 239) Cueillette des myrtilles et citation, à ce propos, d'un discours officiel. 241) Interprétation graphique d'une récolte record de tomates en Floride. (USA)
242: Illustration en pleine page extraite du rapport d'une société spécialisée, notamment, dans la fabrication de rivets pour les constructions aéronautiques et aérospatiales. (USA)
243: Dessin au crayon et photo-collage évoquant le Chili en la personne du président Eduardo Frei. Extrait du rapport 1964 d'un groupe industriel. (USA)
244, 245: Double page (détail et ensemble) extraite du rapport d'une société financière. Une suite de silhouettes représente des scènes de l'histoire coloniale de l'Amérique du Sud. (USA)

238

239

240

241

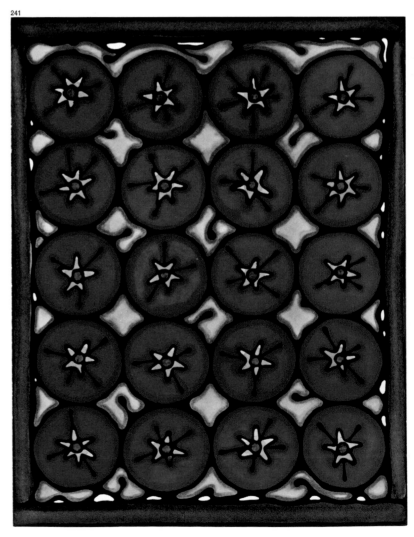

242

243

244

245

DESIGNER:

238–241: The Brothers Bogusky
242: Currie & William Haines
244, 245: Advertising Designers Inc.

ILLUSTRATOR:

238–241: Otis Sweat
242: William Haines
243: Saul Lambert
244, 245: David Pacheco / Advertising Designers Inc.

ART DIRECTOR:

242: Currie & William Haines
243: Robert Miles Runyan
244, 245: Robert L. Steinle/Advertising Designers Inc.

STUDIO – AGENCY:

238–241: M/H/S Inc.
242: Haines Art Studio
243: Robert Miles Runyan & Associates
244, 245: Advertising Designers Inc.

246

247

248

246–250: Covers and illustrations for annual reports of *The Ansul Company*, a corporation engaged in the manufacture of fire extinguishing agents and equipment, industrial and agricultural chemicals. The company's management very early recognized what a powerful communications tool the annual report represents. Prominent graphic artists have been commissioned to illustrate their reports. 246) Cover of the 1961 annual report. The design is an interpretation of Buckminster Fuller's dymaxion projection of the world, symbolizing *Ansul's* interest in–and emphasis on–international marketing. Red, blue and ochre on white. 247) Front and back cover of the 1959 report. Multicolored woodcuts illustrate the entire report. (See 254). 248–250) Two double spreads from the 1966 annual report, and detail of one illustration in actual size depicting aspects of the fire-fighting courses given by the company. (USA)

246–250: Umschläge und Illustrationen für Jahresberichte eines Unternehmens, das Feuerlösch-Chemikalien und -Geräte, Industrie- und Agrarchemikalien herstellt. Die Leiter dieser Firma waren sich schon vor Jahren bewusst, was für ein wichtiges Public-Relations-Werkzeug ein Jahresbericht darstellt. Prominente Graphiker wurden beauftragt, die Jahresberichte zu gestalten und zu illustrieren. 246) Titelblatt des Berichtes 1961. Rot, blau und ocker auf Weiss. 247) Vorder- und Rückseite des Jahresbericht-Umschlags 1959. Farbige Holzschnitte illustrierten den gesamten Bericht (siehe 254). 248–250) Zwei Doppelseiten aus dem Bericht für 1966 und Detail einer Illustration in Originalgrösse, die die von der Firma organisierten Feuerlöschkurse zum Thema hat. (USA)

246–250: Couvertures et illustrations de divers rapports annuels d'une société fabriquant des extincteurs ainsi que d'autres produits chimiques. Très tôt conscients de l'importance que peuvent revêtir ces publications, ses dirigeants font appel à des graphistes du plus grand renom. 246) Page de titre du rapport 1961. Rouge, bleu et ocre sur blanc. 247) Recto et verso de la couverture du rapport 1959, qui est illustré par de très nombreuses gravures sur bois polychromes (voir 254). 248–250) Deux doubles pages et détail extraits du rapport 1966. L'illustration reproduite grandeur nature a pour sujet les cours de lutte contre l'incendie organisés par la société. (USA)

DESIGNER:

246: Chad Taylor
247: Robert Vogele
248–250: Wayne Webb

ILLUSTRATOR:

246: Chad Taylor
247: Antonio Frasconi
248–250: Milton Glaser

ART DIRECTOR:

246, 247: Robert Vogele
248–250: Wayne Webb

STUDIO – AGENCY:

246–250: RVI Corporation
(formerly Robert Vogele, Inc.)

146

249

25

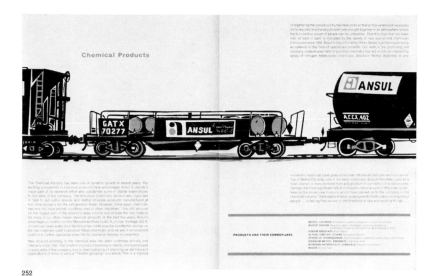

Chemical Products

252

Operating Highlights

253

254

255

251–255: Illustrations and spreads from annual reports of *The Ansul Company* (see also illustrations 246–250). 251) Interpretative painting of one of the company's major product divisions, fire extinguishing agents and equipment. Shown here in actual size as reproduced in the 1965 report. 252, 253) Double spreads from the 1957 report. Two-color woodcuts, olive and black. 254) The 1959 annual report was illustrated in the same colored woodcut technique, by the same artist. 255) Another interpretation from the 1965 report, representing the company's agricultural chemicals division. (USA)

251–255: Illustrationen und Doppelseiten aus Jahresberichten der *Ansul Company* (siehe auch 246– 250). 251) Impression des Künstlers (in Originalgrösse) von Feuerlöschgeräten und -chemikalien, aus dem Bericht für 1965. 252, 253) Doppelseiten aus dem Jahresbericht 1957. Zweifarbige Holzschnitte, olive und schwarz. 254) Der Geschäftsbericht 1959 wurde vom gleichen Künstler in der gleichen Mehrfarben-Holzschnitttechnik illustriert. 255) Diese Illustration aus dem Bericht für 1965 zeigt eine Impression der Agrarchemikalienabteilung der Gesellschaft. (USA)

251–255: Illustrations extraites des rapports annuels d'une société d'extincteurs et de produits chimiques. 251) Rapport 1965: évocation picturale de l'une des principales branches d'activité de la société – les agents chimiques et équipements antifeu (reproduction en format original). 252, 253) Doubles pages figurant dans le rapport 1957: planches gravées en deux couleurs (vert olive et noir). 254) Le rapport 1959 a été illustré par le même artiste, également au moyen de gravures sur bois polychromes. 255) Autre interprétation plastique du rapport 1965, au chapitre des produits chimiques agricoles. (USA)

DESIGNER:

251, 254, 255: Robert Vogele
252, 253: Donald Marvine

ILLUSTRATOR:

251, 255: Leon Travanty
252–254: Antonio Frasconi

ART DIRECTOR:

251–255: Robert Vogele

STUDIO – AGENCY:

251–255: RVI Corporation
(formerly Robert Vogele, Inc.)

Photographic Illustration

Die photographische Illustration

L'illustration photographique

5

Photographic Illustrations

DESIGNER:

256—261: Seymour Chwast / Milton Glaser

PHOTOGRAPHER:

256, 259: André Martin
258, 260, 261: Sol Mednick

ART DIRECTOR:

256—261: Seth McCormick /
Jean Claude Comert

STUDIO – AGENCY:

256—261: Push Pin Studios, Inc.

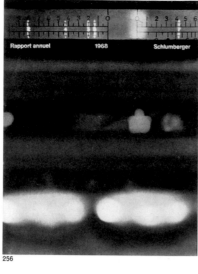

256

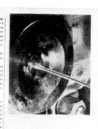

257

258

259

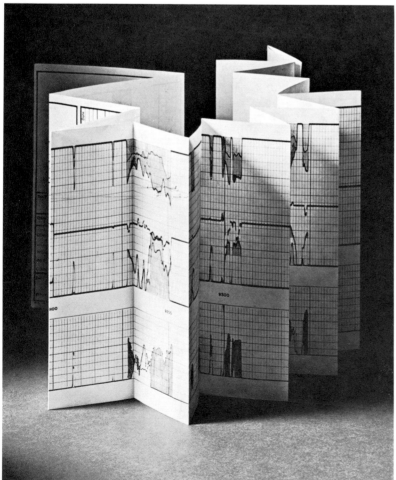

260

256—261: Spreads and illustrations from the 1968 annual report of *Schlumberger Limited*, an international organization whose principal activities are in the oil industry and related fields, in electronics and instrument manufacture. 256) The cover design is a full-color photographic close-up of a recording instrument used on drilling sites. 257, 261) Double page and detail in actual size (261) giving information on a subsidiary of the corporation producing cables and cable connections for various uses. 258) Spread with full-color photographs and text, describing another division making electronic picture tubes (left) and computers for satellite systems. 259) A spread on research and development, with a full-color photographic impression of a measuring device being immersed in a mixture of oil and water. 260) Full-page color photo of a log chart which records different fluids contained in various strata. (USA)

256—261: Doppelseiten und Illustrationen aus dem Jahresbericht 1968 eines Weltunternehmens, dessen Tätigkeit sich hauptsächlich auf die Gebiete der Ölindustrie und verwandte Industrien sowie auf die Herstellung elektronischer Instrumente erstreckt. 256) Umschlag: Nahaufnahme eines bei Erdölbohrungen verwendeten Registriergerätes. 257, 261) Doppelseite und Illustration in Originalgrösse mit Bericht über eine Tochtergesellschaft, die Kabel und Kabelverbindungen herstellt. 258) Mehrfarbige Illustrationen zum Bericht über eine andere Tochtergesellschaft, die elektronische Bildröhren (links) und Computer für Satelliten-Systeme fabriziert. 259) Zur Illustration der Forschungstätigkeit und Weiterentwicklung mit mehrfarbiger Aufnahme eines Messinstrumentes in einem Öl-Wasser-Gemisch. 260) Ganzseitige Farbaufnahme eines logarithmischen Kurvenblattes mit Aufzeichnungen von Flüssigkeiten in Gesteinsschichten. (USA)

256—261: Rapport 1968 d'une entreprise franco-américaine de recherches pétrolières, d'électronique et d'instrumentation. 256) Couverture: photographie en couleurs du tableau d'un appareil enregistreur utilisé dans les forages. 257, 261) Disposition du texte et des illustrations (avec reproduction au format de la photographie en pleine page) relatifs à une des branches de la société, spécialisée dans la fabrication de câbles et de connecteurs. 258) Double page et illustrations en couleurs, au chapitre de la construction d'ordinateurs et d'appareillages électroniques (à gauche, tube à images). 259) Etudes et recherches: à gauche, instrument de mesure immergé dans un mélange de pétrole et d'eau. 260) Photographie en pleine page montrant un enregistrement graphique (log) dont les indications se rapportent à la présence de différents fluides dans les strates. (USA)

262

263

264

265

262–269: *Western Bancorporation*, a group of independently operated banks in Western America, featured in its 1968 annual report an 18-page portfolio entitled "The West". Eight basic industries, which have contributed greatly to the progress of the American West, have their history, growth and future portrayed in photographic art form and in editorial description. Shown here are four spreads: 262, 267) On natural resources, symbolized by oil flowing from barrel. 263, 269) Manufacturing growth, represented by electronic devices. 264, 266) Growth of agriculture. 265, 268) On construction activity, illustrated by a crane hook. (USA)
270, 271: Two full-color photographic illustrations from the 1966 report of *Gulf and Western Industries*, a conglomerate. Top: Picture of a new plating process. Bottom: Electrical capacitors, lying on a mirror, are the subject of this composition. (USA)

262–269: Eine Gruppe unabhängig arbeitender Banken im Westen Amerikas publizierte im Jahresbericht 1968 eine 18-seitige Beilage über «Den Westen». Acht Hauptindustriezweige, die grundlegend zur wirtschaftlichen Blüte des Westens beigetragen haben, werden vorgestellt, jeder mit einer ganzseitigen Farbaufnahme und einem Begleittext über ihre geschichtliche Entwicklung, Ausbau und Zukunft. 262, 267) Diese Aufnahme – aus einem Tank fliessendes Öl – symbolisiert die Naturschätze. 263, 269) Der Produktionszuwachs wird durch elektronische Einrichtungen dargestellt. 264, 266) Fortschritte in der Landwirtschaft. 265, 268) Die Bautätigkeit wird durch einen Kranhaken symbolisiert. (USA)
270, 271: Mehrfarbige Illustrationen aus dem Bericht 1966 eines Mischkonzerns. Oben: neues Plattierungsverfahren; unten: elektrische Kondensatoren auf einem Spiegel. (USA)

262–269: Contenue dans un portefeuille intitulé «The West» et jointe au rapport 1968 d'un groupe de plusieurs banques américaines de la région, une suite de planches photographiques accompagnées de textes en regard célébrait huit grandes branches industrielles, parmi celles qui ont le plus contribué au progrès de l'Ouest du continent. On a reproduit ici (en grand, à gauche, l'illustration photographique seule; en petit, à droite, l'ensemble photo-texte) quatre de ces compositions, qui évoquent, respectivement, la mise en valeur des ressources naturelles (262, 267), équipements électronique pour illustrer le développement des industries manufacturières (263, 269), l'essor de l'agriculture (264, 266) et l'effort de construction (265, 268). (USA)
270, 271: Deux photographies en couleurs du rapport 1966 d'un consortium industriel. En haut: nouveau procédé de placage. En bas: condensateurs électriques réfléchis par un miroir. (USA)

270

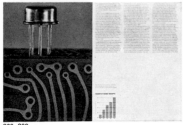

DESIGNER:

262–269: Will Martin

PHOTOGRAPHER:

262–269: Don Jim
270, 271: Art Seller

ART DIRECTOR:

262–269: Will Martin
270, 271: Matthew Leibowitz

STUDIO – AGENCY:

262–269: Will Martin Design

Photographic Illustrations

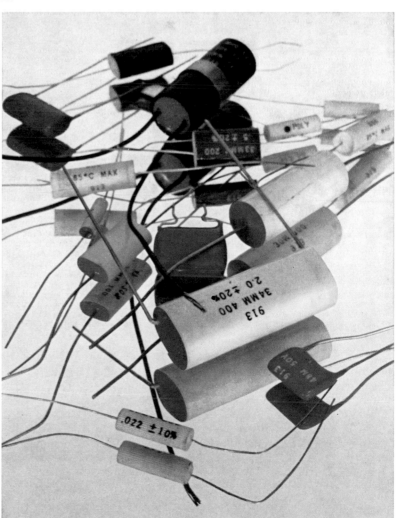

271

272

273

274

DESIGNER – ART DIRECTOR:

272–278: Arnold Saks

PHOTOGRAPHER:

272–278: Simpson Kalisher

STUDIO – AGENCY:

272–278: Arnold Saks, Inc.

275

272–278: *Wallace-Murray*, an industrial corporation, presents in its 1968 report, primarily in photographs, the story of the corporation's activities in its various fields of technology. 272, 275) This spread deals with the manufacture of custom gears. Fig. 275 shows, in a full-page color photo, a giant spiral bevel ring gear being inspected before shipment. 273, 276) The cover subject, which at first glance appears to be an abstract composition, is a close-up color photo of the interior of a new high-temperature testing furnace. 274, 277) Spread and full-page photograph of highly magnified teeth of circular saws, stacked for final inspection and packaging. 278) Double page from the section on building products, showing in full-color photos, from left to right, stacks of gas vent pipes, stainless-steel chimney sections and a photographic study of cut edges of aluminum gas vent pipes. (USA)

272–278: Der Bericht eines Industrie-Unternehmens zeichnet anhand von Photographien deren Aktivität auf verschiedenen Gebieten der Technologie nach. 272, 275) Diese Doppelseite behandelt einzeln angefertigte Kegelräder. Abb. 275 zeigt eine ganzseitige Farbaufnahme eines gigantischen Kegelrades, das vor dem Versand inspiziert wird. 273, 276) Für das Titelbild, das auf den ersten Blick einem abstrakten Bild gleicht, wurde eine Innenaufnahme eines neuen Versuchsschmelzofens verwendet. 274, 277) Doppelseite und mehrfarbige Vergrösserung von Zähnen einer Rundsäge, die für die endgültige Prüfung und den Versand gestapelt wurden. 278) Doppelseite aus dem Kapitel über Bauelemente mit mehrfarbigen Illustrationen, von links nach rechts, von gestapelten Gasabzugsröhren, von Kaminteilen aus rostfreiem Stahl und eine photographische Studie der Schnittkanten von Gasabzugsröhren. (USA)

272–278: C'est principalement par l'image qu'une société industrielle s'est attachée, dans son rapport 1968, à dépeindre les diverses branches de son activité. 272) Composition de la double page où figure ce pignon géant (275), au stade des dernières mises au point. 273) Couverture du rapport avec, en grand (276), son décor graphique, qu'on prendrait à première vue pour une composition abstraite mais qui est fourni, en fait, par un cliché en gros plan de l'intérieur d'un four à haute température servant aux essais de fusion. 274) Disposition d'ensemble et (277) photographie en pleine page: vue fortement agrandie d'un empilement de scies circulaires entreposées avant expédition. 278) Au chapitre des éléments de construction: photographies en couleurs montrant, de gauche à droite, des tuyaux d'évacuation, des sections de canaux de cheminée en acier inoxydable et une étude photographique des formes dessinées, en coupe longitudinale par des tuyaux d'évacuation en aluminium. (USA)

277

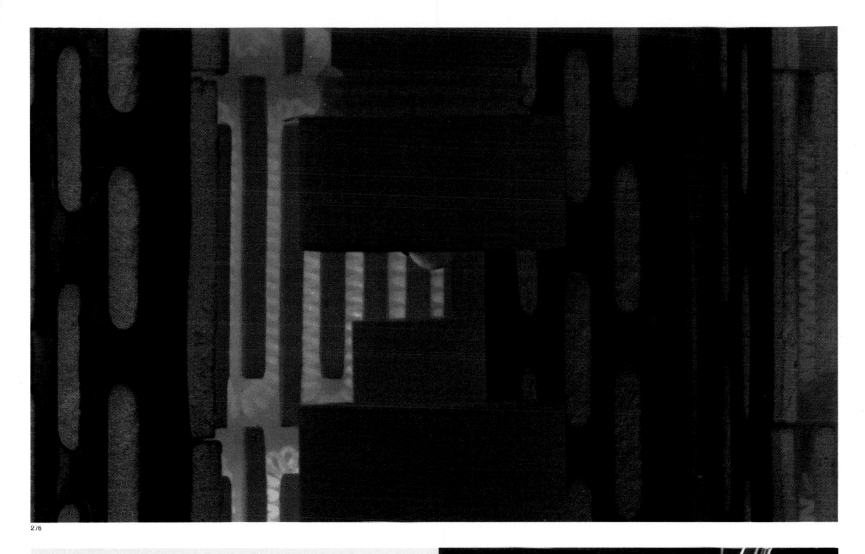

Stacks of Metalbestos gas vent pipes in varying sizes. These advanced designs assure flow of flue gases without drafthood spillage. Lightweight stacks capped with weatherproof "Belmont tops" are parts of venting systems for homes, commercial buildings and industrial plants.

Below: Subdued glow of light reflecting inside barrels of all-stainless steel chimney sections stacked at a warehouse for shipment to plants or homes where they will replace brick chimneys. These factory-built units are made in diameters from 6 to 14 inches in 2½ -foot sections that can be quickly stacked and locked. They may revolutionize this aspect of building.

Right: Reflections of light from cut edges of aluminum gas vent pipes. These Metalbestos parts are ready to be assembled. They will be packaged and shipped for use in apartment houses, buildings and factories.

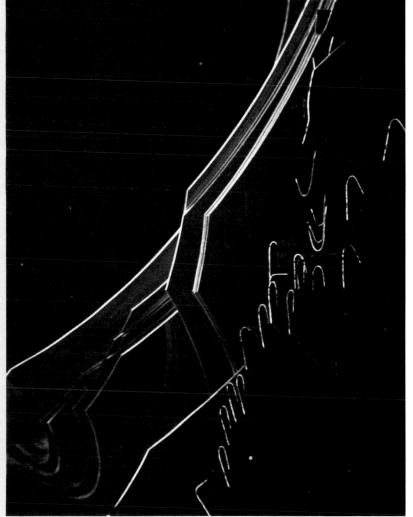

10

Photographic Illustrations
Photographische Illustrationen
Illustrations photographiques

279

280

279–283: The 1968 annual report of *Kimberly Clark Corporation*, producers of paper and paper products, consisted of three sets of enclosures: Contained in a cardboard folder and mailed in an envelope carrying a full-color illustration (279) were a 12-page financial report including the president's letter to the stockholders, six separate cards with glossy, full-color photos on one side and texts devoted to various aspects of company business on the reverse, and a 20-page booklet titled "The new generation". In full-color photographs and a typographic layout reminiscent of a volume of poetry, this section examines the increasing needs of the coming, more mobile new generations for such disposable items as non-woven "textiles" made of paper. Reproduced here are the cover of this booklet (283), two of the photographic illustrations and a double spread (281) to show the typographic arrangement. (USA)

279–283: Der in einem mehrfarbigen Briefumschlag (279) versandte Bericht 1968 einer Papierfabrik enthielt drei Beilagen, die in einer bedruckten Kartonhülle steckten: einen 12seitigen Finanzbericht mit Brief des Direktors an die Aktionäre, sechs einzelne Karten auf Chromo-Karton mit mehrfarbigen Photos auf der Vorderseite und kurzer Beschreibung der Tätigkeit auf der Rückseite und eine 20-seitige Broschüre über «Die neue Generation». Die Aufnahmen mit Begleittext – mit einer an einen Gedichtband erinnernden typographischen Gestaltung – sollen das zunehmende Bedürfnis der kommenden, viel mobileren Generation für Artikel wie z. B. wegwerfbare «Textilien» aus Papier illustrieren. Die Abbildungen zeigen das Titelbild der Broschüre (283), zwei der ganzseitigen Illustrationen sowie eine Doppelseite (281), die die typographische Anordnung des Textes illustriert. (USA)

279–283: Le rapport annuel 1968 d'une fabrique de papiers et produits similaires se composait des éléments suivants: un portefeuille cartonné, posté dans une enveloppe illustrée en couleurs (279); à l'intérieur, a) un rapport financier, introduit par la lettre adressée aux actionnaires par le président de la société; b) six grandes photos en couleurs, sur carton glacé, avec texte au verso, évoquant divers aspects de l'activité de la société; c) une brochure de vingt pages intitulée « La génération nouvelle», commentant à l'aide de photos en couleurs et de textes dont la présentation évoque un ouvrage poétique, le goût croissant que manifestent les jeunes de notre temps, épris de mouvement et de renouvellement, pour des produits éphémères, tels que les «tissus» en papier. On voit ici la couverture (283), illustrations et double page (281) montrant l'arrangement typographique. (USA)

DESIGNER – ART DIRECTOR:

279–283: Morton Goldsholl

PHOTOGRAPHER:

279–283: Erich Hartmann (Magnum)

STUDIO – AGENCY:

279–283: Morton Goldsholl
Design Associates

281

282

The new generation

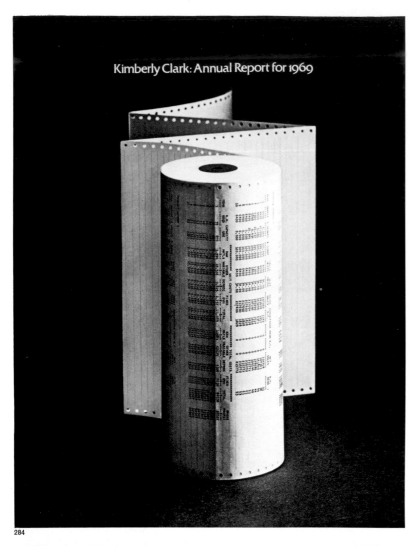

Kimberly Clark: Annual Report for 1969

284

285

287

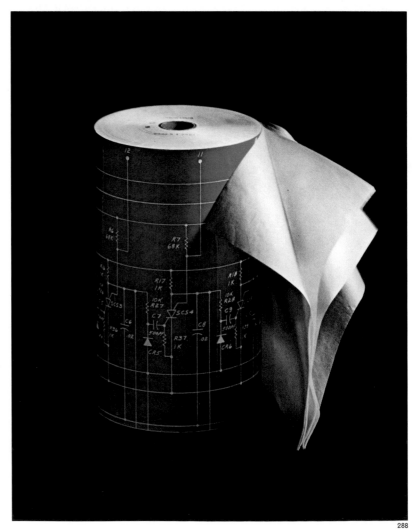

288

286

289

290

DESIGNER – ART DIRECTOR:

284–291: Morton Goldsholl & Associates

PHOTOGRAPHER:

284–289: Morton Goldsholl & Associates

STUDIO – AGENCY:

284–291: Morton Goldsholl & Associates

291

284–291: *Kimberly Clark*, manufacturers of paper and paper products, emphasized their international scope in the corporation's 1969 annual report. Presented in a single unit, the two parts, consisting of the 15-page financial report and a 23-page section titled "A world report", were bound together in an accordion fold and mailed in an envelope which underscored the international theme by having the words "Annual report" printed on it in six languages, including Japanese (291). Shown are the cover pages of the two parts (284, 285), illustrations and a spread (290) from the world report part. These illustrations depict company products and symbolize geographical areas in which the corporation is represented. (USA)

284–291: Der Bericht 1969 einer Papierfabrik legt das Hauptgewicht vor allem auf die internationale Geschäftstätigkeit. Der zweiteilige Bericht in Leporellofalzung besteht aus einem Finanzbericht und einem «internationalen Geschäftsbericht». Auf dem Versandkuvert (291) wird das Wort «Jahresbericht» in sechs Sprachen wiedergegeben, um die weltweiten Beziehungen zu unterstreichen. Die Illustrationen zeigen die Titelbilder der beiden Teile (284, 285), sowie Abbildungen und eine Doppelseite (290) aus dem internationalen Geschäftsbericht. Die abgebildeten Papierrollen symbolisieren nicht nur die Verwendungsmöglichkeiten der Papiere, sondern auch die Absatzmärkte in verschiedenen Ländern. (USA)

284–291: Par la présentation de son rapport annuel 1969, la société productrice de papier et de matières cellulosiques déjà citée aux pages précédentes s'est attachée à mettre en évidence les dimensions internationales de son rayonnement. Ce document se compose de deux fascicules distincts, réunis par un montage en accordéon. L'ensemble est enclos dans une enveloppe où le titre «Annual report» est répété en cinq autres langues (291). On a reproduit ici la couverture de chacune des deux parties (rapport financier de 15 pages – fig. 284 – et rapport d'activité de 23 pages, intitulé «a world report» – fig. 285), ainsi que des illustrations (286–289) et une double page (290) extraites de cette seconde partie. C'est par les variations apportées à un thème iconographique unique (rouleau dressé) que sont évoquées, tout à la fois, la gamme des produits de la firme et les régions du monde où celle-ci affirme sa présence. (USA)

Photographic Illustrations

292

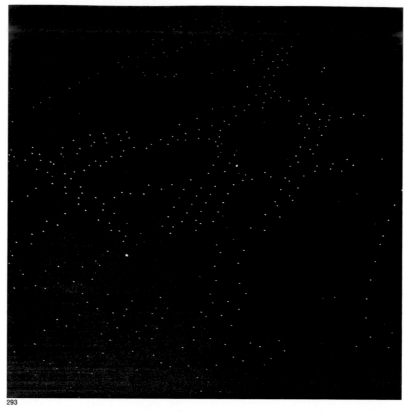

293

294

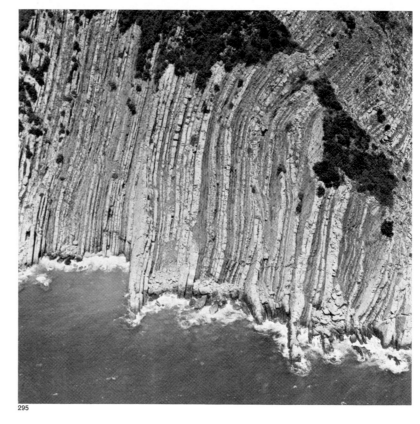

295

DESIGNER:

292–295: George Tscherny
296: Stanley Sollid

PHOTOGRAPHER:

292, 294, 295: Charles Rotkin
293: Robert Perron
296: William Garnett

ART DIRECTOR:

292–295: George Tscherny
296: Paul T. Carey

STUDIO – AGENCY:

292–295: George Tscherny, Inc.
296: Logan, Carey & Rehag

292–295: Illustrations from the 1967 annual report of *Overseas National Airways*. These full-color, full-page aerial views seek to capture a sense of the heightened perception of place which flight brings. 292) The random pattern of a European city. 293) The lights of New York's Central Park mirror the constellations. 294) Pineapple plantation on a Hawaiian island. 295) Erosion pattern of cliffs on the Italian Riviera. (USA)

296: Section of a full-page illustration from the 1969 annual report of *The Crocker Bank*. Aerial view of a California celery field being harvested, highlighting that state's number one business, agricultural produce. (USA)

162

296

292–295: Illustrationen aus dem Bericht einer Fluggesellschaft. Die ganzseitigen Flugaufnahmen sollen einen Begriff vom erhöhten Wahrnehmungsvermögen geben, das die Vogelperspektive vermittelt. 292) Typische Ansicht irgendeiner europäischen Stadt. 293) Das Lichtermeer des New Yorker Central Parks erinnert an den nächtlichen Sternenhimmel. 294) Ananas-Plantage auf einer Hawaii-Insel. 295) Erodierte Klippen an der italienischen Riviera. (USA)
296: Ausschnitt aus einer ganzseitigen Aufnahme eines kalifornischen Selleriefeldes während der Ernte. Mit dieser Illustration wird der wichtigste Produktionszweig dieses Staates hervorgehoben – nämlich die landwirtschaftlichen Produkte. Aus dem Bericht einer Bank. (USA)

292–295: Illustrations extraites du rapport annuel d'une compagnie d'aviation. Ces photos aériennes en couleurs, reproduites en pleine page, tentent de rendre la perception particulièrement vive et pénétrante des sites que donne la vision en vol. 292) Aperçu caractéristique d'une petite cité européenne anonyme. 293) Non pas un ciel étoilé, mais la constellation formée par les lumières du Central Park, à New York. 294) Plantation d'ananas à Hawaii. 295) Falaises de la Riviera italienne, avec leur intéressante structure érosive. (USA)
296: Reproduction partielle d'une des illustrations d'un rapport bancaire: vue aérienne d'une plantation de céléris en Californie – image de la prédominance de l'agriculture. (USA)

297–303: Photographic illustrations for annual reports of the *Xerox Corporation*. 297) The cover of the 1964 report shows a photo of molded polymers, the plastic materials used in making xerographic toners, as they are probed in a research laboratory with the use of polarized light, which brings out the brilliant iridescence displayed here. 298, 299) Full-page, full-color photos, one illustrating a spread on the corporation's educational activities and the other depicting a selenium alloy, a photoconductive material used in *Xerox* copiers, as it goes through a pellet stage on its way to becoming a mirror-like, image-capturing surface. From the '67 report. 300) Double-page spread from the '69 report. Full-color photographs and text highlight the potential of microfilm joined with that of xerography. 301) The cover of the 1968 report is a photographic detail study of the control console of a new, high-speed copying machine made by *Xerox*. 302) A full-page color photo from the same report shows a school girl studying the "new math" as presented in a course which was introduced in elementary grades by a *Xerox* education company after exhaustive tests had been undertaken in major U.S. cities. 303) Photographic cover illustration for the 1970 annual report. This rather abstract visual effect in shades of green, blue and purple was obtained by reflecting light off a flat liquid cristal sheet during a research experiment. The caption refers to the company's expanded research activities. (USA)

297–303: Illustrationen aus *Xerox*-Jahresberichten. 297) Diese gegossenen Polymerstäbe werden im Forschungslabor anhand von polarisiertem Licht getestet, was diese leuchtenden Farbspiele und -effekte erzeugt. Dieses Plastikmaterial wird zur Herstellung des Xerokopierentwicklers verwendet. 298, 299) Ganzseitige Illustrationen aus dem Bericht 1967. Die erste symbolisiert die von dieser Firma ausgearbeiteten Bildungsprogramme. Die zweite zeigt eine Selenlegierung – ein lichtleitendes Material für Xerokopien – in noch körnigem Zustand, vor der Verarbeitung zu einer spiegelglatten, bildaufnahmefähigen Oberfläche. 300) Diese Doppelseite aus dem Bericht '69 illustriert und beschreibt die unzähligen Verwendungsmöglichkeiten von Mikrofilmen und Xerokopien. 301) Detailaufnahme des Regelpultes eines Schnell-Vervielfältigungsapparates; Umschlag des Berichtes 1968. 302) Abbildung – aus dem gleichen Bericht – einer Schülerin beim Lernen der «neuen Mathematik». Dieser Kurs wurde von einem *Xerox*-Bildungszentrum ausgearbeitet und nach ausgedehnten Versuchen in amerikanischen Grossstädten für Elementarschulen eingeführt. 303) Umschlag des Jahresberichtes 1970. Diese eher abstrakt wirkende Illustration in verschiedenen Grün-, Blau- und Lilatönen entstand bei einem Experiment durch Licht, das von der glatten Oberfläche flüssiger Kristalle zurückgeworfen wurde. Mit dieser Abbildung soll die ausgedehnte Forschungstätigkeit dieser Firma illustriert werden. (USA)

297–303: Illustrations photographiques figurant dans différents rapports annuels de la Société *Xerox*. 297) Couverture du rapport 1964: éléments de matière plastique (polymères) soumis, en laboratoire, aux radiations d'une lumière polarisée, qui les fait chatoyer. Ces substances sont utilisées en xérographie. 298, 299) Photographies en couleurs illustrant, la première, les activités éducatives de la société, la seconde, l'aspect à l'état brut d'un alliage de sélénium qui doit à ses propriétés photoconductrices de servir au revêtement des papiers xérographiques (rapport 1967). 300) Double page extraite du rapport 1969. Texte et photographies en couleurs mettent en évidence les multiples applications de la xérographie au service du microfilm. 301) Couverture du rapport 1968: photographie en gros plan des organes de commande d'un nouveau modèle de copieuse rapide. 302) Du même rapport: écolière en train d'étudier les «mathématiques nouvelles» à l'aide d'un cours élaboré, à l'intention de l'enseignement du premier degré, par un centre pédagogique dépendant de la société, sur la base d'une ample expérimentation réalisée dans plusieurs grandes villes des Etats-Unis. 303) Couverture du rapport 1970: ces formes d'apparence abstraite, colorées en vert, bleu et mauve, ont été saisies par l'objectif au cours d'une expérience de laboratoire, portant sur la réfraction de la lumière par les cristaux liquides. Cette photographie symbolise l'activité étendue dans le domaine des recherches. (USA)

297

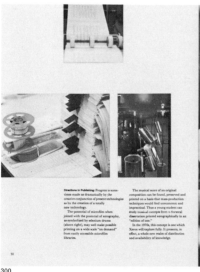

300

DESIGNER:

297–299, 301–303: Thomas Geismar
300: Kenneth MacKay

PHOTOGRAPHER:

297: Jay Maisel
298–303: René Burri (Magnum)

ART DIRECTOR:

297: Jack Hough/Thomas Geismar
300: Rocco Yervasi
303: William B. Sontag

STUDIO – AGENCY:

297–299, 301–303: Chermayeff & Geismar Associates

Photographic Illustrations
Photographische Illustrationen
Illustrations photographiques

301

298

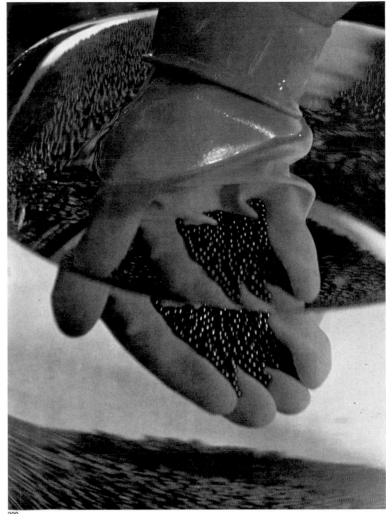

299

302

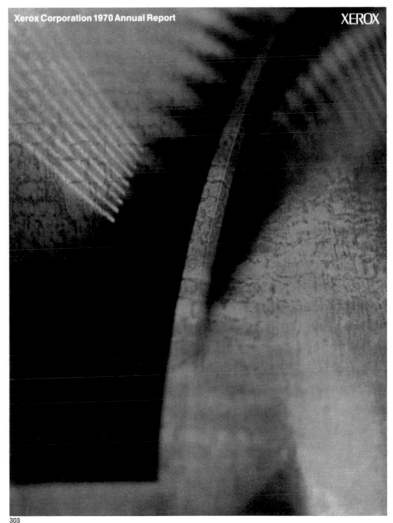

303

304

305

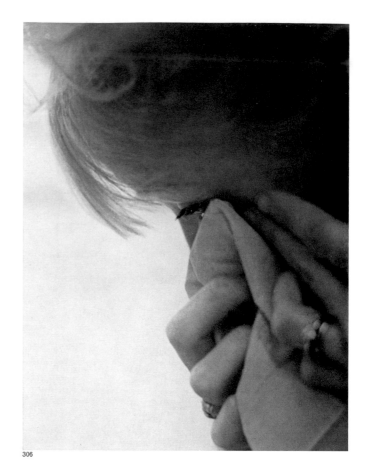

306

307

DESIGNER – ART DIRECTOR:

304, 305: Leslie A. Segal
306–308: Morton Goldsholl

PHOTOGRAPHER:

304, 305: Burt Glinn
306–308: Erich Hartmann (Magnum)

STUDIO – AGENCY:

304, 305: Corporate Annual Reports Inc.
306–308: Morton Goldsholl Design Associates

304, 305: Two full-page color photos illustrating the «Review of Operations» section of the *Olin* 1969 annual report. 304) This photographic close-up refers to a coating developed by *Olin* research, which protects fast aircraft from costly in-flight damage caused by rain and hail. 305) The caption to this composition relates to welded copper alloy tubing for heat exchange and desalination systems, introduced by *Olin* in 1969. (USA)
306–308: *The Kimberly Clark* 1966 report featured a 20-page photographic essay titled "The magical world of everyday". It sought "to explore the part that *Kimberly Clark* plays in this world and in the process to show some of the unexpected beauty and magic that lie within it." 306) Full-page photograph as part of a spread on paper napkins and sanitary products. 307) Another company product: paper for teabags. 308) The photograph opening the essay, the title to which was printed in white on a translucent paper lying on top of this picture. (USA)

308

Photographic Illustrations

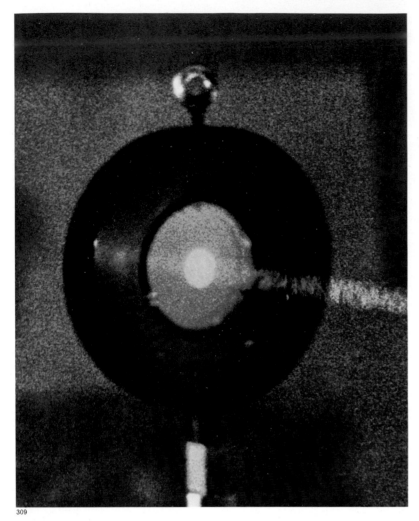

309

310

309–313: Photographic illustrations from annual reports of *Litton Industries,* an industrial conglomerate. 309) Introducing a chapter "Opportunity and the Atmosphere" in the 1963 report, this picture represents the coherent light waves of a single laser beam. 310, 311) These photographic studies from the 1966 report faced a black page which carried quotations by Allan Nevins, a distinguished American scholar. The theme of this report was "Managing Ideas". 312, 313) Two spreads from the 1961 report, which was interspersed with color photographs of people from various walks of life. The captions were reflections on these persons' confrontation with a changing world of advancing technology. (USA)

314–316: Three photographs, all in color and full-page, illustrating the 1969 annual report of *Overseas National Airlines.* 314) An important source of revenue was military cargo, pictured here being loaded aboard an *ONA* aircraft. 315) *ONA* acquired the steamship line operating this vessel. 316) Hull plates of an *ONA* cruise ship under construction. (USA)

309–313: Illustrationen aus verschiedenen Jahresberichten eines diversifizierten Industriekonzerns. 309) Abbildung – Lichtbündel eines einzelnen Laserstrahls – zum Kapitel «Opportunity and the Atmosphere» aus dem Bericht 1969. 310, 311) Photographische Studien aus dem Bericht 1966, zum Thema «Managing Ideas»; die schwarzen gegenüberliegenden Seiten bringen Zitate von Allan Nevins, einem hervorragenden amerikanischen Gelehrten. 312, 313) Doppelseiten aus dem Bericht 1961 mit mehrfarbigen Abbildungen von Vertretern aus den verschiedensten Berufsgattungen. Der Begleittext gibt die Überlegungen dieser Leute wieder, die sie über unsere mit dem Fortschreiten der Technik sich ständig verändernde Welt anstellen. (USA)

314–316: Ganzseitige Farbaufnahmen aus dem Jahresbericht einer Fluggesellschaft. 314) Eine der wichtigsten Einnahmequellen ist der Transport von Militärgütern, die hier gerade verladen werden. 315) Ein von dieser Gesellschaft angekaufter Raddampfer. 316) Platten für die Verschalung des Schiffsrumpfes eines Vergnügungsdampfers. (USA)

314

315

298

299

302

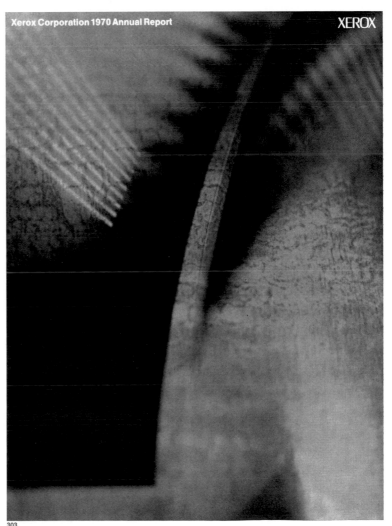

Xerox Corporation 1970 Annual Report

XEROX

303

304

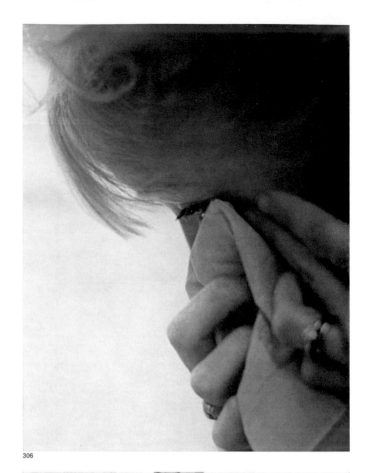

306

305

307

DESIGNER - ART DIRECTOR:

304, 305: Leslie A. Segal
306—308: Morton Goldsholl

PHOTOGRAPHER:

304, 305: Burt Glinn
306—308: Erich Hartmann (Magnum)

STUDIO - AGENCY:

304, 305: Corporate Annual Reports Inc.
306—308: Morton Goldsholl Design Associates

304, 305: Two full-page color photos illustrating the «Review of Operations» section of the *Olin* 1969 annual report. 304) This photographic close-up refers to a coating developed by *Olin* research, which protects fast aircraft from costly in-flight damage caused by rain and hail. 305) The caption to this composition relates to welded copper alloy tubing for heat exchange and desalination systems, introduced by *Olin* in 1969. (USA)

306—308: *The Kimberly Clark* 1966 report featured a 20-page photographic essay titled "The magical world of everyday". It sought "to explore the part that *Kimberly Clark* plays in this world and in the process to show some of the unexpected beauty and magic that lie within it." 306) Full-page photograph as part of a spread on paper napkins and sanitary products. 307) Another company product: paper for teabags. 308) The photograph opening the essay, the title to which was printed in white on a translucent paper lying on top of this picture. (USA)

311

312

313

309–313: Illustrations photographiques extraites de différents rapports annuels d'un même consortium industriel. 309) Faisceau de lumière émis par un rayon laser: page initiale d'un chapitre du rapport 1969 intitulé «Opportunity and the Atmosphere». 310, 311) Rapport 1966: ces études photographiques font pendant à des textes imprimés sur papier noir et composés, sous le titre de «Managing Ideas», de citations empruntées à Allan Nevins, le savant américain bien connu. 312, 313) Deux doubles pages du rapport 1961, où figurent les portraits en couleurs et les déclarations de représentants de multiples profession, exprimant leurs réactions en présence des transformations profondes qu'engendre le progrès des techniques. (USA)
314–316: Trois des photos en couleurs du rapport '69 d'une compagnie d'aviation. 314) Chargement d'équipements militaires (dont le transport constitue l'une des plus fructueuses activités de la société). 315) Ce bâteau à vapeur dessert une ligne désormais exploitée par la compagnie. 316) Tôles destinées au carénage d'un navire de plaisance construit par la société. (USA)

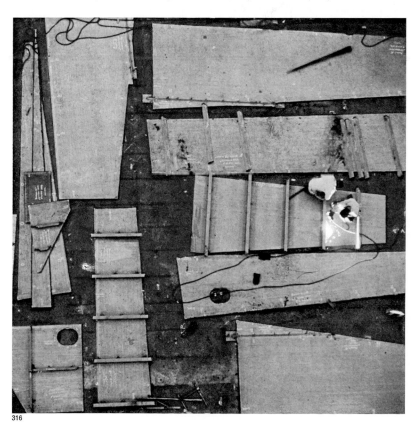

316

DESIGNER:

309, 312, 313: Robert Miles Runyan
310, 311: Maurice Yanez
314–316: George Tscherny

PHOTOGRAPHER:

309, 312, 313: Ovid Neal
310, 311: Art Kane
314, 316: William R. Farrell
315: Bill Muster

ART DIRECTOR:

314–316: George Tscherny

STUDIO – AGENCY:

309–313: Robert Miles Runyan & Associates
314–316: George Tscherny, Inc.

Photographic Illustrations
Photographische Illustrationen
Illustrations photographiques

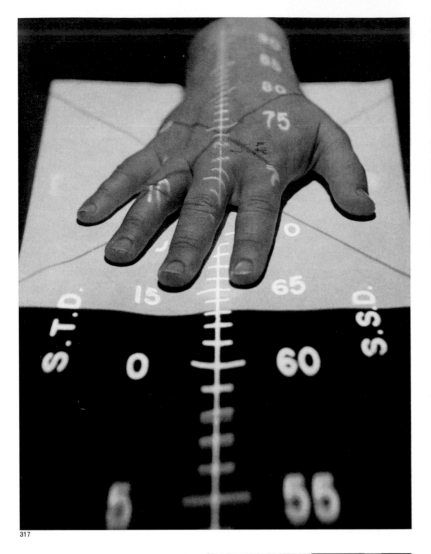

317

318

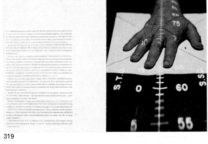

319

321

DESIGNER:

317–319: James Cross
320: Jaqueline Rothman/DLJ
321–323: Arnold Saks
324, 325: Robert S. Nemser

PHOTOGRAPHER:

317–319: Marvin Lyons
320: Erich Hartmann (Magnum)
321–323: Arthur Lavine
324, 325: Burt Glinn

ART DIRECTOR:

317–319: James Cross
320: Jacqueline Rothman/DLJ
321–323: Arnold Saks
324, 325: Robert S. Nemser

STUDIO – AGENCY:

317–319: James Cross Design Office, Inc.
321–323: Arnold Saks, Inc.
324, 325: Corporate Annual Reports, Inc.

Photographic Illustrations
Photographische Illustrationen
Illustrations photographiques

322

320

317–319: "We see new ways of extending the reach of man's helping hand" was the last sentence of the president's report to *International Chemical & Nuclear Corporation's* stockholders. This set the theme for the illustrations throughout this 1969 report: hands. 317) A reference to *ICN* radioactive sources for destroying malignant invaders of tissue. 318) New *ICN* research suggests possible control of aging. All photos full-page size and reproduced in color. (USA)
320: Photograph of 140 Broadway, the location of *Donaldson, Lufkin & Jenrette, Inc.*, illustrating the opening spread of their 1967 annual report. In black and white. (USA)
321–323: These photographs illustrate industries which are financed by *Chase Manhattan Bank*, such as cattle ranching in Panama (322) and turkey farming in California (323). (USA)
324, 325: Full-page color photo of a skyscraper reflected in a Volkswagen windshield, the glass for both of which was supplied by a division of *Combustion Engineering, Inc.* (USA)

317–319: «Wir sehen neue Wege, die Reichweite der helfenden Hand auszudehnen.» Mit diesem Satz schliesst der Bericht des Direktors an die Aktionäre einer chemischen Fabrik. Dieses Zitat setzt auch das Thema für den Jahresbericht fest: die Hand. 317) Die Firma entwickelte Methoden zur Zerstörung bösartiger Gewebekrankheits-Erreger durch radioaktive Bestrahlung. 318) Das Photo illustriert Forschungsarbeiten der Firma auf dem Gebiet der Gerontologie. (USA)
320: Schwarzweiss-Aufnahme des Hauses Nr. 140 am Broadway, dem Hauptsitz eines Vermögensverwaltungsbüros. Aus dem Jahresbericht 1967. (USA)
321–323: Diese Aufnahmen zeigen Industriezweige, die von einer Grossbank finanziert wurden: Viehwirtschaft in Panama (322), Truthahnaufzucht in Kalifornien. (USA)
324, 325: Die Windschutzscheibe des VWs, sowie die Scheiben des Wolkenkratzers, der sich darin wiederspiegelt, wurden von einer affiliierten Gesellschaft einer Kesselbaufirma hergestellt. (USA)

317–319: «Nous apercevons de nouveaux moyens d'étendre l'action secourable de la main humaine.» C'est sur cette phrase que s'achevait l'adresse aux actionnaires rédigée en 1969 par le président d'une fabrique de produits chimiques. D'où le thème général des illustrations de ce rapport: la main. 317) Evocation du traitement des dégénérescences malignes de la peau à l'aide d'agents radioactifs. 318) La recherche autorise de nouveaux espoirs dans la lutte contre la sénéscence. (USA)
320: En frontispice du rapport 1967 d'une société fiduciaire: la photographie de son siège, à Broadway, no 140. Reproduction en noir et blanc. (USA)
321–323: Evocation de diverses branches d'activité auxquelles s'étend le financement d'une grande banque, tels l'élevage au Panama (321) ou l'aviculture en Californie (323). (USA)
324, 325: Les glaces du pare-brise de cette voiture, tout comme celles du gratte-ciel qu'il reflète, ont été produites par une filiale d'une entreprise dont cette photographie illustre le rapport. (USA)

325

323

324

326

DESIGNER:

326–329: Sam Antupit

PHOTOGRAPHER:

326, 327, 329: Bruce Davidson (Magnum)
328: Mort Schreiber

ART DIRECTOR:

326–329: Sam Antupit

STUDIO – AGENCY:

326–329: Hess and/or Antupit

326–329: Cover and two double-page spreads from *The Mead Corporation* 1969 annual report. The company's major products are paper, board, educational and consumer products, metals, construction materials, interior furnishings, pulp and forest products, etc. The caption to the cover photo gives the theme of the report: "A young mind, an open book, the warmth of home ... major themes of *Mead's* endeavor and of this report. Information, education, shelter... three of the great markets of the seventies we are ready to serve." 326, 329) Front cover, reduced, and part of the cover photo in actual size. The picture extended partly over the back cover. 327) A spread on the activities of the interior furnishings group, with a picture of a bedroom set made by this group. 328) Double-page spread describing and illustrating products of the packaging division which designed, coated and impregnated the containers shown. All photos were printed in full color. (USA)

326–329: Umschlag und Doppelseiten des Jahresberichtes '69 eines Mischkonzerns, dessen Produktion folgende Gebiete umfasst: Papier- und Kartonherstellung, Bildung und Erziehung, Konsumgüter, Metallwaren, Baumaterialien, Inneneinrichtungen, Holzverarbeitung usw. Die Legende zur Umschlagphoto setzt gleichzeitig das Thema des Berichtes: «Eine Kinderseele, ein offenes Buch, häusliche Gemütlichkeit ... drei Hauptanliegen dieser Firma und dieses Berichtes. Information, Bildung, Sicherheit ... drei wichtige Forderungen der 70er Jahre, die wir bereit sind zu erfüllen.» 326, 329) Vollständiger Umschlag – Illustration auf Rückseite überlaufend – und Detail in Originalgrösse. 327) Doppelseite mit Schlafzimmer, das von der Abteilung für Inneneinrichtungen entworfen wurde. 328) Doppelseite mit Beschreibung und Illustration von Produkten, die von der Verpackungsabteilung entworfen, verarbeitet und imprägniert wurden. Mehrfarbig. (USA)

327

328

Photographic Illustrations

172

326–329: Couverture et pages intérieures tirées du rapport 1969 d'une entreprise dont la production s'étend du papier et des emballages aux matériaux de construction, aux articles métalliques, en passant par l'ameublement, les biens de consommation et le matériel éducatif. La légende de la photo de couverture définit le thème général: «Un esprit qui s'éveille, un livre ouvert, la chaleur du foyer ... trois inspirations majeures de notre firme et du présent rapport ... Information, éducation, logement ... autant de préoccupations majeures de notre temps, auxquelles nous avons le souci de répondre.» 326, 329) Vue d'ensemble et détail, au format original, de l'illustration de couverture (qui s'étendait en partie sur la face inférieure). 327) Vue d'une chambre à coucher—illustration extraite du chapitre de l'ameublement. 328) Description et reproduction de différents articles conçus et produits par la division de l'emballage. Toutes les photographies sont en couleurs. (USA)

329

330

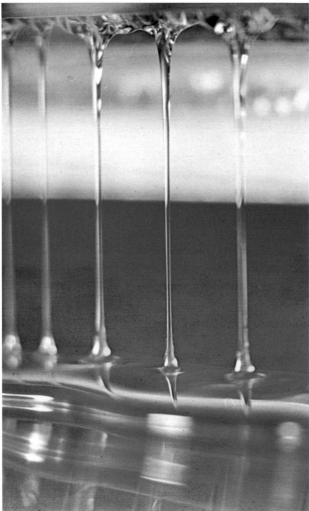

331

332

333

Photographic Illustrations
Photographische Illustrationen
Illustrations photographiques

DESIGNER:

330, 331: Leslie A. Segal
332–335: S. Neil Fujita/Mal Bessen

PHOTOGRAPHER:

330, 331: John T. Hill
332–335: Marshall C. Henis
336, 337: Neal Barr

ART DIRECTOR:

330, 331: Leslie A. Segal
332–335: S. Neil Fujita
336, 337: Jack Robson/Bozell & Jacobs, Inc.

STUDIO – AGENCY:

330, 331: Corporate Annual Reports, Inc.
332–335: Fujita Design, Inc.
336, 337: Bozell & Jacobs, Inc.

334

335

336

VF Corporation 1969 Annual Report

Berkshire International: fashion in hosiery

337

330, 331: *W.R. Grace & Co.* stressed the multinationality of its operations in the 1970 annual report. 5½ × 9″ in size, the 60-page booklet introduced each corporate group with a full-page color photo and a portrait of the group executive. Reproduced here are the cover (330), which illustrates the closure of a newly developed vacuum-sealed bag for cheese, and the photographic illustration which accompanies the report on the corporation's technical group. (USA)
332–335: "The World of *Bristol-Myers*" was the theme of the 1969 annual report of this drug, toiletries and nutritional products company. The cover (332, 334) shows a family unloading shopping bags filled with company-brand products from their station wagon. In full color. 333, 335) This photo illustrates a company-sponsored neighborhood improvement program as evidence of the corporation's commitment to social causes. (USA)
336, 337: Cover and full-page photograph from the 1969 report of the *VF Corporation*, a company operating in the apparel field. Printed in color. (USA)

330, 331: Der Bericht eines Industriekonzerns legt das Hauptgewicht auf die weltweit verbreitete Tätigkeit dieser Firma. Jede Abteilung wird mit einer ganzseitigen Farbaufnahme eingeführt, sowie mit einem Portrait des jeweiligen Abteilungsleiters. Die Umschlagillustration (330) zeigt eine neu entwickelte Vakuum-Verpackung für Käse. 331) Mehrfarbige Abbildung zum Bericht über die technische Abteilung. (USA)
332–335: Der Jahresbericht 1969 eines Unternehmens der Arzneimittel-, Toiletten- und Nahrungsmittel-Branche stand unter dem Thema «Die Welt von *Bristol-Myers*». Der Umschlag (332, 334) zeigt eine Familie beim Ausladen von Einkaufstaschen, angefüllt mit firmeneigenen Produkten. 333, 335) Aufnahme und Text auf dieser Doppelseite weisen auf ein von dieser Firma unterstütztes Programm hin, das die Verbesserung der Wohnverhältnisse in sozial benachteiligten Stadtteilen durch Selbstinitiative der Bevölkerung anstrebt. (USA)
336, 337: Umschlag und mehrfarbige Illustration aus dem Jahresbericht 1969 eines Unternehmens der Bekleidungs-Branche. (USA)

330, 331: Le volumineux rapport 1970 d'un consortium industriel s'attache, d'une part, à mettre en évidence le caractère multinational de ses activités et réserve, d'autre part, à chacun de ses départements, un exposé illustré d'une grande photographie en couleurs et d'un portrait du directeur responsable. On voit ici (330) la couverture, qui montre le système de fermeture d'un nouvel emballage sous vide pour le fromage, et la photographie en pleine page (331) qui introduit le chapitre consacré au département technique. (USA)
332–335: Rapport 1969 d'une entreprise de produits pharmaceutiques, aliments diététiques et articles de toilette. La couverture (332, 334) montre une famille déchargeant des cabas pleins d'articles portant la marque de la firme. Photographie en couleurs. 333, 335) Texte et photo mettent en valeur un programme d'aide sociale, patronné par la société, en faveur des mal-logés. (USA)
336, 337: Couverture et photographie en pleine page extraite du rapport 1969 d'une entreprise de la branche du vêtement. (USA)

Photographic Illustrations
Photographische Illustrationen
Illustrations photographiques

338

DESIGNER:

338–341: Hans Hartmann

PHOTOGRAPHER:

338–341: Fernand Rausser

340

341

339

338–341: Cover, double-page spread and two photographic illustrations from annual reports of a Swiss property insurance company. 338) A full-page color photograph from the company's 1968 report, which devoted five pages, including the cover, to the work of a Swiss photographer. 339, 340) The cover and the four inside illustrations of the 1965 annual report of this company depicted various real estate objects, the remote farmhouse, the closely grouped chalets of a mountain village, the small industrial plant or the city building, all of them risks the company is willing to assume in insuring them. (SWI)

338–341: Umschlag, Doppelseite und Illustrationen aus Jahresberichten der *Schweizerischen Mobiliar Versicherungs-Gesellschaft*. 338) Aus dem Bericht '68, dessen Illustrationsteil dem Werk eines Schweizer Photographen gewidmet ist. 339, 340) Der Umschlag wie die Illustrationen im Bericht 1965 greifen verschiedene Grundbesitze heraus – ein abgelegenes Bauernhaus, Holzhäuser in eng überbautem Walliserdorf, Industriebetriebe auf dem Land und in der Stadt – deren Versicherungsschutz die Gesellschaft gewährleistet. (SWI)

338–341: Couverture, pages intérieures et illustrations de deux rapports annuels d'une compagnie d'assurances immobilières. 338) Ce cliché en couleurs, reproduit en pleine page, fait partie d'une suite d'illustrations photographiques, toutes signées du même auteur, ornant le rapport 1968. 339, 340) La couverture et les illustrations du rapport 1965 avaient pour thème la diversité des biens immobiliers assurés par la société – depuis le chalet de haute montagne jusqu'au building urbain, en passant par la ferme campagnarde et l'installation industrielle. (SWI)

177

DESIGNER:

342: Arnold Saks
343: Bell & Howell

PHOTOGRAPHER:

342: Arthur Lavine
343: Arthur Siegel

ART DIRECTOR:

342: Arnold Saks

STUDIO – AGENCY:

342: Arnold Saks Inc.

342: One of three illustrations from a double-page spread in *Chase Manhattan Bank's* 1967 report, which dealt with this bank's dedication to uplifting the standard of living in the low-income areas of New York. The caption to this photo mentioned the fact that *Chase* donated money to sponsor playstreets, which afforded children in these areas such activities as painting, music and beating the heat with the help of an open fire hydrant. (USA)
343: Actual-size reproduction of the opening picture of an eight-page photographic folio, titled "Deepening our technology", from the 1965 annual report of *Bell & Howell*. The photographs, all taken in *B&H* research laboratories, were chosen for their resemblance to modern art. The pattern shown here was achieved by running magnetic tape at high speed in an experimental tape recorder developed by a company division. (USA)

342: Aus einem Bericht einer Grossbank, der die Bemühungen dieser Bank zur Verbesserung des Lebensstandards in ärmeren Vierteln New Yorks zum Thema hat. Der Text erwähnt eine Stiftung dieser Bank zur Schaffung von «Spielstrassen» für Kinder, wo sie Gelegenheit haben zu malen, zu musizieren und sich nach hitzigem Spiel an einem offenen Hydranten abzukühlen. (USA)
343: Illustration in Originalgrösse aus dem Bericht einer Firma für optische und elektrische Geräte. Die im Forschungslabor aufgenommenen Photos wurden wegen ihrer Ähnlichkeit mit Werken moderner Kunst ausgewählt. Das mit hoher Geschwindigkeit abgespulte Magnetband eines im Entwicklungsstadium befindlichen Tonbandgerätes ergab dieses Muster. (USA)

342: Cette image se réfère aux efforts déployés par une grande banque pour améliorer les conditions de vie dans les quartiers pauvres de New York. C'est ainsi qu'elle a subventionné l'aménagement de rues réservées aux jeunes, qui peuvent s'y installer librement pour peindre, faire de la musique, s'ébattre à leur guise. Il leur est même permis, quand il fait chaud, de se rafraîchir en ouvrant le jet de la borne-fontaine. (USA)
343: Reproduction, au format de l'original, du frontispice d'un album photographique inclus dans le rapport annuel d'une entreprise d'instruments optiques. Il s'agit de clichés pris dans le laboratoire d'essais et choisis pour leur similitude avec l'art moderne (ici, image donnée par une bande magnétique défilant à grande vitesse). USA)

342

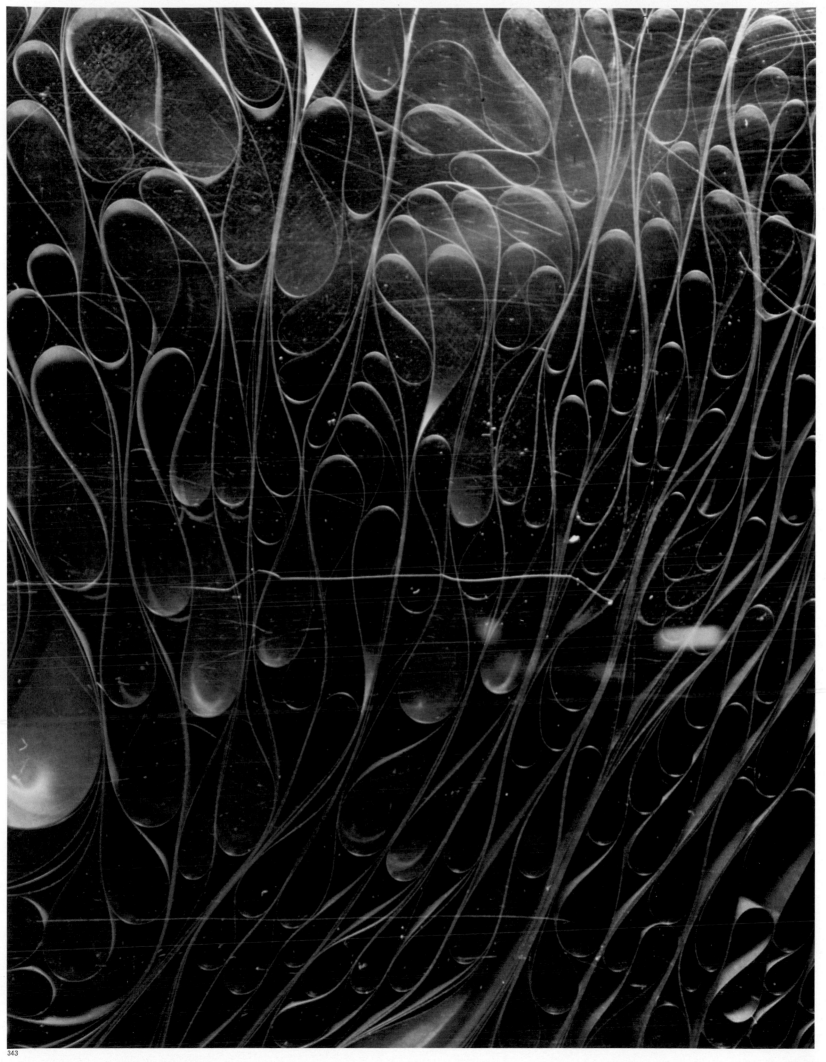

Photographic Illustrations
Photographische Illustrationen
Illustrations photographiques

DESIGNER:

344–346: Gary Hinsche
347, 348: Robert S. Nemser
349: Roger Cook/Don Shanosky

PHOTOGRAPHER:

344–346: Marvin Silver
347: Allen Vogel
348: Morecraft/Oliwa
349: Jon Silla

ART DIRECTOR:

344–346: Robert Miles Runyan
347, 348: Robert S. Nemser
349: Roger Cook/Don Shanosky

STUDIO – AGENCY:

344–346: Robert Miles Runyan & Assoc.
347, 348: Corporate Annual Reports, Inc.
349: Cook and Shanosky Associates Inc.

344

347

348

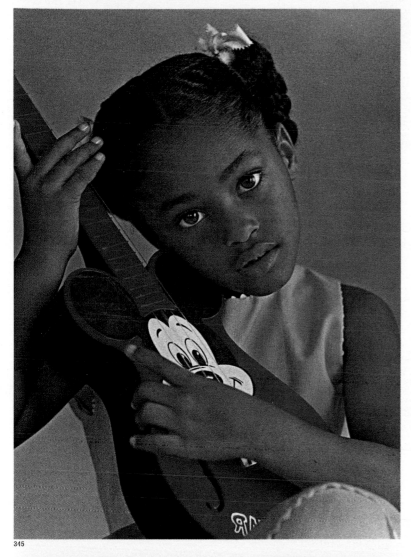

345

346

349

344–346: Full-page photographs from the *Mattel, Inc.*, 1970 annual report. Each page pictures a child with a product of this toy manufacturer. 344) A recent acquisition was a company manufacturing and distributing aquariums, pet products and accessories. (USA)
347, 348: Two pictures from reports of the *American Can Company*. 347) This presentation of disposable cups and food containers was placed opposite the Financial Highlights page in the 1969 report. 348) A toddler enjoying her birthday in the midst of company products. One of fourteen such full-color, page-size illustrations displayed in the 1970 report, most of them depicting scenes of typical family life and incorporating products of the company. (USA)
349: Four color pages with products and samples of advertising matter illustrated the 1965 report of *Duffy-Mott Company*. All were bleed pages and in full color. (USA)

344–346: Ganzseitige Illustrationen aus dem Jahresbericht 1970 eines Spielzeugfabrikanten. Jede Aufnahme zeigt ein Kind mit einem von dieser Firma hergestellten Spielzeug. 344) bezieht sich auf eine kürzlich erworbene Firma, die neben verschiedenen Produkten und Gegenständen für Haustiere auch Aquarien herstellt und vertreibt. (USA)
347, 348: Illustrationen aus Jahresberichten einer Verpackungsfirma. 347) Diese dem Finanzrückblick gegenüberliegende Abbildung zeigt wegwerfbare Becher und Nahrungsmittelbehälter. 348) Ganzseitige Farbaufnahmen zeigen Szenen aus dem Alltagsleben verschiedener Familien, die Produkte dieser Firma gebrauchen. Hier ein kleines Mädchen während seiner Geburtstagsparty, umgeben von Firma-Produkten. (USA)
349: Mehrfarbige, angeschnittene Seiten mit Abbildungen von Produkten und Werbematerial illustrieren den Jahresbericht einer Nahrungsmittelfirma. (USA)

344–346: Hors-texte illustrant le rapport 1970 d'une fabrique de jouets. Sur chaque photo, on voit un enfant avec un jouet ou un objet différent, telle cette jeune personne devant un aquarium, lequel rappelle l'acquisition récente, d'une entreprise spécialisée dans ce domaine. (USA)
347, 348: Illustrations extraites de deux rapports d'une fabrique d'emballages. 347) L'image de ce gobelet et autres récipients «perdus» figurait en regard du bilan chiffre de l'exercice 1969.
348) Fillette fêtant son anniversaire, entourée de récipients et d'emballages fabriqués par la firme. C'est l'un des quatorze hors-texte en couleurs qui ornent le rapport 1970; la plupart dépeignent, de la sorte, des scènes familières, qui sont autant d'occasion de suggérer l'ample usage quotidien qui peut être fait des produits de la société. (USA)
349: Le rapport 1965 d'une fabrique de produits alimentaires était illustré de compositions photographiques en couleurs montrant, comme celle-ci, d'appétissantes nourritures, ou reproduisant des matériels publicitaires. (USA)

351

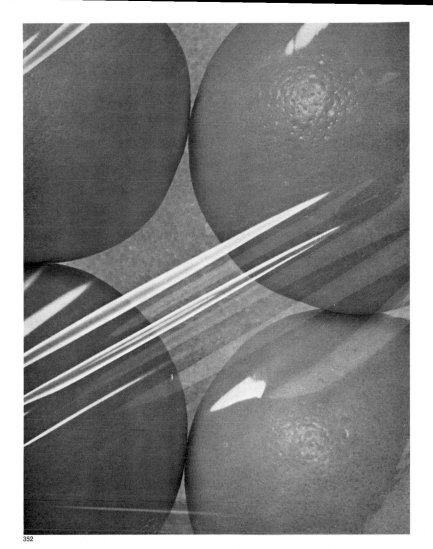

352

DESIGNER:

350, 351: Carol A. Moore
352: Leslie A. Segal
353: George Tscherny

ART DIRECTOR:

350, 351: Carol A. Moore
352: Leslie A. Segal
353: George Tscherny

PHOTOGRAPHER:

350, 351: Wolf von dem Bussche
352: Allen Vogel
353: Mike Smith

STUDIO – AGENCY:

350–352: Corporate Annual Reports, Inc
353: George Tscherny, Inc.

350, 351: The text part of the *Rheingold Corporation's* 1969 report was printed on a buff-tinted, matt stock, whereas the illustrations, all bleeding off the page, were reproduced on a glossy coated paper. 350) This photo opens the section "Review of Operations", which starts with the Breweries Division. 351) Syrup is being drawn from a tank for testing. This picture accompanies the review of the company's soft drink operations. (USA)
352: A double-page spread in the *W. R. Grace & Co.* annual report of 1967 is devoted to the corporation's packaging and plastics divisions, illustrated by this close-up of shrink-film wrapped oranges. Printed in full color. (USA)
353: A spread titled "Reaching the consumer through promotional activities" was illustrated by this photo of sample packages left at a homeowner's door. *Colgate-Palmolive* 1969. (USA)

350, 351: Der Textteil des Jahresberichtes eines Brauerei- und Getränkekonzerns wurde auf getöntem Papier, die angeschnittenen Illustrationsseiten auf Kunstdruckpapier gedruckt. 350) Mit dieser Aufnahme wird der Jahresrückblick der Brauerei eingeleitet. 351) Sirup-Proben werden für verschiedene Versuche abgezapft. Diese Illustration gehört zum Bericht über die Geschäftstätigkeit der Abteilung für alkoholfreie Getränke. (USA)
352: Eine Doppelseite im Jahresbericht 1967 eines Industriekonzerns wurde der Abteilung für Verpackungs- und Plastikmaterialien gewidmet. Die ganzseitige Illustration zeigt eine Nahaufnahme von Orangen, die in Schrumpffolie verpackt sind. (USA)
353: Die Musterpackung an der Wohnungstüre illustriert eine Doppelseite über das Thema «Wie der Konsument durch Werbung gewonnen werden kann». Aus dem Jahresbericht 1969 der *Colgate-Palmolive Company*. (USA)

350, 351: Dans le rapport 1969 d'une brasserie, le texte était imprimé sur papier chamois mat, alors que les illustrations, toutes en hors-texte étaient tirées sur papier glacé. 350) Frontispice du compte rendu général d'activité. 351) Prélèvement d'un échantillon de sirop: illustration du chapitre consacré à la fabrication des boissons sans alcool. (USA)
352: Oranges enveloppées sous film rétractable. Illustration hors-texte (en couleurs) tirée du rapport 1967 d'un consortium industriel produisant des plastiques et des emballages. (USA)
353: Ce sac d'échantillons-réclame suspendu à un loquet de porte illustre une forme d'action publicitaire mentionnée dans le rapport 1969 de la Société *Colgate-Palmolive*. (USA)

353

DESIGNER:

354: Robert Wood
355: Stuart Kipperman
356: Jay Novak
357: Maurice Yanez
358, 359: Leslie A. Segal

PHOTOGRAPHER:

354: Seymour Mednick
355: Arthur d'Arazien
356: NASA Photo
357: Kurt Lenk
358: Bob Philips
359: Simpson Kalisher

ART DIRECTOR:

354: Robert Wood
355: Stuart Kipperman
356: Jay Novak
357: Robert Miles Runyan
358, 359: Leslie A. Segal

STUDIO – AGENCY:

354: Al Paul Lefton Co., Inc.
357: Robert Miles Runyan & Associates
358, 359: Corporate Annual Reports, Inc.

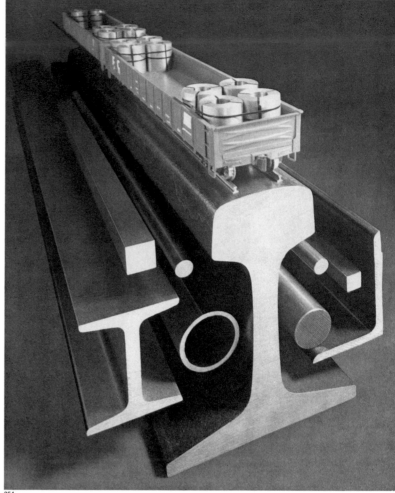

354

354: Full-page illustration from the 1967 annual report of the *Penn Central* transportation company. Printed in full color. (USA)
355: Color illustration from an annual report of the *Celanese Corporation,* showing a chemical tank in one of the company's plants. Reproduced full-page size. (USA)
356: Full-page black-and-white photograph reproduced from the 1964 annual report of the *Northrop Corporation,* depicting an experimental body in a wind tunnel. (USA)
357: Black-and-white page from an annual report of *Teledyne Inc.* (USA)
358: Color page from an annual report of the *Scott Paper Company,* showing dye research. (USA)
359: Full-color photograph of laboratory pipettes illustrates activities of the *Riegel Paper Corporation's* research department. From the 1966 annual report. (USA)

354: Ganzseitige Illustration aus dem Jahresbericht eines Transportunternehmens. (USA)
355: Mehrfarbige Aufnahme eines Riesenbehälters für Chemikalien. Aus dem Jahresbericht einer chemischen Fabrik. (USA)
356: Ganzseitige Illustration aus dem Jahresbericht eines Flugzeugwerkes. Die Abbildung zeigt ein flügelloses Experimentier-Modell im Windkanal. Schwarzweiss. (USA)
357: Schwarzweiss Illustration aus dem Jahresbericht eines Unternehmens für elektronische Geräte und Instrumente. (USA)
358: Diese mehrfarbige Illustration aus dem Jahresbericht einer Papierfabrik zeigt einen Farbversuch im Forschungslabor. (USA)
359: Mit diesen Messpipetten soll die Tätigkeit des Forschungslabors einer Papierfabrik illustriert werden. Mehrfarbige Aufnahme aus dem Jahresbericht 1966. (USA)

354: Hors-texte en couleurs d'un rapport annuel d'une entreprise de transports. (USA)
355: Echelle métallique au flanc d'un réservoir de produits chimiques. Hors-texte en couleurs d'un rapport annuel publié par une société chimique. (USA)
356: Essai en soufflerie. Photographie en noir et blanc illustrant, en hors-texte, le rapport 1964 d'une usine d'aviation. (USA)
357: Photographie en noir et blanc illustrant l'un des rapports annuels d'une société productrice d'appareillages électriques. (USA)
358: Essai de colorants: photo de laboratoire, en couleurs, illustrant l'un des rapports annuels d'une fabrique de papier. (USA)
359: Cette photographie de pipettes graduées évoque le travail de recherche d'une fabrique de papier. Illustration en couleurs du rapport 1966. (USA)

Photographic Illustrations
Photographische Illustrationen
Illustrations photographiques

357

355

356

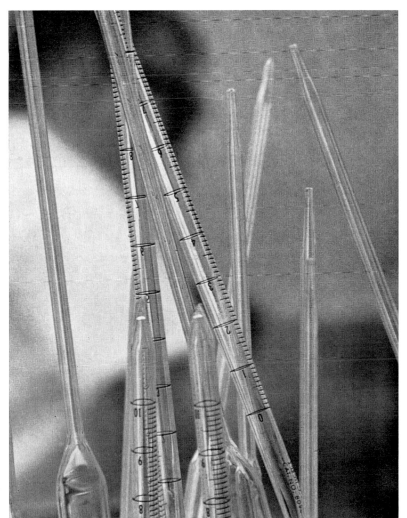

358

359

Photographic Illustrations
Photographische Illustrationen
Illustrations photographiques

360

361

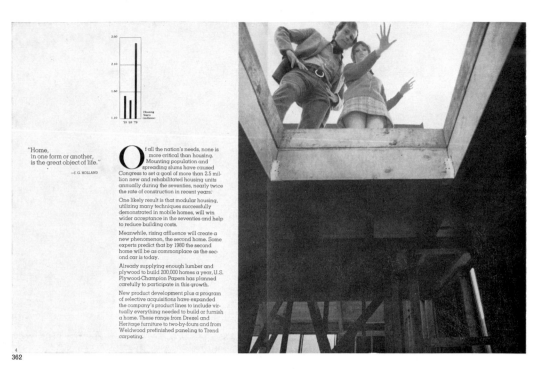

362

364

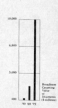

365

360–366: The 1969 annual report of *U. S. Plywood-Champion Papers Inc.* was presented in the form of two separate booklets: Book I, a review of the company's performance in 1969, printed on tinted kraft paper, and Book II, titled "The 1970s: The New Environment", printed on white coated stock and containing the illustrations shown here. The two booklets are stapled to the cover folder in such a way that they lie side by side when the folder is opened (360). 361, 366) Spread on the company's involvement in the area of education, illustrated by a photo of youngsters looking out of a school bus. Each spread shows a graph giving a twenty-year comparison of figures pertaining to the market area discussed, including a predicted figure for the year 1979. 362) A spread on housing. 363) Double page on the world's need for printing paper. 364) The hotel-motel industry is another market area for the company. 365) Spread on a subsidiary manufacturing carpets. (USA)

360–366: Der Bericht 1969 einer Firma für Holzverarbeitung und Papierfabrikation besteht aus zwei Teilen: Book I – Jahresrückblick über die Geschäftstätigkeit, auf getöntem Werkdruckpapier; Book II – enthält mehrfarbige Illustrationen auf Kunstdruckpapier zum Thema «Die 70er Jahre: Die neue Umgebung». Beim Öffnen des Berichtes liegen die beiden Hefte einander gegenüber (360). 361, 366) Doppelseite über die Tätigkeit auf dem Gebiet der Bildung und Erziehung, illustriert durch Knaben in einem Schulbus. 362) Doppelseite über Wohnungsbau. 363) Zur Illustrierung des Weltbedarfs an Druckpapier. 364) Ein weiterer Marktzweig: die Hotellerie. 365) Doppelseite über die Teppichfabrikation einer Tochtergesellschaft. Jede Doppelseite zeigt zusätzlich einen Vergleich der Ausgaben der Jahre 1959 und 1969 für die jeweiligen Marktzweige mit dem im Jahre 1979 voraussichtlich auszugebenden Betrag. (USA)

360–366: Le rapport 1969 d'une fabrique de papier et de produits cellulosiques se présentait sous la forme de deux fascicules brochés en vis-à-vis (360). Le premier, constituant le rapport d'activité proprement dit, était imprimé sur papier bulle; le second, intitulé «Le nouvel environnement», était sur papier couché blanc. Il contenait une suite de doubles pages composées chacune – comme celles qui sont reproduites ici – d'un texte, d'une illustration et d'un graphique mettant en évidence, pour les différents secteurs d'activité de la société, le développement intervenu entre 1959 et 1969, et l'évolution prévue jusqu'en 1979. 361, 366) L'image de ces garçons dans un bus qui les mène à l'école évoque le rôle joué par la firme au service de l'enseignement. 362) Sur le thème du logement. 363) Sur le thème des besoins croissants en papier-journal. 364) Sur le thème de l'hôtellerie. 365) Sur le thème des revêtements de sol. (USA)

The world is swirling with ideas. Political ideas. Social ideas. Moral ideas. Technological ideas. All competing for the mind's attention amid the rising clamor of the times.

Both the quantity of printed material and the quality of paper stock are on a sharply ascending curve as authors and publishers vie for the eye with impressive book and record jackets, enticing magazine covers, attractive advertising, and creative promotional brochures.

Between now and 1980, sales of the printing industry will more than double. And Champion Papers, the number one supplier to commercial printers, has the trained people, the advanced technology, and the basic resources to continue its leadership in sales and quality.

Not to be overlooked is the unsung hero of the printed communication world—the envelope. As any footsore postman will attest, there has been no letup in all kinds of mail. Like most things in today's world, the number of envelopes seems to grow. And Federal Envelope, whose 3.5 billion yearly envelope production makes it one of the leading envelope manufacturers for business uses, expects to do the same.

"Many ideas grow better when transplanted into another mind than in the one where they sprang up."
—OLIVER WENDELL HOLMES

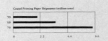

363

DESIGNER:

360—366: Richard Hess

PHOTOGRAPHER:

360—363, 365, 366: Art Kane
364: Joel Meyerowitz

STUDIO – AGENCY:

360—366: Hess and/or Antupit

366

187

Photographic Illustrations
Photographische Illustrationen
Illustrations photographiques

367–369: The photographic illustrations in the 1970 annual report of *National Medical Enterprises, Inc.*, are described in the introductory note as follows: "We have focused our cameras on the various components that comprise health care, on the facets of endeavor that will weave the fabric for a new and revitalized health maintenance concept. We have assembled the basic functional aspects of health care in a variety of structural forms, as would an architect …". 367) The full-page illustrations face text pages, each of which introduces a principal officer of the company in a black-and-white inset. 369) Cover of the report. (USA)

370–372: Cover and two illustrations from the 1969 report of *Sterling Drug Inc.* The theme of the report was "Sterling's Business is Everybody's Health". 370) The cover photo combines the company products which are pictured individually inside the report. 371) Illustration to the spread on consumer products. 372) A newly developed drug for the treatment of snail fever. (USA)

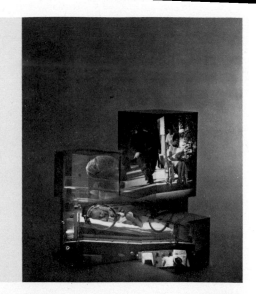

367

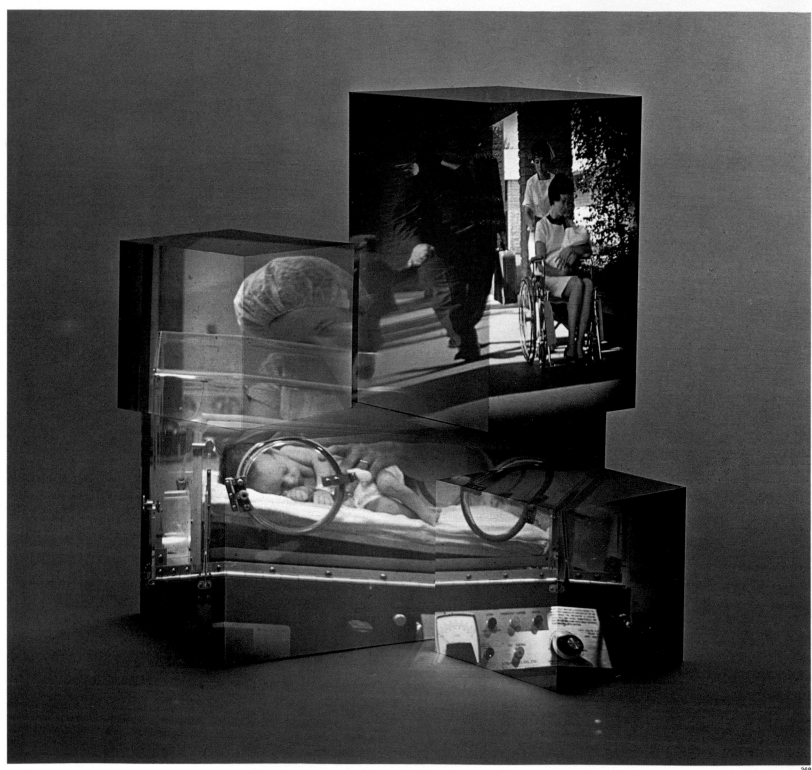

368

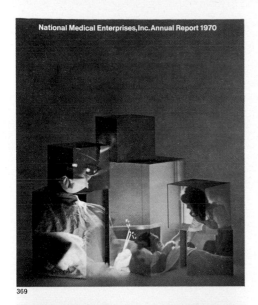

National Medical Enterprises, Inc. Annual Report 1970

369

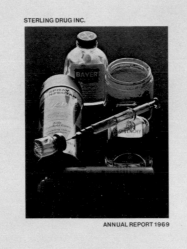

STERLING DRUG INC.

ANNUAL REPORT 1969

370

371

367–369: Der Stil der photographischen Illustrationen im Jahresbericht eines Unternehmens für medizinische Apparaturen und Geräte wurde im Einführungstext wie folgt umschrieben: «Wir haben mit unserer Kamera die verschiedensten Aspekte der Gesundheitspflege festgehalten, haben sie auf die einzelnen Bestrebungen, die auf ein fortschrittliches Konzept zur Erhaltung der Gesundheit hinzielen, gerichtet. Wir haben die grundlegenden Aspekte für eine zweckmässige Behandlung in ihrer strukturellen Vielfalt zusammengebaut, wie das ein Architekt tun würde ...». 367) Jede der den ganzseitigen Illustrationen gegenüberliegenden Textseiten stellt ein Mitglied der Geschäftsleitung vor. 369) Umschlag des Jahresberichtes. (USA)
370–372: Umschlag und Illustrationen des Jahresberichtes einer chemischen Fabrik. Das Thema lautet «Unser Geschäft ist jedermanns Gesundheit». 370) Die Umschlagillustration zeigt einige Produkte, die auf den Innenseiten einzeln abgebildet und beschrieben werden. 371) Aufnahme zur Doppelseite über Konsumgüter. 372) Neuentwickeltes Mittel zur Behandlung von Schistosomiasis. (USA)

367–369: «Tentant de refléter, dans leur diversité, les efforts qui, de toutes parts tendent à en rénover la conception, nous avons assemblé sous des formes structurelles multiples, à la manière d'un architecte, les éléments fonctionnels de l'action sanitaire et médicale ...» C'est en ces termes que le rapport 1970 d'une société productrice d'appareils médicaux explique, dans une note liminaire, le sens des compositions photographiques qui illustrent ses pages. 367) Comme ici, chaque illustration est placée en regard d'une page de texte où figure, encadré, le portrait en noir et blanc de l'un des dirigeants de la firme. 369) Couverture. (USA)
370–372: Du rapport 1969 d'une fabrique de produits chimiques et pharmaceutiques. 370) En couverture: vue groupée de produits dont l'image séparée se retrouve dans les pages intérieures. 371) Illustration hors-texte sur le thème des articles de toilette. 372) Médicament nouveau pour le traitement de la schistosomiase. (USA)

372

DESIGNER:

367–369: Detlef Hallerbach
370–372: Len Fury

PHOTOGRAPHER:

367–369: Robin S. Robin/Don Ornitz
370–372: Phil Marco

ART DIRECTOR:

367–369: Advertising Designers, Inc.
370–372: Len Fury

STUDIO – AGENCY:

367–369: Advertising Designers, Inc.
370–372: Corporate Annual Reports, Inc.

374

375

373–376: Illustrations and spread from *PepsiCo's* 1969 report. 373) Actual-size reproduction of the photograph illustrating the opening spread of the report. It shows workmen scaling the *Pepsi-Cola* pavilion at Expo '70 in Osaka, Japan. The caption to this picture gives details of the company's participation in this exposition. 374) *Pepsi-Cola* cans at one of the canning cooperatives owned by the company's franchised bottlers. 375) A *Pepsi-Cola* television commercial being filmed on New York's lower East Side. The copy points out the fact that for these commercials real-life people in real-life situations are used, such as this wedding party scene. 376) Spread with a full-page illustration showing drums filled with *Pepsi-Cola* concentrate being readied for shipment from the concentrate plant in Puerto Rico, and a smaller photo of a champion tennis player who uses a steel tennis racquet made by *Wilson Sporting Goods*, a subsidiary of the company. All illustrations in full color. (USA)

373–376: Illustrationen und Doppelseite aus dem Jahresbericht '69 der *PepsiCo*. 373) Wiedergabe in Originalgrösse der Eröffnungsillustration dieses Berichtes. Sie zeigt Arbeiter beim Hinaufklettern auf den *Pepsi-Cola* Pavillon an der Expo '70 in Osaka. In der Legende werden Einzelheiten über die Teilnahme dieser Firma an der Weltausstellung erwähnt. 374) *Pepsi-Cola*-Dosen in einer den konzessionierten Abfüllfirmen gehörenden Dosenfabrik. 375) Ein *Pepsi-Cola*-Fernsehwerbefilm, der in einem New Yorker Stadtquartier gedreht wird. Der Text streicht heraus, dass Leute von der Strasse die Rolle der Schauspieler übernehmen und dass nur Szenen aus dem Alltagsleben – hier eine Braut – aufgenommen werden. 376) Die ganzseitige Illustration dieser Doppelseite zeigt mit *Pepsi-Cola*-Konzentrat gefüllte Behälter, die in einer Konzentrat-Fabrik in Puerto Rico zum Versand bereit stehen. Die kleinere Aufnahme zeigt eine Tennisspielerin, die mit einem Stahlrakett spielt, das von einer Tochtergesellschaft der *PepsiCo*. hergestellt wird. Alle Illustrationen sind mehrfarbig reproduziert. (USA)

373–376: Du rapport 1969 de la société *PepsiCo*. 373) Reproduction, au format original, de l'illustration placée en frontispice. On y voit des ouvriers gravissant le sommet du pavillon édifié par la société dans le cadre de l'Exposition universelle d'Osaka. 374) Boîtes neuves prêtes à quitter la fabrique d'emballages métalliques pour l'une des nombreuses firmes concessionnaires de la marque *Pepsi-Cola*, où s'opèrera le remplissage. 375) Prise de vues pour un film publicitaire *Pepsi-Cola* destiné à la télévision. Le commentaire insiste sur le caractère direct et « nature » des bandes tournées à cet effet, qui sont composées de scènes de la vie quotidienne prises sur le vif, comme cet épisode d'un mariage célébré dans un quartier populaire de New York. 376) Double page illustrée, en horstexte, d'une photographie montrant des barriques pleines de concentré de *Pepsi-Cola*, prêtes à quitter l'usine de Puerto Rico qui produit ce composé essentiel; en regard, dans le texte, photographie d'une championne de tennis équipée d'une raquette en acier fabriquée par une entreprise rattachée à *Pepsi-Cola*. Toutes les illustrations sont en couleurs. (USA)

376

DESIGNER – ART DIRECTOR:

373–376: Eisenmann and Enock, Inc.

PHOTOGRAPHER:

373–376: Simpson Kalisher

STUDIO – AGENCY:

373–376: Eisenmann and Enock, Inc.

Photographic Illustrations
Photographische Illustrationen
Illustrations photographiques

Photographic Illustrations
Photographische Illustrationen
Illustrations photographiques

DESIGNER:

377: Graphics
378, 379: Robert S. Nemser
380: Georg Vetter
381: Hanspeter Fritschi
c/o Gebrüder Sulzer
382: George R. Woltz

PHOTOGRAPHER:

377: Morton Beebe
378, 379: Burt Glinn
380: Georg Vetter
381: G. Derungs, c/o Gebr. Sulzer
382: John F. Gilbert

ART DIRECTOR:

378, 379: Robert S. Nemser
381: A. Meyle, c/o Gebr. Sulzer
382: George R. Woltz

STUDIO – AGENCY:

377: Graphics
378, 379: Corporate Annual Reports, Inc
380: Georg Vetter
381: Gebrüder Sulzer
382: Design for Industry

377

377: Full-page color illustration from the 1969 annual report of the *Transamerica Corporation*, a multi-market service organization. This particular photo of a couple strolling along a beach in Hawaii illustrates the company's growing number of travel-related services. (USA)
378, 379: Two photographs illustrating the 1968 annual report of *Northeast Utilities*, a power supply group. 378) This full-color bleed page shows a radar approach control screen at a Connecticut airport. The text mentions the dynamic growth of this airport at the hub of *NU*'s service territory. 379) The report stresses the point that the company is taking steps to protect and enhance the environment. This illustration shows *NU* personnel going down to the sea with clipboards and frogmen suits to study the marine environment of a shore area. The purpose of these studies is to establish basic data for subsequent comparison with ecological observations when warm water released from a new nuclear power project enters the area. (USA)
380: Stacked die-cut aluminum sheets lent their shapes to this photographic study illustrating the inside back cover of the 1969 report of a Swiss combine in the aluminum industry. (SWI)
381: Assembling the tubes for the rectifying column of a heavy-water production plant. Color illustration from the 1968 report of a Swiss industrial corporation. (SWI)
382: Color photo of a modern diesel engine in a freight yard of the *Norfolk and Western Railway Company*. Full-page illustration from the 1963 annual report. (USA)

377: Ganzseitige Illustration aus dem Jahresbericht einer diversifizierten Dienstleistungsorganisation. Das an einem Strand in Hawaii schlendernde Paar symbolisiert die wachsende Zahl der von dieser Organisation geführten Reisedienst-Betriebe. (USA)
378, 379: Illustrationen aus dem Bericht eines Energieversorgungswerkes. 378) Diese mehrfarbige Aufnahme zeigt den Schirm eines Radaranfluggerätes in einem Flughafen Connecticuts. Der Text erwähnt die rapide Ausdehnung dieses Flughafens im Zentrum des Versorgungsgebietes der Gesellschaft. 379) Der Bericht betont ausdrücklich die Umweltschutzbestrebungen dieses Unternehmens. Die Illustration zeigt Froschmänner bei Wasseruntersuchungen, die eine Grundlage für weitere ökologische Forschungen schaffen sollen, vor allem in Hinsicht auf ein geplantes Atomkraftwerk, das Warmwasser in diesem Gebiet ausfliessen lassen würde. (USA)
380: Stapel von ausgestanzten Aluminium-Platten bilden das Sujet der Illustration auf der dritten Umschlagseite des Jahresberichtes 1969 der *Alusuisse*. (SWI)
381: Einsetzen von Röhren in einer Rektifizier-Kolonne für eine Anlage für Schwerwasser-Erzeugung. Mehrfarbige Illustration aus dem Jahresbericht '68 der *Gebr. Sulzer AG*. (SWI)
382: Farbaufnahme einer modernen Diesellokomotive im Frachtbahnhof eines Eisenbahn- und Transportunternehmens. Aus dem Jahresbericht 1963. (USA)

377: Photographie en couleurs illustrant le rapport 1969 d'une organisation commerciale à vocations multiples. Ce couple longeant une plage à Hawaii évoque l'extension donnée par la société à ses activités dans le domaine du tourisme. (USA)
378, 379: Deux photographies extraites du rapport 1968 d'une compagnie productrice d'électricité. 378) Ecran radar en service dans un aéroport du Connecticut. 379) Le rapport insiste sur le souci que porte la société à la protection du milieu naturel. Dans ce contexte, on voit ici une équipe d'hommes-grenouilles chargée de procéder à des relevés sous-marins dans une zone côtière où l'on projette de déverser l'eau chaude provenant d'une centrale nucléaire; il s'agit de pouvoir vérifier, le moment venu, que cette décharge n'entraînera pas de conséquences écologiques néfastes. (USA)
380: Cet empilement de feuilles d'aluminium estampées fournit le décor photographique de la face interne de la couverture du rapport 1969 de la société métallurgique *Alusuisse*. (SWI)
381: Assemblage de tubes constituant l'un des organes essentiels d'une installation pour la production d'eau lourde. Illustration en couleurs du rapport 1968 de la Société *Sulzer*. (SWI)
382: Locomotive Diesel de type récent en service dans un poste de triage. Photographie en couleurs illustrant le rapport 1963 d'une compagnie ferroviaire. (USA)

380

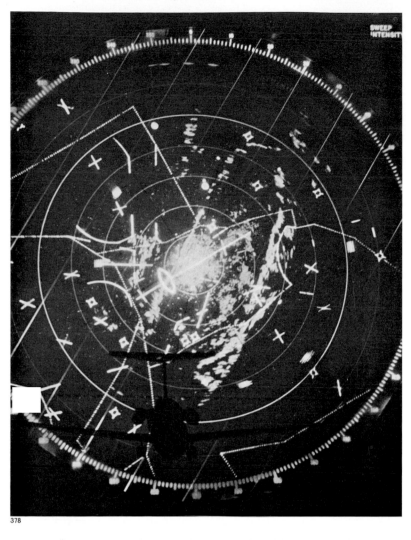

378

379

381

382

Photographic Illustrations
Photographische Illustrationen
Illustrations photographiques

383

386

383: *ECL Industries* is an international holding company managing growing operations in North and South America. In this double-page spread from its 1968 annual report, a full-color photograph illustrates the company's program to encourage independent local farmers to grow barley, which resulted in a record crop for malting purposes. (USA)
384: Illustration from the annual report of the *International Minerals and Chemical Corporation*. (USA)
385: Full-color illustration from an annual report of the *Cummins Engine Company, Inc.* (USA)
386: *Sperry Rand* autopilots, flight instruments and compass systems are used by more than 100 airlines, including those flying the Boeing 747, shown here in a full-color wide-angle photograph reproduced from the corporation's 1970 report. (USA)
387–390: Photographs illustrating annual reports of a French glass manufacturing combine. 387, 389) Photographic studies of reflections in glass were used in the 1968 report. 388, 390) The 1966 report used more realistic compositions of articles made by the corporation. All in full color. (FRA)

383: Doppelseite aus dem Bericht einer internationalen Holding, die aufstrebende Industrien in Nord- und Südamerika betreut. Die Farbaufnahme – Mälzen von Gerste – illustriert ein Programm, das unabhängige Farmer zu vermehrtem Anbau von Gerste ermunterte, was eine Rekorderne brachte. (USA)
384: Illustration aus dem Jahresbericht eines Unternehmens für Mineralien und Chemikalien. (USA)
385: Mehrfarbige Illustration aus dem Jahresbericht einer Motoren- und Maschinenfabrik. (USA)
386: Automatische Piloten, Fluginstrumente und Kompass-Systeme der *Sperry Rand* werden von über 100 Fluggesellschaften verwendet, auch von denjenigen, die mit der Boeing 747 fliegen, die hier mit einem Weitwinkelobjektiv aufgenommen wurde. Mehrfarbig reproduziert. (USA)
387–390: Aus Berichten eines Glashütten-Konzerns. 387, 389) Photographische Studien von Lichtwiderspiegelungen auf Glas; aus dem Bericht 1968. 388, 390) Der Bericht 1966 zeigt realistischere Illustrationen von verschiedenen Produkten. Alle mehrfarbig gedruckt. (FRA)

383: Double page extraite du rapport 1968 d'un holding finançant des entreprises de culture dans les deux parties du continent américain. La photographie (en couleurs) se rapporte à l'action menée avec succès par la société en vue d'encourager les exploitants indépendants à développer la culture de l'orge. (USA)
384: D'un rapport annuel publié par une entreprise de produits minéraux et chimiques. (USA)
385: Illustration en couleurs d'un rapport d'une entreprise de constructions mécaniques. (USA)
386: Boeing 747. Comme de nombreux autres appareils en service sur plus de cent lignes aériennes, ce géant est muni d'instruments de bord produits par une société connue notamment pour ses systèmes de pilotage automatique. Photographie en couleurs, prise avec objectif grand-angulaire. (USA)
387–390: Photographies en couleurs extraites de deux rapports de la société *Boussois-Souchon-Neuvesel*. 387, 389) Jeux de lumière réfléchie dans le verre – thème des illustrations du rapport 1968. 388, 390) En 1966, un style plus réaliste avait été adopté pour mettre en valeur différents produits. (FRA)

384

385

387

388

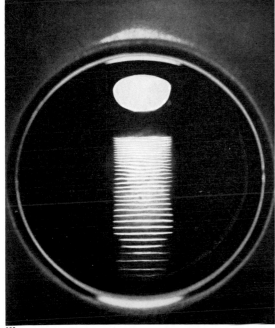

389

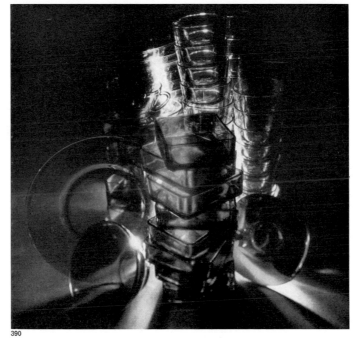

390

DESIGNER:

383: Bruce Blackburn
384: Morton Goldsholl
385: Paul Rand
386: Dominic Arbitrio
387–390: Robert Sadoux

PHOTOGRAPHER:

383: Bernard Wolf
384: Gordon Coster
385: Carl Turc
386: Barry O'Rourke
387, 389: Pierre Berdoy
388, 390: Morris Smith

ART DIRECTOR:

383: Bruce Blackburn
384: Morton Goldsholl
386: Dominic Arbitrio
387–390: Robert Delpire

STUDIO - AGENCY:

383: Chermayeff & Geismar
    Associates, Inc.
384: Morton Goldsholl
    Design Associates
386: Page, Arbitrio & Resen
387-390: Delpire-Advico SA

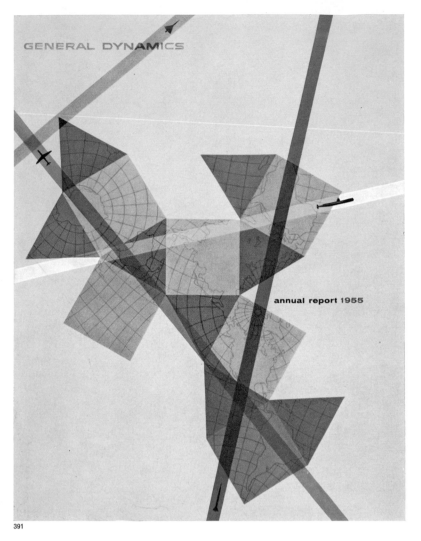

391

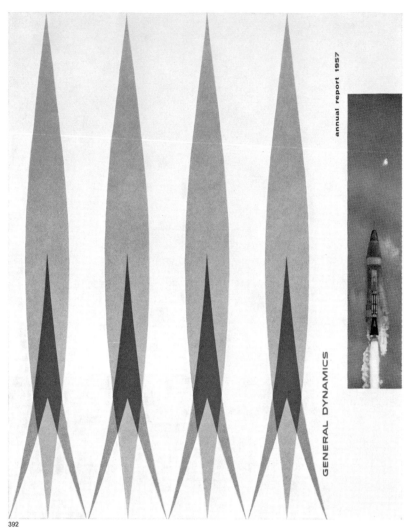

392

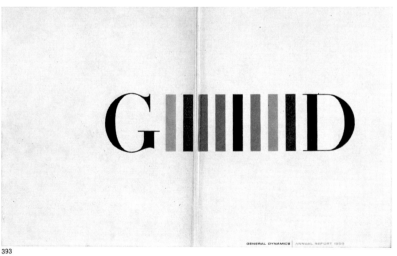

393

391–397: In recognition of the pioneering work done in the field of annual report design, the last two double pages of this book are devoted to some early reports of *General Dynamics Corporation*, designed in the 1950's by Erik Nitsche. These examples should also prove the fact that yester-year's avant-garde is today's accepted standard. Other companies, such as *IBM, CBS, Litton Industries, Xerox, Ansul*, etc., were in the forefront of this avant-garde, and the convincing graphics of their annual reports exerted a wide influence on designers and corporation executives at a time when visual excitement was far from the norm in annual report design. 391) Cover in full color. 392) Cover. Graphic design in greys on white, photographic inset in full color. 393) Front and back of 1959 cover. G and D in black, bars multicolored. 394) Cover of 1958 report. Blue, green and gray. 395–397) Cover, detail and inside page with chart from which cover design was derived. (USA)

391–405: In Anerkennung der Pionierarbeit, die die *General Dynamics Corporation* auf dem Gebiet der Jahresberichtgestaltung leistete, wurden die letzten vier Seiten dieses Buches einigen der in den 50er Jahren von Erik Nitsche gestalteten Berichten dieses Unternehmens gewidmet. Die Beispiele sollen zeigen, dass die Arbeiten der gestrigen Avant-Garde dem akzeptierten Standard von heute entsprechen. Weitere Firmen, wie *IBM, CBS, Litton Industries, Xerox* und *Ansul* gehörten ebenfalls in die Reihen jener Avant-Garde, die die visuelle Gestaltung der Jahresberichte des folgenden Jahrzehntes wesentlich beeinflussten. 391) Umschlag, mehrfarbig. 392) Umschlag. Graphik grau, Photo mehrfarbig. 393) Vorder- und Rückseite des Berichtes 1959. G und D in Schwarz, Balken mehrfarbig. 394) Bericht 1958. Umschlag in Blau, Grün und Grau. 395–397) Umschlag, Detail in Originalgrösse und Innenseite mit graphischer Darstellung, der das Umschlagmotiv entnommen wurde. (USA)

391–405: En hommage à l'œuvre de pionnier accompli par la *General Dynamics Corporation* dans le domaine du design des rapports annuels de sociétés, nous avons réservé les quatre dernières pages du présent ouvrage au rappel de quelques-uns des travaux exécutés par Erik Nitsche au cours des années 50 à la demande de la *GDC*. Entre autres mérites, ces exemples ont celui d'attester que les audaces de l'avant-garde d'hier sont si bien passées dans les mœurs qu'elles font aujourd'hui figure de règles en la matière. (D'autres firmes, telles que *IBM, CBS, Litton Industries, Xerox* et *Ansul*, ont également fait école, de longue date, à cet égard.) 391) Couverture polychrome. 392) Couverture. Eléments graphiques en gris, photographie en couleurs. 393) Couverture du rapport 1959. «G» et «D» noirs, bâtons multicolores. 394) Couverture du rapport 1958. Bleu-vert et gris sur blanc. 395–397) Couverture (détail reproduit au format) et page où figure le diagramme d'où est dérivé le motif du frontispice. (USA)

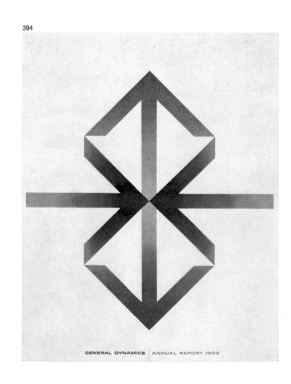

394

395

396

GENERAL DYNAMICS annual report 1956

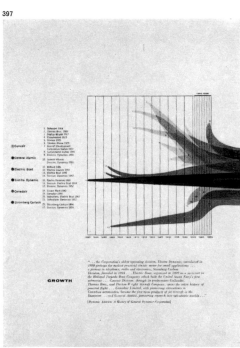

397

DESIGNER:

391—405: Erik Nitsche

COMPANY / FIRMA:

391—405: General Dynamics Corporation

A Design Pioneer of the Fifties

DESIGNER:

391–405: Erik Nitsche

COMPANY / FIRMA:

391–405: General Dynamics Corporation

398

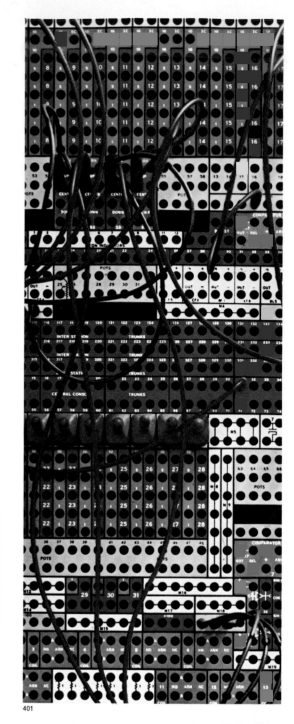

401

399

400

402

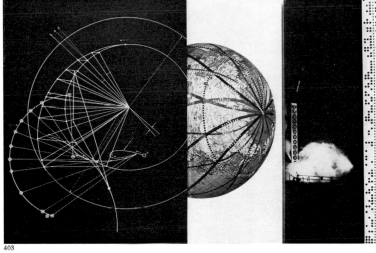

403

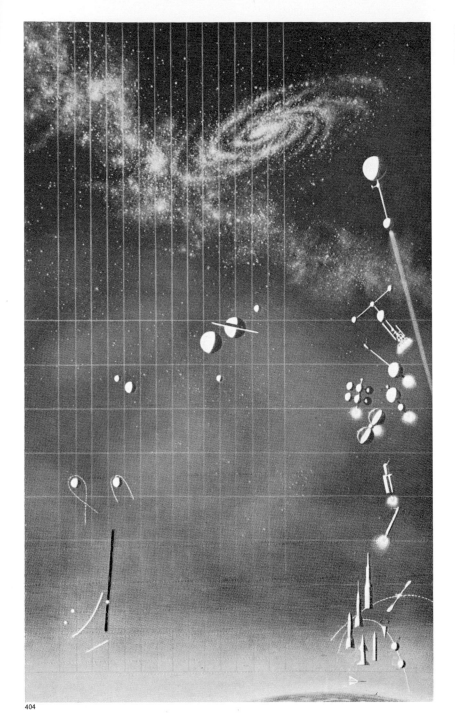

404

405

398—405: See introduction on previous page. 398, 399) Two double-page spreads with right-hand gatefolds from the 1957 report. Photo on left side in black and white, on gatefold page in full color. 400) Full-page illustration from 1957 report, showing an electric power unit being assembled. Black and white. 401–403) Spreads and detail from the 1958 report. Between two black-and-white photos were placed two half-pages bearing full-color illustrations and text (401 shows detail of 402). 404) Color page from the 1956 report. It illustrates the corporation's purpose: The profitable translation of the basic forces of nature into useful work under the sea, on the sea, on land, in the air, and in space beyond the earth's atmosphere. 405) Cover illustration from the 1953 annual report, depicting the first nuclear-powered submarine "Nautilus", which was designed and built by *General Dynamics*. (USA)

398—405: Siehe Einleitung auf vorangehender Seite. 398, 399) Zwei Doppelseiten mit Ausklappseiten rechts, aus dem Jahresbericht 1957. Linke Seite mit Schwarzweiss-Aufnahme, Ausklappseite mit mehrfarbiger Illustration. 400) Diese Aufnahme zeigt den Zusammenbau eines elektrischen Triebwerkes. 401–403) Detail und Doppelseiten aus dem Bericht 1958. Zwischen zwei Schwarzweiss-Photos wurden zwei Halbseiten mit Farbphotos und Text eingeheftet. (401 zeigt Detail von Abb. 402). 404) Farbseite aus dem Bericht 1956. Sie soll Zweck und Ziel dieses Unternehmens illustrieren: Gewinnbringende Umwandlung von Naturkräften in nutzbare Arbeit unter dem Meer, auf dem Meer, auf dem Land, in der Luft sowie im Weltraum. 405) Die Umschlagillustration des Jahresberichtes 1953 zeigt das erste atomgetriebene Unterseeboot «Nautilus», welches von dieser Gesellschaft gebaut wurde. (USA)

398—405: (Introduction: voir page précédente.) 398, 399) Rapport 1957: deux doubles pages avec volet dépliant sur la droite. La page de gauche est en noir et blanc, la page de droite en couleurs. 400) Rapport 1957: montage d'une turbine électrique. 401–403) Deux doubles pages du rapport 1958 (la fig. 401 est un agrandissement partiel de la fig. 402). Entre deux photos en pleine page, en noir et blanc, étaient insérées deux demi-pages avec texte et photos en couleurs. 404) Hors-texte en couleurs du rapport 1956. Composition symbolisant la mission essentielle que s'est assignée l'entreprise: capter et transmuter les énergies de la nature au service de l'effort humain – en mer, sur terre, dans les airs et dans l'espace. 405) La couverture du rapport 1953 représente le «Nautilus», premier sous-marin propulsé au moyen de l'énergie atomique. (USA)

Index to Designers
Verzeichnis der Gestalter
Index des Designers

Index to Photographers and Illustrators
Verzeichnis der Photographen und Illustratoren
Index des Photographes et Illustrateurs

Index to Art Directors
Verzeichnis der Art Directors
Index des Directeurs Artistiques

Index to Studios and Agencies
Verzeichnis der Studios und Agenturen
Index des Studios et Agences

Index to Companies
Verzeichnis der Firmen
Index des Entreprises

As a rule, corporations are pleased to send out annual reports to anyone who requests them. Write the Corporate Secretary and ask him to send you one or more copies of their annual report.

In der Regel liegt den Firmen daran, all jenen ihren Jahresbericht zu senden, die ihn verlangen. Richten Sie Ihre Bitte um Zusendung der Exemplare an das Generalsekretariat (Corporate Secretary) der Firma.

Les entreprises tiennent à envoyer leurs rapports annuels à tous ceux qui les demandent. Ecrivez au Secrétariat Général (Corporate Secretary) et demandez-le de vous envoyer les rapports désirés.